STRUGGLE AND
PROMISE

The Carnegie series in American education

The books in this series have resulted from studies made under grants from the Carnegie Corporation of New York and, occasionally, studies supported by The Carnegie Foundation for the Advancement of Teaching. These books are published by McGraw-Hill in recognition of their importance to the future of American education.

The Corporation, a philanthropic foundation established in 1911 by Andrew Carnegie for the advancement and diffusion of knowledge and understanding, has a continuing interest in the improvement of American education. It financed the studies in this series to provide facts and recommendations which would be useful to all those who make or influence the decisions which shape American educational policies and institutions.

The statements made and views expressed in these books are solely the responsibility of the authors.

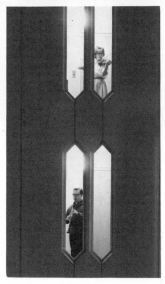

STRUGGLE AND PROMISE:

A future for colleges

MORRIS KEETON
CONRAD HILBERRY

McGraw-Hill Book Company

New York   St. Louis   San Francisco   London
Sydney   Toronto   Mexico   Panama

The authors wish to thank the
schools profiled in this book for
permission to use their photographs.

This book was set in Optima by Monotype Composition Company, printed
on permanent paper by Halliday Lithograph Corporation, and bound by
Maple-Manchester. The designer was Betty Binns. The editors were
Frederic Hills and Helen Greenberg. Adam Jacobs supervised the production.

PREFACE

T HIS study of the future of liberal arts colleges came about through
the initiative of the Carnegie Corporation and with its financial
support. In February, 1965, Dr. Peter Caws, then executive associate
of the corporation, asked Morris Keeton to consider conducting a
study on threats to the survival of private colleges and to propose
how such a study might be done. The corporation provided a planning grant to develop these ideas during 1965, and in the fall of 1965
funded a two-year study for the academic years 1965–66 and 1966–67.

The study has consisted of five main projects, only a portion of
which are reflected in this book. These projects have included a close
study of twelve colleges to develop the portraits that appear here;
work on trends affecting the future of the colleges by sociologist
Everett Wilson; the meetings, seminars, and a study on public policies
affecting the colleges conducted by Christopher Jencks and Marcus
Raskin in Washington, D.C.; a program of development activity
within the Great Lakes Colleges Association; and a study by Conrad
Hilberry and Victor Ayoub of student cultures in three colleges not
included in the original twelve. In addition, Leona Nelson worked for
a semester studing the applicability of our findings to colleges lacking
some of the advantages of those depicted here.

Our early thinking about this book was influenced by an address
given by the late Dean William C. DeVane of Yale College in May,
1964. At that time he said:

**There are prophets abroad in the land today who foresee the early demise
of the liberal arts tradition in higher education in America, and the consequent**

vii

end, or at least the drastic revision, of the college which has been the home of that tradition. . . .

What is most needed now . . . is for some of our most eminent universities and strongest colleges to take time and make a major effort to understand the situation the college is in, and from that understanding to set up models of their conception of what the college ought to be and how it must function if it is to justify its position in the total plan of the country's educational establishment.*

When we came to enlist "some of our . . . strongest colleges" in preparing these profiles, however, we deviated in one important respect from the second part of his prescription. We have not seen in these profile colleges models of "what the college ought to be," but rather models of how a college can be what it ought to be. Another college wishing to make appropriate use of these profiles should not simply choose a school depicted here and try to become like it, but rather, note ways in which these colleges have developed aims and practices distinctively right for them. Then it can choose its own aims and practices in light of its particular clientele, traditions, location, and resources.

Although our study focusses upon private colleges, two colleges set within public universities were also studied, in part to keep our perspective healthy and restrain the tendency to overgeneralize and in part to indicate our belief that private and public colleges are complementary parts of a system which owes much of its utility to their mutual presence and interaction.

Three criteria were used in selecting colleges for the profiles: (1) the schools had to differ from each other in kinds of students attracted, in educational programs and attitudes, in religious and social commitments, and in location; (2) they had to be reasonably strong examples of their kind, to the extent that this could be judged in advance; and (3) most of them had to be "free-standing" liberal arts colleges (not professional or technical schools or junior colleges) although a couple could be colleges attached to multipurpose universities. In accordance with these criteria, St. Thomas, Earlham, and Wheaton represent Catholic, Quaker, and conservative Protestant religious positions; Ripon's educational stance is conservative, Goddard's experimental; Berea and Morehouse serve somewhat special clienteles, Appalachian and Negro; Simmons is distinguished by its location, its all-women student body, and its vocational bent; Oberlin and Amherst, one Midwestern and coeducational, the other Eastern

* "A Time and a Place for Liberal Education," *Liberal Education*, vol. 50, no. 2, May, 1964, pp. 198, 212.

and all male, are the most elite of the group if eliteness is measured in terms of endowment, College Board scores of students, and faculty salaries and publications; and Monteith and Ball State are colleges within public universities, one an enclave somewhat separate from the rest of the university, the other sitting squarely in the middle of its parent institution. The profiles are written in the narrative present tense and refer, except when the contrary is specifically indicated, to the colleges as our teams observed them in 1965–66. Both the countable facts and other conditions have changed *in some measure* since that time, so that a profile may not be properly read as describing a particular college *now*.

Our own reflections and recommendations, stimulated by the profiles but going well beyond them, appear in seven chapters. We have arranged these editorial and recommendatory statements among the profiles, in part because the profiles illustrate in greater depth than is appropriate within a chapter the problems and opportunities that concern us, in part because the significance of the profiles is highlighted by the issues considered in the chapters. This alternation reflects the process of alternating between observation and interpretation which we as authors used in order to gain some insight into the future that colleges should have. In Chapter 1 we emphasize five trends to which we think colleges will be obliged to respond in the next decade. In Chapters 2 to 6 we reflect upon key elements in the shaping of a college—its purposes, the mix and culture of its students, its faculty, its curriculum, and its leadership. In these chapters we suggest some principles helpful in creating the future a college wants; but because each college's situation and resources are unique, we view these ideas as requiring different application in different colleges. In Chapter 7, however, which discusses the national context for American colleges, we venture explicit recommendations for which we seek some form of trial in use. In the chapters as in the profiles, references to events and conditions in the profile colleges are in the narrative present tense and refer to the academic year 1965–66.

An enormous number of faculty, administrators, trustees, alumni, and students have assisted us in one way or another in this study, some of whom are named in Appendix A. We mention them here in order to emphasize a further feature of the study. We suspected from the outset that the thinking and action generated among study participants would have more significant effects than anything we say editorially; we therefore designed the study to combine observation and reflection with action. For example, we conjectured that associations of colleges will be most effective when faculty have a major voice in program and priority plans. A working paper to this effect was presented to the Board of Directors of the Great Lakes Colleges Association; the Board proceeded to test the idea by creating an association-wide Faculty Council—the first, to our knowledge, with its form and influence.

In this spirit of combining study with action, the findings of this investigation were exposed, as they were being developed, to three meetings of the Association of Governing Boards of Colleges and Universities during 1966–67. The public policies project of the study was carried out largely in Washington, D.C., where it would be possible to consult legislators, government administrators, and representatives of higher educational associations; and the seminars from March to May, 1967, that climaxed this effort were used to expose the merits of controversial proposals for the reform of higher education to the criticism of public officials and influential educators.

The director of the study enjoyed the counsel of an advisory committee, the members of which met on several occasions for full-day sessions; some of them also contributed ideas by correspondence. The core of the advisory committee was supplied by the Commission on Liberal Learning of the Association of American Colleges. The commission also generously opened the agenda of a number of its own sessions to the task of critique and counsel for the study.

Morris Keeton, Director of the Study
Conrad Hilberry, Associate Director

CONTENTS

CHAPTER 1
STRUGGLE AND PROMISE:
A FUTURE FOR LIBERAL
ARTS COLLEGES

T HE typical private liberal arts college of the mid-twentieth
century is obsolete. Its sovereign isolation, its protected students, the one-track careers of its faculty, its restrictive curriculums
and teaching, and its tepid purposes make it unsuited to the needs
of the decades ahead. To have a bright future, private colleges
must struggle to surmount these defects in a context of significantly
altered purposes.

Survival for the sake of survival, however, is a purpose unworthy
of America's liberal arts colleges. They are only instruments of liberal
education. Liberal education was never more needed in our society
than it is today, but it can be provided in many ways. Unless liberal
education can be better-achieved with the help of these colleges
than without, it is time for their demise. What the future of liberal
arts colleges should be is thus not a question of survival, but one
of their function and significance in the world that is emerging.

In affluent America, survival without legitimate function is entirely
possible. At the very time Jacques Barzun is expressing his fear that
the traditional function of the colleges is being sapped away, they
prosper. New colleges—public and private, free-standing and em-
bedded in complex universities—are created each year. Many others

1

are achieving their first accreditation. Some that were on the verge of financial ruin begin to swarm with students and to shine with the glass and steel of new buildings. Within the Council for the Advancement of Small Colleges, initially composed almost entirely of unaccredited colleges, the last decade has brought steady and substantial increase in numbers and ability of students, in number of faculty and percentage of doctorates among them, in salaries, endowment, buildings, and expenditures per student.

These achievements have not come easily. Some colleges face setbacks today and a harder time tomorrow. But for the majority of our colleges, "struggle" no longer means the worry over filling beds and meeting a minimum payroll. There is no doubt that the liberal arts college, as a visible set of facilities and activities, is surviving.

Should it survive? Are private colleges prospering only because more efficient and equally effective public institutions cannot yet accommodate everyone who can profit from education? Precisely what is surviving at these colleges—a fun culture? prevocational workshops? an outlet for adolescent unrest and discontent with contemporary society? Or is a competent probing in idea and act into the nature and possibilities of men and society surviving?

To repeat, the familiar free-standing, four-year liberal arts college of the mid-twentieth century is already obsolete. Emerging within it is a new set of institutions. In these institutions there should be—we do not know whether there will be—an increasing commitment to liberal education. There should also be—we do not know whether there will be—more room for private initiative and diverse control patterns. Diversity of purpose and philosophy there will surely be. On this score, at least, "will be" coincides with "should be."

The good college a decade hence should be distinguished in five ways from its typical counterpart of the recent past:
1   By intricate and active engagement in a network of educational opportunities beyond its old campus boundaries.
2   By the variety of its students and the large responsibilities these students will carry in the tasks of education, administration, research, and public service.
3   By the colorful and diverse careers of its faculty.
4   By the individualization, the sophistication, and the rich rewards of its life of learning.
5   By the complexity of purposes that will enliven its learning and teaching.

An educational network *Why, first of all, the need for greater interdependence of colleges and other institutions of our society? The world of the 1970s and later can already be defined as a world of greatly increased numbers of people, a rising rate of change, more frequent changes of work and residence, a more complex social order within and among national cultures, more varied vocations, of which an increasing proportion will require collegiate education, and lives of greater leisure. If a person is to realize his fullest potentialities, these conditions will demand that he appreciate a much wider range of experience than before, adjust to more varied contexts and shape them, reopen and reconsider opinions once settled, reevaluate commitments once appropriate, and act as these reflections may guide him in reordering his life. But these are precisely the concerns at the core of liberal education.*

The faculty talent that once sufficed for undergraduate education is no longer adequate. Those colleges that try to make do as self-sufficient teaching communities are either feeling the inadequacy of their staffs or deceiving themselves. Colleges today are arranging exchanges to increase their access to diverse competences, providing for temporary student sojourns elsewhere, enriching their troupe of visiting scholars, or piping the specialist's voice and face in by tele-lecture and television. In short, eagerly or reluctantly, the campus has opened its borders to traffic both going and coming.

Some people feel strongly that this is a development to be resisted, an erosion of the core function of liberal education and a withering of the colleges preliminary to their final demise. Thus a Wesleyan University committee has argued that the colleges must become small university-like institutions or perish. A college can indeed meet some of the emerging needs by transforming itself into a small university, but this is neither the only viable response nor one that will arrest the increase of interdependence.

Another response to this pressure is to form associations and confederations, make contracts for special services, engage in neighborly barter. These arrangements form a network of educational services upon which the student may draw. The college continues to be his educational home. Here he is, or should be, well-known to one or more members of the faculty, for whom his education as a whole is the primary concern and the principal vocational mission. They give, or obtain access to, whatever diagnostic, teaching, and evaluative services he needs.

Some colleges are combining the network idea with a half step toward becoming a university. This sometimes works. For example, a few M.A.T. or M.A. programs in large departments or in interdisciplinary programs may be efficient without vastly enlarging and depersonalizing the campus. In general, however, the term "small college" no longer means what it once did. The average institution of higher education today has about sixteen hundred students. The popular idea that universities can divide into subcolleges to combine the advantages of the small and the large is only partially correct: It repeats a mistake made by many small colleges that fail to gain quality by getting larger. For example, if the subcolleges fail to attract strong faculty or if the strong faculty who take part continue to have their primary associations and loyalties elsewhere, the intended advantage of their presence is not realized.

In another variation on the network theme, some colleges are choosing to offer special programs running only from the student's third to fifth years. This option holds down the increase in total size, retains the interest of most scholarly faculty, and also permits a wide array of specialists, but it usually involves a high cost per student. Furthermore, it may surrender the concept of liberal education as a counterbalance against overspecialization and narrowness in discipline. To place the responsibility for liberal education in the first two years of college is to embrace a misconception, for liberal education is not a task that may legitimately be cut off at a certain age or grade level or left thereafter to chance. A third- to fifth-year program should have its own way of continuing liberal education—at a more advanced level than in the opening years of college and surely not as an isolated program of courses, but as an explicit and high-priority mission of professional education. Otherwise, this "solution" indeed represents the demise of a liberal arts college. For example, a student of economics with aspirations to be an economic adviser in industry or government is ill-served by upperclass or graduate study in which his exposure to the methods and theory of political science, sociology, or biological sciences is treated as peripheral to his own discipline. If he cannot engage in probing debate with specialists in other such disciplines about the relevance of their fields to the matters on which he will be advising, he is not only illiberally educated, he is a poorly equipped specialist.

As already suggested, some of the most devoted champions of liberal education view trends toward interdependence within educational networks as a potentially fatal threat to liberal education. We believe that interconnectedness can be reconciled with the objectives of liberal education. It can further the freeing of the individual from the normal limitations of his local and cultural particularity. It can permit students to have both familiarity and strangeness, a college or subcollege where they know people and feel at home and periodic exposure to Harlem or an industrial research organization or a Washington office or an archeological dig in Jordan where they may feel very alien indeed. Thus the network can help a student to discover the distinctive values of his own locale and cultural origins and thereby to see his own identity and greatest potential.

But the network idea is no cure-all. It creates hard choices for the colleges themselves. Every link that a college establishes with a place off campus costs money and talent. Anyone who has sent students to Sierra Leone or to the National Institutes of Health or even to the college or university in the next county knows what an appalling amount of planning and managing it takes. A college could easily go bankrupt setting up off-campus programs promiscuously. It must choose. And every time it chooses one link in the network rather than another, it defines its own character. A college might emphasize collaboration with research institutes, sending students to Oak Ridge or the Argonne Laboratories or Ohio State or Dow Chemical and thus developing a really high-powered program of professional preparation in the sciences. Or a college might form a number of links with a foreign country, as Earlham College is doing with Japan. Or it could develop associations with a city, as Antioch is beginning to do with Washington and Philadelphia, sending students there on jobs, recruiting students from some of the slum neighborhoods, planning programs—for example, in theater and art—in cooperation with the city school system. But a college cannot do all these things at once. It will have to decide what traffic within the network will be most appropriate to its students and its mission and what arrangements will better the ratio of educational benefit to cost. Thus the development of the network will require colleges to become more distinctive—to decide what they really want to do and can manage well and what they should leave to someone else.

The responsible student The second major recommendation is two-pronged: Colleges should first prepare to serve a greater variety of students than they now do and should then thrust greater responsibilities upon these students.

Recent studies show that what we measure as "intelligence" can be raised with appropriate educational opportunity, and that during both the preschool and in-school years, home and community environments can depress or elevate learning potential and accomplishment. In coming decades, educators will find new ways to raise the level of learning in both normal and exceptional children and youth. The array of talents viewed as worth cultivating will increase. High school dropouts may have high verbal intelligence that is not measurable on today's scholastic aptitude tests. Students who are not verbal may have much-needed artistic, mechanical, and intuitive abilities that amount to alternative modes of intelligence. The rising affluence and know-how of our society will make it possible for us to cultivate these students. Already federal legislation provides measures to remove inequities in educational opportunity for "handicapped children," children of poverty, those needing certain kinds of vocational education, those in "federally impacted areas," victims of racial and social discrimination, children of war veterans and teachers, and other categories. All these trends combine to produce students who have more varied talents and backgrounds than those we are now educating and who require diverse educational programs.

Why new responsibilities for students? For one thing, the numbers of today's students, the declining proportion of staff available to work with them, and the effects of modern upbringing usually render it futile to try to impose yesterday's protective rules.

Concurrently there are changes on campus and in the culture that foreshadow a new pattern of student life. On campus there are politically activist minorities, groups dominated by the yearning for service and social significance, and those who seek to have a say about the organization and content of their own education. At the same time, society is increasing in complexity. Men are more and more interdependent. Our knowledge about the workings of matter, life, and culture grows ever more rapidly. Consequently, there is an enormous extension in both the good of which we are capable and the evil that we may unwittingly do. These conditions call for men and women who are prepared to decide and act responsibly in every role, from citizen to professional.

If we relate these trends, symptomatic of important human needs, to the meaning of liberal education, a major new level of educational opportunity emerges. A liberal education aims not only at self-knowledge and an appreciation and knowledge of one's heritage, as we indicated in discussing the network idea. It also aims to cultivate self and culture. This cultivation means not merely preserving the best of the past but also criticizing and transforming both self and culture to achieve still better possibilities. In the past, most colleges have been far too protective, both of students and of traditional institutions and practices, for this fundamental part of liberal education to be well-served. We ought to give greater responsibilities to students in those matters over which the college itself has control—teaching, research, and some kinds of public service. Again, there are pitfalls. But the possibilities for learning and for student growth in maturity are tremendous.

Of course, given substantial freedom, students can make ridiculous, sometimes even destructive choices, for they are novices in freedom, and they lack the vested interests which make their elders more cautious. To evoke their best from students, we must take them as they are—and trust them with significant tasks. Although, from the jaundiced perspective of an older generation, students may not seem ready for much responsibility, they should be obliged to take it; for if they do not, they will remain immature.

If students are to learn through participation in college governance, enormous time must be set aside for student-faculty-administration deliberations. If the appropriate time and talent are invested, the return can be handsome; but if not, it would be better never to make the gesture. A pattern of student-initiated courses can be chaotic or creative, and sometimes both. Students can confuse responsible freedom with making the campus and dormitories a kind of legal sanctuary in which self-destructive and socially harmful practices take root. Or they can use that freedom to achieve a quality of community that no corps of deans could impose. Colleges may be tempted to offer students the sop of student government with much fanfare and little substantive responsibility. This arrangement is one that has already had its day and failed. Students can and should take greater responsibilities.

Undergraduate education in the past has been more indoctrination than inquiry. Youthful exuberance has been drained off in such minor destructiveness as spring riots and painting the founder's statue. If ever this energy is turned predominantly toward intellectual discovery, it is sure to bruise more deeply the proprieties and the consciences of both professors and the public. As a society, we have not been sufficiently mature to bear more than a few Harvards and Berkeleys, Reeds and Swarthmores. In the coming century, however, the costs of racism, parochialism, and nationalism will be too heavy and too immediate to go unchallenged; students can be effective allies in pressing the challenge as an integral part of their own education if colleges can provide the essential leadership.

The faculty-to-be   *The homogenized faculty and the one-track system of faculty careers are also on the route of the dodo and the dinosaur. The strong college of the future will not frown on faculty who consult for the government, take research leaves, and run up monstrous long-distance telephone bills. Nor will the faculty all be Ph.D.s. It does not take a "distinguished" faculty to make a distinguished college, for distinction, as defined by papers read at professional meetings or published in quarterly journals, may have little to do with the faculty's fitness to serve the primary purpose of the liberal arts college.*

Why is this radical change called for? First, the explosion of knowledge has outdated faculties whose numbers, teaching loads, and style of life are those of the typical contemporary college. In many a small college, a professor teaches four or five different courses each semester but serves only a few students in each course. He is thus both overworked and underproductive. Whereas a well-managed clinic may have seven supporting staff members (secretary, technicians, nurses, etc.) for three doctors, even an affluent college will have an average of less than one such staff member to free each teacher for truly professional duties. How then can the professor keep abreast of new findings and new methods in his field, stay in touch with professional colleagues, or contribute to the growth or reinterpretation of knowledge? Keeping up, moreover, is a matter of more than specialized competence. The students today represent a mixture of cultures and a breadth of experience in travel, work, and out-of-hours sophistication that make a narrowly competent scholar look naïve.

Second, the learned community has begun to achieve some solid knowledge about learning and how it best occurs, although the literature continues to abound with trivial questions and data disclosing "no statistically significant differences." At least we understand better how to ask questions about what matters in learning—about inducing student motivation, about organization of available knowledge for convenient access and effective use, about respect for teachers' individualities and styles, about the interplay of campus culture and learning, and about the dynamics of firsthand experience interacting with vicarious experience. All this, with the emerging revolution in educational technology, means that teaching as a profession is in for epochal developments. It is clear that differentiation of functions and roles among faculty will shortly become common. There will be preceptors, lecturers, discussion leaders, programmers, evaluator-examiners, educational technologists, and consultants of many stripes, as well as supporting technicians for the subprofessional tasks within teaching. The person who sees himself as an educator, and not simply as one of this array of specialists in teaching, will be concerned with complex problems of designing environments and tasks to further learning, enlisting students who will contribute significantly to one another's learning, and fostering the efforts of his fellow faculty to improve teaching.

Finally, our society has increasing needs for the services of faculty away from campus—as consultants, as evaluators of proposals for public funding or sponsorship, as staff of industry and government on leaves of absence, as producers of new knowledge, and as teachers in off-campus settings.

Hazards abound in these new challenges for faculty. Preoccupation with any one of the growing demands can lead to neglect or weakness in the others. Great mobility in the faculty can destroy the stability of a college, its program, and its climate for learning. Fads in educational technology may turn a teacher who did well intuitively into a confused mentor trying to do well deliberately. Pay and status for new tasks may draw talent away from the long-range social need for better undergraduate instruction.

The hazards, however, are also opportunities. Faculty have never before had such wide alternatives for renewal of their flagging intellectual interests, for upgrading their disciplinary competence through temporary leave in universities or in field work away from home, and for studying teaching through institutes, summer workshops, and externally financed experiments at the home campus. A teacher's grasp of the relevance of his special competence to the society's needs and his ability to make that relevance clear to students can be enhanced by appropriate use of the new career possibilities.

Tomorrow's curriculums A fourth trend to which colleges should respond selectively and critically is the trend toward constant innovation in curriculum and instruction. In response to social changes and internal pressures, colleges are altering their conceptions of what a college education is and ought to be.

Most of us have taken it for granted, at least in our actions, that being educated means mastering one discipline and knowing a smattering of other subjects. Virtually all our colleges are organized with this ideal in mind, by departments. But students are beginning to insist there must be other ways. They see knowledge increasing at such a rate that they will never be able to master chemistry or mathematics or English literature. Mastering a discipline sounds like an endless preparation, leading where? To the chance to impose the same discipline on students of their own? To some students this prospect sounds sterile or incestuous—as if zoology bred only zoologists and zoologists created nothing but zoology. They are repeatedly asking that their learning be "relevant." Students want to know what their learning is good for—not particularly what job it will enable them to get, but what social utility it will have. What will they be able to do after they have mastered Middle English that they could not do before? (The answer, of course, is "read Chaucer.") History and political science and psychology must have uses, and if they do, students ask, why can we not begin using them now, right away, in Watts or Chicago or Cleveland, or on our own campus, where we know there are problems that need solving?

The new technology will contribute to this experiential, even utilitarian concept of education. Television and the computer will lead us to put less premium on storing up information in our own heads. The machines can do it better. The function of education may be to teach us what questions to ask and how to interpret the answers, what techniques or approaches are appropriate for what sorts of problems, and how to develop the social, political, and intellectual skills we will need to size up a job, go after it, and get it done.

Other social changes press similarly for expression in the contemporary conception of college education; the impact of student concerns and that of technology are but illustrative. We do not mean to overstate the prospects just sketched. The world will continue to respect people who really know something; we will not begin producing all-purpose entrepreneurs. But the direction seems clear. There will be less emphasis, at least in undergraduate education, on "knowing a field" and more emphasis on confronting pressing social or personal problems where they are and figuring out some way to get a handhold on them. Different colleges, of course, will lead their students to different kinds of problems: Some will consider student participation in the regular operation of the college a legitimate educational venture, worth the time and trouble it requires; others will emphasize student participation in research, real investigation of social or scientific problems, such as the National Science Foundation is already sponsoring; others will encourage students to campaign for social reform, by lobbying, *writing papers on national or local policy, demonstrating, inviting public officials in for discussion; others will arrange for students to undertake special assignments in the public schools—in the arts, perhaps, or in science.*

New purposes for old *If the developments we envision do materialize—the networks of educational services, more various and colorful faculty careers, a wider range of students and growth of student responsibility, and transformation of curriculum and instruction—college leaders will still face the difficult and complex task of integrating these developments in a way that gives them sense and significance. Actually achieving this integration will be far more difficult than conceiving statements of purpose and policy that make the changes seem congruent. The real problem will be to secure coherent and mutually supportive commitments on the part of the people who make up the colleges.*

To be worthy of the name, a liberal arts college must go beyond recognition of the trends we have described. It should look further than to their immediate uses in, and adaptations to, the college's traditional programs. It should probe for intimations that we, like Newman clothing his idea of the university in the terms of nineteenth-century British ideals, have conceived our colleges too narrowly. While the mission of liberal education, in its concern with inquiry, appreciation, and criticism, transcends particular times and cultures, the implications and applications of that mission call for substantial change or replacement of the institutions that have served it.

WHEATON
COLLEGE
(ILLINOIS)

Wheaton College has a double aim: liberal
education and Evangelical Christianity. For the
majority of students, it provides solid training,
increased awareness of the artistic and
intellectual world, more sophisticated Biblical
and philosophical undergirding for their religious
beliefs, and more flexible social and political
attitudes. Being affiliated with no one church,
it is (as alumnus Billy Graham put it) "a citadel
of Evangelical faith and fervor."

WHEATON College has a double concern: liberal education and Evangelical Christianity. The first issue of *Critique,* an off-campus magazine published by Wheaton students, opens this way:

It was a Christian college president who stated recently, "I never want to hear it said that a student came to [this college] and lost his faith. While it is true that this is a liberal arts college, we will never sacrifice a person's faith for academic learning. This college will be a place Christian parents can send their children to with the confidence that their faith will be established and not shaken."

We would not quarrel with the man's sincerity or his motivation; we would however regard as artificial his implied conflict between the Christian faith and a liberal education.

The student author argues that Christian commitment is "in no way antithetical to the liberal arts attitude in education; on the contrary they are inseparable."

In many people's minds, Wheaton's Georgian brick and limestone campus, in one of the westernmost suburbs of Chicago, stands as an island of conservative Protestantism in a secular area. Affiliated with no one church, it is "a citadel of Evangelical faith and fervor" (as alumnus Billy Graham puts it) to Christians of many denominations—Baptists, Presbyterians, Brethren, members of the Assemblies of God, the Evangelical Free Church, the Christian and Missionary Alliance, and dozens of independent churches. According to one student, Wheaton is the "Evangelical Vatican."

The college is determined not to go the way of some other colleges by allowing the religious cast, first of the student body, then of the faculty, and finally of the administration and Trustees to be eroded away. Though Wheaton's constituency is interdenominational, there is nothing uncertain about its position. Members of the faculty subscribe annually to a nine-point doctrinal statement, distinguished by its emphasis on the Scriptures "as verbally inspired by God, and inerrant in the original writings, and . . . of supreme and final authority in faith and life," by its expectation of the "imminent return" of Christ, and by its conviction "that man was created by a direct act of God and not from previously existing forms of life, and that all men are descended from the historical Adam and Eve, first parents of the entire human race." From their first contact with the college, faculty are aware of its religious stance. The questionnaire which faculty applicants fill out asks, "When did you accept Jesus Christ as your Savior?" "Are you prepared to lead another person to accept Christ as his Savior?" "Do you subscribe fully to the 'Statement of Faith'? Have you any reservations?" "Describe your conception of the relation of a teacher to the moral and spiritual lives of his students."

These explicit doctrinal requirements assure a measure of unanimity and common understanding among the faculty seldom found in secular colleges, though it would be a mistake to conclude that the faculty is monolithic. Individual members differ in styles of life and thought, in social and educational convictions, in the rigidity of their doctrinal positions. And adherence to a creed does not prohibit teaching about theories contrary to that creed; the biologists, for example, teach about evolution as a theory currently favored by a large part of the scientific community. Still, the college is built on some common convictions.

No formal doctrinal commitment is required of students, but the college takes some pains to let them, too, know what to expect. This question, for example, appears in the application form: "The following is part of an assumed dialogue between a Christian and a non-Christian: 'I believe that the message of Jesus Christ is not relevant to the problems and needs of my life and our day. If his message is pertinent, why—after two thousand years—isn't there greater evidence that the Gospel of Christ is the solution to our problems, individual and social?' How would you respond to this question in terms of your own experience with Jesus Christ?"

Though the college does not limit the belief of students, it does restrict their conduct. All students must annually sign "the pledge," an agreement to refrain from "gambling, dancing, attendance at the theaters (including moving picture theaters), the use of playing cards, alcoholic liquors and tobacco, and membership in secret societies." (These restrictions apply to administration, faculty, and staff as well.) The college recognizes that these prohibitions are not explicitly scriptural, that they are generally a matter of mores rather than morals, and that some Wheaton students had greater freedom of conduct while they were living at home. And, in fact, these prohibitions are being modified gradually. A number of years ago, attendance at the opera became acceptable. In 1966, regulations were modified to permit drama, which has long been studied in Wheaton literature courses, to be performed on campus. Some commercial movies are now shown on campus, and students predict that the movie ban will be relaxed and removed before long. (Television, never prohibited, may already have made the movie ban anachronistic.)

Wheaton students chafe at these restrictions in much the same spirit as students at more liberal colleges chafe at not being permitted open visiting between men and women in the dormitories or at being required to wear shoes or ties to dinner. But students sign the pledge and, with some exceptions, adhere to it. Undoubtedly it helps to attract a student body and create a campus atmosphere quite distinct from those at any of the other colleges represented in this volume.

Wheaton's self-definition has not been limited to matters of doctrine and conduct. Until 1965 Wheaton avowed conservative political, and economic, as well as theological, views in its catalog. Recently, however, it has taken a more open view of the social outlooks compatible with its faith. All elements of the college community—Trustees, administration, faculty, students—are strongly Republican. There are Democrats on the faculty, but they are so few that other faculty, after a moment's thought, can name them.

The essential atmosphere   Explicit statements of college position indicate limits within which the institution works, but they give little feeling for the way religious conviction and action permeate the campus. To sense that, it helps to talk with students who have transferred to Wheaton after a dramatic religious experience has converted them to Evangelical Christianity. (Some of these are disappointed to discover that students gossip even at Wheaton or that few people at Wheaton understand the difficulty of dealing with parents who call themselves Christians but have not really accepted Christ as their Savior.) It helps to talk with students back from a weekend with a gospel team or back from a Sunday of skid-row work on Chicago's Madison Avenue. It helps to talk with a student who regrets that religious meetings are less spontaneous than those in her home church: At Wheaton, speakers may use a text instead of letting the Spirit speak through them.

A prayer meeting, billed as "Quaker style," provides a glimpse of one side of Wheaton religious life. It was held from seven to eight o'clock on a Tuesday evening in Pierce Chapel. Perhaps 150 students (out of a student body of about 1,800) showed up. At seven, a young man stood and said that this was to be an informal meeting at which people could say whatever they were moved to say. He proposed a loose structure—twenty minutes of hymn singing, twenty minutes of testimonials, and twenty minutes of prayer—a pattern which the meeting followed. From various parts of the chapel people called out the numbers of hymns, someone with an ear for pitch started them, and everyone joined in. Sometimes standard Protestant hymns like "Fairest Lord Jesus" or "Holy, Holy, Holy" were sung, sometimes gospel hymns like "Brighten the Corner." The singing was full and spirited.

With no formal transition, hymn singing stopped and testimonials began. A boy spoke with engaging enthusiasm of a Crusade he and other Wheaton students had made to Purdue University. They had felt the Lord with them, leading them to students there who were searching for Him. And they met, he said, with an amazing response. When the Purdue students asked questions, the Holy Spirit gave them answers; he said that he found himself quoting Scriptures he did not even know. At this, the students at the prayer meeting laughed, but sympathetically. Another student told, with similar excitement, of a six-man Crusade to the University of Illinois: In a week they brought one hundred people to Christ. (The girl sitting next to me looked over and said, "Wow.") Some of the testimonials and prayers were more personal, but the tone of none of them was openly emotional or revivalistic.

Study and the uncertainty of college life came up often. At home, one student said, you can depend on your family or the church; but at Wheaton you have to depend directly on the Lord. Dependence on the Lord became a recurring theme, particularly in the prayers. Many students asked that they might let Him do the work, let Him lead their steps. These prayers carried a convincing sense of relief and renewal—an antidote to anxiety that many college students might envy. One boy said he had wondered whether he could take time off from studying to come. He had stopped by the chapel before the meeting began and had gone on and tried to study. He could not, and he returned. Now he was glad that he had come back, because the Lord was here.

Outside, at the end of the hour, a girl told a friend whom she met on the sidewalk that it had been a "wonderful prayer meeting."

Academic quality Faculty from more liberal colleges are tempted to conclude, on hearing of Wheaton's religious position, that no education can be occurring there. What self-respecting college teacher would permit an institution to tell him that he must not drink or smoke or go to movies? Worse yet, who would submit to signing a doctrinal loyalty oath every year?

Questions like these reflect a kind of reverse provincialism, an unquestioned assumption that no one who accepts arbitrary limitations on his behavior or who publicly subscribes to a religious platform can be well-educated and intellectually alive. Wheaton's restrictions on behavior and belief do create strains, but there can be little question of Wheaton's academic respectability and vigor.

The entering students rank high on the conventional measures of ability and accomplishment. The median student scores close to the 600 mark on the College Board's Scholastic Aptitude Test—slightly above 600 on the mathematical portion and slightly below 600 on the verbal portion. Sixty-one percent of the men and 82 percent of the women come from the top tenth of their high school classes, and virtually all come from the top quarter. According to information collected by the Educational Testing Service's College Student Questionnaire, about 70 percent of the entering students say they definitely or probably will go to graduate school; another 10 percent report that they have not thought about it enough to say. Eighty-two percent of the freshmen say that their high schools did a very good or at least a fairly good job of preparing them for college (whereas only 14 percent of college freshmen in the ETS comparison group from a variety of colleges and universities look with that much respect on their high school training). But even with this confidence in their background, 91 percent expect a great deal of competition for grades at Wheaton (as opposed to 63 percent of the comparison group), and when asked what problems they anticipate in college, the Wheaton freshmen name difficulty in handling their courses almost four times as often as they mention any other problem.

The competition that the freshmen foresee is not an illusion. Students are aware of grade-point averages, their own and other people's. The college makes competition formal by awarding three scholarships strictly on the basis of grades—$1,000 each to the freshman, sophomore, and junior with the highest grade average for the year. As one might expect, grade consciousness takes some odd forms: Some students will reel off, on demand, the percentage of A's, B's, C's, D's, and F's recorded by each department in the college.

This is not to say that academic work at Wheaton is simply a race for grades. A student who transferred to Wheaton from a state university in Ohio (after a personal meeting with the Lord and a decision to enter the ministry) reported that the work itself was no more difficult at Wheaton but that the atmosphere, which the students created, was much more intellectual. He spoke with admiration of dormitory discussions of Kant and Hegel, generated by a philosophy course. As for himself, he was "just trying to battle through it, much less discuss."

One evidence of students' accomplishment at Wheaton is their performance on Graduate Record Area Tests. In the humanities area, Wheaton students rank well above the average of students from the twenty-two colleges and universities in the Educational Testing Service norm group; in natural sciences, they rank noticeably above the norm group; in social sciences, they rank a shade lower than the norm group. It may be that this relatively strong performance in humanities and sciences reflects the strength of the faculty. (The most distinguished departments, by something like campus consensus, are the science departments, literature, and philosophy.) Or it may be that religiously conservative students are more at home with science and the humanities than with the social sciences.

On Graduate Record Advanced Tests, too, Wheaton seniors score consistently higher than seniors in the widely representative comparison groups, and Wheaton graduates are now sought by graduate and professional schools and by employers of all kinds. (In the past ten years, about fifteen hundred graduates have become certified teachers; in 1964–65 the college received twelve thousand inquiries from school districts wishing to employ graduates.)

Wheaton students gravitate to fields that combine academic rigor with clear opportunity for service—medicine, nursing, education, social work, and the ministry. Of the 377 Wheaton students who took the Medical College Admission Test from 1953 to 1959, the median student ranked at the 85th percentile on the verbal portion of the test, at the 96th on the quantitative portion, at the 90th on the science portion, and at the 62d on the portion labeled "modern society" (reflecting the relative weakness in understanding or analysis of society). Of the 114 graduates who attended medical school from 1949 to 1959, only 4 withdrew during that period. In recent years, 20 to 25 graduates have gone to medical school each year. About half of the current graduates go on for advanced work of one sort or another.

The impression these statistics convey is of an abler-than-average student body, competently trained, going on to successful graduate work or jobs, often in fields that incorporate an element of "Christian service." But the faculty, I believe, would not concede that that description does justice to the students. Repeatedly, faculty who have taught elsewhere praise the Wheaton students. "Sometimes things get rough around here. Then you say, 'Oh, but those great kids! It's worth staying.' "

Why this appeal to their instructors? The students combine quick intelligence with a readiness to work, but so do students at many colleges. More unusual is the combination of solid conviction and a kind of energetic innocence they bring with them to college. Wheaton often introduces students for the first time to the ideas of anthropology, psychology, or philosophy. Here, the teacher can play the questioner doubting old certainties—a role that is less appropriate, or at least more difficult, in colleges where students come having been weaned on Fellini and bringing with them subscriptions to the *Realist* and *I. F. Stone's Weekly*. The Wheaton faculty enjoys its part in the transformation of bright but inexperienced freshmen into seniors who know what attitudes and issues move the non-Evangelical world and who can talk with some sophistication about their own positions.

About 45 percent of the faculty hold Ph.D. degrees. Over half are Wheaton graduates, and many of the rest are graduates of schools closely allied with Wheaton in the Evangelical movement—Westmont, Taylor, Houghton, Gordon. This proportion is not likely to decrease. The truth is that very few people prepared to teach in college are also prepared to subscribe to the Wheaton creed and standards of conduct. Those who have that double qualification are, as often as not, Wheaton graduates. This situation may be described as "inbreeding," but there is an element of tradition as well. Many of the faculty have connections with Wheaton going back a generation or two; more of them have been associated with Wheaton one way or another all their adult lives. For these people Wheaton is not just an office, a teaching assignment, a roomful of students; it is a mixture of recollection and hope, of conviction and frustration intricately woven into their own lives.

Probably the Wheaton faculty are best-known outside the Evangelical world for their work in science and literature. For example, Howard Claassen, chairman of the Department of Physics and Mathematics, has carried on research regularly at the Atomic Energy Commission's Argonne National Laboratories 15 miles away—every summer and two full years. Professor Claassen was one of a group first to combine xenon with fluorine—a major breakthrough. In 1964 he won the Chicago Man of the Year in Science award and in 1966 a Guggenheim fellowship.

Another example: In October, 1963, excavation for an artificial lake on the property of Judge Joseph Sam Perry in Glen Ellyn, some 3 miles away from Wheaton, uncovered a large bone. Wheaton geologists heard of the find and helped excavate what proved to be an excellently preserved skeleton of an American mastodon, roughly eleven thousand years old by carbon dating. The bones, about 60 percent of those in the original skeleton, have been identified and laid out in a special room at the college; Wheaton students in geology, anatomy, and art are now engaged, under the direction of Prof. Donald Boardman, in the exacting work of reproducing the missing bones by sculpturing a mirror image of the same bone from the other side of the animal. In the process, Professor Boardman and Richard Rush, a Glen Ellyn commercial sculptor, have developed a technique for casting reproductions of the bones in fiber glass that has attracted the attention of museums and science supply houses throughout the country. Eventually, the reassembled mastodon will have a place in the new science building proposed for the college.

In literature, the best-known member of the faculty is Clyde Kilby, chairman of the English Department and author of frequent reviews in the *New York Herald Tribune* and elsewhere, a widely praised biography of Jonathan Blanchard (nineteenth-century educator, Evangelist, reformer, and President of Wheaton and Knox colleges), and the first major study of the work of C. S. Lewis.

The bookstore devotes a whole section of shelves to Lewis, and sells as many Lewis books as it does all trade fiction works combined. Interest in him, reinforced by Professor Kilby's studies over a number of years, shows no sign of diminishing. Two Wheaton students have done Ph.D. theses on Lewis. Even though his Anglicanism places him about as far from Wheaton's Fundamentalism as an orthodox Christian can get, short of Rome, Lewis apparently answers an urgent need on the Wheaton campus for a lucid, intellectually sophisticated defense of Christianity, free from both theological involutions and revivalist naïveté.

Professor Kilby hopes to give scholarly substance to this interest in Lewis by building at Wheaton a research library of materials on Lewis and his circle. He and his colleagues and students have begun the work of finding and purchasing manuscripts and first editions and already have what is one of the finest collections of Lewis material in the country. (The 1966 senior class made a gift of over $2,500 to be used for purchases for this collection.)

This is the sort of project that could be taking shape, Professor Kilby believes, in many Wheaton departments—a natural development of student and faculty interests. A glance at the 14-page, single-spaced list of faculty publications from 1960 to 1965 supports Professor Kilby's contention that most of the writing is either technical or Evangelical. There is little in the middle where religion and scholarship meet.

Finances and spending policies
Wheaton's ability to attract scholars and give them the time and facilities they need to work productively will depend in part upon its financial strength. There, Wheaton's position is an enviable one. In the last half-dozen years it has worked aggressively to increase its endowment and gifts for operating expenses, particularly stressing annuity and special contract arrangements whereby donors receive an income during their life from securities assigned to the college. (The college itself realizes an average income of 2.42 percent on annuity funds in its management after payments to the donors have been made.)

The college now has eleven men whose job is to keep in touch with its constituency, reminding them that Wheaton will accept gifts in any number of forms. Incredulous money-raisers from other colleges ask Public Relations Director David Roberts how he can afford to send field men out to the farms to talk with little old ladies and come back with a $10 bill. Roberts replies, "Yes, but what if they come back with the farm?"

In 1964–65 they came back with the farm often enough to increase the college's assets by more than $3,500,000. At the end of August, 1965, investments in endowment, annuity, and special contract funds had a book value of $22,179,000 and a market value of over $26,500,000. Of the educational and general expenditures of about $3,000,000, gifts and income from endowment and annuity contracts paid about $1,000,000. As a result, Wheaton's tuition has remained lower than that at many private colleges. For 1965–66, the charges were $1,120 for tuition and fees and $790 for room and board.

In spite of the college's relative affluence, faculty salaries, until 1966, have been distressingly low. This has resulted partly from the college's policy of keeping tuition charges as modest as possible, partly from extremely conservative habits of budgeting. Though the budget approved by the Trustees at the year's beginning may show only a modest surplus or even a small deficit, things usually turn out better than predicted, and the college ends the year with a considerable surplus. (In 1964–65, it was $229,736.) This money is spent, of course, but instead of being spent for salaries, it is generally spent on campus improvements. As a result, the campus has always been attractive and carefully maintained, even though many of the faculty (or their wives) have taken second jobs to help meet expenses in this rather high-priced suburb of Chicago.

In 1963–64, the median salary for all faculty was $6,875; in 1964–65, $7,200; in 1965–66, $7,800, with a high of $11,300 and a low of $5,600. Professors' salaries have consistently been $2,000 or more below the American Association of University Professors averages for liberal arts colleges. Now the college is making an effort to catch up. In their contracts for 1966–67, full professors found increases averaging almost $2,000. (One professor sent his contract back to the President's office, assuming the figure was a mistake.) For associate professors, increases averaged over $1,000; for assistant professors and instructors, about $400 or $500. These increases will leave the college still below the AAUP average for liberal arts colleges, but they will certainly help persuade faculty that the college is doing something about salaries.

Tensions At Wheaton, the Trustees are an important force in the network of stresses that gives the college its shape. Individually and collectively, they embody the Wheaton tradition. Herman A. Fischer, the abrasive, generous, widely respected Chairman of the Board of Trustees, provides continuity from the very beginnings of the college. His grandfather was Jonathan Blanchard, the fiery founder of the college and its first President (1860–82); Charles Blanchard, the second President (1882–1925), was Fischer's uncle. His father was, for fifty years, a member of the Wheaton faculty and college treasurer. Mr. Fischer himself graduated from the college in 1903. He became a Trustee in 1925 and began an uninterrupted forty-year tenure as Chairman of the Board the following year.

The college bylaws call for ten-year terms for Trustees, but the Board, apparently from the beginning, has felt free to renew the terms of the members, so that many are in their second, third, or fourth decade. According to a bulletin published by the college, the average tenure of members of the Board in 1966 was 19.1 years.

The Board is very much part of the college's present as well as its past. Fourteen of the twenty members of the Board live in Wheaton or nearby, and they feel an intense concern for all the decisions that determine the character and future of the college. Not only do the Trustees supervise the financial affairs of the college and the building program; they recognize that the spiritual integrity of the college lies partly in their charge and feel it their responsibility to challenge changes that might erode its religious or moral character. Thus the Board sometimes finds itself dealing with matters that would ordinarily fall to the President, another administrative officer, or the faculty—e.g., what sort of stories may appropriately be published in a Wheaton literary magazine? May the philosophy faculty be organized as a separate department, distinct from the Bible faculty?

Perhaps the pulls at work within Wheaton can best be seen by reviewing specific incidents, though these may give the mistaken impression that the college is constantly absorbed in politics. It is not. Students learn mathematics or history, train for football, go on dates; faculty prepare lectures, write articles, or counsel students. And occasionally, both groups have something to say about college policy.

The first incident seems to have been resolved in a way satisfactory to all parties. In the spring of 1965, a group of students proposed to organize a chapter of the National Association for the Advancement of Colored People on campus. When they brought their proposal to the faculty committee that considers and approves new campus organizations, the President interrupted the process to ask for a more elaborate investigation than the committee would ordinarily give. His procedure, in fact, was to call the FBI to ask whether the NAACP was subversive or Communist-dominated or otherwise dangerous. When the FBI declared the NAACP free of anything un-American, the President returned the matter to the faculty committee, and the chapter was approved. Since then, the college's action has been challenged by one or two Trustees and some alumni; but, fortified by the FBI, the President has been able to argue, first, that the NAACP is an appropriate campus organization and, second, that decisions of this sort are the proper prerogative of the faculty and administration.

A second incident is more ambiguous. As part of the college's 1964–65 concert series, the Warsaw Symphony Orchestra (along with the Roger Wagner Chorale and the Philadelphia Orchestra) performed in Edman Chapel. While the orchestra played Brahms' Fourth Symphony and the Chopin E Minor Piano Concerto, some twelve or fifteen pickets, reportedly members of the John Birch Society, paraded in front of the chapel to protest this intrusion of communism into the sanctum sanctorum of Evangelical Christianity. In his public comments, President Edman attached little importance to the pickets. But the following season, when it was suggested that the Moscow Symphony appear in the Artists Series, the administrative officers decided by vote that the college's religious and patriotic convictions made inappropriate its playing host to an Iron Curtain group. The Associate Dean of Students, a Wheaton alumnus newly returned from graduate work at Michigan State, introduced this issue in faculty meeting, proposing that the faculty vote to reverse the administrators' decision. In the discussion that followed, both Dr. Armerding, recently appointed President, and Dr. Edman, now Chancellor, defended the prohibition. Dr. Armerding's argument, essentially, was that the proceeds from the concert would support Communist propaganda in the United States; Chancellor Edman suspected, further, that the orchestra might be serving as a front for Communist snooping of some sort. After a somewhat tense debate, the Associate Dean's motion lost. Some faculty have speculated about what would have happened if it had passed. President Armerding contends that there would have been no constitutional crisis—that the inviting of outside performers is an administrative responsibility and that the faculty action, had it passed, could be viewed only as advice and exhortation to the administrative officers.

Free speech and received doctrine In almost all colleges, the newspaper and the literary magazine are internally stimulating. They are a place for the airing of grievances, the defining of positions—a church door on which anyone can nail his theses. The *Record,* the Wheaton student newspaper, and *Kodon,* the literary magazine, are these things and something else besides. At Wheaton, as at few other colleges, the publications raise issues and also *are* the issue.

By their very presence, the publications persistently raise important theological questions: Within what limits can a faith-affirming college encourage open debate, free advocacy of any position honestly held? What if the search for truth leads temporarily or permanently away from Biblical Truth? Is there such a thing as Christian art? If so, how is it distinguished from non-Christian art or from

Christian polemic? Can art depicting the sordid or depraved properly be sponsored by a college that hopes its students will serve the Lord in confidence and joy? So there remains tension between commitment and inquiry, between the eye of the Christian and the eye of the artist, between faith and learning.

This tension, in varied guises, has underlain the intense, sometimes bitter, sometimes comic cold war between Wheaton and its student publications. Going back only to 1962, one can find skirmishes as various as these: a *Kodon* editor warning his readers that an issue of the magazine would be controversial (he was right) and in the next issue responding to some of the anguish caused by the controversy by writing an open letter "to the woman who came to my office and wept"; the student members of a student-faculty-administration publications board jockeying to find meeting times when faculty or administration members would be out of town; the Board of Trustees formally considering a motion to ban *Kodon* permanently and passing a motion to suspend it for a year; students going off campus to Glen Ellyn to publish an issue or two of *Critique,* a journal of essays directed toward a Wheaton audience, before the editors were asked to leave school (since then, one of the editors has reportedly been fired from the Peace Corps for trying to introduce free speech into the Turkish school system); an instructor in anthropology being asked to explain to the Board of Trustees his reasons for writing an essay on race for *Brave Son,* a short-lived student forensic magazine; a Trustee appearing in the *Record* office to protest what he took to be a deliberate delay in printing a letter he had written to the paper; a *Kodon* story intercepted by the printer but allowed to appear after a long note had been added to make clear that the story was a Christian allegory; a new *Kodon* editor resolving not to let the magazine be banned again though it might mean not printing some of the most skillful stories submitted.

To an outsider, the intensity of this contest over publications seems ironic. First, the Wheaton publications seem, to non-Evangelical eyes, to be one of the brightest ornaments of the college. In 1964–65, the *Record, Kodon,* and *Tower,* the yearbook, all won all-American awards in the Associated Collegiate Press competition—*Tower* for the fifteenth consecutive year. The *Record* carries news stories that are consistently well-written, well-organized, and free from editorial intrusions, reviews that give more than perfunctory treatment to real books, varied and vigorous letters to the editor, and editorials that can be matched by few college papers for lucidity of statement and sophisticated discussion of genuinely difficult issues. *Kodon,* too, assembles a remarkable collection of undergraduate stories, poems, essays, and artwork. Its 1965–66 editor was the first person ever to win awards for the best poem and for the best story the same year in the *Atlantic Monthly's* Annual Creative Writing Contest.

The second irony: Though student writers are sometimes critical of college action or inaction, they invariably argue from Christian assumptions. Even *Critique* and *Brave Son* debate only the applications of a conservative faith or the proper means of fostering it and accommodating it to a liberal education; they never undercut or ignore the faith itself. One writer attacks the Wheaton chapel speeches as "sacred vaudeville, spiritual patent remedies, and amateur psychiatry." But he goes on to ask, "Could it be that diatribes given on the world's problems do not fit our crying need as a student body? We stand between the Resurrection and Parousia in dire need of the word-act of the living God. What we need, if we will but admit it, is not talk about Christ, but an encounter with Him."

The Adam and Eve footnote
While the publications tug-of-war raises basic questions, the faculty (except for members of the Committee on Publications) generally stand aside from these disputes, involving themselves only to the extent of hoping that the students might mix a modicum of prudence with their logic or that the Trustees might act on principle, not pique. But another issue, "the addendum," touches the faculty very deeply indeed. If one wishes to get a sense of the forces contending for the college's future, he can hardly do better than to follow the history of the addendum.

In 1926 the Trustees adopted an official Statement of Faith for Wheaton; every year since then the Trustees, the administrators, the faculty, all the secretaries, buildings and grounds workers, etc.— everyone but the students—have reaffirmed their commitment to its nine doctrinal points. The fourth of these points states that man is created in the image of God; nothing further is said about man's beginnings. But Wheaton scientists and Biblical scholars have often been asked to explain what they think about evolution, to reconcile a fairly literal reading of Genesis with fossil evidence and the rest. Wheaton's chief spokesman in this matter has probably been Prof. Russell Mixter, chairman of the college's Biology Department. In 1959, he edited a book entitled *Evolution and Christian Thought Today,* which brought together essays by some American scientists of Evangelical persuasion. The book was well-received within the conservative community: *Eternity* magazine recognized it as the outstanding Evangelical book of the year.

In February, 1961, four contributors to the book took part in a so-called "origins symposium" on the Wheaton campus, a record of which appears in the *Journal of the American Scientific Affiliation*, June, 1961. Some of the speakers sounded as though they would cheerfully have done with the whole evolution dispute, at least in conventional terms, because it has distracted attention from more exciting and significant scientific work, because it has alienated some potentially Christian scientists, and because it has done less than justice to the processes of divine creation. Here, for example, are two passages from the paper read by Walter R. Hearn, professor of biochemistry at Iowa State University. After talking enthusiastically about Dr. Sidney Fox's work in forming protein-like substances from amino acids, he said:

I know that Dr. Fox continually comes in contact with Christians—at least by correspondence. His work has been widely publicized in the popular press, and he told me he has a huge scrapbook full of letters, some highly emotional, some denouncing him for monkeying around with God's Word (he receives Bibles in the mail regularly), and some calling him a fool for denying God by trying to do something anybody knows only God can do [i.e., create life].
Now I ask you, if you are an Evangelical Christian, is that the way you would go about trying to witness to Sid Fox?
I hope not. That's not the way I'm trying to go about it anyway.

The following day, he became somewhat more theological:

Many Christians have gotten into the habit of thinking of God's direct action in nature as always of a sudden, instantaneous type—never a steady type involving processes which could be studied by the scientific method. "Processes" are considered "natural" and instantaneous events "supernatural." This sort of thinking inevitably leads one to a "God of the gaps" philosophy, no matter how sophisticated he may be about the nature of the present gaps. I am for a "science of the gaps"—that's exactly what science is for, to fill in gaps. I am also for a "God of Creation," who is involved directly in all natural processes. . . . I am baffled by the idea that God is "in" some events more than in others.

One name for the view of creation espoused by Professor Hearn and others at the symposium is "theistic evolution," the belief that life and man were created, not *ex nihilo* by instantaneous acts, but over a period of time by a God-directed process. The more conservative Evangelicals consider this doctrine to conflict with Biblical truth, and though the statements at the symposium were explicitly those of the speakers, not of the college, word began to circulate in the

Evangelical world that Wheaton was abandoning the doctrine of direct creation.

Wheaton heard from a good many of its constituents who wanted to know whether or not it had swung over to theistic evolution. After intense discussion, the Trustees decided to clear up any uncertainty that might exist by appending to article 4 of the Statement of Faith, in January, 1962, an addendum, composed at the Trustees' request by a group of five members of the faculty. It reads, "Wheaton College is committed to the Biblical teaching that man was created by a direct act of God and not from previously existing forms of life; and that all men descended from the historical Adam and Eve, first parents of the entire human race."

The Trustees intended this simply as a clarification and reaffirmation of what Wheaton had believed all along. To some of the faculty, it appeared to be more. One member of the faculty, chairman of the Division of Science, went on leave the following year and eventually resigned rather than subscribe to the addendum. The others signed, but some of them with uneasiness.

The uneasiness led, in May, 1964, to a resolution, passed 80 to 10 by the faculty, urging the Trustees to remove the addendum and suggesting five other "safeguards" for the orthodoxy of the faculty. Basically, this resolution once again affirmed the substance of the addendum but made it not so absolutely a part of the formal Statement of Faith; some leeway was left for present or future faculty to phrase their own statements of belief on this point.

In a meeting with a special faculty committee, the Executive Committee of the Board said that it would be unwise to delete the addendum at that time (when President Armerding had just taken office, succeeding President Edman) but that the Board would consider the resolution at a later date. Ten months later, in January, 1966, the faculty presented its resolution again, urging affirmative action.

The Trustees, after discussion with various members of the faculty and debate in Executive Committee and in the full board, ruled that the addendum would remain. Two arguments appeared to be central in the decision: First, the addendum only clarifies what has always been implicit in the Statement of Faith; to *remove* this clarification would appear, at least, to be a change from the college's historical position and would be so interpreted by some parts of the constituency. Second, if the faculty genuinely believe what is stated in the addendum, then is not the resolution a great deal of unnecessary fuss? If they do not believe what is stated there, why do they not frankly say so?

Before any discussion of the range of faculty opinion on the issue, it might be well to make clear some elements of the official Wheaton position on science and particularly on creation. In the first place, the college is not obscurantist. It values scientific discovery not only for the sake of knowledge itself or for the uses it may be put to but also as a revelation of God, a complement to the special revelation of the Bible.

On the question of creation, Wheaton (insofar as the college is unanimous) believes that the Bible is silent regarding the age of the earth and of man. "No statement is made anywhere in Scripture that affords us a conclusive and reasonable basis to calculate the time that elapsed prior to Abraham," according to Dr. Samuel Schultz, chairman of the Biblical Education and Philosophy Division. As far as I can discover, no one at Wheaton insists the world was created in six literal days. Instead, the prevailing view is that of "progressive creation," which holds that God created various forms of life at various moments in the geological history of the earth. Many of these created forms have undergone considerable evolution, as studies of paleontology and genetics make clear. But the gaps in the fossil record are so pronounced that one is not obliged, scientifically, to believe that all species are descended from a few forms or one, or that man is descended from lower creatures.

What, then, of faculty reactions to the addendum—the "Adam and Eve footnote," as one member of the faculty calls it? The faculty may be divided almost symmetrically on the issue. One group, perhaps a quarter or a fifth of the faculty, welcomes the addendum as a healthy clarification of the college's position. At the other end, another quarter or fifth of the faculty, many of them in science, philosophy, or Biblical studies, are seriously uncomfortable with the addendum. A number of them would contend that the addendum position, though one good possibility, is not the only one: "The first man was enormously different from the animals, in that he had a soul. At some point—we don't know when—God created man. Whether He used the already-evolved body of an ape or whether He made a new creation is a minor point. Since I believe fairly literally, I would say God started over again and created man much like the apes. But if someone else wants to say He used a living body, OK. That is an option."

Between those who actively welcome the addendum and those

who chafe under it is a large group of faculty, many of whom will go part way with the dissenters for other reasons. Some of the faculty have spent decades at Wheaton working on those very questions of Biblical and scientific interpretation, and do not feel party to the decisions. This has little to do with evolution but much to do with professional dignity and the political operation of the college. At this writing, the President and the Trustees are looking for new ways to keep in touch with the faculty and make Wheaton's government more genuinely consultative.

More basically, the addendum concerns many "middle" members of the faculty because they see in it a possible sign that Wheaton is wrapping itself more tightly in the doctrinal cloth. If the addendum points toward a more closed faculty, if it means fewer scholars with reputations outside the Evangelical world, if it means fewer teachers who understand and take seriously points of view unlike their own, if it means more "pat-answer people" (to use the phrase of one teacher), then it will mean a diminution of the Wheaton to which they have linked their lives. No one can say, at this short range, that the addendum will have any such effect. But this, I believe, is why the faculty cannot let the issue rest.

Patterns of student life The recent flowering of beards, drugs, and bare feet on many campuses has helped bring home the fact that there are such things as student cultures, distinct from adult cultures, which differ remarkably from college to college. The distance between Goddard and Wheaton may be almost as great as the distance between Samoa and Middletown.

Student cultures can be compared in any number of ways. A useful scale, I believe, is one which arranges them according to their formality, the amount of organization they impose on a student's life.

On all counts, Wheaton's is a formal campus. One evidence of this is the formation of discernible groups, or clusters, of students. The athletes are one cluster, a large one since Wheaton traditionally fields strong teams in all the major sports and some out-of-the-way ones like soccer, wrestling, and gymnastics. Athletic events are social occasions, and athletes enjoy a good deal of prestige. Perhaps the tightest and most audible group is the "vocal minority," the intelligentsia, many of whom frequent the student government and student publications offices on the third floor of the student center. Though this group speaks for the student body in student publications, in press conferences with the President, in chapel, and on other occasions, students are inclined to consider it somewhat sharp in its criticism of the school and view it with a mixture of suspicion and awe. Another cluster centers its loyalty in the Christian Service Council, the agency for Wheaton's Evangelism and social service; as many as a thousand different students may work with CSC at one time or another during the year. The Men's Glee Club, which regularly makes European tours, singing and witnessing, has become a social as well as a musical entity; one student spoke of it as "a fraternity in disguise," and another reported that it was the glee club that kept him at Wheaton.

Two other categories of students might be mentioned (they cannot properly be called groups)—"yukkers" and "fundies." The yukker likes to laugh and feels free to entertain himself at the expense of whatever people or institutions are at hand. The fundy is more earnest. (The word "Fundamentalist," as used at Wheaton, often connotes excessive piety and naïveté. "Evangelical" is the preferred term.) One student defined a fundy as "a person who will ask you, in the shower at 7:30 A.M., what the Lord has done for you this morning."

For the most part, the formality of Wheaton's campus is entirely appropriate to its students. Most of them come from families that imposed a good deal of order on their lives, and they may operate best, for the time being, in a setting where structure is conspicuous. But as it affects relationships between men and women, Wheaton's formality troubles some of the people there. A man wanting a date for a Saturday night basketball game will ordinarily call on Monday or Tuesday; Wednesday would be considered a trifle late. For occasions like a concert in the Artists Series, men report, "You'd better ask about a month before." Even the mixing of men and women at meals is largely prearranged.

Aware that they may never again be surrounded by bright Christians of their own persuasion, Wheaton students feel some pressure to find a mate while the candidates are plentiful, and many succeed. This sense of urgency about finding a husband or wife, coupled with the formality of Wheaton social life, creates anxiety for some students. Even impromptu dating is likely to become stylized.

If Wheaton has not yet found a social structure that will bring together men and women naturally, easily, and not in pairs, it has developed institutions which meet other needs with striking appropriateness and success. The annual May nominating convention to choose candidates for president of the Student Council, for example, becomes a kind of rite of spring, in which inhibitions are momentarily relaxed and the Lord of Misrule reigns for a day. In addition to serious candidates, the convention hears from mock candidates advocating elimination of dorm hours or burning of meal tickets, and aisles are filled with delegations carrying placards and parading to a rock and roll band. Conventions often go on in high spirits until two or three in the morning, eventually nominating serious candidates for the presidency, but in the process allowing students to say what they think under the sanction of ritual. It is, as a student said, "our little modified Berkeley affair."

Wheaton's formality does not mean coldness or indifference. On the contrary, formality is associated with unusual friendliness. According to freshman responses on the College and University Environment Scales, Wheaton ranks in the 90th percentile, in relation to a national sample of colleges and universities, on "propriety," or orderliness of behavior; but also, it ranks at the 96th percentile on "community." Students may feel confined at Wheaton, but they do not feel the anonymity or aimlessness that sometimes besets students on less formal campuses, the feeling that the world is equally indifferent to their presence or absence.

Student development Any estimate of a college's success must rest on a description, however rough or subjective, of the kinds of students drawn to the college and the kinds of changes the college encourages in them.

In many ways, Wheaton students are a typical college population. According to information gathered from a sample of 150 of the 1965 freshmen on the College Student Questionnaire, about a third of the students live in suburbs, only 4 percent (as opposed to 13 percent in a comparison group from colleges and universities of all kinds) in a city of over 500,000 people. The rest are scattered among cities and towns of less than 500,000, with 8 percent (twice as many as in the comparison group) coming from farms or ranches. Of the students' fathers, about half have completed a bachelor's degree and 20 percent have gone on for advanced degrees—figures higher than for the comparison group (35 percent and 10 percent) and higher, I would guess, than for any other Evangelically inclined college in the country. Occupationally, their fathers range from unskilled workers to physicians, lawyers, and business executives. There are a few American Negroes in the student body, and some African and Oriental students.

Family incomes are slightly higher than those of the comparison group—11 percent under $6,000 and 13 percent over $20,000. Possibly because they come from fairly prosperous families, the students themselves put little emphasis on making money. When asked about their prospective careers, 26 percent say they would prefer an academic life, 25 percent a professional life, 21 percent a life centering on home and family. Only 4 percent say they would prefer a business life.

If these students are to be distinguished sharply from those at other private colleges, it is by their political, social, and religious attitudes. When asked about their parents' politics, 61 percent say their parents favor conservative Republicans, 20 percent liberal Republicans; only 7 percent see their parents siding with Democrats of any description.

But not all student attitudes fit with a conservative stereotype. The Wheaton students are more concerned than the comparison group with poverty in the United States, with the lack of opportunity for non-WASPs in the United States, with the welfare of the elderly. Even though Wheaton is not at all pacifist (two years of ROTC are required for men), 36 percent of the sample, twice the proportion in the comparison group, "strongly agree" that conscientious objectors should be excused from military service.

Nearly all the Wheaton students went to public high school, did good work there, and took part in extracurricular affairs. But socially they were distinct. Seventy percent "never, or almost never," went to a movie during their last year in high school, and 45 percent listened to no popular music, or almost none. About half dated not at all or not oftener than once a month—sometimes, no doubt, because their parents discouraged dating outside their church.

There are no statistics to identify the religious attitudes that characterize entering Wheaton students. Almost without exception they are "conservative Evangelicals." This term will have slightly different content from church to church, but generally it means belief in the Bible as the inspired and inerrant word of God, acceptance of the vicarious atonement of Jesus Christ, and expectation of the Second Coming. For many students it implies daily devotions and witnessing or testifying to their faith. For almost all of them, it means an attempt to see life in religious terms that is rare among college students.

What happens when these students get to Wheaton? For one thing, they discover that Evangelical students come in more varieties than they had supposed. Students from rural schools and isolated sects encounter students who have been leaders in enormous suburban high schools and affluent churches. A student whose parents would not tolerate lipstick or jewelry may find himself rooming with one whose parents or whose friends' parents gave cocktail parties. A student whose church claimed to have a corner on Biblical truth is confronted by students of other denominations and somewhat different beliefs whose conviction and skill in Biblical exegesis match his own.

For many students, campus life itself opens windows in all directions. During 1965–66, University of Chicago theologian Martin Marty, English historian A. L. Rouse, and commentator Howard K. Smith spoke on campus, and staff members from Martin Luther King's Southern Christian Leadership Conference came to the college to discuss plans for a summer End-the-Slums movement in Chicago. The Artists Series brought the Cleveland Symphony, the Robert Shaw Chorale, the Netherlands Chamber Orchestra, Rudolph Serkin, and Nathan Milstein. (A member of the freshman class performed a piano composition of his own with the Boston Symphony.) *Record* editorials argued that the cancellation of Cassius Clay's Illinois bout was a flagrant violation of his right to free speech, and that "anyone who would consider Emerson or Matthew Arnold spiritually more sound than Sartre or Kafka simply does not understand the implications of these writers' thoughts." Several writers debated whether Scripture could be adduced to support a liberal political position, a conservative one, or neither, and a columnist writing under the name Pangloss neatly roasted all the sacred cows in sight.

Wheaton sends students off campus, too. Some study abroad; thirty-one served as student missionaries in eighteen countries during the summer of 1966; many have tutored high school students in a program planned in cooperation with Chicago social agencies; others have worked with deprived children on Chicago's South Side. And not all the off-campus work is Evangelism or service. One member of the faculty observed that the parents of these students "would have gone to Bible conference in the summer and stayed around the fringe of American society." But the students, or some of them, want to be involved in that society. Recently this desire has led to active politicking in national or regional groups like the National Student Association or the Young Republicans.

On campus and off, Wheaton lays before its students a landscape of ideas and experiences more various than most of them have seen before. But the toppling and rebuilding of convictions, the basic reexamination of religious and intellectual positions essential to these students' growth, seems to begin, usually, with course work. In philosophy classes there are "no unaskable questions," and students often find themselves contending for their faith with Hume or Bertrand Russell. Sociology, anthropology, and psychology suggest interpretations of human behavior that do not sit easily with the simpler versions of Fundamentalism. Bible courses make clear the historical context in which the Scriptures were written and relieve students of extravagantly allegorical or naïvely literal readings their local preachers may have burdened them with. In this process of rethinking their beliefs, students look particularly to faculty who take a clear position themselves but who are not defensive or dogmatic about it, who invite students to get inside religious or philosophical positions other than their own, acknowledging their strengths and defining their limitations. Instructors ask students to read and take seriously non-Evangelical theologians like Paul Tillich or Karl Barth, and existentialist writers like Camus or Sartre. Some are willing to discuss, without evasion or oversimplification, the problems that persistently trouble students: Does scriptural religion oblige one to take some kind of social or political action? Can one separate Evangelical doctrine from the restrictions and expectations of Evangelical culture? What is to persuade one that the Bible is not just a literary, historical, or anthropological document? What if the proofs for the existence of God *are* invalid? Aside from simple competence, this openness among the faculty, the willingness to ask hard questions, is the quality that seems to draw greatest respect from Wheaton students.

Some students, including some of the most able ones, find Wheaton's confinements intolerable and leave. But for almost all those that stay, the college has, I believe, a liberalizing effect. For the majority of students, probably, Wheaton provides solid training, increased awareness of the artistic and intellectual world, more sophisticated Biblical and philosophical undergirding for their religious beliefs, and more flexible social and political attitudes. When they go back to their homes and churches, they will be uncomfortable with some of the opinions and reasoning they encounter, but they will continue to be essentially Evangelical in doctrine and culture. For others, often those with intellectual inclinations, Wheaton precipitates a deeper questioning of received doctrine and greater impatience with what they see as the narrowness, the fearfulness, the inconsistency of Evangelical practice. Though they usually remain orthodox Christians, these students often leave their home churches for more liberal denominations and abandon many of the Fundamentalist mores.

However they emerge, Wheaton students are obliged to put together belief and conduct in a systematic way. Through a remarkable combination of intellectual stimulation and tenacious opposition (on the part of the President, the Trustees, and some faculty) to any departure from Evangelical faith or practice, the college creates discussion as intense, perhaps, as any to be found on American campuses, and as consistently directed to ultimate issues.

Perhaps one can best sense the kind of development that may overtake a student by following a single individual as he comes, changes, and goes. The student whose Wheaton years are summarized here emerged from a background fairly typical of Wheaton students, but he is more intellectual than most and went through more dramatic changes; most Wheaton students remain loyal to Evangelical Christianity and conservative politics.

Although I grew up in Latin America where my parents were missionaries, I came to Wheaton with the social and political attitudes—if without quite the comfortable affluence—that most Wheatonites share. In high school I took the pietistic emphases of our tradition quite seriously, having devotions of prayer and Bible-reading probably an hour a day and attempting to further the process of sanctification (interpreted as continuous inner joy, peace, love, and freedom from unworthy thoughts and intents). "Witnessing" or "testifying" to my faith was essential in furthering what was seen as the Christian's first duty: evangelization, "leading others to the Lord." The Christian life entailed "separation from the world," except for occasional forays to "preach the Word to the world" through distribution of tracts or streetcorner preaching. (We were often told to carry our Bibles on top of our books to school so as to get a chance to testify.)

During my freshman year at Wheaton, I kept my daily devotions, joined Student Missions Forum with its World Focus prayer groups, attended weekly prayer meetings, directed an Evangelistic service for Spanish-speaking prisoners in the local jail every Sunday night, and taught a Sunday school class at a Spanish-speaking church in a nearby town. I attended the local Fundamentalist churches whenever possible.

But as early as my senior year in high school, I had become discontented with the erratic nature of my spiritual life and uncomfortable at the hypocrisy of professing what I knew darn well I didn't have in terms either of "spiritual fruits" or of repentance for sin. Most frequently, the Fundamentalist professes his joy and closeness to Christ, his peace of mind, his spiritual victories through Bible-reading and prayer, his successes through trust in God. . . . Most of this, I am convinced, is the well-meaning but usually psychologically impossible effort to impose an inherited set of infinitely detailed categories on one's experience. The consequence is secret and inadmissible frustration and defensiveness about fundamentalist mores, doctrines, and terminology.

My rejection of what I came to consider false and hypocritical "humble-pie" came near the end of my freshman year after a semester in an honors introduction to philosophy section and lots of contact with friends who were taking anthropology and psychology and were talking about cultural or psychological determinism. I recall that I felt miserable as the objective pillars of my faith seemed to crumble away. . . . When I asked myself, "How do I know that I know God?" I could find no answer. I think it was my encounter with the pragmatism of John Dewey in my philosophy course which sealed the matter, as I applied the pragmatic test for truth to my own experience and found it wanting. But more than that it provided me with a positive framework within which I could reorient my experience and values in freedom, without a rigid and stifling list of categories to structure them by. I remember that when I could at last positively affirm that I did not believe in God, it was like a great burden rolling off my back leaving me with an exhilarating sense of freedom. At last I could be myself, be honest; and I soon discovered that it was both fun and intellectual to be a trenchant iconoclast.

This new identity was undoubtedly one of the most significant events in my intellectual development, for it brought me into contact with the keenest minds on campus and pushed me into much more vigorous thinking and academic work. And it would not have been possible without the stress on uncompromising honesty by a few professors. Although I can now look back and see some of the more superficial motives of my behavior, I do believe that by and large my newfound "search for Truth" was quite sincere. It certainly excited me about a liberal arts education, and made me seek out the best teachers and students in order to match my mind with theirs. An honors course in literature was especially stimulating, and courses in anthropology and psychology pushed me on in my pursuit of a naturalistic basis for human values. And through all this, ultimate values which could give convincing direction both to my life and to society remained my first concern; here one can see the intense need to discover ultimate norms for human existence that is characteristic of Wheaton's education. I was still seeking for Truth with a capital T. But this search meant reading Albert Camus, Jean-Paul Sartre, Feodor Dostoevsky and Francois Mauriac, as well as John Dewey and Julian Huxley. And there came the rub.

I think it was these existentially-oriented writers (together with my lit prof's criticisms of my humanistic literature papers) who first made me realize that the problem of evil was not merely an intellectual one . . . but an intensely personal one: why are some people lonely and neurotic while others are not? How does a bland, optimistic religion of humanity and progress (á la Huxley) help them? Is not a world in which six million Jews can be slaughtered in cold blood an absurd one? Does not death itself make all our hopes and values absurd? To paraphrase Ivan Karamazov, isn't anything possible morally in a world where God does not exist, yet where men find themselves free? As I read theologians like Paul Tillich, these questions began to bite deeper and deeper, making a naturalistic ethics seem almost farcical in its naïveté. The existential dilemma of No Exit and The Flies became intensely personal, and Byron's Manfred became the foremost symbol of my alienation from the entire world, including myself. . . .

It was during this experience that the answers of Dostoevsky and Mauriac took on new significance and when my reading of great non-Fundamentalist Christian theologians like Paul Tillich, Donald Baillie and Emil Brunner led me to a new assessment of Christian faith. The compassionate and understanding encouragement of a couple of teachers was particularly helpful in enabling me to see Christianity in a new light, making it philosophically attractive and even compelling. I think it was the discovery of the concept of grace as unconditional love that took me beyond the emotionally loaded legalistic view of God as the cosmic tyrant or as an effete meek-and-mild Jesus acting like Uriah Heep.

I have changed somewhat since then. I have come to a new appreciation of the theological distinctives of Fundamentalism—the solicitude for clear-thinking consistency and truth, the sense of moral antithesis and the unescapable necessity of radical choice, the forthright emphasis on the doctrine of redemption as God's solution to the problem of evil, and the encouragement of a strong lay role in the mission of the church. But I am not and cannot be a Fundamentalist. I continue to feel that Fundamentalist ethics are unrealistic and even un-Christian, since they produce a new legalism of faith and works in place of the strong Biblical emphasis on grace and freedom, out of which responsible discipleship alone can arise. I do have other theological differences, of course, and plan in fact to be confirmed soon in the Episcopalian church. I will be attending Yale Divinity School next year under a Rockefeller Theological Fellowship. Yet I respect the ethical conflicts of Fundamentalists and feel that it is this pietistic seriousness which gives Wheaton its intense sense of ultimacy and reflects itself even in Wheaton's rebels.

Politically and socially my attitudes have undergone changes as well. I think I came here a Goldwater supporter, but by the end of my sophomore year I was quite liberal politically (not just in terms of Wheaton but of the national spectrum as well). I think President Kennedy's death was something of a catalyst to new attitudes. A summer of work as a door-to-door salesman in southwest Georgia particularly convinced me of the justness of the civil rights cause. Now I personally have a great deal of sympathy with the radical left, while most Wheaton students are just getting used to the NAACP. I hope to work eventually in Latin America, probably in social development programs (where my Christian witness will certainly come to bear).

The future Like other colleges, Wheaton has recently introduced significant structural changes. The curriculum has been reorganized so that students normally take only four courses at a time; a Faculty Senate has been created to carry on many of the policy deliberations and conduct much of the business formerly entrusted to the faculty as a whole; tutorial work and honors work have become prominent features of the instruction in many departments. And other changes have been proposed—for example, a new academic calendar that would permit the college to be in session a greater proportion of the year, regular programs of study abroad or off-campus work and service, and the institution of graduate work outside the School of Theology, particularly in education. Some supporters have urged the college to follow the example of St. John's College and set up a twin Wheaton in another part of the country. (President Armerding observes that Westmont College in Santa Barbara has become something like a West Coast Wheaton without Wheaton's doing anything about it.) The President himself has publicly discussed the possibility of organizing a "cooperative university," sharing the resources of strong Evangelical colleges to offer solider and more varied graduate programs than any one college could support. These proposals and others will be debated in the next years, and some will be adopted.

But few people at Wheaton feel that the future of the college will be made or marred primarily by structural changes of this sort. Wheaton's future will be contested on other ground. One of the contestants will be the Trustees, speaking for the college's tradition, for more conservative members of the faculty, and for the constituency. In the spring of 1966, the *Wheaton Alumni* magazine published replies by nine Trustees to the question, "What do you see in Wheaton's future?" What they see, in addition to new buildings, improved faculty salaries, and a modest increase in enrollment, is a Wheaton that will continue to produce well-rounded graduates doing the Lord's work in secular occupations and in churches, schools, seminaries, and missions throughout the world, a Wheaton that has "the heart and will to continue against all efforts either from within or without to water down or compromise its century-old belief in the eternal Word of God." Again and again they warn against "apostasy," against "infidel leavening, subtle infiltration, and un-Biblical intellectuality," admonishing their readers to remember other colleges that began with Christian commitment but drifted into secularity. They emphasize academic quality but always in a Biblical context—"the finest in scholarship with a close adherence to the Holy Scriptures" or "safe and sound scholarship."

The Trustees see it as their own function to resist pressure and to "take a positive stand upon issues where their faith in God and His Word will conflict with concepts of the 'intellectuals of the hour.' " To be sure that it will take that stand, the Board intends to "guard jealously its membership, so that never will there be one man on the Board who is not a Bible-believing, born-again Christian, completely dedicated to promoting the College's spiritual and academic welfare." In the impressive unanimity of the Trustees' statements, only one paragraph suggests that times and students may have changed, and not altogether for the worse. It is written by the Chairman of the Board: "I look for a student body of the character and caliber of those now in Wheaton. I have no doubt that my editorials, when editor of the *Wheaton Record* in 1902–3, would seem stuffy to today's editors. In fact, they would seem stuffy to me could I reread them. Similarly, some recent editorials, to my aging eyes, seem presumptuous or even juvenile. Yet they reflect basic taste and character in the authors."

Those student authors, presumptuous perhaps but commanding respect, make it abundantly clear that the Trustees are not the only group wishing to have their say about the college's future. For a substantial portion of the student body and a good many of the faculty, the danger is not apostasy but rigidity. They warn that if the college imposes restrictions on its members' behavior without convincing reasons, if its language is a generation out of date, if it does not welcome debate on all points of political and religious doctrine, then it will lose some of its most vigorous students and faculty and make cynics of some of those who stay. (This fear, they argue, has present substance. In 1965–66, perhaps a half dozen of the faculty, among them some of the ablest, took other jobs, partly at least because of the addendum and what they read as other signs of retrenchment. This is not numerically a high rate of turnover, but it caused concern on campus.)

This segment of Wheaton is convinced that the college has the tradition, the money, the faculty, and the students to lead its constituency. In the winter of 1962–63, one of the editors of *Brave Son*, often critical of Wheaton, visited fourteen Evangelical colleges from coast to coast. His conclusions, in part, were these: "Where do we stand at Wheaton? Cast in the lead role. Our campus, for better or worse, is far more alive intellectually than any other campus visited. There is less ignorance, more discussion; less apathy, more activity. [A visitor] remarked to me during his stay on campus that there is a tension building within the whole Evangelical world and its focal point is Wheaton College." The more liberal people at the college would like to be sure this tension leads to new explorations and applications of Biblical truth.

More specifically, these people would like to see the college hew out a philosophy of culture and a philosophy of art—or at least provide a setting in which to discuss the patterns of conduct and the kinds of artistic expression appropriate to Evangelicals. They would like to see the college recognize that more and more of its students will bear witness in secular occupations and social service rather than missions work. (A large display case outside the administrative offices lists, class by class, all the alumni who have served with foreign missions. The number rises gradually through the 1930s and 1940s to a high of 100 alumni from the class of 1947; then it falls off until only 6 names are listed for 1964. On the other hand, a number of recent graduates have gone into the United States Foreign Service, and 20 percent of the 1965 freshmen say they "definitely" or "probably" plan to enter the Peace Corps.) With this recognition would come greater attention to social problems and fuller discussion of the kinds of service or social action, if any, required by Biblical Christianity.

Most basically, this portion of the Wheaton community insists that inquiry be free, even if it leads to skepticism or requires attitudes more ambiguous or complex than the ones Fundamentalism usually espouses. Free inquiry is the element that comes first to mind when Wheaton students think of liberal education. "I still don't know what a liberal arts education is," a student wrote in *Brave Son*. "But I really think it has something to do with freedom to find your own answers and honesty to express them and responsibility to do something about them." A large proportion of the students would concur.

The vision of Wheaton that moves the more liberal students and faculty is not the vision that sustains the Trustees. What looks like Christian liberal education from one angle may look like apostasy from another. It is thus hard to see how Wheaton, in the next years, can be placid—unless the students grow silent, the faculty stop reading, and the Trustees lose interest in doctrine. But while the contest goes on—and partly *because* it goes on—students will continue to come to Wheaton from Evangelical homes and receive excellent training in chemistry, music, psychology, biology, or whatever. They will get to know books, arguments, and styles of life they might never have met otherwise. They will begin to see America's problems as their own, to be analyzed and worked at, not just deplored. And repeatedly, intensely, they will examine their beliefs—defending, doubting, testifying, insisting that their experience yield meaning.

Conrad Hilberry, associate director of this study and professor of English at Kalamazoo College, was the author of the Wheaton College Profile. His associate was Morris T. Keeton, director of this study and Academic Vice President of Antioch College. Peter Veltman, chairman of the Department of Education and now Dean of the College at Wheaton, was Wheaton's representative. The student observers were Ronald Lehmann and Ruth Mesing of Knox College and Claudene Oliva of Antioch.

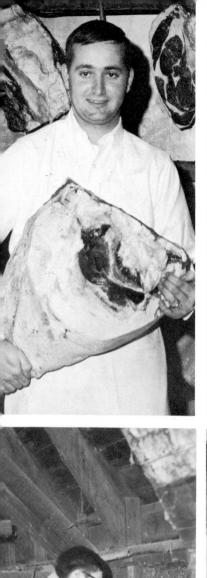

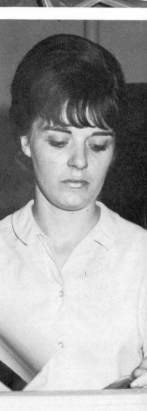

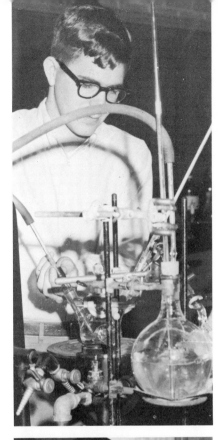
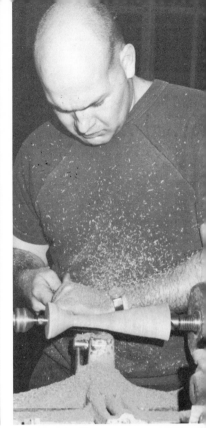

Berea College is well known for its strong liberal
arts curriculum, its work program, its free-tuition
policy, its endowment, and especially its
dedication to the higher education of young
men and women of its geographical area. The
nondenominational, humanitarian, and democratic
atmosphere of Berea embodies ideals to which
lip service is paid in most colleges but which
seldom exist in fact.

BEREA College, a coeducational liberal arts college of approximately 1,350 students, is located in the town of Berea, Kentucky, in the foothills of the Cumberland Mountains. Many visitors to the region have pleasant memories of the college, of the campus shaded with beautiful trees, of the surrounding hills, and of the excellent food served by students in the college-owned Boone Tavern. Possibly, too, they have acquired gifts made by students in one of the college industries. Today Berea College is well-known for its strong liberal arts curriculum, its work program, its free-tuition policy, its endowment, and especially its dedication to the higher education of the young men and women of its geographical area.

The roots of the past In many ways a unique institution, Berea has been remarkably true to its past, and two features of the college in particular—its emphasis on interracial service to its area and its student work program—go back to 1855, when a small one-room nondenominational church school was established on the Berea Ridge. John G. Fee, an abolitionist minister under whose auspices the school was established, saw in it the beginnings of an institution "which would be to Kentucky what Oberlin is to Ohio, anti-slavery, anti-caste, anti-rum, anti-sin." Later Fee wrote, "We ... eventually look to a college— giving an education to all colors, classes, cheap and thorough."[1] In

[1] Elisabeth S. Peck, *Berea's First Century*, University of Kentucky Press, Lexington, 1955, p. 8.

1859 a constitution was drawn up for the college by Fee, a young Oberlin graduate named John A. R. Rogers, and others. The constitution laid down principles which Berea has preserved through the years—that the college should be under a Christian but nonsectarian influence, that thorough education should be furnished at least possible expense, the facilities for manual labor should be provided, and that opposition should be brought against "slaveholding, caste, and every other wrong institution or practice."[2]

Almost at once, hostility erupted toward Fee and his abolitionist friends, and the college was not finally incorporated until 1866. That year, of 187 students, 96 were Negroes and 91 were whites.

Berea was known as a "college"; in fact, however, until the 1890s, it was little more than an elementary and preparatory school. The first college graduating class in 1873 numbered only 3, and in 1890 only 28 of a total enrollment of 355, were in the college.

The free-tuition policy for which Berea is famed was not established until 1892. Also in the 1890s occurred an expansion of the labor program, which at Berea had been an outgrowth of the manual labor schools of the 1830s and 1840s. While labor programs in other colleges were eventually abandoned, Berea's grew; it flourishes today.

During the 1890s, Berea struggled hard but successfully to retain its white students and remain a biracial school. Suddenly, in 1904, the Day Law was passed by the Kentucky Legislature, making it unlawful to operate a school or college where both Negroes and whites are received for instruction. The act was aimed specifically at Berea, which was the only mixed college in the state. Even before the segregation law was upheld by the U.S. Supreme Court, Berea began to plan for a new Negro institution; President Frost raised funds equal to the Negroes' share of the Berea endowment, and in 1910 the Lincoln Institute was established for Negroes. Not until 1950, when the Day Law was amended, did Negroes and whites again attend Berea together. Through the years, however, the college continued to promote interracial understanding in an attempt to remain true to its heritage.

Student labor program   The concept of manual labor as a vital part of the educational experience has had probably greater and more lasting success at Berea than at any other college. Certainly, it has been successful partly

[2] *Ibid.,* p. 13.

because the labor program has enabled the college to keep costs to its students at the extremely low level demanded by their financial circumstances. A great deal of credit has to be given to the students, whose work has been efficient enough to maintain the competitive position of the industries. In this respect Berea's program is quite different from the typical student aid program maintained by most colleges, in which the chief objective is financial aid with work efficiency only a secondary factor.

Berea's work program involves all students for a minimum of ten hours per week. A student may work longer, with a labor load adjusted to his academic load. The pay scale varies with duties and responsibilities, but ordinarily the student carrying a full academic load is able to earn enough to pay for about one-half of his term bill for room, board, and fees.[3]

A special work program for the student with greater financial need may enable him to work twenty-four hours a week, but he must then reduce his classes to approximately three-fourths of a normal academic load. Students in the special work program are also given $100 each semester to be applied to the term bill.

The range of student occupations involves work in administrative and departmental offices, preparation and serving of meals, care of buildings and grounds, and work in the industries (bakery, candy kitchen, college press, needlecraft, weaving, woodcraft, dairy, broom making, and the college inn). During his college career, a student may work in one or more of sixty-four different departments.

Berea's work program differs from Antioch's work-study program, which employs alternating periods of work and study. At the same time, both Berea and Antioch recognize that work experience can play a vital role in the process of liberal education. Such experience engenders habits and attitudes which should transfer to later employment and also to living in general. As one observes the Berea students at work, he is impressed by their diligence and their apparent acceptance of the "Berea way," with its emphasis upon the ready assumption of responsibility, respect for others, and friendliness toward colleagues.

Characteristic attitudes and values   Approximately 90 percent of Berea's students are from the eight states of Alabama, Georgia, Kentucky, North and South Carolina,

[3] While in terms of actual dollars this is so, in practice the students find that their pay goes for travel, clothing, and incidentals, even at the increased hourly rates made possible through the U.S. Office of Education.

Tennessee, West Virginia, and Virginia. These states are rapidly becoming more urban. However, many of their urban centers are still relatively small cities; and the Berea student's capacity for hard work and his clearly defined vocational aspirations stem in part from his desire to escape from a life which offers narrow prospects of vocational satisfaction. Upward social mobility also operates as a powerful incentive for students aspiring to a life in business or one of the professions in a prosperous urban area. The majority of the almost twelve thousand alumni and former students of Berea have left Appalachia and are scattered widely across the country and around the world.

A substantial number—over four thousand—have retained strong ties with home and community and have returned to serve in both rural and urban areas of Appalachia—most frequently, perhaps, as teachers. Service to the people of Appalachia remains a substantial motivating force to many students, paralleling the service mission of the college.

Certainly the Protestant ethic, which we are told is dying or dead in much of the country today, is anything but dead at Berea. The Berea way of life has many points in common with the traditional Protestant ethic as Weber described it.[4] This way of life stands in sharp contrast to the alienation and lack of commitment supposedly characteristic of a large part of this student generation. At the same time, it does not conform entirely to the ethic and outlook of southern Appalachia.

One might venture, as a hypothesis, that Berea exerts a powerful effect upon the student's value structure because of the social climate of the area from which most of its students come. The college still gets its students largely from a population resembling that of the rural United States in the nineteenth century, from which many private liberal arts colleges drew so heavily. As a result of rapid urbanization and increased prosperity, these colleges today tend to attract an urban, upper-middle-class student body, but Berea does not. This suggests that Berea represents a more stable community than most liberal arts colleges. Much of the liberal Protestant outlook of the late nineteenth and early twentieth centuries seems to have been retained, including the values of thrift, sobriety, social service, and moral earnestness. Although cultural change at Berea goes on as it inevitably must in a community which is not too isolated and although students are made aware of competing philosophies and of

[4] Max Weber, *The Protestant Ethic and the Spirit of Capitalism*, Charles Scribner's Sons, New York, 1958.

social trends, there has so far been little change in the fundamental value structure. Questions may be raised and doubts expressed, but Berea changes much more slowly than the strongly urban-influenced college. In its basic values, the community calls to mind ideas of progress, democracy, and Christian humanism characteristic of an earlier day. In short, Berea is contemporary without having discarded the past. Such a value complex may be instructive and pertinent for tomorrow as well as today.

Knapp and Goodrich have done a study in which they see scientists as being frequently drawn from situations which provide few competing vocational opportunities, where traditional occupations are sharply restricted and where science may be regarded as an avenue to improved social and economic status.[5] In a more recent study by Knapp and Greenbaum, *The Younger American Scholar,* Berea was listed in the top 50 of 377 institutions on the basis of an index of male recipients of scholarships for graduate study.[6] The only other Southern colleges listed in the top 50 were the University of the South and William and Mary. Berea's indices in the social sciences and the humanities were not high enough to place the college in the top 20 in either of these categories; in science, however, Berea placed *seventeenth* among 377 institutions and was the only Southern college to place in the top 20.

There are a number of dramatic examples of students who come to Berea from small high schools where they have been poorly prepared in science and mathematics and emerge four years later to enter one of the nation's leading graduate departments in science. Consider Larry Blair.

Larry Blair graduated from Oil Springs High School in Kentucky first in his class of fifty-five, identified by his principal as the best pupil in his eight years' experience. Larry's father is dead; his mother, an elementary school teacher, earns enough to provide a modest living for Larry and his younger brother, also a Berea student. Although the family income is below the Berea average, Larry could have received scholarship aid to attend one of a number of colleges. He chose Berea because he was convinced by Berea graduates that the college provided the best liberal arts program in the state. Larry did not come to Berea well-prepared in science or mathematics (he found it necessary to start his mathematics with a course in algebra and trigonometry), but he did come with an interest in learning and doing scientific work, an interest generated by a highly inspiring, moderately informed chemistry teacher. Larry listed medicine first and teaching second among his occupational goals.

[5] R. H. Knapp and H. B. Goodrich, *Origins of American Scientists,* The University of Chicago Press, Chicago, 1952.
[6] R. H. Knapp and J. J. Greenbaum, *The Younger American Scholar: His Collegiate Origins,* The University of Chicago Press, Chicago, 1953.

At Berea, Larry took all the science and mathematics courses he could in addition to the required general studies and German. Except for his freshman year, when he worked for the Audio-Visual Aids Department, Larry has spent his time on the work program in the Chemistry Department; he has also been moderately active in student affairs (sophomore-class president and member of the Student Senate). He spent the summer after his freshman year at Berea taking a required course in the social sciences and a course in speech. He spent his second summer at the University of Louisville extracting an enzyme from mosquitoes, work supported by a National Science Foundation undergraduate research participation grant. His third summer he worked, at high pay, as a chemist for DuPont in Wilmington.

As a senior, Larry is using his considerable talents with great effectiveness. He has been granted one of the much-coveted National Science Foundation fellowships and will begin graduate work in chemistry at Stanford University in the fall. He has been preceded at Stanford by a Berea chemistry graduate who has already published two papers in his first year and a half as a graduate student. Larry knows that his own abilities are comparable and has few apprehensions about graduate school. He and a Berea senior in elementary education have tentative plans for marrying about a year after graduation.

Probably Larry Blair could have made the transition from rural high school to graduate work in science at any one of a number of colleges. It is not equally clear that Larry could have found himself in so many ways at another institution. His general education courses, in particular the required courses in the humanities, were sources of stimulation and satisfaction. He found himself enough in tune with his fellow students to assume, despite a disinclination toward self-assertiveness, positions of leadership. The models provided by his science teachers at Berea have given a direction to his career that, unless deflected by his graduate experiences, will lead him to college teaching. Berea has done more than train a chemist; it has assisted the development of a young man toward broad social usefulness.

Berea is also a productive institution in terms of the total number of graduates going on to receive a Ph.D. degree—not only in the sciences but in the humanities and social sciences as well. While it is difficult to assess the relative contributions of the characteristics of entering students and the characteristics of the college environment toward this result, one has the strong impression that Berea does well in maintaining and enhancing student ambitions.

The students   In one sense Berea's students are highly selected; in another sense they are not. About 80 percent of the entering students rank in the top fifth of their high school graduating class. On the other hand, Scholastic Aptitude Test scores, while they appear to be rising, are not as high as one would expect to find in a selective college.[7] These

[7] Mean scores for the class entering in 1965 were as follows: verbal, men 455, women 478; mathematical, men 496, women 467.

two facts tell us something significant about Berea's students and indicate the complexity of the educational task of the college.

Obviously, most of the students entering Berea have competed successfully in high school. They have formed a habit of success which is often a good index of future achievement. That their Scholastic Aptitude Test scores are generally not superior may be less a reflection upon their basic aptitudes than upon the quality of the instruction they have received at the primary and secondary levels. The southern Appalachian region has not been financially capable of supporting many high-quality school systems, and it is understandable that many Berea freshmen enter with some academic deficiencies in comparison with national norms. The college is then faced with the task of bringing these ill-prepared students within a four-year period to an academic level which will enable them to compete successfully in the graduate and professional schools to which approximately 55 percent of those receiving degrees go for further study.

Berea accepts the students with the highest academic qualifications from the group that meets the requirement of need established by the college.[8] Students from outside the region are limited to 10 percent of the student body, and competition among these applicants for admission is very keen. However, since these students from outside the region are an able group intellectually and represent diverse social backgrounds, they make a significant contribution to campus life.

Most of the students are from middle- or lower-middle-class families of the numerous small communities of the region. Of 418 freshmen enrolled in 1965, only 32 were from states other than those included in the southern Appalachian area, and 4 were from foreign countries. The average family income is reported to be under $4,000 per year. Many of the students feel that without Berea a college education would be impossible for them, although a growing number of public institutions are now becoming available, which changes this picture somewhat. Some students have chosen Berea because of its academic reputation, and others have been impressed by the reputation of the institution for Christian service.

Many students, faculty, and administrators are severely critical of what they refer to as "the barefoot image" of Berea. Despite efforts by the college to present a balanced, true image to its public, newspaper and magazine writers have almost always stressed the poor,

---

[8] Berea College policy is to accept only those students coming from families with income too low to pay a significant amount of tuition.

hardworking, and talented young man from the hills who badly wants a college education but has no money. Berea's free-tuition policy and work program are then presented as the answer to his prayers. While Berea does indeed wish to provide for these students, it wishes to provide for students from other locales in the region as well, and *what* it sees itself as providing is not a philanthropic hand-out, but a college education of some excellence. Bereans resent the extreme emphasis upon the "do-good" aspects of the college at the expense of the intellectual and academic aspects, of which they feel they can be justifiably proud.

One cannot fail to be impressed by the general activity level of the students. Course loads average fifteen to seventeen hours a week, plus two more hours for laboratory classes on the average. To these must be added ten hours of work. If we allow four hours a day for study six days a week (and this may be a low estimate), we arrive at a fifty-one- to fifty-three-hour week, which would seem to leave little time for extracurricular affairs. Typically, however, students are in-volved in a wide variety of time-consuming activities—sports, dra-matics, publications, an interdormitory "College Bowl," a little United Nations Assembly, movies, student government, a variety of arts and crafts projects—and these by no means exhaust the list. Since Berea has no fraternities or sororities, students are not burdened with the time demands that these organizations entail. Social activities tend to center in dormitory groupings, which are less formal in their orga-nization than fraternities and sororities would be.

The following brief biographical sketch, which may be regarded as typical in at least several respects, illustrates some of the facets of the background and campus experience of the Berea student.

Wilda Baldwin came to Berea from Logan County, West Virginia. However, unlike many Berea students, she graduated from a large city high school.

At the time Wilda applied to Berea College, her family (mother, stepfather— a retired coal miner—four younger children) had an annual income which was about average for Berea students, paid no federal or state income taxes, and paid a property tax of only $4.50. On her application form Wilda said that she wished to "become a teacher," that she chose Berea "because it is a religious college and it teaches one the importance of responsibilities." Her answer to the question, "If you are accepted, what will be your attitude toward the practice of racial equality?" was supported by the brief statement, "God created all men equal."

Although Wilda graduated eighth from the top of a high school class of about four hundred and had been a member of an advanced learning group, during her first two years at Berea she did not do especially well academically. Arriving at college with primary interests in science and mathematics, she soon found herself moving toward sociology and philosophy. Part of this shift

resulted from a more realistic appraisal of her interest and abilities, but part can be ascribed to the combined repulsion exerted by the required course in the physical sciences and attraction exerted by the introductory humanities and social science courses.

The humanities course that Wilda took in her sophomore year is "designed to reveal in correlation three mediums of man's creation—music, the visual arts, literature." For Wilda (as for all of the Berea students we talked to), this course, with its discussion groups, studio work, and frequent listening to music, "opened up a new world." Berea students, from a region with a strong tradition in a limited range of music and dance forms, frequently feel an intense excitement as they observe and participate in a broader sweep of human artistic expression. For Wilda the course was not enough; she began piano lessons.

Two one-semester courses in the Bible are required of all candidates for the A.B. degree. The first, "Literature and Religion of the Hebrews," Wilda took during her first semester; the second, "New Testament Literature and Religion," she studied in her fourth semester. Many students are shocked and upset by the factual objective treatment of ideas and happenings that they have always met in a highly emotional atmosphere. Wilda denies that she herself found the experience traumatic, but does feel that she was better able to talk about the significance of religion in her life after these courses.

Sometime during her second year, Wilda decided to major in sociology. Her third year was devoted almost exclusively to work in her field, and her fourth year was divided about equally between work in sociology and in the humanities, with a little time set aside for an elementary course in design and some continued evening work in crafts. It is not hard to understand Wilda's choice of field. The study of sociology promised to help her attain two ends that are strongly valued at Berea—awareness of the relation of the mountain culture to the rest of the world and an increased ability to be of service to others.

Wilda spent her first two years on the work program as a typist in the Vice President's office, and the junior and senior years as secretary to one of the professors in the Department of Philosophy and Religion. The second job was valuable to her in getting to know this much-admired teacher. Wilda volunteered that there were three members of the faculty she felt she could "go to with any problem."

Each summer, about seventy-five Berea girls work as helpers to families in Connecticut. Wilda spent two summers this way, one in a family with seven children. The $25 to $35 per week that the girls receive in addition to room and board is a significant contribution to the $300 they must pay each semester for room, board, and fees. However, Wilda was as pleased by the opportunity to study a family and a community so different from her own as she was by the wages.

What are some of the contributions that Berea has made to Wilda's growth during her college years? First, she has found the language, concepts, and detachment necessary to talk about herself. If we can judge from her autobiographical sketch (required of all applicants), she was nearly inarticulate about her hopes and plans when she applied to Berea. Four years later, she can discuss herself, her family, and her environment in terms adequate for the task. She can say that her values have changed from "instrumental and materialistic" to "intrinsic" and explain quite clearly what she means by these phrases. She tells of her plan to spend the summer following her graduation living with an Egyptian family in Cairo under the Experiment for International Living, and of the letter she wrote seeking advice from a prominent Southern author who lived for a time in Egypt. She has enough confidence to ignore his advice, "Don't go." She has a clear direction for the next few years—to train herself for some form of child welfare work—and has been given a traineeship in child welfare by the University of Tennessee Graduate School of Social Work. She will receive $2,000 plus tuition, and the appointment is renewable for a second year.

At the same time that she finds it easier to communicate with a range of people, she finds it harder to talk with her family. It seems unlikely that Wilda will go back to serve the people in the mountain counties, but very likely that she will be of service to some of the emigrants from these counties as they try to adapt to city life.

Wilda might be described as a student who has built on the values of Berea and adapted them to her own life.

Students at Berea are pleasant in manner, and friendliness is one of their most obvious and impressive characteristics. On the whole, student relations are democratic and unpretentious.

A number of informal groups can be distinguished within the Berea student body. Any classification of such groups must be based on somewhat arbitrary criteria, and must recognize their fluid and constantly changing composition. However, within these limits, one student observer felt that the following groups could be rather easily recognized.

Typical Berea students. Students making up this large group (possibly 70 percent of the student body) show considerable diversity, yet it is possible to identify several shared characteristics. These students are best-described as serious, hardworking, capable, alert, and well-motivated. Their tolerance and permissiveness create a student culture which accommodates individuals of widely differing attitudes and needs without imposing overly stringent group mores.

Activists. These are probably the most visible people on the campus. Their names are generally known. They are the self-confident students who tend to run things and spend a great deal of their time conferring with one another. There seems to be an unusually high representation of students from outside the region in this group. While in one sense "activism" is a term which characterizes Berea in general, here it refers more particularly to leadership in campus activities.

Apathetic students. Several tables are occupied in the afternoons and evenings by students who spend a great deal of time playing cards. These students do not seem to be deeply involved in academic or campus activities. In general, they may be characterized as apathetic, although the apathetic group certainly includes more individuals than just those who play cards. The picture of apathy that these students present, while it could probably be duplicated on any campus, does constitute a serious challenge to the college.

Aesthetes. There is an arty crowd, loosely composed of a number of English majors and students in dramatics, crafts, and music, who entertain themselves with such activities as amateur folk singing. These talented students form a group which tends to overlap with the campus activists and the cosmopolitan liberals.

Cosmopolitan liberals. This is a fairly small group deeply involved in political and social causes. Many of these students come from outside the region. A number of them plan to continue on to graduate school; others are interested in the Peace Corps, teaching and study abroad, etc.

Negro students. Since no records of the students' races are kept, it is impossible to say exactly how many Negro students there are in the college. A rough estimate, however, would place the number at about seventy-five. Both in and out of the classroom, Negro students tend to group together.

Students from outside the region. Some students say that they can easily spot a student from outside the southern Appalachian region. While the individuals who make up this rather small group of students mix frequently with the rest and do not stick closely to one another, there seems to be a general awareness of their identity. A number of them tend to emerge as campus leaders, particularly in the first two years.

In the area of race relations, Berea students appear to accept, at least passively, the traditional liberal position of the college. It is difficult to believe that many would act in a discriminatory manner with members of a minority group. On the other hand, many students come from towns in which racial attitudes are quite conservative and traditional. These students may then find themselves caught in a conflict of ideologies which can be expressed in rather subtle ways. Thus dating between Negroes and whites is rare, and is perhaps regarded as too flagrant a violation of the mores of the region. At the same time, there seems to be no conscious feeling of discrimination.

Most students take a moderate rather than activist position on civil rights. They feel that race relations at Berea approach the ideal, and they would deny that they are apathetic about the plight of the Negro. The motto of the college, "God hath made of one blood all nations of men," is frequently referred to as portraying the attitude of the college community without cant or hypocrisy.

Student relations with the faculty are on the whole easy, open, and informal, particularly in the smaller, upperclass courses. A number of the faculty make it a point to invite students to their homes, and students and faculty have an opportunity to become well-acquainted with one another through the work program. In general, while the faculty exhibits a strong personal interest in the students, students seem to regard a certain distance in their relationships with faculty as quite proper. This distance, arising perhaps from mountain mores, is based upon respect for the position of the professor, his experience, and his professional qualifications. The authority of the professor carries considerable weight with students, and they show little inclination to challenge his statements in class. They express the feeling that students who talk too much in class and raise too many questions are simply wasting a good deal of class time. On the other hand, in discussion classes, students may disagree quite violently with one another. The informality of such classes is often refreshing.

Student-administration relations are generally good. One hears some complaints about paternalism, but for the most part students seem to accept rules and regulations as necessary and desirable. Rules regarding chapel attendance, women's hours, and smoking arouse little organized protest. The drinking rule, however, does come in for some criticism, primarily because the students feel that it is not adequately enforced. A member of the faculty explained that the negative attitude on smoking, which is allowed only in specified places, was less on moral grounds than on the basis of unnecessary extravagance; drinking is still seen as a moral issue by a few. There is evidence that the rules are generally tempered by consideration and understanding and that there is on the part of students and faculty alike an appreciation of the good, simple life which Berea seeks to cultivate.

Courses of study The curriculum has been designed with the particular needs of Berea students in mind. There is, for example, a strong emphasis upon "core" courses, or general education courses designed to draw together "broad divisional fields" and to provide each student with a minimum level of knowledge, skill, and understanding in these areas. Placement tests are given at the beginning of the freshman year so that each student may be put in the basic courses for which he is prepared. Berea's stress on basic education seems more appropriate for students from culturally limited backgrounds than it would be in a college serving students from upper- and upper-middle-class families.

Many students feel that the humanities course is the most significant and enlightening in the curriculum; others think that it is at least the best general course. What is more surprising is that while we heard a few negative comments regarding some aspects of this course, we heard none that was generally unfavorable, despite the strict grading. It may be that such an offering would be equally successful on other campuses. On the other hand, it is perhaps more likely that the course is admirably tailored to the needs of students who have for the most part been deprived of the cultural advantages which the urban center provides in the fine arts, music, and literature.

Not all the core courses are highly regarded by students; in particular, the one in physical science fails to evoke much favorable comment from nonscience majors. However, Berea is like most colleges in having failed to discover a satisfactory solution to the problem of science instruction for the general student.

The required Bible courses tend to shock many students who have not been used to approaching religion in a reflective manner. Religion and theology evoke considerable interest on campus, which is reflected in discussions of Barth, Tillich, and Niebuhr and the utopian behaviorism of Skinner's *Walden Two*.

A course which illustrates the regional concern of the college is "Problems of the South." Others with a somewhat similar orientation are "Rural Community Development" and "Community Leadership and Action." The preoccupation with regional problems and interests comes out again and again in references made in class in a variety of subject-matter fields. The faculty appears to attempt to tie topics in with the experiential backgrounds of the students and to indicate relevance of particular subject matter to the region.

Thus in an urban sociology class for seniors, the central question raised on the day of our visit was "To what extent is the growth of cities contiguous to Appalachia the result of a repulsion exerted by the mountains, to what extent an attraction exerted by the cities?" The students are the test bodies probing such fields; little reference is made to statistical evidence bearing on the issue. In a Southern literature class, the teacher explored the authenticity of dialect in a story by having a student from the author's county read the story out loud, which she did fluently, unabashed by the scatter of apostrophes. In a philosophy class in theories of international relations, points were made, mountain style, by the use of stories featuring the granddaughter of the professor.

Some students decry this emphasis on regionalism in their classes, preferring the more cosmopolitan treatment they consider characteristic of a college with a national clientele. The professors, about half of whom are from far "out of territory," are very much aware of the regional characteristics of their students and find it natural and educationally sound to use such convenient resources.

If Berea seems to emphasize liberal learning, it by no means neglects special or vocational education. In addition to the degree of bachelor of arts, degrees are offered in agriculture, home economics, business administration, industrial arts, and nursing. About 40 percent of recent graduates have been prepared to teach. Programs are offered leading to certification in elementary education and in secondary education. Here again is evidence of the college's desire to serve not only the special needs of its students but those of the region as well. From a financial standpoint, it does not appear sensible for a small college to undertake such diversity in programs; offerings do make sense, however, when seen in the light of the general service aims of the institution.

The distribution of majors is interesting. The largest major is business administration, which is followed closely by English and elementary education. The combined Department of History and Political Science has a large major group, and it is followed by nursing and home economics. Biology, chemistry, and mathematics are about equal in size and have about the same numbers as sociology. Next in order come agriculture, industrial arts, and psychology. The major group in physics, while slightly smaller than that in psychology, is substantial in relation to those in other liberal arts colleges. Economics, art, languages, philosophy, religion, and music have relatively small numbers.

This distribution reflects the strong vocational interests of many students. The arts fields, while well-developed in terms of curriculum, seem to attract few students with professional ambitions. On the other hand, the sciences generally fare very well, with unusual strength in biology, chemistry, and mathematics.

Berea students are serious, conscientious, and highly motivated, and for the most part they appear to enjoy their academic work. Many of them report having to work very hard during the first year or two, and typically they find the last two years of concentration in a major field somewhat easier.

In addition to the previously mentioned tendency to draw on the regional background, a wide variety of classroom techniques is used in teaching classes of various sizes and different levels. Lecture classes are fairly popular, and students attending them are attentive and seem bent upon getting complete sets of notes. One complaint often registered, however, is that some of these classes are too large. The smaller discussion classes are more interesting to an observer, since much of the discussion is of a freewheeling variety in which students state their positions and defend them against one another. In some of these classes, students feel free to speak up without first being recognized by the professor.

Faculty Berea's faculty is drawn from many colleges and universities, both Northern and Southern. Several members of the faculty are Berea graduates. About one-third have the Ph.D. degree, and most of the others have a master's degree.

Faculty are frequently attracted to Berea by reports of the college and its program which have aroused their curiosity. Some investigate and are impressed by what they see. Some men join the faculty feeling that Berea will certainly be a place in which they can gain good experience and from which they may move to a higher-paying institution. Then, after two or three years at Berea, many a man finds that he has no real desire to leave. He enjoys the community, the teaching, and the advising responsibilities, and something of the dedication and high purpose of the institution gets into his blood.

Certainly it is not high salaries which keep a strong faculty at Berea. While the salary scale has improved considerably in recent years, salaries are still not high. The average salary of $7,970 paid in 1965–66 is considerably less than in most colleges of comparable stature. Substantial increases were made, however, between 1966 and 1969 to sustain Berea's access to faculty.

The emphasis at Berea falls heavily upon teaching and close personal contact with students. The man who sees himself as first of all a teacher is likely to find such a situation rewarding, whereas the man whose primary interests lie in research is likely to leave after a few years. Only a few of the faculty express the feeling that the college should provide greater research opportunities than it has in the past. In general, those who take this position are the scientists, who are naturally interested in research and can argue that with the rapid expansion of knowledge it is difficult to stay abreast in one's field without keeping up a regular research program.

As in most small colleges, the faculty is deeply involved in committee work and a great variety of extraclass activities. Schedules seem to be at least as heavy as in most colleges, if not heavier. A student-faculty ratio which is slightly under 14 to 1 appears to be reasonably favorable. Teaching loads, averaging between twelve and fifteen credit hours per week, are certainly not light; yet one hears few complaints about the overall work load, and efforts since 1965 have resulted in bringing standard teaching loads down to the twelve-hour level.

In general, the faculty seems fairly relaxed even though obviously quite busy, and the atmosphere remarkably free of the tensions which are common in university life and which seem to be growing in many small colleges. For most of the faculty at least, Berea seems much less a job than a way of life—that of the dedicated teacher serving a particular group of students within a particular framework of values.

A look at the future Over the years, the cause of Berea has appealed to many people, some wealthy and many in moderate circumstances, who have given generously to support the college and its ideals. As a result, the college today has an endowment with a book value of over $32 million and a considerably higher market value. This may make Berea appear to be one of the wealthiest of American colleges if we think of endowment only; but, since no tuition is charged, endowment has a special significance for Berea. In addition, the college is receiving increasing support through its alumni fund, which now yields approximately $125,000 a year. The average gift from the individual alumnus has increased steadily, and it is hoped will continue to do so. Total gifts for current operating expenses approach the striking level of $1 million a year.

Endowment remains, however, as the critical factor in the financial picture at Berea. This fact is recognized in a projection of the endowment fund which anticipates its virtual doubling within a twenty-year period and considerably greater growth when contemplated appreciation is taken into account. Significant changes in enrollment, in the program of the college, or in general business conditions could have profound financial effects.

An analysis of the budget indicates that nearly sixty percent of the current educational and general income is from endowment. Student fees account for slightly less than 5 percent, student industries 2 percent, student aid 5 percent, and rentals another 4 percent. Gifts for current operating expense total about 25 percent of the annual educational and general income.

Berea's free-tuition policy is made possible by two factors: Costs are kept low (less than $2,000 per student) through careful management, and income from endowment and gifts is considerably higher than that of most small colleges. Since buildings, including dormitories, are obtained as gifts, student cost for room can be kept to the minimal figure sufficient for maintenance of the dormitories. Board is charged at cost, and here the use of student workers results in lower costs for both the college and the students.

One big question that Berea must face is whether it will be possible in the future to maintain the free-tuition program. As costs climb, the college may be forced to adopt a small tuition charge; there is also the possibility that government support in some form may make such a charge unnecessary. Another possibility might be a tuition-loan plan, with the amount borrowed to be repaid over a period of years.

At present, costs are so low at state universities that from a purely financial standpoint there is increasingly less advantage to the student in attending Berea. Students who have transferred to state schools, however, attest that the advantage is still heavily in favor of Berea when social, recreational, lodging, and clothing costs are included. Only if the student lives close enough to a state university or a community college to commute is his apparent cost somewhat less than it would be at Berea.

One of the most impressive things about the college is its demonstration that private initiative is still capable of providing valuable and badly needed services to underprivileged young men and women. While government support in one form or another will undoubtedly aid colleges in the future, one need not think of the government as the only source of support for a program of higher education designed for those who are unable to meet full educational costs.

A nagging practical problem is whether Berea can continue to recruit a strong faculty in the future. The answer will depend in part on the ability of the college to pay higher salaries. The college does not need to compete with leading liberal arts colleges on a dollar-for-dollar basis, since there are several strong nonfinancial incentives that will attract the young teacher to Berea. On the other hand, the salary gap cannot be increased without possible serious consequences; in fact, it should probably be *decreased* if Berea is to retain the quality of its present faculty. This will not be easy to accomplish. Most strong colleges can still raise tuition in order to provide the needed dollars without pricing themselves out of the market. Berea, having no tuition charge, must raise the dollars in some other and obviously more difficult way. While the financial resources of the college are considerable, they will have to be increased appreciably to meet rapidly rising instructional costs.

In the long-term future, the relevance of Berea's special mission to the young people of Appalachia may change. At one time the need for secondary education was probably far greater than the need for a college program, and Berea's Foundation School, separate but closely affiliated with the college, was established for this purpose. In recent years, secondary education has improved to the point that the school has become unnecessary. It will soon close, and its boarding students will be taught in a new cooperative high school. The obvious question is whether Berea College's special orientation may in time become equally obsolete and out of step with the needs of the actual world.

Families have lived under adverse conditions in the southern Appalachian region for a long time, they probably will continue to do so for a long time to come, and there is no indication that the needs of the region will cease to exist. There is a possibility, however, that state and federal support will enable these needs to be met more adequately in the future. In this event, Berea may well decide to reexamine its role in American higher education.

Certainly, part of the college's great appeal lies in the high quality of its instruction. Except for its devotion to the region, Berea could easily recruit on a nationwide basis and offer a liberal arts education that few colleges could match. If the college chose to take this road, given its resources, it might quickly become one of the most selective liberal arts colleges in the country. To move from its present role, however, to that of an extremely selective, high-cost college would mark a sharp break with its past. In view of the circumstances under which many large bequests have been made to the college, it is difficult to believe that such a decision could ever be reached. Certainly, the service motivation that has characterized Berea throughout its long history cannot easily be given up, nor can one easily substitute the concept of service to higher education for service to the people of the geographical region.

Possibly a greater need for technical education will emerge in the future, and the college may decide to operate as a technological institute on the pattern of MIT or the California Institute of Technology. While social and economic trends may make such a move desirable, this would hardly appear today to be a significant possibility. The present combination of liberal arts and vocational programs seems admirably suited to the present situation and that of the immediate future.

What aspects of the Berea program appear to hold the most promise for developing institutions and, in particular, new colleges? Most significant, perhaps, is the regional emphasis, which could be adapted to the special needs of other geographical areas. While a number of such colleges might be developed for rural regions, others might be aimed more directly toward the needs of underprivileged urban groups. While it is true that community colleges and branches of many of our great state universities are now doing a great deal for the urban population, it could be argued that there is still room for high-quality private colleges offering low-cost education to a highly selected and intellectually able student body. The greatest problem, of course, for any private, regionally oriented college serving an economically underprivileged group would be that of keeping down the cost to the student. Berea's almost unique free-tuition policy hardly seems to be a possibility for the new or developing colleges, even though Berea's dedication to a service ideal has brought it great financial support over a long period of time. With today's costs, there is only the remotest possibility that even the most dedicated college could muster the support for a free-tuition policy. At best, such an institution might hope to charge tuition not too far out of line with that of the state universities.

The work program, which has been most successful at Berea, could be adopted by almost any college so inclined. Building local, student-operated industries would be a difficult but not insurmountable task. The work program, however, need not be patterned too closely on the Berea model. Several other types are now in operation, and recently there has been a resurgence of the idea that work experience can play a vital role in liberal education; in recent years, for example, such work programs have been developed at Beloit and Kalamazoo. It is interesting that in spite of the long-standing success of the work programs at Berea and Antioch, American colleges have been rather slow to extend the approach through additional practical programs. There seems to be a fertile field here for further investigation.

The nondenominational, humanitarian, and democratic atmosphere of Berea embodies ideals to which lip service is paid in most colleges but which seldom exist in fact. The particular spirit and tradition of Berea are in a sense unique and can never be transplanted to new soil. One cannot help being deeply impressed by the fact that Berea's traditions have continued uninterrupted for over one hundred years.

The dedication of men to an ideal, however, can find its expression in a number of different ways, depending upon varying cultural, political, and economic circumstances. Colleges like Berea contribute to the diversity that is one of the great strengths of higher education in America, and perhaps help to foster still other ventures in diversity elsewhere.

The principal author of the profile of Berea College was Parker E. Lichtenstein, Dean of the College at Denison University. Acting on behalf of Berea was James R. Bobbitt, associate professor of art; Dr. Lichtenstein's associate was Albert B. Stewart, professor of physics at Antioch College. The student observers were James Reed of Ripon College and Marilyn McNabb of Earlham.

CHAPTER 2

THE CHOOSING

OF COLLEGE PURPOSES

THE founders of the country's first colleges had important
choices to make—to what extent their training should be
clerical and to what extent civil;* how tolerant their Puritanism
should be, where the institutions should be located (for a time the
school which became Yale actually operated in three places at
once). But they were confronted with nothing like the range of
choices that face a new college today—alternatives in the variety
of students to serve, in the array of intellectuals available for faculty,
in communities wanting to be their hosts, in curriculums to offer,
in resources to muster, and in the range of complementary functions
in research and public service that might be creatively combined
with undergraduate teaching. Each of these choices involves both
risk and opportunity. In this forest of possibilities, how can a
college find the maximum opportunity for success in the risk it takes?

Our study has convinced us that safety for colleges in the future
lies in greater risks—not thoughtless gambling, but deliberate
chancing of socially important and hitherto unmet responsibilities.
Almost a decade ago, Earlham College decided that its vision of a

* In 1724 a friend of the college suggested that William and Mary be officially
recognized as a school of civil service training and that from each graduating
class there be appointed surveyors, clerks to the colonial government, and
county clerks (Frederick Rudolph, The American College and University, Vintage
Books, Random House, Inc., New York, 1965, p. 7).

71

world community implied a commitment to non-Western studies at the undergraduate level—a commitment generally regarded as too expensive and too disruptive for a small college to fulfill. Only large universities could do a good job in non-Western studies, it was said. Yet Earlham took the gamble. It sought a partner college, then an association of partner colleges in the Great Lakes area, then partners overseas. Today, it challenges the provincialism and nationalism of its students with one of the most sophisticated programs of foreign study available. Again and again the initial vitality of the colleges we studied could be traced to a critical risk, often a distinctive moral commitment. Wheaton in Illinois began in a battle against slavery, oath-taking, and secret societies. Oberlin fueled its early zeal with feminist, antislavery, and Evangelical missionary concerns. Monteith at Wayne State combined commitment to a special approach to liberal education with a concern for the children of laborers and immigrants in the inner city of Detroit.

How is a college to recognize a great risk that is also a promising one? We know no easy answer to this question. Our study, however, suggests some clues.

Beyond the true, the good The first clue is this: A college may find a promising risk in committing itself deliberately not only to critical inquiry but to other values as well. It would seem almost self-evident that liberal education must concern itself with discovering and holding to what is good, with asking why it is good and how it might be better. To know oneself and one's environment is to appreciate the forms of worth achieved and still to be achieved. Yet there is a strong trend in intellectual circles today toward ethical and religious neutralism; it is commonly thought that the commitment to critical inquiry can be served well only if all other commitments are subordinate to it. As recently as the autumn of 1966, the American Association of University Professors reflected the aspiration toward neutralism in its proposal to the American Council on Education and the Association of Governing Boards of Universities and Colleges. The statement on government of campuses reads:

When an educational goal has been established, it becomes the responsibility primarily of the faculty to determine appropriate curriculum and procedures of student instruction.

Special considerations may require particular accommodations: (1) a publicly-supported institution may be regulated by statutory provisions, and (2) a church-controlled institution may be limited by its charter or by-laws.

When such external requirements influence course content and manner of instruction or research, they impair the educational effectiveness of the institution.

This statement confuses two ideas. True, the faculty should be primarily responsible for implementing college goals, but that does not mean that the goals should have no influence upon curriculum and instruction. Any goals that are not vapid will necessarily have some such bearing. The question is how goals can be implemented so that learning is most productively advanced.

Similarly, accreditation examiners often assume that religious commitment in a college, if genuine, unavoidably interferes with liberal education. Their question then is simply whether the pressure for academic excellence manages to circumvent or overcome that religious commitment. One of our reasons for studying Wheaton College was to find out how its intense Evangelical Protestant commitment interacts with its academic aspirations. Indeed, we brought with us to Wheaton the usual preconceptions—that inquiry would be restricted to "safe" subjects, that inculcation of doctrine would take precedence over free examination of issues. In some respects we found this to be so. Radical speakers are not often given audience on campus, the literary magazine does submit to a kind of censorship, and some scientists are embarrassed and perhaps hampered in their work by the Trustees' insistence on a simple and explicit doctrine of creation. But far more important, we felt, was the impetus that religious conviction gives to students' learning. The brighter students, at any rate, read philosophy, psychology, anthropology, and theology with a passion that we have seldom encountered at secular schools. These are not simply studies. They are arguments that will confirm or challenge the beliefs on which the students' lives are built. Instead of closing them off from learning, Evangelical Christianity drives many Wheaton students into persistent and rigorous consideration of difficult philosophical, religious, and social questions.

The profile writers found something similar at Earlham. Earlham's traditional convictions—its internationalism, its opposition to war, its trust in decision by consensus, its stress on "community"—all these, in our observation, are likely to stimulate inquiry rather than stifle it. Colleges may doubtless be so rigidly doctrinaire that they shut off learning, but we think this danger has been overemphasized, with the result that some schools eschew convictions that might have fired controversy and discovery on campus. As long as students and faculty feel free to quarrel with received doctrine, secular or

*religious, and know where to find support for contrary opinions, a
college can well risk standing for something.*

*Everett Wilson, sociologist on the study staff, offers this speculation
about the relations between moral concern and liberal learning.*

**The morally concerned are more likely to have goals toward which academic
work, conventionally conceived, can be seen as useful, if not indispensable,
means.**

**The morally concerned will be anxious to build an intellectual underpinning
making their commitments stronger and surer. (. . . I note in passing a separate,
and obvious, problem: the conscious—or more dangerous, the unwitting—
selection of evidence to support one's predispositions.)**

**No problem lacking a moral component is likely to be as compelling, as
effective in stimulating inquiry or generating vigorous debate as one in which
the moral aspect is salient.**

**Probably moral concerns heighten the need for integrating one's knowledge,
for achieving closure, for developing personal integrity.**

**Since all enduring human relationships have a mandatory aspect, an oughtness,
about them, sensitivity to men as valuing creatures is particularly relevant for
students in the humanities and social sciences. Nor are such aspects irrelevant
for the student in biological and physical sciences, for the organization and
support of scientific work and the use of scientific findings pose moral problems
in these fields as well.**

The uses of tension *A second clue derives from the first: A college may well risk
espousing goals or values that are in tension with one another. In
fact, if the goals or values are not platitudinous, they are almost
sure to create tensions. At Wheaton and, to a lesser extent, at
St. Thomas, an accepted creed pulls constantly against the demands
of free inquiry. At Goddard, the commitment to an extraordinary
conception of education is sometimes at odds with the faculty's
desire to achieve prestige in the disciplines or students' demands
that they be systematically prepared for graduate work. Many
students at Monteith enter college with a fairly clear ambition—to
prepare themselves to get a good job. But immediately they find
this ambition contested by the Monteith faculty, who are determined
to catch them up in a tenacious investigation of difficult social
and intellectual questions, and never mind the job. This conflict may
simply lead to frustration on both sides; but when students and
faculty manage to stay with one another, it can lure students into
a much richer education than they intended for themselves and
often into a reconsideration of what constitutes a "good job."
Similarly, in the present decade some students who might otherwise
have a low commitment to learning have such strong aspirations*

*toward civil rights and social justice that the door to inquiry can be
opened by faculty through this approach.*

*Admittedly, tensions within an institution are risky. They can
destroy as well as create liberal education. The colleges in which we
found the tensions to be healthy, creative, and conducive to learning
appear to have three features in common. First, the commitments
were not contrived, but reflected genuine concerns shared by
the great majority of persons making up the college. Students and
faculty may have come together in response to an explicit statement
of creed, as at Wheaton or St. Thomas, or an explicit task, as with
Berea's call to Appalachia. At Oberlin the professionalism of the
faculty strikes a responsive chord in student aspirations; at the
same time a strong extracurricular student culture, linked with the
college's reformist tradition, supplies an acid criticism of both the
professionalism and the society it staffs.*

*Second, the commitments and the tension are not petty, but bear
upon both the lives of students and the future of our society.
Campus tension based on bickering among faculty, logrolling
between departments, and small-time politics cannot be expected to
yield much education. But the struggle at Morehouse between the
bitter rejection of white society and the drive for Negroes to achieve
American-style success as lawyers, researchers, corporate managers,
politicians, and teachers is far more than a local struggle; it is a
piece of twentieth-century history.*

*Third, the interplay of commitments must lead to inquiry. Inquiry
itself need not be one of the initial aspirations, but it must be an
outcome if liberal education is to occur. A religious, political, or
ethical dogma can make for concealment of evidence and a closed
mind. If, however, such a dogma requires constant inquiry regarding
the meaning and relevance of the faith for us and our circumstances
or if it is conceived as only an approximate grasp of an insight
requiring constant refinement and revision, then it can actually
energize and sustain inquiry.*

Who shall be admitted? *A third clue: A college may risk choosing a student body on some
basis other than academic ability alone. This choice will be difficult
to make. College examiners tend to view a rising College Board
score for entering freshmen as an essential mark of an improving
college. And faculty will predictably (and understandably) resist any
selection procedure that rejects able and well-prepared students
in favor of less able or less well-prepared ones or that sets out to*

recruit anything but the best students that can be found. Recently, however, a great deal of attention has been directed to groups that are somehow isolated by poverty or history—urban minorities, rural Southern communities both black and white, and so forth. Colleges that address themselves to groups of this sort—or to students of some other distinctive character—may be plotting an interesting and rewarding future.

Of the colleges represented in this book, Berea defines its clientele most self-consciously. Its decision to focus upon students in need of full financial aid and native to Appalachia colors the entire culture of the college—its governance, its rules, its curriculum, the vocational aspirations of its graduates, the persons considered and available for faculty appointment, and such features of the college community as its Boone Tavern, its craft industry, its ties with area schools, and its expectation that all students will work. These characteristics of Berea, in turn, contribute to its teaching effectiveness; they give Berea its interest, its drive, touchstones for critique of the world outside, and a perspective from which to organize students' experiences.

Other institutions have no doubt been doing something comparable, less deliberately or with less public notice. Dr. Leona Nelson argues, in a paper prepared for this study, that Anderson College in Indiana, sponsored by the Church of God, has from the beginning been serving "disadvantaged" students—first-generation college students from low-income families—without thinking of them as that. They are simply the young people of the church. Only about 15 percent of the student body score above the national mean on SAT verbal aptitude tests, but of those 15 percent, a higher proportion go on to graduate school than from the same ability range at Antioch College. By serving its own clientele well, Anderson has almost surely been more useful socially and more confident in its identity than if it had tried to climb the SAT ladder.

Some vanishing myths   A fourth clue: Colleges may well risk violating some of the myths about teaching that dominate college operations. Almost everybody wants a low student-teacher ratio. Almost everybody thinks that grade-point averages are necessary impedimenta of colleges. Almost everybody seems to think that encounters in the classroom are the primary source of college learning. Almost everybody thinks undergraduate colleges should enroll students for four years, ages eighteen to twenty-two. And it is almost a dead certainty that deviations from these myths could produce vitality in places that need it.

Undergraduate liberal arts colleges have frequently lamented the loss of good teaching that is supposed to accompany a faculty's preoccupation with research. Recently a number of colleges—some very strong, others in their infancy—have proposed to build a liberal education upon apprenticeship of nonmajors to specialists who teach the apprentices through participation in research. It is too early to know the outcome of this topsy-turvy plan; but it has just the right mixture of reason and disruption of prejudice to be a promising risk.

Another set of colleges—the Union for Research and Experimentation in Higher Education—has conceived the idea of establishing temporary beachheads for service and study in unlikely places, such as the inner city of Philadelphia, or Kauai in the Hawaiian Islands. The idea is to expose students to situations of great need and challenge, to do so with as little "establishment" as possible, and thereby to allow students a major voice in control of the studies. Naturally these beachheads will not be equipped with the usual proportion of "generals," supply depots of books, and other modern matériel. Again, however, a temporary sojourn in that ill-equipped world may give students incentives, awarenesses of relationships that make study relevant, and understandings that they cannot get by handout from any supply rooms.

Just as many colleges feel their activities can no longer be confined by campus boundaries, others feel a college education cannot be confined to a four-year segment of a person's career—particularly since the time given to education in a typical career has expanded so dramatically. Goddard College offers a degree program to adults who come to the campus for two weeks twice a year and pursue an individually arranged course of study in between visits. Simmons's Career Center will help women think more than a few years beyond graduation and will keep access to education open to them as their families grow up and their ambitions change. Some colleges offer extensive programs of graduate work in special areas as a way of reaching others besides "college-age" young people. Simmons, building on its experience with vocationally inclined undergraduate programs, offers graduate work in library science, social work, urban education, publication, medical technology, physical therapy, and other fields.

Service to society   *A fifth clue: A college may well risk the performing of some direct services to society in addition to its indirect service through the education of students. Robert A. Nisbet of the University of California at Riverside said to the 1966 meeting of the American Council on Education:*

If there is a single transcending challenge before university presidents today—the successful meeting of which will alone place them in the heavenly choir now occupied by the William Rainey Harpers, the Charles Eliots, and the Daniel Coit Gilmans—it is that of somehow keeping the university in a vital relationship to a political and industrial society that, by reason of its infinite complexity, is insatiable in appetite for professional information, advice, and operational knowledge, and, at the same time, protecting and nourishing those fragile, life-giving activities within the university that are not primarily concerned with giving professional advice to society and that require relative autonomy from the demands of society as the condition of intellectual creativeness. . . .

The great minds in the history of Western thought have been minds concerned first and foremost with intellectual problems drawn from the practical needs of society, with their own individual relation to these problems and needs frequently that of professional consultant. This was as true of a Plato and Aristotle, who never disdained to draw philosophical problems and principles from their practical consultantships in the service of kings, as it was fifteen hundred years later of the powerful Roman law teachers in the medieval university who, in their own consultantships with struggling monarchs, helped to found the national state and create, incidentally, the basic problems of modern European moral and political philosophy.

We have spoken already of examples of social concern that dictated a particular choice of student body, curriculum, or religious mission. This concern can also call colleges to address questions and problems for which no answer is at hand. Thus concern about the fate of cities has impelled some colleges to search for a program which will do for the cities what the Morrill Act did for rural America and incidentally for higher education. The concern for better ways to resolve international conflict and to reach decisions in a peaceful world has produced institutes, "world colleges," and even one college afloat.

One of the initial questions of the Liberal Arts Colleges Study was this: Are the differences among good colleges merely superficial? In other words, is there only one ideal form of liberal arts college beneath all the outward variety? There is, we think, something common to all good colleges—namely, that they induce inquiry and discovery in their students, deepen the power and grasp of these students' ideas, widen and enrich their intrinsic satisfactions, free them from some of their initial biases of origin, and open them to continuing development in their ideas and concerns. But precisely because of this common impact on a widely differing spectrum of individual students, these colleges themselves must differ essentially in their forms and functioning. Not only is there no ideal liberal arts college; there cannot be one.

OBERLIN
COLLEGE

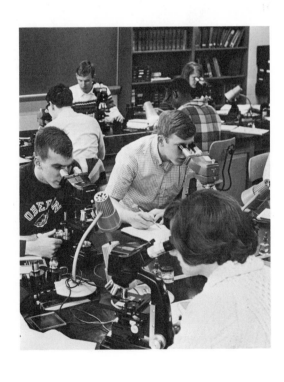

*The distinctive thing about Oberlin is the climate
of expectation that it somehow creates in students.
It is a community of exceptionally able students,
screened and self-selected by unusually high
intellectual and academic criteria, already
motivated or habituated to academic routines,
anticipating or discovering and accepting high
scholarly standards, and attaching the greatest
prestige to academic distinctions.*

WHAT makes Oberlin "different?"

**The distinctive thing about Oberlin is the climate of expectations that it
somehow creates in students. Students expect to work outside of regular class
assignments and academic obligations. They work on dates, over the weekends,
anytime. They take assignments as a challenge, not as something to complain
about or to try to go over as lightly as possible. And they take it for granted,
most of them, that they will go on to graduate school.**

This answer came from a member of the faculty of long standing.
It reflected not merely his personal or professional experiences on
the campus but also systematic surveys over a period of years made
by him and his students in psychology. The answer, furthermore,
confirms the impressions gained by a campus visitor after many conversations with students, faculty, and administration. A description of
Oberlin, whether of the instructional program, social activities, or
extracurricular events, begins best with an appreciation of the intensity of the academic life.

"Pressure" is a word very likely to be used by students or faculty
when they are asked what Oberlin is like. A student who speaks
about courses that require from 400 to 600 pages of reading a week
appears to be boasting as much as complaining, and he is likely to
be telling the truth. "Necessarily," stated a senior, "the Oberlin
experience is tense."

It seems there can be no rest, no reprieve, no relenting of the grind once it has begun. . . . You get used to it. . . . It gets to be fashionable . . . a peculiarly Oberlinian syndrome in which we find ourselves constantly trying to top each other's study loads. . . . Any Oberlinite knows what it's like to read along constantly watching the page numbers decrease, by tens, and then by twos, as the rainy afternoon draws to suppertime. Which will come first—six o'clock or the end of the article?

Oberlin life is not all that frantic, that serious, or that austere, but as a cartoon this image of the Oberlin student catches an essential truth. This is, in fact, a community of unusually able students, screened or self-selected by unusually high intellectual and academic criteria, already motivated or habituated to academic routines, anticipating or discovering and accepting high scholarly standards, and attaching the highest prestige to academic distinctions. The freshman, knowing that he is in competition with exceptional classmates, strives to demonstrate to himself and to his peers that he can make the mark; the senior may share with his classmates his "panic" about the quality of his grades and their effect on his admission to graduate school. Postgraduate study is so generally the normal prospect of Oberlin students that the senior who intends to go into business or schoolteaching may feel he is disdained by those who seek a doctorate. Oberlin's "score" for Woodrow Wilson "winners" for 1966 was seventeen fellowships and twenty-six honorable mentions— which was, to the dismay of many, a considerable drop from the twenty-four fellowships won the year before.

A long tradition   A second factor that makes Oberlin different is the thoroughness with which its history has been integrated into its present life.[1]

Oberlin was founded in 1833 by a colony of Christian families in northeastern Ohio, about 10 miles inland from Lake Erie, at a location which today is better identified as a small town rather close to the Ohio Turnpike and about 20 miles from the Cleveland Airport. The college halls, the buildings of the Conservatory of Music, and the quadrangle of the Graduate School of Theology are grouped around a square that touches on the town business district at one corner. The square is named Tappan for an important early donor

[1] This profile deals with Oberlin College only, not with the conservatory or with the Graduate School of Theology (now transferred). The college and the conservatory are distinct, with about 2100 students and 140 faculty in the College of Arts and Sciences and about 450 students and 60 faculty in the conservatory. The distinction between college and conservatory is important for an understanding of organization and of educational procedures, though in most ways the two institutions constitute one community.

to the Oberlin enterprise—the name of a family famous in ante-bellum America for its philanthropy to radical social causes.

A social historian who is familiar with the place of Oberlin in the history of the religious and social crusades of mid-nineteenth-century America may attach undue significance to the fact that its theological seminary, once the crowning institution of its various departments, was dropped by the Trustees as an Oberlin enterprise during 1965, and at the beginning of 1966 was merged with the Divinity School at Vanderbilt University. To most of the faculty and students at Oberlin today, this event seemed to be more significant for how it occurred than as a major change. In its true perspective, the closing—or rather the transference—of the School of Theology and the taking over of its buildings for college purposes seems to have been the logical conclusion of a process of secularization under way for some forty years. The college has long had its own Department of Religion, and contacts between the School of Theology and the college have been progressively lessening. A milestone along this path was the year 1927, when for the first time since 1851 a layman was installed as President of Oberlin. Oberlin students, however, are still expected to attend, at least eight times a semester, an assembly that meets in the Charles Grandison Finney Chapel. Though these convocations are almost invariably secular, a voluntary religious chapel also meets each Tuesday.

Secularization has not meant indifference at Oberlin. Oberlin's character still appears to be affected by the kind of social forces symbolized by Finney, a leading Evangelist of the great revival of the 1820s and a propounder of an unconventional theology that blended religious zeal with humanitarian causes and social reform.

A radical stand at Oberlin may be taken in the name of conservatism, and change may be invoked in the name of Oberlin tradition. The Oberlin community is still proud that it first established co-education and that it had no color line from the beginning. The cemetery contains a Negro memorial to three men who died with John Brown at Harper's Ferry; a great Memorial Arch on the campus recalls the Oberlin missionary martyrs who died during the Boxer Rebellion. Tank House, today a student cooperative dormitory–dining facility, was originally constructed late in the nineteenth century to provide housing for missionaries on furlough and for their children who were living in the community in order to pursue an American education. A senior member of the faculty, himself a student during the 1920s, notes that that was a period of transition from a school that was intensely religious in quality before World War I to a more secular institution, and that in the years immediately after World War I such characteristically Protestant-Puritanical social restrictions as those against smoking and dancing were eliminated. Nevertheless, the older missionary religious motivation continued as a more secular kind of commitment, and the activist tradition at Oberlin which was there at the beginning has never been lost. As recently as 1964–65, an official statement for the college declared that "throughout . . . its history Oberlin has been an avowedly Christian college . . . has sought to be liberal and open-minded, to lead in those types of changes which represent true growth and yet to hold fast the essential spiritual values." The statement noted that the college still regarded development of the religious life of its students as one of its aims and maintained "courses of study in the field of religion," as well as "extensive services of the Young Men's and Young Women's Christian Association."

While such a specific commitment to religious responsibilities embarrasses or is not entirely acceptable to a significant proportion of the Oberlin community, the seriousness of educational purpose, the considerable involvement in contemporary social and political concerns, and the preparation for vocations or professions that lead to "service" are consistent with earlier chapters in Oberlin history. The five students who in 1966 received the highly respected Shansi fellowships to teach in Tunghai University at Taichung, China, or to serve at Madurai and elsewhere in India were direct successors in a tradition of Oberlin missionaries in China which had continued from the 1880s until brought to an end in 1950 following the victory of the Chinese Communist regime. Recently Oberlin was selected by the U.S. Office of Education as an East Asian Language and Area Center under the provisions of the National Defense Education Act. An analysis of the occupations of the parents of Oberlin students showed that the second largest category was the field of religion, outranked only by science and engineering.

On the basis of a long tradition, Oberlin has within the lifetime of its senior faculty become increasingly firm in its academic emphasis, gathered and maintained a strong teaching faculty[2] which remains extraordinarily productive in the field of scholarship, and intensified its academic standards while becoming an institution not merely Midwestern but national in its composition and increasingly heterogeneous in its student body.

[2] During the academic year 1965–66, 90 percent of the faculty (exclusive of physical education teachers and part-time lecturers) had the doctorate.

Academic quality and the curriculum Faculties at most colleges would be envious of a student body like Oberlin's. Generally the faculty at Oberlin are pleased and proud, and sometimes they themselves are amazed. Occasionally some professors wonder whether their students are not too academically conforming or even meek; the heterogeneity of students' origins, the variety of their opinions, their assertiveness in college affairs, and their independent action for "causes" might not seem to bear out these suspicions. But the role of the professors does seem to be highly respected, and many of them as persons are regarded with genuine awe. And, in the words of one thoughtful senior, some students "seem to be perpetually trying to decide what the professor's opinions are on the issues being discussed in class," with the result that students "eventually begin to believe opinions just because they are held by a respected professor." It would be unfair and untrue to characterize an entire student body as being pressured to scholarship by such external influences, but the ultimate authority of a professor may be considerable if the life goals of a student will be affected by the graduate school he is able to choose or the fellowship for which he is recommended.

"Blue books," the campus term for examinations, accent the rhythm of a student's life. Papers are assigned and tests occur frequently—and, some faculty believe, too regularly. The intensity of the final examination period is suggested by the schedule of the Oberlin radio station at the ending of one semester, when it arranged for a 280-hour "classical-music marathon"—which also suggests the bias of Oberlin students toward the academically respectable. During the next semester a petition carrying fifteen hundred signatures was presented to the faculty Committee on Educational Plans and Policies for a relaxation of the final examination schedule. A proposal from the committee which would have eliminated two examinations for a student in one day was rejected by the faculty, but apparently because of technical features of the plan rather than because the faculty was insensitive to the students' anxieties.

The examination peaks at Oberlin are also steep because of the general zeal for good grades. The registrar's report for 1963–64 summarized the grading pattern since the postwar year of 1947. Generally, 12 to 13 percent of the students rather consistently got A's; approximately 45 percent got B's; approximately 34 to 35 percent got C's; approximately 6 percent got D's; consistently less than 2 percent and more than 1 percent got F's. The attrition rate for academic reasons at Oberlin is low. However, the distribution of high grades ran significantly lower than the maximums which were permissible in accordance with the guidelines suggested by faculty action in 1956.[3] Concerned that lower grades put Oberlin students at a disadvantage when applying to graduate schools, the faculty in 1966 adopted more generous policies for its grading procedures: The guidelines were modified to increase the percentage of A's and B's that were recommended and to decrease the proportion of lower grades that formerly had been suggested. While these standards are not compulsory, it is presumed they will affect faculty grading practices, and give new instructors, in particular, a measure against which to compare their own grade distribution. At the same time, the faculty voted to give academic honors to all students with a B average or better, instead of limiting the distinction to the top 10 percent of each class. So that other institutions might not misinterpret transcripts from Oberlin, the unusual 7-point grading system was also made to conform to the more common 4-point system, in which A is weighted as 4 and F as 0.

More radical was action taken by the faculty to eliminate any grading at all under certain circumstances. In December of 1965, it voted to give a three-year trial to a system of nongraded courses. After two semesters, students may now elect each term to enroll for one course on a "Satisfactory-Unsatisfactory" basis. The option must be indicated by the student before classes start and does not extend to courses in the student's major. "Satisfactory" is defined as C— or better; "Unsatisfactory," though appearing on the student's record, does not count toward graduation or toward class rank. In May, 1966, it was further announced that eleven courses had been specifically listed as "no-grade courses" for the academic year 1966–67. All students enrolled in these courses must expect not to receive grades at all. The purpose of these changes was "to encourage students to choose some courses where the grade earned would not be the prime consideration." It was hoped this would increase the range of courses elected by students and "decrease the tension sometimes produced when a student is working for grades."

Such modifications of traditional teaching practices reflect the awareness of many Oberlin faculty that studies ought in their own right to be intellectually thrilling and pleasurable. Easing of the examination and grading routines should work toward reducing the more mechanical aspects of academic pressure.

Students maintain that the Oberlin faculty are extraordinarily con-

[3] A, 16 to 8 percent; B, 50 to 33 percent; C, 46 to 30 percent; D, 10 to 4 percent; and F, 3 to 0 percent.

servative in educational matters. Indeed, at first view, the curriculum and general pattern of instruction at Oberlin have remained relatively static for more than three decades. Under the basic plan of the Oberlin curriculum adopted in 1930, a student is expected to fulfill requirements of thirty-six semester hours according to the following pattern:

1 A year course with laboratory work in a biological or physical science.

2 Two courses in social sciences, in two separate departments.

3 Three semester hours in English composition.

4 One year of study in a foreign language above the elementary course level, unless the student passes a proficiency examination.

5 One semester course in art or music.

6 A year course in literature, English or foreign.

7 A semester course in philosophy.

8 A semester course in religion.

During the spring of his sophomore year, the student selects a major. The number of credit hours which a student can offer in his major toward the degree must be at least twenty-four but is limited to a total of forty, though he may take more if he graduates with more than one hundred twenty-four hours.

While as an overall educational program this is conventional, it does not adequately reflect modifications which have occurred at the departmental level, nor does it reveal the academic riches available to the student in a number of special programs. During the summer, Oberlin College operates programs in France, Spain, Germany or Austria, and Russia. At home, the campus during the summer provides undergraduate research opportunities in several science departments and operates an eight weeks' summer program designed to enrich the educational opportunities of a small number of selected students by intensive independent studies.[4]

Within the relative autonomy of departments, the upperclass programs have come to present considerable variation. In addition to the summer Honors Program cited above, there are the following:

1 Composite majors approved by a faculty committee.

2 An Honors Program which varies from department to department

[4] In recent years, summer activities at Oberlin have included an Honors College, an Oberlin Summer Theatre, a master of arts in teaching program, a Peace Corps teacher training program, and a high school student-enrichment program which has brought nearly one hundred high school students from secondary schools in the county to the Oberlin campus.

but always includes independent study, characterized by private reading, special research projects, and preparation of papers and reports.

3 A program of senior scholars, appointed by a Committee on Honors, consisting of a small number of highly qualified students who pursue their own program of independent study.

4 A private reading program in which two or three hours of private reading with a department professor may substitute for conventional course work.

In the spring semester of 1966, the Educational Plans and Policies Committee proposed that for a trial period of four years all formal course requirements for graduation be suspended. No more than forty credit hours would be taken in one department, except that honors students might take forty-five. Otherwise, instead of the specific academic course requirements, students would be asked to select "a broadly based" course of study by following "appropriate guidelines" in consultation with their advisers. These guidelines would "resemble present requirements," and advisers could reject programs that seemed "unwise." Not only would requirements become more flexible but "the burden of formulating a program would be shifted from the catalogue to the student."

The most striking recent trend in Oberlin's educational program has indeed been toward more and more independent senior studies and senior Honors Programs. The significance of this development can be appreciated only in the light of recent developments in the academic economy of the college. In 1959, the college faculty adopted a motion for increasing student enrollment from sixteen hundred to two thousand without at the same time enlarging the faculty. A change in the student-faculty ratio, concurrent with higher tuition charges, would make possible desirable increases in faculty salaries. The student body accordingly grew to two thousand. In 1962, the faculty reaffirmed the action of 1959 but recommended the addition of up to five faculty over the period 1962–65. In November of 1965, the Dean of the College sent to department chairmen a rather searching inquiry regarding what had happened to department enrollments, course changes, curricular changes, class size, teaching loads, and faculty activities. On the basis of the answers, decisions were to be made regarding the addition of faculty for the academic year 1966–67.[5] Early in 1966, it was announced that while an increase

[5] Administrators will not be surprised that seventeen departments asked for an additional member and one department asked for two, all on persuasive grounds having to do with teaching load or subject-matter coverage.

in the student body was not anticipated "in the near future," six additional faculty would be appointed during the next academic year—two for history and one each for religion, government, biology, and sociology. In addition, physics was to receive an extra instructor who was to be supported by "outside grants."

During this period in which the student enrollment thus increased by 25 percent and the faculty by 11 percent, the ratio of students to faculty moved from somewhat less than 13 to 1 to somewhat over 15 to 1; the time, talent, and energy of the faculty seem to have become proportionately devoted more to upper-level than to lower-level instruction. Independent studies have increased significantly; greater use has been made of special reading programs and of seminars; and for all types of instruction, the proportionately greatest increases reported by departments have been in the number of students invited or accepted for course work in honors. Departmental analyses speak rather approvingly of this development, at the same time indicating that such programs consume a great deal of faculty time.

These changes, as one would expect, have not been consistently the same in all departments. The departments have also varied in the ways they have saved time in the allocation of faculty for lower-level courses. A review of the departmental reports indicates such devices as the consolidation or even the elimination of lower-level offerings, the use of double sections for occasional lecture meetings, team teaching, use of programmed learning, utilization of more students as departmental assistants, the requiring of fewer papers and examinations, and the use of general assignments rather than individually tailored projects. To some extent, the reduction of departmental effort at the lower levels was made easier because from 1959 to 1966, the effect of the Advanced Placement Program[6] became considerable. By 1966 it was possible for the Mathematics Department practically to eliminate one of its lower-level course sequences. In the English Department, enrollment fell in introductory courses, while rapidly increasing at the upper level. In history, the number of Advanced Placement students was only nine in 1959; it increased to seventy-one by 1964. It fell back again to forty in 1966; numbers of this size, however, are significant. Departmental reports also affirm that during this period professional scholarly production, research, writing, and publication increased.

[6] This is a nationwide program that permits entering freshmen to obtain credit or waiver without credit for college-level work done in high school.

These considerations suggest to the observer that during this recent period, Oberlin College may have been moving to something that might be called a graduate school economy,[7] including strong approval of faculty research and publication, with increased attention to specialized studies at the advanced level and with frequent savings of faculty effort at the lower levels. The report of the President issued in 1965 revealed that twenty-seven faculty would be on leave for the academic year 1965–66. Seventeen pages in this report were given to an appendix listing college faculty publications during the year.

During this increase in the size of the student body and relatively smaller increase of the faculty, the physical sciences did not hold their own. If all the sciences (chemistry, physics, biology, geology, mathematics, and psychology) are lumped together, the enrollment increase was directly proportional to the overall increase in college enrollment, which was 22 percent. However, in the physical sciences (physics, chemistry, and geology) and mathematics the increase was only 5 percent, so that relatively these sciences fell behind, while biology and psychology were growing at a rate greater than the college generally. Oberlin's problems in this area are representative of difficulties that all liberal arts colleges now encounter in recruiting good science faculty, supporting research, and attracting the most able science students. That a college of Oberlin's strength and reputation should also be affected by this trend is significant.

The faculty role in college governance

For many years, Oberlin has been noted for the broad powers that the faculty exercise in the governance of the college. Probably the greatest single influence in its early history came from the migration to Oberlin of the famous "Lane rebels," who seceded from a seminary in Cincinnati at which the Board of Trustees had suppressed the free discussion of the slavery issue. The continued presence of these students and the support of their valuable Eastern patrons was ensured only after alleviation of concerns about Trustees' interference and assurances regarding the choice of certain faculty. From this early

[7] The reference here is to the undergraduate program. Oberlin College offers graduate work to the master's level, but the scope of the program is small and most faculty are not enthusiastic about the standards of the graduate work now done. The prevailing view is that except in a few fields, prospective graduate students who are good enough to do graduate work should go to a Ph.D.-granting institution. Those not that good would probably have a hard time competing with Oberlin undergraduates. There is some division of opinion regarding the advisability of doing graduate work at all. The continuation, the abrogation, or the extension of graduate work at Oberlin is not, however, a lively issue on the campus.

event and others, a strong tradition of faculty government came to be established. One of the senior members of the Oberlin faculty maintains that the faculty's power has fostered corresponding responsibility. In the long run it has, he believes, reduced interdepartmental jealousies and aggressiveness and developed a common concern to strengthen weak departments.

Over the years the role of the President may have depended more on his administrative or scholarly ability, leadership traits, and personal influence than on well-defined constitutional authority. Ernest Hatch Wilkins, who was President from 1927 to 1946, has been cited as an example. The reputation of Oberlin for academic excellence was to a considerable extent confirmed during his long executive tenure.

However, during Wilkins's regime, certain direct involvements of the faculty in administrative decisions began to disappear. The faculty no longer acted on the budget line by line and ceased voting in general faculty sessions on the specific recommendations for salaries and promotions. This tendency toward reducing the faculty's voice on financial details continued thereafter. Evidently the budget, on which the faculty once had a considerable say, is now largely prepared by administrative officers who, after consultation with departmental chairmen and certain other members of the faculty, make their final decisions and report to the faculty; discussion is thus post facto. In recent years there have been some rather tense situations because the procedures are not entirely clear and the powers not well-defined for a coordinate exercise of administrative responsibility and faculty authority.

Yet faculty authority still works vigorously in academic affairs. The limits placed on this authority by budgetary restrictions would perhaps be greater if the college finances were tighter.[8] Admittedly a potential weakness in the Oberlin operation is that considerations of financial prudence or feasibility may not enter directly into the rather autonomous faculty deliberations on primarily academic matters.

The most important committee agency of the faculty at Oberlin College[9] is the College Faculty Council, consisting of the President,

[8] The library operations illustrate this point. There are no library allocations by departments; there is enough financial leeway so that no absolute ceilings have to be set.

[9] Administrative lines at Oberlin have been complicated by the need to coordinate the affairs of college, conservatory, and Graduate School of Theology. There has been a General Faculty Council, consisting of the President, Provost, Deans of the three institutions, and seven elected members of the faculty. The discus-

the Provost, the Dean, and eight members elected by the faculty. This council is particularly active in personnel decisions: When a teaching vacancy occurs, this body authorizes a new appointment. Within the rank and salary communicated by the Dean, the departmental chairman seeks candidates, who after approval by the Dean are invited to Oberlin for interviews. Council members as well as the department chairman and other faculty in the department participate in interviewing the candidates. Formal approval by the council may or may not follow upon recommendation from the department chairman. Similarly, the council acts to make changes in rank, tenure, and salaries and reports its action to the faculty. The decision in 1966 to increase the size of the faculty was made in the College Faculty Council. Though candidates and new members of the faculty may sometimes have found this involvement of general faculty representatives in all personnel decisions a cumbersome procedure, it is general faculty opinion that the exercise of the faculty's authority in this way has worked well.[10]

Next to the College Faculty Council, the most important committee of the faculty is the Educational Plans and Policies Committee. Its importance was enhanced a few years ago by making it elective instead of appointive, and its prestige now stimulates its members to more intensive committee work. It is anticipated that from joint meetings of the council and the Educational Plans and Policies Committee, a kind of Faculty Senate may evolve. Given the present structure, however, it is not clear how faculty influence may bear directly on such matters as tuition, scholarship funds, salary scale, and dormitory planning—areas in which administrative officials may proceed rather independently.

Oberlin, like many other colleges, is discovering that greater size, more internal diversity, and multiplying external contacts have tended to confuse and complicate the making of decisions; a consensus is less readily achieved. When more complex decisions need to be made more frequently and with greater speed, the natural tendency is to proceed less by general debate and deliberation and to depend

---

sion above relates only to the organization of the college, and in doing so may somewhat slight the role of the General Faculty Council, particularly regarding salary scales and certain other common concerns. There has been a conscious effort in recent years to revitalize the role of the General Council.

[10] Criteria for evaluating faculty are elastic. Department chairmen and senior members of the faculty rarely visit the classes of new instructors. Reliance is placed upon student comments, observations made in some courses where teaching is shared by other faculty, and the impression made when members of the faculty present papers before their colleagues.

more on communication and negotiation emanating from permanent administrative agencies.

The "power structure" at Oberlin is a frequent topic of discussion, and uncertainties, suspicions, or even fears about the role of the Board of Trustees are often voiced. During the spring of 1965, students formally went on record expressing their concern about the "increasing degree of control by the Board over the internal life of the College to satisfy the demands of the external world." And many faculty do perceive in the Oberlin community an increasing Board intervention in the internal affairs of the college, with a resulting tendency, whether or not by design, to enhance the authority of the President and other officers in the administration.

Misunderstanding of the formal or nominal versus the real distribution and delegation of power at Oberlin seems to occur readily. Though the Board has carefully avoided interfering with the routine affairs of the college, there is general uncertainty regarding what occasions or circumstances may bring about its involvement in the making of decisions.

The student role in governance The governance of the Oberlin community is at present greatly affected by the on-campus political activities of the students. The students have long shared with the faculty, on several boards and committees, the responsibility for purpose, management, or regulation of campus programs, dormitory life, dining-hall behavior, student affairs, and, more precisely, the sexual conduct of students—which, until rather recently, most colleges had presumed lay within the area of their institutional responsibilities. It will best serve the purposes of this report to describe the Student Congress which occurred in the spring of 1965, not only because it was dramatic but also because its deliberations were substantial and its recommendations wide in scope.

Early in the academic year 1964–65, campus leaders developed a plan for a representative assembly of students through which they might present their ideas, opinions, and studied conclusions on practically all the programs, policies, and organizations of the college. In February, the student body elected about 275 delegates to the Student Congress. During the month preceding the plenary sessions of this congress, March 14 and 15, 1965, most of these delegates did considerable work on committees, which solicited information and opinions from faculty and administrative officers and prepared resolutions for the deliberations of the congress.

Fifty-six resolutions touching on almost every phase of college life were adopted and embodied in a 39-page report that the leaders of the congress presented to the administration, the faculty, and the Trustees. The specific proposals ranged from improved communication between the students and the alumni, Trustees, and President, through autonomy of dormitories and greater student authority in rule enforcement, to a smaller student-faculty ratio and stronger emphasis on seminars and independent study. Any précis of these resolutions would fail to communicate the students' seriousness, studiousness, and strength of commitment to intellectual and ethical standards, to personal freedom and open discussion, to the democratic process, and to social service.

The impact of these resolutions upon the Oberlin campus during the twelve months succeeding the event undoubtedly was reflected in some of the faculty and administration actions which already have been described in this profile. As President Carr himself reported, the students provided "an admirable checklist of College policies and problems, deserving of careful and honest review by those responsible for Oberlin's operation and welfare."

After receiving this report from the congress leaders, the President, along with the faculty, took steps to bring into being a so-called "Four-Four-Two" Committee comprising four faculty, four students, and two administrators, which was charged with responding appropriately to the proposals of the congress. Unfortunately, the favorable impression made by the thoughtfulness and thoroughness of the proceedings that had culminated in the resolutions of the Student Congress was spoiled to some extent when the chairman of the congress presented the report to the Board of Trustees. It seemed to the Board that student leaders insisted on two "demands." One was for the Board immediately to appoint a committee of faculty, administrators, and students to consider the congress proposals and to submit recommendations to the Board in June. The second "demand" was that Trustees should "accept as binding" whatever action the faculty took at its April meeting regarding the expansion of "co-op" residences. When the Board failed to take action on these two matters, students marched on the President's house and presented other demands for immediate action. They also picketed the administration building. A rather tense crisis was weathered without the disorders which some anticipated, and more deliberate consideration of the issues propounded by the students was begun by the Four-Four-Two Committee as well as by other faculty and student agencies.

The foregoing narrative alone could give an altogether false impression of Oberlin as the scene of discord and instability. On the contrary, even during periods of turmoil Oberlin seriously and studiously carried on its normal activities.[11] Indeed, certain of the most significant aspects of the community were not at all threatened, but were in part even reaffirmed. Among these were the academic Honor System, the traditional aversion to fraternities and sororities, the rule against student cars, the character of extracurricular activities, and the important custom of having the men sudents eat in dining rooms in the women's dormitories.

Extraordinary riches in extracurricular experiences abound on the Oberlin campus. One senior, who felt he had got a broad liberal education at Oberlin, indicated that much of it had derived from extracurricular activities and the student interaction involved. Between the various college departments and student organizations, the community is provided with an uninterrupted and frequently overlapping succession of important public figures, distinguished scholars, authors and critics, performing artists, and musical and dramatic events from beyond the campus, and these are supplemented by the talents of the Oberlin faculty itself. The stimulating effect of this continuous flow of presentations must be considerable.

Though the academic program is demanding and is genuinely given priority by nearly all the students, a number find that their studies leave them considerable time for participation in the activities of student groups. Characteristically, most students do become involved in at least one extracurricular activity. A sociological study done recently on the Oberlin campus discovered at least seventy student organizations or activity groups.

Of these many organized student activities, however, only twenty-six were listed under the categories of "athletic," "collegiate traditional," and "student government." Fifty-four of them were in the categories of "academic," "aesthetics," "professional," "religious," "service," and "activist," either "active" or "intellectual." These facts again emphasize the self-direction of Oberlin students toward the thoughtful, the serious, the creative, and the intellectual, with implicit commitments to social service or social criticism and, in general, to activities that would particularly receive approbation in an academic community. A quantitative summary of the extracurricular life of the Oberlin students does not do justice to its quality, to the ambitious

[11] In the very hotly contested elections that occurred in spring, 1966, for members of a new Student Senate, only two-thirds of the students voted.

scope of some of these activities, or to the courage required for others. One can illustrate by noting that the Cinema Arts Association was planning a two months' shooting of two documentary films and that the Newman Club announced that it would sponsor a contest on the campus to compose a Mass in English in an effort to help build a new tradition of Catholic liturgical music in the vernacular. Altogether, the choices that Oberlin students make for expending leisure time are what one would expect from students who preferred a college which they knew ahead of time had very high academic standards and which had deliberately denied to itself the more conventional social life associated with fraternities, sororities, and automobiles.[12]

"Activism is an Oberlin tradition." There is a volatile contradiction in such a statement, since activism disturbs the traditional, but for Oberlin, the paradox is nevertheless true. At Oberlin's commencement in June of 1965, Martin Luther King, Jr., gave the commencement address. The President of Oberlin in his annual report for that academic year summarized a long list of involvements by Oberlin in social action, ranging all the way from those which were officially and formally sponsored by the college to those in which students or faculty were involved at their own individual option. During the year, Oberlin had served as a center for Peace Corps training, had operated a special educational opportunities program under a grant received from the Rockefeller Foundation, and had taken advantage

[12] It may be well to present here a few statistics about the Oberlin student body. The freshman class entering in September, 1965, consisted of 695 students from forty-five states and eight foreign countries. The average SAT scores were 640 verbal and 655 mathematics. The freshmen were chosen from 3,165 applicants. Seventy percent of them had graduated in the top 10 percent of their high school class; 200 of them entered with scholastic credit from enrichment courses in high school or from advanced placement courses, and almost 100 were able to waive the required English composition course. For the freshman class entering in 1964, 185 had been active in student government and 80 had been editors. Only 30 of the men had earned letters in football, and 30 had earned letters in basketball. For the freshman class entering in 1964, 116 of the men had been awarded scholarships, while only 66 of the women had been awarded scholarships. The difference in scholarship awards reflects the fact that for some time Oberlin has tended to attract more strong men applicants than women applicants. Of the seniors graduating with the class of 1964, definite plans for advanced study were reported by 66.5 percent of the men and 41.2 percent of the women; 24 seniors were awarded Woodrow Wilson fellowships, and 5 won National Science Foundation awards. For the class graduating in 1965, the President reported that "Oberlin students continue to receive exceptional outside recognition. One graduating senior received a Fulbright award; 22 June graduates and two who were graduated earlier received Woodrow Wilson Fellowships."

of another grant from the Rockefeller Foundation to admit needy students who would otherwise not have been able to attend a college of high quality. The YMCA and YWCA of Oberlin College had sponsored activities such as the tutoring and befriending of deprived children in the county where the college is located; the students had conducted a major tutorial program for children in the grade schools and had visited the friendless in retirement areas. Students had worked at a rehabilitation center in Lorain County, and twenty-one Oberlin freshman women were "big sisters" to a group of Negro girls of high school age. An Oberlin group called Carpenters for Christmas undertook to assist in the rebuilding of a burned-out church in Ripley, Mississippi. Another band of students participated in a sit-in at a construction site at the Federal Office Building in Cleveland, thus demonstrating against racial discrimination in hiring practices; and some of these students were arrested. Other students made a trip to Erie, Pennsylvania, to protest a decision of the Hammermill Paper Company to build a new plant at Selma, Alabama, and some of the Oberlin students in this demonstration were arrested also.

The academic year 1965–66 witnessed similar activities, including lively and studious discussions on the Oberlin campus protesting the involvement of the United States in the Vietnam War. Vietnam protest took more active form when in March a considerable number of the students participated in a demonstration in Cleveland. When the college administered the draft deferment examination on its own campus in May, about three hundred "sit-ins" and pickets caused the locale of the examination to be changed from Finney Chapel to the gymnasium. It was the judgment of President Carr that since the students had refrained from a "final effort to obstruct the administration of the test," their conduct "fell within the always broad limits of discussion and dissent that must be permitted in an academic community." The President informed some eight or ten students who were blocking one doorway that they might be subject to expulsion if they interfered with the administration of the test; but it was an inaccurate interpretation of the facts that led the Student Senate to censure the President because he allegedly had threatened to expel the antiwar demonstrators.

The official position of the college is one to which hardly any academic liberals could take exception. In the *Oberlin Alumni Magazine* of May, 1965, the President cited the student and faculty activity in the antislavery movement, in campaigns for equality of opportunity for all persons, and in various efforts to promote peace and international understanding. President Carr noted:

In the course of protesting laws and practices they believed unjust, they have been arrested, and yet society has eventually come to accept the justice of their cause. In the light of Oberlin's continuous tolerance of persons in the academic community who choose to become active in support of social causes, there is no compelling need now in 1965 to reaffirm this tradition. It is part of the very air we breathe in Oberlin.

In view, however, of the widespread public notice which had been taken of the participation of Oberlin students in demonstrations, the President felt obliged to go further and to make this clarification:

I wish to state to the best of my knowledge, no disciplinary action has ever been taken by the College against students or faculty members for such participation. . . . Indeed, in all its practices and policies regarding the activities of its students in off-campus political activities and social protest movements, Oberlin has always acted in a manner consistent with the highest standards of freedom and due process of law.

Speaking to a student visitor on the campus, the president of the Young Democrats described Oberlin generally as a "liberal school" but declared that there was a definite distinction in the community between the "ultraliberals" (i.e., the demonstrators, anti-Vietnam-draft "types") and the more moderate "liberals" like himself, who actually at that time were supporting the administration's Vietnam policies. In his opinion, the so-called "ultra" group was not large but very active and very visible. One of the important controversies during the last year and a half on the Oberlin campus was concerned with whether the college should or should not recognize and subsidize as an official Oberlin student publication a periodical called *Activist*. This relatively new journal of politics and opinion is published by a student staff. However, there is also an advisory and editorial board, the members of which need not be associated with Oberlin College. Also, many of the articles published by the *Activist* admittedly come from non-Oberlin students. Certain quarters would have preferred that the "caustic political ideology" of the *Activist* not receive the "support and privileges implied by official College recognition." After considerable discussion, the *Activist* did receive the recognition necessary to procure funds from student fees.

Social patterns: toward greater student control

Social patterns in the dining rooms and dormitories at Oberlin are particularly important because of the virtual absence of any other kind of organization which is social for its own sake. Indeed, the mores and folkways of Oberlin dormitories may be more important for an understanding of college life than on most campuses.

In October of 1965, a visitor to Oberlin, having heard that by Midwestern standards this college was in most respects rather avantgarde, was genuinely surprised when he ate his first meal in one of the larger Oberlin dormitories. The men went to dinner in coats and ties. The women were neatly dressed, went in first, and stood alternately around the tables. The men followed. A junior student, the "chaplain," spoke a grace, after which the students were seated. The meal was served and proceeded decorously, and everyone remained in place until formally dismissed by the rising of the adult director of the dormitory. Even at the "co-ops," which had a reputation for more casualness, a grace was spoken, although it consisted of a quotation on "separateness" carefully attributed to Erich Fromm, giving one the impression that either the scholarly amenities were to be followed or that this popular contemporary deserved the same kind of awe as a verse from the Holy Scriptures. Research revealed that this much of such behavior existed in formal regulations: "Dining at Oberlin is considered a social occasion, and the students should be well groomed in the dining halls at all times. Men wear coats and ties, and women wear dresses or skirts and blouses for all dinner meals. Acceptable sport clothes may be worn for informal meals on Saturday and Sunday."

Considerable light has been thrown on the social controls affecting dormitory life by the discussion it received at the Student Congress in the spring of 1965 and by the continuous editorializing about it in the student publications. Also, the writer had the advantage of perceiving the conduct of Oberlin students through the eyes of two students from another college who lived on the Oberlin campus in the student dormitories, dining halls, recreational quarters, and classrooms for five days.

Dormitory autonomy was a major issue during the deliberations of the Student Congress. Early in November of 1965, the faculty-student board which had jurisdiction over such matters made a significant concession in this direction. It was provided that the individual dining halls should determine by majority vote their own rules on such matters as dress, "dismissal," smoking, and premeal meditation. A revisit by this writer the following spring indicated that the result was a considerable relaxation of the previous formality.

However, dining-room folkways are probably less critical and easier to modify without controversy than other social customs or rules or even the physical structure of the students' living quarters. The following issues have come in for much discussion: women's hours, rules regarding alcoholic beverages, the visiting of men in women's rooms, the visiting of women in men's dormitories, supervision of "dating parlors," and the integration of men and women into so-called "co-ed dorms." On these matters, the principle of establishing dormitory autonomy has so far been rejected, and only minor modifications in the general rules have occurred during the current academic year. In this area, response of faculty and administration has fallen considerably short of the proposals, or "demands," made by the Student Congress in the spring of 1965.

Early in the academic year 1965–66 the college did make what would at one time have been regarded as a radical change in its social regulations. Students criticized the existing marriage rule, which required that students who contemplated marriage must give official notice to the college through the Dean of Men or Dean of Women under "ordinary circumstances" at least three months in advance. In October the Committee of Deans, in response to a proposal coming from a joint board of faculty and students, abrogated the three months' notice previously required and substituted a statement of policy which reiterated the idea that Oberlin was the kind of academic community best-suited to the single student.

Toward midyear there came into effect what to many of Oberlin's alumni and Trustees was a radical departure from its previous rules on drinking. In accordance with a decision made by the faculty the year preceding, in January of 1966 on the Oberlin campus the Rathskeller Beer Co-op began operations, serving 3.2 beer.

At Oberlin, as elsewhere, it has been increasingly difficult to agree upon the standards of conduct or rules which would maintain the order most conducive to an intellectually untrammeled community. The administrators realize that the college is in the difficult situation of trying to compel "entering students . . . to give up personal freedoms which they have come to enjoy during their high school years, both in terms of what their parents have allowed them and what the secondary schools now recognize and permit." On the other hand, there are still students who are personally loyal to the "conventions," and some approve even the older piety of the college and believe there has been an overemphasis in student agitation on issues of social controls. There are still some freshmen who come from what others term a "sheltered" background and who experience initial shock with the "freedom" they find on the Oberlin campus. These students are then faced with "moral decisions"; for them, the regulations provide standards, however shaky, that support them while they are seeking for rules by which to govern their own personal conduct.

The regulations are shaky because they are publicly attacked, because they are privately resented, and because they are widely evaded. But even some who break the rules believe they are necessary, the rules as well as the infractions being acceptable as long as the infractions are kept down to a "reasonable level."

Another insight into the unrest of many Oberlin students is offered by a senior: "Another game we often feel forced to play is the 'Analyzation Game.' . . . At Oberlin it takes the form of criticism of everything. Nothing is sacred. Anything can be torn apart. It gets a bit tiring, but nonetheless, I often feel that we indulge in these intellectual trifles because we feel we ought to rather than because we really want to."

"It gets a bit tiring." This revelation complements the suggestion made by some students, by a professional counselor, and by thoughtful visitors that a large number of Oberlin students are lacking in the ordinary social skills and are insecure in the more usual social situations—afraid that they "can't hack it in the mainstream of life where one has to compete with looks, social charm, and wealth, not intellect." It may be that Oberlin attracts students, particularly men, who believe that on this campus they can escape social involvements where they are ill at ease and avoid the kind of competition that elsewhere would be offered by fraternities, parties, automobiles, and athletic status. Some girls go so far as to say that more than a usual number of Oberlin men are "socially retarded." At Oberlin it is quite proper to be too busy to play. Activities that are simply fun do not flourish on the campus, even though some students express the desire or need for them.

On the Oberlin campus, as on many others, the search for privacy provides the uneasy motivation for a considerable amount of student unrest, and at Oberlin it particularly motivates the agitation over social regulations and for dormitories that are smaller, more informal in structure, and autonomous in their social controls. In the large building which houses Oberlin's student union and many of its recreational facilities, the college has provided twenty to thirty rooms which are set aside as "dating parlors." This is a contrived solution, and the arrangements for using the dating parlors are awkward, but they do meet to some extent the students' need to escape from uninterrupted association with large groups. They also provide a place for intimacy, which otherwise is likely to occur in more conspicuous locations, not infrequently to the embarrassment of the students themselves. (There could be some merit in the suggestion, alleged to have been made by a former Oberlin President, that the real solution to this problem would be to put a large number of automobiles on jacks and park them in a suitable place.)

Students regard it as a proper return to the traditions of the college that the new dormitories to be constructed on the campus will be small. Eight small resident houses will accommodate about forty students each. Three of them will serve as language houses, two of them as women's honor dorms, and three of them as upperclass dormitories for men. They will contain a higher proportion of single rooms than has characterized recent dormitory planning at Oberlin, and the double rooms will be partitioned to permit the separation of sleeping and study areas. Each of the new residence halls will have its own dining room, though all eight will be served by a central kitchen. The closing of the Graduate School of Theology makes available to the college the "quad," which is scheduled to become a coeducational upperclass dormitory in which thirty-five men will live in one wing and forty-two women in the other.

It is the cooperatives that have provided for a large segment of the Oberlin students the model for student living facilities. The first of these was started in 1950 and a second one added subsequently; in response to student requests, a third cooperative was established in 1966. In spring of 1966, there were 528 applications by students to live in cooperatives and only 239 places available. There is now agitation for a fourth cooperative. These cooperatives are not merely a device by which students may make substantial savings in board and room. Many students consider them a panacea for college ills.

Membership in a cooperative consists partly of students who have previously been members and partly of students who "draw" the opportunity of being admitted. Though the drawing adds an element of chance, it works out in practice that a group can pretty much stay together throughout college, and a very intense in-group feeling does develop. As perceived by some members of the community, "co-opers" are a somewhat cliquish, bizarre, or "way-out" group. Co-op students, on the other hand, look down at another group of students, the so-called "jocks," who are stereotyped by the co-opers as being athletic, fatuous, and notorious for evading the drinking rules.

Within recent years there has been some concern on the Oberlin campus regarding the "image" of the co-opers and their failure to abide by the general expectations of behavior and appearance on the Oberlin campus. In 1963, a thorough investigation of the co-opers was made by a special Trustee task force, consisting not only of Trustees but of students, faculty, and administrators as well. This study confirmed that a significant proportion of the co-opers were characterized by nonconforming behavior or unconventional dress habits and that they were probably more likely than students in general to be vocal and aggressive or hypersensitive about their status and their rights. But it also found that the reputation of the co-opers as being agitators or "troublesome" was undoubtedly exaggerated. Careful analysis disclosed that the students who requested and were accepted for cooperative living were more likely than others to be the higher-achieving students in academic work, less likely to be involved in actions which resulted in suspension or withdrawal from school, and more likely to be active in the official or regular extracurricular activities of the college. In both graduate work and occupational activities there was no significant difference between Oberlin students who had lived in the co-ops and those who had other living arrangements on the campus. The co-op students were very likely to hold leadership positions which were activist, particularly in areas which showed a concern for getting something done on the campus as well as for community service, and to place a major emphasis on issues agitating both the national and the international scene. They were strongly identified with intellectual activities, campus affairs in the areas of the arts and music, and literary work. As a consequence of these discoveries regarding the co-ops, the decision was reached not only to continue them but to add an additional cooperative residence hall. Measures were also taken in an effort to bring the somewhat casual life of the students who lived in the co-ops into closer conformity with the behavioral patterns existing on the rest of the campus.

More student control over social governance was partially achieved under a new constitution that was worked out by the Four-Four-Two Committee resulting from the Student Congress. In effect the Student Senate now has the authority to initiate legislation in the nonacademic areas; the faculty has the power to veto. It is too soon to determine how this delegation of authority will work. Already there is some speculation on the campus that under this arrangement, the faculty will share with the administration the suspicion that students formerly felt toward the administrative officers. Formerly, students generally felt that in a pinch the faculty would always stand by them against the administration. In the new definition of student-faculty authority, open student-faculty confrontation now appears possible.

Students and control of the academic program

Student leaders were greatly disappointed over faculty response to the section in the new constitution that proposed to involve students directly in the control of academic affairs. The Student Congress of the spring of 1965 had indicated a desire for student participation in the decision-making process in all areas of the college, including the academic program, the structure of the curriculum, the kinds and number of the faculty, and the construction of college buildings. The original draft of the new constitution, as it came from the Four-Four-Two Committee, provided that the Student Senate would appoint two regular members from the student Educational Plans and Policies Committee who would become regular voting members of the faculty Educational Plans and Policies Committee. There was substantial faculty opposition to this proposal, particularly among well-established but younger faculty. It was apparent that while they were in favor of allowing students to have a larger role in determining student social rules, they were opposed to sharing with students the exercise of the academic powers of the faculty.

After considerable discussion, the faculty voted that the two students should not be regular members of the committee but that, instead, two members of the student committee might be invited to join the faculty committee from time to time for consideration of major changes in educational policy.

Student determination to have a say in college policy is not likely to go away. Here, as elsewhere, two Oberlin traditions pull against each other: on the one hand, the jealously guarded tradition of faculty government; on the other hand, the college's traditional partisanship for the disenfranchised—women, Negroes, students. What forms this contest will take or how it will be resolved one cannot say. But being grounded solidly in the college's past, the contest will not be frivolous, and by putting traditions to a present test, it may do much to keep Oberlin resilient and alive.

Author of the Oberlin profile was Hermann Muelder, then Dean of Knox College; his associate was Conrad Hilberry, associate director of this study and professor of English at Kalamazoo College. They were assisted by David L. Anderson, chairman of the Department of Physics at Oberlin, on behalf of the college. Ann Bolt and Richard Bolt of Antioch College were the student observers.

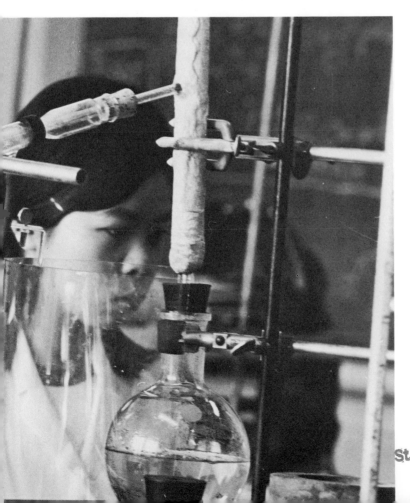

The new developments at Simmons are in large measure a consequence of external forces, especially the changing role of women in our society and the new motivations which bring educated, middle-class women into the world of remunerative employment at a relatively early age.

A T Simmons you have the best of two worlds—the advantages of a small college and the opportunities offered by a great city." The attractive, articulate senior who said that, from a small town on Cape Cod, echoed the sentiments of many of her fellow students: At Simmons there are small classes, an interested faculty, and warm human relationships—and there is "the city."

The city The city is Boston, and the immediate location is the Fenway. Across the parking lot from the main Simmons building stands the venerable Boston Latin School, established in 1635—one year before Harvard. Across the street, on one side, is the Isabella Stewart Gardner Museum; on the other side, Emmanuel College. Down the street, a few minutes' walk along Avenue Louis Pasteur, the Vermont marble buildings of the Harvard Medical School rise before the distinguished Peter Bent Brigham Hospital. Turn one corner and you stand before the State College at Boston. Walk past the English High School and turn right and you find yourself in the midst of one of the nation's greatest centers for child medical care and research, the Children's Medical Center, including the Children's Hospital and the Judge Baker Clinic. From the front steps of the main Simmons building you can look across the Fenway and see the Boston Museum of Fine Arts. Within a half-mile radius are also the Harvard schools of Public Health and Dental Medicine, Wheelock College, Wentworth Insti-

113

tute, Massachusetts College of Art, Massachusetts College of Pharmacy, the Winsor School, Boston Lying-In Hospital, Beth Israel Hospital, New England Deaconess Hospital, Angell Memorial Hospital, and the Forsyth Dental Infirmary.

A bit farther on, within a mile, are Boston University and Northeastern University, the New England Conservatory of Music, Garland Junior College, and Hebrew Teachers College, and Symphony Hall, as well as the Massachusetts Health Center, Robert Breck Brigham Hospital, New England Baptist Hospital, and the Boston VA Hospital. Add another mile and you bring into the circle of neighboring institutions the Massachusetts Institute of Technology, Boston University Medical School, the Boston branch of the University of Massachusetts, Massachusetts Bay Community College, the Boston Public Library, the Institute of Contemporary Art, and the Children's Museum, plus Boston City Hospital and University Hospital.

Within a ten-minute subway ride are the large department stores, the insurance and financial districts, the concert halls and theaters, the throbbing life of a great city surrounded by a metropolitan area heavily populated by educated, sophisticated suburbanites. Within the city itself the urban problems of twentieth-century America seethe—slums and urban renewal, racial ghettos and de facto segregation, a "mystery" strangler and frequent crime, new roads in and out of the city that cannot keep pace with rising traffic figures. Problems of public transportation, an astonishingly high real estate tax, scandal in public office—these are all part of an ever-changing city.

The same ten-minute subway ride will take you to the Freedom Trail. Here you can walk from one piece of ground to another, from one building to another, to trace colorful events in early American history, to see cemeteries with tombstones bearing distinguished names, churches celebrated in verse, the site of the Boston Massacre and the site of the Boston Tea Party. Or you can take a short bus ride to Lexington and Concord; or you drive in an hour to Plymouth Rock.

Does it mean anything very special to go to college in this environment? The girls at Simmons affirm with consistent enthusiasm that it does—that they came to Simmons in part because of its location or, if they did not, that the location has now become of great importance to them. Several of them felt that they could not again live in a small town or medium-sized city.

The city means different things to different students. For some, the hospitals are an important part of the curriculum—nursing, physical therapy, medical technology, orthoptics, and dietetics. For the girls in art there are cooperative relationships between the college and some of the museums. For all students, Boston provides a variety of rich cultural opportunities that only a few other American cities can equal or surpass. And a recently completed survey demonstrates that the Simmons students take substantial advantage of these opportunities. Moreover, Simmons has joint programs and cooperative relationships with nearby colleges. Students work in the slums, teach in the ghettos, learn in the social welfare agencies. "I love this city," said a sophomore from Connecticut, "especially the chance to sing in choirs and to hear good music performed." Then she added, "My grades aren't good. . . . I spend too much time at concerts. . . . but I don't regret it. . . . I couldn't stand a rural college and rolling hills."

But for many girls the city means yet another thing, and they speak of it with understandable enthusiasm. "Most of the girls here date quite a bit," said a sophomore from North Carolina. "If you don't," she added, "you're quite miserable." Apparently not many are miserable. The men in the area, who constitute a large pool of desirable husbands, greatly outnumber the women. "I absolutely adore Boston" is followed a few minutes later by "Social life is overwhelming. You could have six dates on one weekend." No figures are available, but college officials report that the marriage rate is high between Simmons girls and men from MIT and Harvard (especially the Medical and Business schools), as well as Boston University.

The mission, then and now   In 1867, at the age of 71, John Simmons made his will. While the money was left in a number of different trusts, the final legatee of the three major trusts was to be Simmons Female College, as he chose to call the institution that was to bear his name. In the spring of 1899 the Massachusetts Legislature granted a charter of incorporation to a group of men and women constituting the governing board, called then and still called "the Corporation." In the fall of 1899 the new Corporation received from the trustees of Mr. Simmons's estate about 1 million dollars in the form of real estate and an additional half million in other assets, including cash and investments in mortgages.

John Simmons had been dead for thirty-two years when, in 1902, the first President of Simmons College, Dr. Henry Lefavour, addressed the first class of students and some attending dignitaries on the occasion of the opening of the College. "We are come together this morning to inaugurate a new educational institution. . . . This College is unique, in that it is the first to stand in New England for a utilitarian education for girls, while aiming not to neglect any influence that may broaden the students' outlooks and deepen their lives."

Dr. Lefavour and those who presided over the establishment of Simmons College chose deliberately to found a school at which the primary aim would be utilitarian instruction for young women. At the same time, like the author of the Morrill Act in 1862, they kept ajar the door for the inclusion of liberal studies within the curriculum.

Simmons has had only three Presidents in its history. Following Dr. Lefavour, Dr. Bancroft Beatley, whose presidency extended over the difficult years of depression and war from 1933 to 1955, retained the initial emphasis on training in those fields in which women college graduates were most likely to find employment—library science, home economics, nursing, social work, and business. He also encouraged some expansion of the curriculum into newer fields, especially publication, social science, and the paramedical fields. But most important, his presidency witnessed a growing emphasis on the desirability of balancing the practical with the liberal. Dr. Beatley saw no conflict between the two; in fact, he saw little difference between them if they were planned and taught as he defined them. He emphasized what he conceived to be the four major aspects of a college education for women: (1) the personal life of the individual, (2) life in the community, (3) home and family life, and (4) occupational life.

In 1955, Dr. William E. Park became the third President of Simmons, and in the tenth year of his presidency the college once again modified its educational philosophy—not with a sharp break from the past but with a substantial change in emphasis. The change, which will be described more fully later, adds up to this: The college will retain its dedication to educating students for careers, but the more utilitarian courses will focus on basic knowledge and concepts and give but scant attention to such skills as quickly become obsolete or are easily learned on the job. The curriculum planners are sensitive to changing needs in college education for women, changing roles of women, and changing motivation of women who return to careers outside the home when the children are in school (and when the women themselves may be young enough still to hold jobs for twenty-five years or longer).

Thus under three Presidents, Simmons has followed a line of development that, while always faithful to the will of the founder, has reflected both changes in the larger society and recent changes in the intellectual and social backgrounds of its own students. However, the pace of change has grown more swift under each succeeding President.

How a college resists change
As everybody associated with Simmons knows, the college is changing rapidly. Consider this chronology: President Park appointed a Self-Study Committee in June of 1963; the committee issued a substantial interim report in June of 1964; a "Working Paper on the Simmons Curriculum" appeared in the early fall of 1964; a carefully thought-through final report reached the faculty in the late fall of 1964; and in January of 1965, though not without real reservations here and there, the faculty unanimously adopted the final report of the Self-Study Committee. Many of the changes recommended in the report were implemented within the year; a timetable for the next three years provided for the full development of the rest of the proposals. For an institution of higher education, such a sequence of events represents extraordinary speed.

On the other hand, climbing enrollments demand expansion of physical facilities, and Simmons has expanded its physical plant with an agonizing slowness—even to the point of jeopardizing the quality of the education it offers because of inadequate space and obsolete facilities. This refusal to put up essential buildings as needed can be understood, though not justified, from the fact that the Corporation at Simmons follows the lead of a few other private schools in the East in its extreme reluctance to borrow money. It is particularly opposed to borrowing money from the government of the United States. The student newspaper regularly needles the Corporation and the President on this matter, with articles, editorials, and photographs of federally financed buildings going up at other colleges around the corner—so far, with no effect.

If those who administer the institution have slowed the rate of growth by excessive economic conservatism, the faculty have not until recently adopted a constructive, innovative position regarding curricular modification. Indeed, before the recent creation of a Faculty Council, the faculty had no adequate voice for influencing change even had it so desired.

Finally, the administrative organization of the college could scarcely have blocked change more successfully if it had been deliberately designed with that goal in mind. Chapter VI of the June, 1964, Interim Report of the Self-Study Committee informs us that no formal procedure was then in existence at Simmons for adding or dropping courses and that such changes usually reflected the coming of a new member of the faculty or the departure of an old one. There can be no doubt that the chairmen of the schools and divisions of the college, vested with remarkably large powers over faculty and curriculum, had no desire to witness the creation of procedures for effective curricular modification. Nor can there be any doubt that these powerful chairmen, especially in the professional schools, played the role of deans of professional colleges in a university and effectively inhibited college-wide curricular planning. Now in the newly reorganized structure of the college, these barons have been stripped of their power—which means, quite simply, a corresponding increase in the power of the President and of the faculty.

How a college changes: Simmons students today

The new developments at Simmons are in large measure a consequence of *external* forces, especially the changing roles of women in our society and the new motivations which bring educated, middle-class women into the world of remunerative employment at a relatively early age.

For example, one-third of all mothers in the United States who have children under eighteen now hold paid jobs. Work opportunities for mature, educated women are excellent. Although most Simmons women, some 99 percent of them, want and expect to marry, they also expect to work—before marriage; after marriage and before the first child arrives; and, finally and most important, from the time the children are in school (when the mother may be in her late thirties) until retirement (which for many women may mean until sixty-two, when social security benefits begin). In short, quite apart from the need and desire to work in the early years after graduation from college, college-educated women in substantial numbers look forward to a lengthy career in later life.

No college for women can wholly ignore these facts. For Simmons, with its long tradition of combining the professional and the liberal, the response to these changed needs and desires of women came more gradually than might have been expected. But when it finally did come, it was greeted with enthusiasm, imagination, and a determination to bring outside reality and internal curriculum into harmony.

However, changes in the outside world—in the ways in which educated women now seek to order their lives—represent only half the story behind the large innovations approved at Simmons in 1965.

The other half of the story has to do with changes *within* the college—specifically, changes that have taken place in the composition of the student body.

The composition of a student body in any college may change because the college has changed its goals or its character or its curriculum. The whole matter has to be turned on its head at Simmons: The student body changed first, and the modifications and revisions in other aspects of the college changed as a consequence.

The scores made by students admitted to Simmons on the College Board examinations mirror the changes taking place. The size of the freshman class has in recent years remained almost stationary, fluctuating from 308 in 1955 to 354 in 1960 to 366 in 1965. Median scores on the verbal aptitude test have climbed each year, from 493 in 1955 to 564 in 1960 to 601 in 1965; median scores on the mathematics aptitude test have risen from 467 in 1955 to 544 in 1960 to 594 in 1965. With test scores like these, the Simmons student should do well. And she does: No more than 10 percent will fail out of school; of the final grades made by freshmen, more than 40 percent are A's and B's. A good majority of those who are admitted come from the upper tenth of their high school class.

It is obvious that the entering freshmen have been brighter, as measured by Board scores and high school rank, with each passing year and that this fact has in turn created pressures for curricular revision. Equally obvious is the fantastic change in the ratio of commuting students to resident students as Simmons slowly built new dormitory space. In 1940, 63 percent of the students were commuters; only 37 percent were residential. By 1954, the figures were almost reversed, to 40 percent commuters, 60 percent residential. In the class that entered in the fall of 1965, only 15 percent were commuters. The implications of this change are clearly reflected in a more vigorous social life on campus and the development of such extracurricular activities as clubs, art displays, student publications, career panels, dramatics, and guest speakers in the evenings. Quite simply, Simmons has become a campus school with an active, vigorous, and diverse pattern of out-of-class experiences.

A generation ago, the fathers and mothers who sent their daughters to Simmons were not themselves college graduates or engaged in professions requiring advanced education. Many were immigrants; many others were the children or grandchildren of immigrants. They lived in Boston and its immediate suburbs, and their daughters could commute by subway train, trolley car, and bus. It is probably correct to say that the majority of these parents were hardworking, ambitious inhabitants of the city.

In contrast, the parents of many Simmons girls today are likely to be middle-class suburbanites of Boston who can afford to have their daughters live in the residence halls. Other students come from elsewhere in Massachusetts, well beyond commuter range; and 204 of the 366 freshmen who entered in the fall of 1965, came from outside Massachusetts. Studies of the student body reveal a high percentage of families in which the father is a college graduate (60 percent) and a smaller percentage in which the mother, too, is a college graduate (40 percent). Moreover, the family has to be moderately well-off. 1965–66 tuition was $1,400 a year; room and board, another $1,000. Add a few miscellaneous fees and the things on which adolescent girls have to spend some money apart from tuition, room, and board, and it becomes clear that Sally Simmons has to come from a home that is comfortably middle class. At least, most Simmons girls do. There are, of course, many girls at Simmons who need and get help from the college: about one-fourth of the students receive such financial assistance as a loan, a scholarship, a part-time job, or some combination of these aids.

However, Simmons is now less accessible to the kind of student who once made up the majority of the student body. Changing residential patterns reduced the number of potential commuters within the city. Increased tuition—a rise of $800 in ten years—priced some prospective students out of the market. Limited enrollments and increasing numbers of applicants raised entrance requirements substantially. It is easy to feel nostalgic regret for the passing of the ambitious local girl from a poor family; but Simmons today is different. The students changed; the larger society changed. Finally, the college itself changed.

The new program As indicated earlier, once the college became aware of the need for change, it moved with speed and with sound planning. The Final Report of the Self-Study Committee won unanimous approval of the faculty. The changes were so long overdue that everybody recognized the need for them. The proposals had the support of the President, the Provost, and the Vice President of the college. Moreover, there grew up in the atmosphere of Simmons a feeling of inevitability about the whole thing.

The committee recommended modifications in objectives. The first was that each student be required to achieve a broadly conceived education with substantial work in the liberal arts and sciences, specialization in a field, and additional work in depth in one of the liberal arts and sciences—something like a combination of a generous liberal education, a major field for career preparation, and a kind of additional minor in the arts and sciences. The second modification was that while "career preparation" would continue to be a basic goal of the Simmons curriculum, the phrase should be broadly construed to take account of the many different roles which the college-educated woman will play at various times in her life—a job, a family, personal fulfillment, intellectual growth, responsible citizenship. As a third modification, the curriculum had to reflect the fact that, increasingly, Simmons graduates will go on to graduate or professional schools for further training. Finally, the curriculum had to be made more rigorous, and it had to provide more frequent opportunities for the student to be creative, to develop her imaginative and critical faculties, and to engage in independent study, field work, and interdisciplinary seminars.

The committee also called for the awarding of a bachelor of arts degree in addition to the bachelor of science degree, hitherto the only degree awarded at Simmons. It recommended more cooperation with neighboring institutions, more field work, more independent study, and closer involvement for instructional purposes in the problems of the city of Boston. To overcome previous shortcomings, the committee asked for increased emphasis on career counseling for undergraduates, greater flexibility to permit changes of major, and the introduction of additional graduate programs leading to the master's degree in several fields in which the college has appropriate faculty and library resources. The recommendation for the admission of more students who are highly motivated but culturally deprived has been reinforced by the adoption, in March, 1966, of a detailed report of the faculty Committee on Disadvantaged Young People.

In April 1965, the Corporation adopted recommendations for proposed organizational changes to ensure the success of the curricular proposals—a faculty structure to process in an orderly fashion recommendations for changes in the curriculum, and more democratic processes through the abolition of school and division chairmen and the development of faculty committees.

Many of the proposed changes have already occurred: September of 1966 witnessed the opening of the Career Planning and Counseling Center. The primary purpose of the center is to assist students in making thoughtful choices of career goals and in selecting appropriate majors and courses. The center provides academic guidance with the help of general and departmental faculty advisers. Professional counselors are available for personal counseling.

The Continuing Education program at Simmons is consistent with the college's concern for the adult woman who wishes to gain additional education and training after a fairly prolonged interruption in her education. The women taking part in it are mostly in their late thirties and married. Some wish to complete the requirements for an undergraduate degree; a smaller number seek graduate training. For these women, most of whom have family and other commitments, it is necessary to provide flexible, part-time programs. Many of them need careful help in planning, and some of them, in initial interviews, must be directed elsewhere. Frequently, too, these women have doubts about their ability to compete with the adolescent undergraduate, and they need reassurance and encouragement until they find, as most do, that they can more than hold their own.

How the students see themselves and their college

The change in emphasis in the curriculum—the change that comes closest to touching the student in some direct way—has created no anxiety for the more professionally oriented student; nor has it brought great joy to the heart of the girl who worships at the altar of the liberal arts. The changes now in progress at Simmons seem to impress students only as being in some vague way part of an atmosphere of ferment. Yet they are introspective and communicative about themselves and their college.

The girls are far from alike. Indeed, they were selected for interviews because of their differences—the civil rights activist; the Goldwater girl who heads the Conservative Club; the "antiadministration" girl; the commuter and the on-campus resident; the student government girls and those who could not care less; the Jews, Italians, Greeks, Irish, and WASP's; the pragmatist in dietetics and the English major who, if she needed a miracle, "would rather pray to Wylie Sypher than to God." But for all these differences, they collectively fashion an image of themselves and of their college which is surprisingly uniform. The girls agree that though they have strong interests in specific issues, they are not generally interested in partisan politics. They do get involved in those issues that engage the loyalties and stir the idealism of many college students in the 1960s. They go to Selma, protest American military policies in Vietnam, spend a summer in Project Head Start, or join the Peace Corps.

Still, this kind of involvement is important in the lives of a relatively small number. More appealing to the general run are such projects as a school committee election in Boston (with strong racial overtones), volunteer work in local hospitals and in ghetto schools, and internal matters such as changes in the college calendar and the introduction of a reading period. A Simmons girl from Yellow Springs, Ohio, whose father is on the staff at Antioch, put it this way: "Antioch kids jump into big things like Vietnam about which they can't really do anything. Simmons girls work on local things and really accomplish something."

Why is the Simmons girl either lacking in awareness or, if aware, more inclined to involvement in local issues than in large national or international matters? Perhaps, because many of them come from the Boston area, they would naturally have a strong interest in local issues or in local aspects of national issues. This sounds plausible and may even be true, but none of the girls mentioned it. Instead, several students said that the Simmons girl is simply more concerned about her social life than about other people's problems. Certainly there is ample evidence that the Simmons girl cares about her social life and that she has a good deal of it. But the evidence also shows active participation by many girls in humanitarian (if nonpartisan) causes— the girl who spent one summer as a nurse in Nigeria and would like to spend a year on the Ship of Hope after she graduates; the sophomore from Connecticut who plans to join the Peace Corps; the Negro girl from Boston who organized a civil rights group on campus; the junior majoring in English literature who is actively promoting Students for a Democratic Society, mostly because she opposes the war in Vietnam; the girl from a small town in Massachusetts who was an "active demonstrator while in high school," is deeply involved in civil rights matters, and is proud of the fact that her brother is active, though not a leader, in similar concerns at Berkeley.[1]

There is again uniformity when the students talk about their studies—indeed, here there is virtual unanimity. Student after student repeats the same refrain: "We are conscientious; we study hard; we do our work; we like our classes; we like our teachers. But we aren't intellectuals. In the dorm, we talk about dates but not about books." "When a Harvard man wants a fun date, he calls a Simmons girl. If he wants intellectual talk, he calls a Radcliffe girl." "I thought I was

[1] Responding to a College Student Questionnaire item about future job preferences, 35 percent of the 1965 entering class chose, among nine alternative responses, "Opportunity to be helpful to others and/or useful to society in general."

coming to an intellectual mecca, but the bull sessions are all gossip." Observations, interviews, and evidence from the College Student Questionnaire suggest that the students at Simmons, while bookish and bright, come from middle-class homes in which the professional aspects of a college education are still valued more highly than the intellectual—and homes, moreover, where there has been less attention to the arts and music and foreign travel and a certain kind of upper-class respect for the mind than one might encounter in the home backgrounds of the girls at Wellesley or Radcliffe.

In essence, the girls see themselves as not very partisan in political matters; conscientious and bright but not intellectual; fun to be with socially but conventional; humanitarian but not ideological; helpful in local community projects but suspicious of national movements with remote headquarters; interested in both a career and marriage and determined to have both at one time or another.

The students see their college very much as they see themselves. They regard the administration as beyond criticism in such matters as freedom of the student newspaper and academic freedom for the faculty. They quite rightly see the admissions policies as wholly free of any suggestion of racial or religious bias. Yet they regard the administration as a bit prissy in some of its rules and regulations, too cautious in spending money for new buildings, too slow to respond to such student requests as later hours in the library and permission for library dates. They laud the small classes and respect their faculty. They like—perhaps most of all—the balance in the curriculum between the professional and liberal, and they refer to this most frequently in response to the question, "Why did you come to Simmons?" The girls, typically, see their college as not on a par, in its prestige or in its intellectual demands on them, with some of the distinguished women's colleges, and yet they regard the college as right for them. What is ultimately of greatest value to the girls, as repeated over and over by almost every girl interviewed, is that the college is not a grim, competitive place, that they are happy there, that it is a place in which they can grow in wisdom and maturity without the stresses that seem to beset so many students in other colleges with high admissions standards.

How an outsider sees the college We know from the College Board scores that Simmons girls rank high in verbal and numerical skills. Indeed, there is some outspoken concern among faculty that the admissions criteria be broadened to accommodate the girl who may not rank quite so high on Board scores but who gives evidence of originality, creativity, or special commitment of some kind. We know from CUES (College and University Environment Scales) that the girls not only see themselves as, but doubtless are, conventional young people in a somewhat conventional academic environment. Again, there is a feeling among many of the faculty that greater hospitality should be extended to the applicant for admission who is less conventional and more innovative. And there is, moreover, a disposition among the faculty to blame themselves—surely a most significant harbinger of change—for the complacently conventional atmosphere reflected in a 93d percentile placement on the CUES "propriety" scale. Should admissions criteria be modified along the lines suggested by this thinking, the rather low 33d percentile placement on the "awareness" scale of the CUES ranking might well rise.

Using the scores determined by Alexander W. Astin (*Who Goes Where to College*, 1965), we find that the girls at Simmons, when compared with their counterparts at such other Massachusetts colleges for women as Smith, Radcliffe, and Wellesley, indicate much less interest in pursuing graduate work, reflect substantially less interest in literature and the arts, come from families of more modest socioeconomic status, and have a much greater interest in academic work leading toward a career. In terms of intellectual ability, the Simmons girls are somewhat lower; in terms of the major academic disciplines, the Simmons girls show greater interest in the natural and social sciences and less interest in the humanities. Again, this information conforms closely to what the girls at Simmons say about themselves. The changes now in progress at Simmons will soon alter this picture, and in a decade the scores of the girls at all four institutions referred to above will probably be much more nearly alike. Nevertheless, there is a strong determination at Simmons that the college shall not lose its special character, that the concern for intellectual achievement shall not obliterate President Beatley's philosophy of comprehensive concern for all the roles that women play at all stages of life. And this philosophy, in turn, will mean continuing and even broadening the welcome extended to girls of diverse backgrounds and to girls with fairly strong career interests.

What else does an outsider see, or think that he sees? Most striking is the probability that the new curriculum with its greater emphasis on the liberal arts and basic sciences, the new faculty resolve to make the courses more rigorous, and the greater expressed desire on the part of the students to go on to graduate and professional schools—will all produce an atmosphere of greater academic competitiveness, along with all the related changes that competition generates. Whether that will be counted gain or loss will depend on the educational philosophy of the one making the judgment. Greater competition, if it comes, could imperil the Honor System. At present, the system, as all the students agree, works well in the academic domain: Students write their own papers and do not cheat on examinations. Instructors do not proctor examinations.

The girls at Simmons have made it plain that they now wish to be as free in certain matters of dress and behavior as the girls at Radcliffe are. Nobody who takes a close look at the students and administrators at Simmons today can doubt that some interesting changes lie immediately ahead. And if the admissions office should deliberately seek to increase the number of students having primarily innovative rather than conventionally academic talents, the changes will be all the more drastic.

Nevertheless, the present fact is that the Simmons girls, though they speak with candor about behavioral matters and are certainly not immune to newer student moods in the nation, are basically prudent. They say so themselves, and outsiders who have had the opportunity to observe them intimately confirm this judgment. The circle of hospitality for innovation grows inevitably larger, but the extending radius is limited by certain basic facts: Girls are more conservative than boys in behavioral experimentation; middle-class students (with a large percentage of immigrant grandparents) have a substantial respect for the opinions of others about their standards of deportment; in the last analysis, whatever grievances they may have or may think they have, the issues are not now, for most of the girls, of sufficient magnitude to warrant even a mild revolution.

The student weekly newspaper reflects this mood well. Wholly uncensored, it bewails the failure of the administration to get on with a student union and a science building with the aid of federal funds. Yet no issue of this essentially serious paper is completely devoid of a quiet and rather charming humor or disarming spirit of resignation regarding an administration that lacks the wisdom to follow the advice of the editors. Liberal in spirit, it champions the cause of civil rights, and it supports those who oppose the American military policies in Vietnam. Yet most of its space is devoted to social and educational events on campus and in the Boston area.

If the paper is the Simmons-Boston world passing in weekly review, another publication reflects the wide world of scholarship and of history. *Essays and Studies* appears twice a year, and each issue of this attractive periodical carries five or six articles, papers prepared for courses. Consider the range of titles—"Leopold Bloom's Sensuality"; "The 'Fall' of the Roman Empire in the West"; "The State of Innocence in *Paradise Lost*"; "The Political Theory of B. F. Skinner"; "Dream and Reality: An Evaluation of Napoleon III"; "Truth and Certainty in Hume and James"; "Crashaw as a Devotional Poet"; " 'Childlessness' and Divorce"; "Meaning: Its Quest and Attainment in Two Novels by Albert Camus"; "Innocence and Experience in Hawthorne." Almost all the pieces are characterized by careful reasoning, forceful writing, and full documentation. Any undergraduate school in the country could be proud of this publication: perhaps, after all, a Harvard man would not find it so difficult to have an "intellectual date" with a Simmons girl.

Most of the academic activities and many of the extracurricular programs move forward in a whirl of activity in the main academic building, a large, rambling building erected in 1903–04 and enlarged subsequently by several wings. The corridors seem to go on endlessly, and through them hurry crowds of eager young women, upstairs and downstairs, on the elevator, in the "attic" rooms of the top floor with their sloped walls, through the basement (the "dungeon" is what most of the girls call it) crowded with equipment, supplies, students, faculty, a cafeteria, crates, machinery, hats and coats and boots and books. The walls seem to vibrate, and the whole building seems to hum.

Attached to this antique structure in 1961 was the Lefavour Hall–Bancroft Beatley Library complex, stunningly handsome in its architecture, efficient and functional and cheerful. It houses a library with more than 100,000 books, well-lighted stacks, study rooms, lounges where students can read a new book or magazine while listening to good music, classrooms and offices, and several academic departments. In the library the atmosphere is always relaxed. The girls there are reading and taking notes, smoking, chatting, listening to music—and crowding the telephone booths.

The residence halls are small enough to be friendly and warm and yet large enough to be moderately efficient. Grouped together in a triangular pattern, the dormitories constitute a residential campus quite separate from the main academic building. Though the two centers are not very far apart, there is frequent expression of regret that not all the buildings of the college can occupy a single plot of land.

With a willingness to borrow money from sources other than its own endowment, the college could build the additional dormitories it must have if the enrollment is to grow. Similarly, it could build a much-needed student union on a long-range, self-liquidating basis. But neither the President nor the members of the Corporation seem to appreciate the significance of a student union for a satisfactory social life for the students, especially in view of the limited recreational and athletic facilities now available.

As regards the physical plant, the most important single need of the college at this time is to replace the antiquated science facilities in the main academic building with a new science building. Belatedly the college has initiated planning which, it is hoped, will produce such a building between 1970 and 1972.

As already suggested, the slow pace of new construction reflects the conservatism of the Corporation. Limited to twenty-four members, the Corporation is a self-perpetuating body. While four members are elected for six-year terms on nomination by the Alumnae Association, the others serve for life or until they choose to retire. Moreover, election to the Corporation requires the favorable vote of three-fourths of the membership. Perhaps these facts explain why the composition of the Corporation does not adequately reflect the "ethnic mix"[2] which in many ways lies at the heart of the admirable vitality and variety that help to give Simmons its special character.

In recent years, the major source of additional funds has been an average annual increase in tuition of $100. Apart from the fact that an ever-higher tuition rate places Simmons beyond reach of desirable applicants, it is no substitute for an active, aggressive, long-range, carefully planned program of fund-raising on a major scale. Present evidence is that those who guide the destinies of Simmons are unable or unwilling to act with heroic vigor to raise money from sources other than tuition.

On the other hand, everybody associated with Simmons is agreed that the members of the Corporation believe deeply in academic freedom. A former president of the local chapter of the American Association of University Professors asserted that no faculty could enjoy more complete academic freedom. And reference is made with pride to an incident of some years ago when a member of the faculty summoned before a Senate subcommittee received the full support of the Corporation and the administration. Nineteenth-century liberalism, respect for individual freedom, and suspicion of strong

[2] Religious variety is one indication of the varied backgrounds of Simmons students. Returns on the College Student Questionnaire show an equal proportion of Jewish and Protestant students (35 percent each) and only a slightly smaller proportion of Catholics (23 percent).

government—these, in conjunction, have an honorable history and continuing power at Simmons.

The Faculty Council, now that the powerful school and division heads have been reorganized out of their positions, provides an opportunity for the faculty to approach the administration with something like a single voice instead of the many voices it formerly brought to faculty-administration relationships. Moreover, the council, with its power to appoint certain committees and conduct studies and to confer with the President on important issues and advise him on appointments to administrative committees, represents a large infusion of democracy into the academic governance of the Simmons community. Indeed, the change is so great that the members of the faculty are only slowly learning how to use their new responsibilities and opportunities. No one can doubt that the faculty will now contribute, indeed, is already contributing, to the strengthening of Simmons in many ways that in the past either were not possible or seemed not to be possible.

The word "relaxed" seems to describe most of the faculty as well as most of the students, a situation which is somewhat surprising in an institution undergoing rapid change and for a faculty among whom certain sources of frustration inevitably exist. The explanation seems to lie in the words of a young member of the faculty who said, "I've only been here two years, but I feel a very deep sense of loyalty to Simmons. I think I will want to remain here indefinitely after I get my Ph.D." Similar expressions of loyalty emerged from conversations with numerous other faculty, almost all of whom are normally somewhat reserved. In a period when so many university administrators grumble that their best people are more loyal to their discipline than to their institution, this kind of affection for one's college is a source of great strength in a small, private liberal arts institution like Simmons.

One of the issues of concern to the Faculty Council is financial aid to students. If Simmons is to continue to keep its door open to a reasonable number of promising local students and preserve its stimulating variety of ethnic, religious, and class differences in the face of rising tuition and other costs, fairly generous financial assistance in varied forms will be required.

Also important is the feeling of some faculty that they are not sufficiently aware of what is happening or about to happen. Here again, the situation is changing markedly, in the activities of the new council and in the early planning for a new science building. More important—though perhaps more the criticism of an observer than of the people at Simmons—is the lack of close and frequent and regular meetings of administrators with the President of the college. Such meetings, even in small colleges, provide guidance for the president and open important channels of communication.

Despite these few negative matters, faculty morale is, as indicated earlier, high. The salary scale is one contributing factor. Hitherto far too low, it ranged in 1966–67 from a minimum of $6,000 for an instructor to a maximum of $18,000 for a full professor. This brings up another grievance, one advanced rather mildly by a few of the faculty. Although promotions from one rank to another come along with reasonable frequency—perhaps at something like five-year intervals for the abler teachers—there is a feeling, supported by the evidence, that the associate professorship is the terminal rank for too many people and that even those who do make it to full professor must wait too long for the last promotion. To the extent that these assertions are true, they clearly diminish the attractiveness of the salary scale. To offer but a single statistic: There were at the beginning of the 1965–66 academic year twenty associate professors who had been at Simmons more than ten years.

Simmons in summary It is the odd combination of words "private land-grant school for girls" that comes closest to describing the adaptive and practical liberal education which has in the past given Simmons its special character and is emerging with new emphases in the late 1960s.

To one who has had a close look at the place, Simmons emerges at one level as a good private liberal arts college for girls, offering a fairly broad range of courses and curriculums for a small school, requiring sound and rigorous work in the liberal arts and sciences, providing the opportunity to prepare for a professional career—all in an exciting, urban environment. At this level, one would go on to say that it has a splendid faculty, reasonably small classes, a generally happy social life, a strong extracurricular program, physical facilities that are inadequate in some respects, and a concern for quality that will probably make the life of the girls more competitive and perhaps less relaxed in the next few years. But that is only one level, though surely the most important one. At another level, Simmons is a unique institution, as indigenous as the junior college, as varied and unpredictable as the land-grant school, as exciting as the American dream of moving, through higher education, into a world that broadens the horizons, sharpens the critical faculties, awakens the imagination, liberates from parochial influences, and yet narrows in on an area of specialization producing both pride and competence. Above all, inherent in every important decision and spoken or assumed in every discussion about the college is the one fundamental commitment to providing education of high quality and appropriate balance for bright young women (these are always the key words: "bright young women") for life in the closing decades of the present century and the early decades of the next.

If there are many roads that lead to excellence in private liberal arts education, Simmons College has, since its founding, followed its own route without seeking to model itself after some real or ideal pattern. It has been true to itself and honest with its students. In any future histories of Simmons, 1965–66, the year of adoption of the new program, will be the year of a great turning in the road. And those who may some day write such histories will surely dwell with understandable pride on the changes now under way.

Edward B. Blackman, Assistant Dean of University College of Michigan State University, was the author of the Simmons College profile. Conrad Hilberry, associate director of this study and Professor of English at Kalamazoo College, served as his associate. J. Garton Needham, Vice President of Simmons, was college liaison. Mimi Luebbermann of Goucher College was student observer.

A look at the twelve campuses described in this volume is all
it takes to make one suspicious of generalizations about
college students—statements that they are "rebellious" or "sophisticated" or "idealistic" or "conforming." One of the surprises of
the study has been the extent to which customs, attitudes, ambitions,
and conceptions of college vary from campus to campus.

From many ways   *Between two given colleges there may be no overlap; for example,*
and wide apart   *in a Wheaton graduating class there may be no student who could
have enrolled at Goddard with reasonable happiness and success,
and at Goddard no student who would have thrived at Wheaton.
Not all the differences are equally dramatic, but many of them are
striking. A Simmons girl would find at Oberlin almost nothing
she could recognize as social life—few dances or parties, little
opportunity for dinner in the city or an evening at a professional
play. And many Oberlin students would be uncomfortable in a
college like Simmons or Wheaton, where social life means dates
formally contracted for rather than the casual encounter over
breakfast or at a meeting of a committee planning a discussion of
black power or a performance of electronic music. A Berea student
would feel at home with the earnestness and social informality of*

the Oberlin campus (after recovering from his surprise at finding beer served in the college rathskeller), but the fierce pace of the Oberlin academic life might oppress him, and the strident quality of some of the student protests might strike him as unseemly.

Better or worse? If these differences are as important as we believe them to be, what do they imply for evaluation of colleges? How would one set about arguing that Oberlin is better or worse than Simmons or Berea? Which comes higher on the pecking order, Wheaton or Goddard? If Amherst students' Scholastic Aptitude Test scores average 700 and Morehouse students' scores average 400, does it follow that Amherst is the superior school? Who is the ideal student and where does one find him?

Our answer to these questions, we believe, will be shared by almost all college people in theory, but in practice by many fewer: A college should be judged by its impact on the students it serves. If, with the college's help, students become more inclined to look behind events for causes and behind judgments for reasons and better able to grasp concepts and put them to work, if they discover satisfactions that had been closed to them and find themselves freed from some of the limitations of their community, social class, and national culture, if they move toward a more inclusive scheme of ideas than they could manage before and as a result are better able to resolve problems and make complex choices—in short, if liberal education has occurred—the college must be regarded as good. On the other hand, if students leave with the same unexamined attitudes and intellectual skills they brought, the college must be considered poor, no matter how much the faculty may publish or how bright or amiable the students may be.

Impact The difficulty with this criterion of excellence, of course, is that impact is not easily measured. It is much simpler to discover the percentage of students in the top quarter of their high school class or the percentage of Ph.D.s on the faculty. But if student development is the most reasonable criterion for judging colleges, we must find methods, even if we cannot measure such development quantitatively, at least of getting some reliable impressions of whether it is occurring and in what ways.

Some effective instruments and techniques are already at hand. Standard area tests and achievement tests, of course, measure a complex variety of intellectual skills; and questionnaires of many kinds can show changes in opinion, attitude, or personal needs. Careers and accomplishments of graduates are also relevant. In preparing the profiles, we made use of any information of this kind that was available at the colleges and supplemented it with extended interviews with students, conducted both by adult members of the teams and by students from other campuses who lived along with the students at the profile colleges, attending classes, eating in the dining halls, sitting in on bull sessions, getting acquainted with a variety of individuals and groups. These interviews gave an emphatic, if not a statistically defensible, sense of the kinds of changes that may overtake students at a given college.

In this chapter we are interested in the operation of student cultures as a force making for student development. Our impression, as we have looked at the profile colleges, is that student society can press very hard on its members, influencing how they act, what they talk about and how they talk, what range of opinions they take seriously; in fact, every student culture we have seen, even the most resolutely individualistic, pulls and pushes its members, though the manner of the pulling and pushing varies greatly. The power of a student culture to shape actions and beliefs can speed, enrich, and complicate the process of liberal education—or it can retard it, even reverse it, neutralizing the best efforts of the faculty.

Whether a student culture is thought to move its members toward or away from liberal education will depend to some extent, no doubt, on the biases of the observer who is making the judgment. But this much seems clear: A culture that draws its members into a persistent tug-of-war between conflicting attitudes or opinions— so long as the combat is not bitterly destructive—will be more likely to produce liberal education than one that offers unanimity or only petty disagreement or rivalry. Fruitful confrontation may grow out of the students' history. At Berea, though students resent the "barefoot image," it is inevitable that there must be a real pull between their loyalty to the Appalachian region and their desire to let their education carry them out into more prosperous territory. Morehouse students undoubtedly feel a comparable tension between racial pride and personal ambition, between contempt for the white man and desire to inherit his earth. At Wheaton, students are caught between their Republican, pietistic home churches and the secular world they encounter when they leave home. But the debate need not depend primarily on the background of the students. Recurring discussion of the pacifist position, of political detachment or engagement, of educational experimentation, of personal morality and meaning, of any sizable issue that can draw in students and set them to reading and thinking, will reinforce liberal education. A culture that directs attention primarily to small distinctions between social groups or affirms the untested opinions students have inherited can effectively circumscribe that education.

Mix and match We are persuaded that a campus culture is most likely to help a student to liberal education when four conditions prevail.

Liberal education is likely to occur, first, when a student feels somewhat at home, his attitudes and background shared by enough others so that he is not altogether an alien, so that at least in some group his gestures and tone of voice are immediately understood and his beliefs seem natural. Without a home base where a student can draw confidence from familiar sounds, he may simply back off from his surroundings, taking little from them and giving little in return. Thus Larry Blair flourished in the familiar landscape of Berea as he might not have done at a college where he felt like a rare mountain bird.

But, second, the familiarity must be mixed with enough strangeness to force a student's ideas and competences to expand and to challenge his attitudes. If Larry Blair had simply been comfortable at Berea, he would not be on his way to Stanford and a professional career in chemistry. Strangeness may mean instruction that raises the curtain on new scenes—like Berea's humanities course or Wheaton's instruction in philosophy, theology, or literature. Or it may mean living and talking with people unlike anyone a student has been close to before: The Midwestern high school boy at Oberlin is educated partly by the missionary's son who has lived much of his life in India, the Jewish girl from the Bronx, the Texan back from a bitter stint in Vietnam—and they by him. Or it may mean new surroundings: For a small-town girl at Simmons or a farm boy at Morehouse it means Boston or Atlanta.

Colleges have seldom erred by offering their students too much strangeness. The more common error has been an overdose of familiarity, a powerful soporific. If we are right in predicting that colleges will become part of a network which will permit students to move fairly readily out from their home campuses and back, then strangeness may be more easily come by than in the past. A student finding himself an alien in Tokyo or a Cleveland settlement house or a mental hospital or an industrial research laboratory or even .

another college will be stirred to new discoveries about himself and what is around him. Since every link in the network costs something, a college will have to choose carefully the sorts of off-campus work and study it holds open for its students. Certainly, strangeness should be one criterion in the choice: The college should see to it that its students find, off campus if necessary, the stimulation and bafflement they need to grow on.

Third, a college is likely to foster student growth, we contend, if it demands of students greater responsibility than they have been asked to carry before. In recent years, of course, the demands have come from the other direction, from students demanding greater freedom, greater influence on college policy. And the forms that student responsibility or leadership take are changing. Students are less interested than they once were in holding largely routine offices or in making "decisions" that they regard as pro forma. Quite properly, student responsibilities will vary from college to college, but they will be, and should be, more genuine and less perfunctory than in the past. The responsibility may be academic— responsibility for initiating courses, conceiving and carrying out independent study projects, or, as at Goddard, even organizing and rationalizing whole chunks of one's education. It may be social— helping to define and enforce the regulations that order the community. Or it may be political—taking a hand, formally or informally, in the government of the college, or trying through demonstrations, lobbying, or sit-ins to influence national or local policy. Not all students are equally ready to take charge of their own or other people's affairs. Undertakings that an Oberlin student body can manage, like a three-day Student Congress to recommend changes in college policy or a Christmas expedition to Mississippi to help rebuild a burned Negro church, might be difficult for a student body with less experience.

And for any student body it takes time. The author of one of the college profiles suggested that students may have to recognize college politics as part of their "load," the more active ones staying somewhat longer to get the formal academic work for a degree. At any rate, students in every college we visited are speaking more loudly and being listened to more attentively than in the past. They assume that their judgment should figure in college decisions, that learning can result from action as well as from study. In general, we find this new self-assertion on the part of students consonant with liberal education.

But—and this is the fourth condition—if student responsibility is to yield maximum education with minimum chaos, someone must take time to deliberate with students about issues and political processes. This is a long and difficult assignment, which eventually will have to be figured into faculty teaching and committee duties. And it is work with which most faculty are uncomfortable or impatient. There are opposite dangers—that faculty will use "deliberations" to exercise informal control and to subvert student responsibility or that they will abandon the students whenever the students make what looks like a foolish decision. But when student-faculty consultation is genuine, as in Oberlin's Four-Four-Two Committee, it can help students to foresee the consequences of choices, to develop the skills and call on the resources to make an enterprise go—or to discover, gently, that social institutions change only through intricate political processes and that change at best comes slowly.

Ingredients of a student culture

Under everything this chapter has said thus far lies the assumption that student life outside the classroom contributes significantly to a student's education* and that a college can hardly afford to ignore the student culture it creates. What, then, are the elements that shape student society, and what, if anything, can a college do to alter them?

The most important ingredient in a student culture is the most obvious one—the kinds of students who enroll. Most people, including many members of the faculty and students, take it for granted that a college creates a certain kind of student body by selecting in some deliberate if mysterious way among the students who apply. But as far as we could observe, the process of selection is effective only in that it admits students who are likely to do well, or passably well, in college courses. (Even there, the selection process is less effective than we ordinarily suppose.) Where the political attitudes, social or religious habits, and intellectual concerns of campuses differ, it is because the students themselves have chosen—not because the colleges have selected their students to achieve some beautifully balanced social orchestration.

* If evidence of this point is necessary, Everett Wilson's study of the people and events that Antioch students identified as their important "teachers" will supply it (Theodore M. Newcomb and Everett K. Wilson, *College Peer Groups*, Aldine Publishing Co., Chicago, 1966, pp. 89–91). Only about a quarter of these "teachers"—influences most important in their development while at college—were faculty or had directly to do with faculty or academic work.

The director of admissions at Oberlin, for example, reports that the college receives about twenty-five hundred applications a year. Of these, all but perhaps fifty or one hundred are from students who appear able to succeed academically. In choosing one thousand from the remaining twenty-four hundred applicants, does he look for some special Oberlin qualities, we wondered? Well, no. As far as he knows, they are selected very much as they would be selected at Williams or Wellesley or anywhere else. In fact, in the early 1950s the number of applicants fell off rather sharply, so that for several years the college was admitting nearly all the men who applied. But as far as the faculty could tell, there was no change in the quality or character of the students.

Probably two things are at work. Most students must acquire a surer sense than we ordinarily suppose of the campus society they are getting into, picking up cues from campus visits, from comments of friends attending the college, from counselors, even from the catalog. At the same time, adolescents are malleable, and a student culture tends to shape its members to its own specifications. In any event, while student cultures differ markedly, it is seldom because of deliberate selection on the part of the college.

There are a few exceptions. Berea insists that 90 percent of its students come from the Appalachian counties and from families with low incomes. No matter how many applications it receives from merit scholars in Cincinnati or New York City, no more than 10 percent of the entering class will be from out of the region. Berea is one of the few colleges in the country which consistently turn down students with CEEB scores a couple of hundred points higher than their average. Wheaton's explicit and emphatic doctrinal stand limits its student body in a comparable way, as do Morehouse's Negro history and Goddard's educational practice. But even in these colleges, the choice is made largely by the students, not by a college admissions committee.

Colleges may well feel a certain helplessness in this situation, especially since a fuller description of a college (like those in this book) may tend to fix the character of its student body or make it more homogeneous than before. A substantial change in program seems to be the only lever capable of dislodging a well-settled college image. And even such a change may work in ironic ways: Kalamazoo College, seeing that its students came largely from suburbs and towns in Michigan, Illinois, and Indiana, devised a program that would send all students off campus to work, often in Eastern cities, to study abroad, and to pursue independent senior *projects—a program to cure provincialism. But immediately the program began to attract students from New York and Washington, some of whom had lived in France for a year and hankered to go back, students who had long since shed their provincialism.*

Architecture   *Though architecture is what one sees first at a college, he often stops looking at it before its significance has registered. The truth is that students can interact only as the architecture permits. Goddard's sixteen-man dormitories create a social life quite different from that in Ripon's forty- to seventy-man fraternity houses. And Wheaton's new five-hundred-fifty-man dormitory will house a society unlike either of those. Depending on their surroundings, people will eat by ones or twos or fours or eights and may feel quite alone or part of a group of twenty or forty others. Oberlin students have insisted tenaciously that the smaller dormitories for women with dining rooms attached—men coming in for their meals—encourage sustained discussion and shelter special groups, as the more economical large dormitories and dining rooms cannot do. And Oberlin's "dating parlors"—those rooms in the student union which couples may use by signing up in advance—create social patterns not duplicated elsewhere in these colleges. At Morehouse and Simmons, which have no student unions, one gets less sense of campus life than at Earlham, for example. When Simmons students are not in class or laboratory, they can choose to be in the library, in the dormitory, in a makeshift snack bar, or in the city. Of these, the dormitory is most likely to sustain groups. Perhaps this explains, in part, the Simmons girls' acute consciousness that they belong to one house group or another, and the near trauma at room-drawing time. The Simmons campus offers few homes for groups that might compete with the dormitory-based society.*

Architecture can be important symbolically as well as functionally. The limestone walls of Wheaton's Blanchard Hall stand as firm as the Epistle to the Romans. Between the academic buildings and the dormitories at Simmons stands another college altogether (Emmanuel College). That architectural interruption must have something to do with the distinction, probably clearer at Simmons than at any of the other eleven schools, between social life and study: weekends and the dormitories are for social life, weekdays and the academic buildings for study. At Oberlin the academic buildings, some of them striking pieces of architecture, stand around the college square announcing their individuality. They range from the beautifully simple First Church through the Italian Renaissance of Finney Chapel to Minoru Yamasaki's new conservatory buildings grouped around a reflecting pool. (Even Peters Hall, ballooning like alma mater about to give birth, is an extraordinary example of turreted eclectic.) A student could hardly live with these buildings for four years without absorbing part of their message—that elegance can take more than one form and that art is likely to be individual, unpredictable, bizarre. On the other hand, Goddard's converted farm buildings growing in the Vermont hills speak of egalitarianism and simplicity. And students get the message: A student driver, bringing guests from the airport, stopped in front of President Pitkin's silo office and called out, "Hey, Tim. They're here!"

Institutions   *Student life finds much of its variety and texture in institutions within the college. Some of these may be organized and financed by the college itself—glee clubs, football teams, college newspapers, theater organizations, student governments, mock conventions, professional fraternities. Others get their sustaining energy from some source other than the college staff—religious or political groups affiliated with a church or a party, student-run musical organizations or unofficial theater groups, "co-op" houses, fraternities and sororities with national ties, coffee houses or taverns frequented by students. Still other institutions may bring together students only briefly and informally—a folk-dance group, a mimeographed newspaper that lasts only as long as the editor and his friends can supply copy and money, a cribbage enclave in one of the dormitories, a klatch of motorcyclists, a handful of film makers, a group mobilized to protest college administration of draft tests. Some colleges—notably Goddard among our twelve—will run to informal groups, the college organizing no intercollegiate athletics, no student publications, no extracurricular clubs. At other campuses, for example, Wheaton, even student protests may be more or less formally sponsored by the college. Each style may be appropriate to the students who live with it.*

The questions to ask are whether the institutions sheltered by a college are varied enough to give students a chance to try out many skills and sample a number of different ways of thinking and acting, and whether they are open enough so that a student can move in and out of groups of many complexions, finding out about his own talents, preferences, and convictions as he goes.

Regulations *Like buildings, college regulations establish structures within which student life takes place; for example, the no-car rule at Oberlin and Berea, the prohibition of movies and dancing at Wheaton, and the requirement at many colleges that students live in the dormitories make it certain that some activities will not occur, some groups will not form. Further, requirements concerning dress, behavior in the dormitories and dining rooms, drinking, smoking, dormitory hours, and so forth are sure to affect the tone of the campus, making it more or less proper, creating or not creating a slow burn of antagonism toward the rule givers.*

Though colleges vary remarkably, students were pressing for the relaxation of one regulation or another on every campus we visited, and gradually the regulations were wavering or falling. Extrapolating freely, one can see a time not too far in the future when many colleges will make learning and recreation available to students but will do little to impose it on them or to regulate their lives. But since people presumably need some system of limits and demands, our speculation is that other agencies, both larger and smaller, will gradually replace the college as a whole in structuring students' lives. On one hand, misconduct—excessive drinking, misuse of drugs, disorderly behavior—may become more and more the business of civil authorities. The appearance of privately owned dormitories and apartments near university campuses is speeding this process. On the other hand, the setting of expectations for intellectual achievement and social conduct, the fostering of a set of political or religious attitudes, and the cultivation of a style of life may become the business of groups smaller than a whole student body. This has happened long since on university campuses, of course: The boys in the Phi Psi house do not expect to have anything in common with the inhabitants of the Baptist student center or the theater crowd or the "co-opers" or the Hillel group. And at the colleges, fraternities, dormitory groups, or other enclaves have been semiautonomous and powerful in their effect on their members. But the process seems to be speeding up and overtaking colleges that had thought of themselves as entities.

Whether increased pluralism would be a good thing is another question. Professor Laurence Barrett of Kalamazoo College argues that it would not.

The colleges seem to me to be a highly artificial, highly ritualized, transition stage between childhood and adulthood. They are constantly playing the double role of family and state, and the ambiguity of this role is reflected in the language which we use. We stand <u>in loco parentis</u>, in some respects legally

and in many respects ritually. We talk about alma mater, house mothers, big sisters for the freshmen, fraternity brothers, and college family. We also stand in loco civitatis and we have our faculty senates, our student elections, our judicial councils, our procedures for appeal, and our constitutions—rewritten every student generation or so—for student activities. This produces a confusing but fruitful ambiguity in a host of areas. Discipline is aimed at the well being of the child as it is exercised in the family, but in the state, law is aimed at protecting the public.

Part of the process of transition must be a ritual of cutting the umbilical cord, a revolt of some sort against the parent. Since this cannot generally be achieved in a family oriented culture without traumatic guilt, the revolt is often symbolic. The girls revolt against a house mother or a motherly dean—I am pretty sure that quite unconsciously we select these people to play this role—and the men at Bowdoin march in a body to tear down the flagpole. I am constantly impressed by how often the struggle between students and faculty seems to reflect the old contention between children and parents about what one must eat, what one must wear, and when one must go to bed. When I see these students going barefoot, for example, I hear my wife telling the children to put on their rubbers.

The genial quarrel between the adults of the college community and the students seems to me, therefore, to play a very healthy role and I am not made happy by the suggestion that the colleges may abandon it at last and leave the parents to stand in loco parentis and the civil authorities in loco civitatis. A certain amount of pecking at the shell from within strengthens the muscles and enables the emerging chick to stand. Some of the pullets and young cockerels at the most "liberal" colleges seem to me to be flopping around as if they hadn't had quite enough to peck at.

There are other options, no doubt, besides rigid all-college rules and complete acceptance of whatever behavior students choose for themselves. Some colleges may try variations on the Harvard house system, bringing faculty and students together in groups that can exert some adult influence over their members. The time may even be coming when adults—union members, maybe, or middle-management people in one business or another—will be coming to college or back to college in sufficient numbers so that college communities may be a more natural mixture of ages, a few middle-aged insurance brokers or plumbers leavening the adolescent lump. However that may be, colleges in the next few years will be deciding and redeciding what controls and expectations should govern student behavior and what agency—the state, the college, the houses—should set and sanction them.

The configuration of a culture

As with any other culture, the elements of a student culture do not exist independently. The entering students, the architecture, and the local institutions and regulations hang together to make an elaborately intermeshed society. One can see roughly how this may be, though any brief description is sure to be grossly oversimplified.

To take Oberlin as an example: Oberlin students come largely from the families of scientists and engineers, college teachers, ministers and missionaries, and other professional people. Schoolwork is easy for them, and they expect to do well in it. Many of them know they are headed for academic professions. Though they are competent academically and have taken the lead in high school newspapers or student government, they are inclined to be somewhat awkward, or at least not sophisticated, socially (though the sophomore woman who spoke of the entering men as "socially retarded" no doubt overstated matters). Oberlin's location, the no-car rule, the dearth of parties—the "austerities" the catalog speaks of—give it little attraction for students seeking conventional social life.

When the students get to Oberlin, the college mobilizes their energies in at least two quite clear ways. The first is easy enough to describe. The faculty, themselves as "professional" as some university faculties, expect a great deal of reading and a high level of straight academic achievement from the students. Since the students have always excelled in school and feel that their future depends in part on their college record, they are willing to work intensely and unremittingly.

The second way of channeling student energy is more complicated. Since the students tend to be uncomfortable with formal dates, social life is often combined with something else—with discussion in the small dining halls scattered over the campus, with studying in the library or in the dating parlors, with work in the newspaper office, in the theater, in musical organizations, in Students for a Democratic Society or the Young Republicans, in YMCA-YWCA groups, in a tutoring program or a peace group. Instead of frivolity or simple relaxation, social life becomes a sort of self-generated program of general education. This does not mean that Oberlin students find the campus grim; many of them find it exhilarating. But the place is organized so that when one turns from study to recreation, he may find the recreation as serious and instructive as the study itself. If one is determined to relax or waste time, he will have to invent his own apparatus for doing it; the system will not show him how.

The result is students who are well on their way to professional careers but who have acquired, informally, a good deal of information and some opinions about politics and recent history, about music and the other arts, about social movements, religion, and psychology. The college increases their social confidence, but at the same time it fortifies their basic seriousness and quickens their enthusiasm for causes. Generally, it will confirm them in their choice of a professional—particularly an academic—life.

In summary, a student is changed not just by teachers and studies but by an intricately coherent web of attitudes, expectations, traditions, and surroundings that give a college its character. And somehow, though we recruit and legislate, that character persists and changes in its own time, reserving some of its mysteries to itself.

AMHERST
COLLEGE

In any description of Amherst, "affluence" must
be a key word, encompassing not only endowment
and gifts but the varied riches that often
accompany these—prestige; faculty with national
reputations; students with high aptitude scores,
excellent records in school, and well-educated
parents; a low student-faculty ratio; relatively light
teaching loads; and excellent buildings and
facilities.

THE setting is New England. The town of Amherst has a New England look, as do the farmland and woodland of the Connecticut River Valley in which it is situated. And Amherst College men are predominantly Eastern. Of the students admitted in 1967, more than one-third came from New York or Massachusetts. This figure might well be higher if admissions policy did not limit the number of students from these two states. The four states of New York, Massachusetts, Connecticut, and New Jersey together accounted for approximately 53 percent of those admitted. The addition of three more states—Pennsylvania, Illinois, and Maryland—brings this percentage to about 69. The remaining 31 percent of the students admitted in 1967 came from twenty-seven other states and six foreign countries—generally, from one to three students from each. Interestingly enough, in the light of Amherst's national reputation, only eight students were admitted from California.

Yet Amherst is by no means educationally isolated. It is an important circumstance that Amherst belongs to a four-college community. The University of Massachusetts is located in the same town. In Northampton, 7 miles west, is Smith College. Mount Holyoke College lies 10 miles to the south in South Hadley. The proximity of the four colleges creates a community with impressive resources—for example, the resources of half a dozen libraries, more than a million and a half books.

151

Amherst is an affluent college; in any description of the institution, "affluence" must be a key word, encompassing not only endowment and gifts but the varied riches that often accompany these—prestige; faculty with national reputations; students with high aptitude scores, excellent records in school, and well-educated parents; a low student-faculty ratio; relatively light teaching loads; excellent buildings and facilities. The issues discussed in the profile and the resolution of them proposed by the college can best be understood in this context.

To those familiar with the usual state of college finances, a few figures will serve to convey Amherst's situation.[1] In 1967, Amherst's endowment stood at $72,100,000. In 1966–67, income from it came to about $2,700,000, or about 34 percent of total income. In comparison, income from student tuition and fees in that year was about $2,100,000, or about 27 percent of the total. If board and room charges are added, the total of student receipts accounted for about 41 percent of income. Gifts and grants for current use furnished approximately another 14 percent of the total 1966–67 income of $7,738,000.

Under the will of Henry Clay Folger, the Trustees of Amherst College administer the Folger Shakespeare Library in Washington, D.C. In return, the college shares substantially in the library's income, in 1966–67 receiving $246,000 from this source.

Amherst's substantial income is accompanied by substantial expenditures. Even though the fees are high ($2,900 for tuition, room, board, and fees in 1967–68), every student at Amherst College is the beneficiary of a considerable subsidy: It is estimated that the education of each student actually costs the college more than $7,000 per year.[2]

About one-third of the students receive financial aid in the form of scholarships and loans. For the academic year 1966–67, a total of more than $493,000 was awarded in scholarships to 379 students, of whom 92 were freshmen; 183 students received loans totaling more than $81,000.

The Amherst physical plant is impressive. In addition to the thirteen fraternity houses, which accommodate about 47 percent of the upperclassmen, there are four freshmen dormitories and seven other dormitories for upperclassmen. Several dormitories have their own

[1] For a detailed account, see *Amherst College Treasurer's Report*, Amherst College, Amherst, Mass., June 30, 1967.
[2] See *Costs and Financial Aid at Amherst*, Amherst College, Amherst, Mass., August, 1966, and September, 1967. Tuition and fees alone amounted to $1,925. The total cost to a student for a freshman year was estimated at $3,475.

libraries, and in each dormitory group there is a well-equipped recreation room. The main college library holds more than 380,000 volumes. Laboratories are numerous. For example, in the Moore Chemistry Building, built in 1929, are five laboratories for the elementary courses and two set aside for honors students. The Biology Department has six laboratories devoted to undergraduate courses and a new greenhouse for the study of plant growth. An underground vault containing radioactive cobalt permits radiation research. Geology has four laboratories. Physics has six laboratories, among them special facilities for optics, electronics, and low-temperature research. There are laboratories for experimental psychology, including a new laboratory with closed-circuit television and audio equipment. A new music building with recital hall, rehearsal rooms, practice spaces, and classrooms has just been completed. In addition to these facilities, a new center for the physical sciences was finished in 1968, at an approximate cost of 7 million dollars.

Athletic facilities are similarly adequate. In addition to the large gymnasium, which includes the swimming pool, there are football, soccer, lacrosse, and baseball fields, a track, twenty-five tennis courts, and an artificial ice rink for skating and hockey.

The campus as a whole gives an impression of harmony and good grooming. In addition to the newer buildings there are the original college buildings, constructed in the early nineteenth century and maintained in excellent condition.

As might be expected, Amherst is among the top ten institutions in the country in terms of faculty salary levels. For the year ended June 30, 1967, average faculty salaries plus fringe benefits were as follows: professors, $20,435; associate professors, $15,036; assistant professors, $11,274; instructors, $9,428. These salaries represent substantial increases over the past five years—from a 29 percent increase for professors to a 36 percent increase for associate professors during the period.

Among other ways in which affluence may contribute to the success of a college enterprise is the maintenance of a low student-faculty ratio. The *Amherst College Bulletin* for 1966–67 lists 161 faculty, of whom 18 were on leave for the year and another 2 were on leave for one semester. Part time off for research and the like probably means that the number of full-time–equivalent faculty would be fewer than the 141 faculty who were on campus. It would seem clear that Amherst's effective student-faculty ratio must be about 9 to 1.

In addition to the ratio, absolute number of faculty is important;

there need to be enough faculty members to ensure a suitably rich program and to provide a suitably stimulating intellectual community. Probably most Amherst teachers would agree that the size of the faculty is sufficient to achieve the "critical mass" of intellectual resources required.

Who goes to Amherst? In the somewhat yeasty ferment of today's campuses, what of Amherst students? First, a few statistics.

Enrollment now is about 1,200. This represents a modest increase over the 1950s and early 1960s, when enrollment was about 1,050. In the 1930s, Amherst had about 800 students.

In 1967, Amherst's 306 freshmen were selected from a pool of 2,141 who completed applications for admission. In 1960, Amherst drew 270 freshmen from a total of 1,888 completed applications. This high ratio of applicants to freshmen admitted is a relatively recent development. Before the war, Amherst was admitting about four out of every five applicants. In the immediate postwar years, the ratio had moved to about one out of three.

Amherst admissions policy emphasizes "imagination, initiative, resolution, and independence." An attempt is made to select those students who stand out in some special way—for example, in extracurricular interests and accomplishments. Since Amherst aims for the "thinkers and doers," the important information about an applicant concerns what he has done. Within the limits imposed by the need for sufficient academic promise to complete the Amherst course of study successfully, rank in class and College Entrance Examination Board scores are not decisive factors.[3]

While Amherst does not keep a detailed record of the socioeconomic background of its students, about two-thirds of them manage without financial aid. In a recent year, about 44 percent of the Amherst students came from families in which the father's education included a postgraduate degree. The fathers of an additional 30 percent of the students were college graduates. Of the students admitted in 1967, 35 percent came from private secondary schools.

Regarding the distribution of students by major field, the following figures for the class of 1967 are fairly representative. About one-quarter of this class were majors in mathematics or the natural sciences; half of this group, or 13 percent of the total class, were

[3] Nevertheless, in recent years, about 85 percent of the applicants admitted to the freshman year have ranked in the top quarter of their high school classes.

majors in biology, reflecting the prominent place at Amherst of the premedical program. In the humanities and social sciences, American studies with 10 percent, economics with 8 percent, political science with 13 percent, and English with 13 percent were popular selections. About 4 percent of the students elected history as a major—rather fewer than in recent years, and less than half the percentage of history majors as compared with some ten years ago.

The career choices of the class of 1967 showed some 13 percent of the students planning to go into business. Another 20 percent planned careers in law, and 16 percent careers in medicine. Thus nearly half the class elected business, law, or medicine. Twenty-eight percent planned to go on in education.

The student-life controversy   Some interesting sidelights on the quality of campus life can be gained from what may be called the "student-life controversy," centering around the 1965 Report of the Sub-Committee of Faculty to Study Student Life, or Student-Life Report.[4]

This report saw disillusionment and a sense of frustration as prominent features of student life at Amherst. It recognized that:

Much disillusionment, of course, is the result of impossible expectations. But probably most conscientious students inevitably, justifiably, find themselves harassed—by work to be done, books to be read, friends to talk to, grades to be achieved. A student's feeling that he has too little time in which to make too many decisions is, in one sense, merely a sign that his education is having some effect. Yet the sense of frustration is undeniably real, and even for the most capable student too often incapacitating.

Part of the difficulty may also be due, according to the report, to discrepancies between what the student expected from college life—"the grand intellectual adventure"—and what he finds college actually to be—"a game whose goal is grades." One way in which the student may react is to withdraw from the game as defined by the institution and play instead an alternative game called "beating the system." The report noted:

Then he may turn his attention and energy to extracurricular activities, more or less worthy, where the chance of intellectual competition is minimal.

4 In the course of studying the curriculum at Amherst, the Committee on Educational Policy came to the conclusion that "the quality of the curriculum cannot be considered apart from the quality of the life of the students who experience it." Hence the committee appointed this Sub-Committee to Study Student Life, less formally known as the Student-Life Committee. Its report may be found in *Amherst Alumni News*, special issue, Winter, 1965.

He may, in the happiest instances, work for causes for moral rewards which enable him to withdraw with self-respect. In the least happy instances, he may with self-contempt deliberately scorn the very values that have brought him to Amherst in the first place.

The report found that the students tend to divide activities into two parts, one called "work," the other called "social life." This division was held not to be consistent with the ideals of liberal education. Also, each of the parts is in itself somewhat unsatisfactory:

Many [students] agree that their social life seems to have lost occasions for civility and grace. Many of the social institutions and extracurricular activities that have survived from a preceding era seem to have diminished in the standards of excellence, the exercise of wit, and the achievement of significant self-expression, and these values are now assigned to the classroom if anywhere.

Students work hard at their courses, and often achieve remarkable results. But too often they do so joylessly, cynically, grudgingly, and for narrow utilitarian ends. A vague sense of disquiet and frustration pervades both students and faculty. Few would assert with confidence that Amherst is fulfilling its potentials.

Such conditions are not unique. Reports on student life at other institutions of higher education echo many of the same themes.

The report proposed a program aimed to remedy the problems it outlined. Currently on the campus, student extracurricular life is structured by a system of fraternities and dormitories. The Amherst campus is strongly fraternity-oriented, though the fraternity system is different from that of many campuses. Freshmen are not allowed to live in the fraternity houses, and they do not pledge until just before spring vacation. The system features so-called "100 percent rushing"; that is, every man who wishes to join a fraternity may do so. In most recent years, the percentage of each freshman class pledging has been somewhat over 85—the others being, by their own choice, independents. In recent years, from 75 to 80 percent of the eligible upperclassmen have been active members of fraternities, but the thirteen houses accommodate only about 47 percent. The rest of the upperclassmen live in the dormitories.

An important part of the Student-Life Committee proposal was that the college move away from the fraternity-dormitory system to a basic structure made up of eight so-called "societies." Regarding the fraternities, the report inquired:

How can one promote that discourse which is the heart of the College when so much time is spent debating the existence of institutions which now have little relevance either to education or the modern world? We came unanimously to the conclusion, then, that the fraternities at Amherst have become an anachronism, that the possibilities for their reform have been exhausted and that they stood directly in the way of exciting new possibilities for student life.

The Student-Life Report was also critical of the dormitory arrangements, feeling it unlikely that any enriching common activities could be organized in this context. The committee called for the creation of a "new way which will . . . achieve new dimensions for life at Amherst."

The new way proposed by the committee was the creation of eight societies—the resident membership in each to range from 90 to 130 students, plus a proportional freshman membership for each. Freshmen would be integrated into the societies from the beginning. On the basis of a descriptive statement about each society, the prospective freshman would send to the college the names of three or four societies, not in preferential order, which interested him. He would then, before his arrival, be assigned to one of the various societies by the administration of the college, with an effort being made to accommodate his preferences.

Among other features of the societies would be some integration of faculty activities and interests with their functioning, the proposal being that each society have a group of four faculty associates to work with it. The committee's hope was that this would achieve some improvement in what it viewed as the deterioration of faculty-student relations.

It is difficult in short compass to convey adequately the spirit and intention of the societies as the committee envisaged them. Perhaps the best brief summary that can be provided here is the following statement from the Student-Life Report:

> This Committee does not wish to lay out a single pattern of facilities for each Society, or a standard pattern for all of them. Our hope is rather to seek diversity not only within each Society but between the various Societies. One Society might wish to stress music by assembling a record collection, building a listening room, and a practice room, and providing occasional evening performances. But another might develop an active, if thoroughly informal, little theatre. Still another might emphasize interests in social issues or political action by a program of visitors, debates, forums, trips, and public agitation. Perhaps a boat house on the Connecticut, a cabin in the hills near ski slopes or a joint program of activities with a Smith or Mount Holyoke house might provide distinctive features of some Societies. The possibilities and the interests would vary from one Society to another. But it seems clear that the possibilities for a more interesting student life would be greater in any one of these Societies than could ever be the case in one of the existing fraternities or dormitories.

As interesting as the report itself was campus response to it. In the light of the subject matter and tone, perhaps the most striking thing about the student response was its mildness, at least as far as organized reaction is concerned. Indeed, an impression gained from talking to a few students was that perhaps the report was not taken very seriously by the student body as a whole.

One explanation may be that student life on the Amherst campus as the students experience it does not correspond very closely to the picture painted by the committee. One gets the impression that the representative student, although he may find things to complain about from time to time, is fairly well-satisfied with his situation at Amherst. The all-faculty committee which issued the report may not have had as close contact with the realities of student life as might have been desirable for the task at hand.

In December, 1965, the interfraternity House Management Committee published a Memorandum to the Trustees of Amherst College on the Student-Life Report. In the view of the authors of this memorandum, the fraternities provide a desirable way in which to organize the extracurricular life and activities of the students—certainly a more desirable way than would be afforded by the societies. On this score, the following statements (which the authors of the memorandum admit to be overdrawn) are illuminating:

The Report's discussion of the role of Faculty Associates in the proposed Societies seems to envisage assigned faculty direction of what, perhaps not too unfairly, might be characterized as spoon-fed intellectualism in the students' own time.

... We think the Report's proposal would take far too much control of the student's nonclassroom life out of the hands of the students—this we oppose.

We are certain that in the Faculty Sub-committee's thinking, the "good life together which the members of any Society could develop" would not in any way resemble a reversion to their prep school days. Yet as we read the outline of their proposal, it seems to us that there is a fine line indeed between the Societies as they describe them and an adaptation of a faculty-led prep school organization.

Another fraternity response to the Student-Life Report is to be found in the December, 1965, statement "A Commentary on Student Life," adopted by Kappa Theta Fraternity. The major effort in the commentary is to come to grips with the Student-Life Report's characterization of the basic difficulties with student life at Amherst. The commentary agrees that there are some basic difficulties but does not agree with the Student-Life Report as to what they are. The commentary focuses upon what it terms "the displacement of academic relevance."

The initial cause we perceive for the student's lack of motivation to pursue his intellectual interests with complete enthusiasm is that in several ways the educational environment does not encourage the student to establish relevance between academic study and his own goals and values. Furthermore, it seems to us that the formally structured academic environment of Amherst actually inhibits the discovery of this relevance.

The commentary notes that the academic environment is very different from the environment in which most of the students will be operating once they leave Amherst. It agrees that the academic approach is Amherst's primary distinctive contribution and that the students should continue to apply the academic approach throughout their lives. But this approach should somehow be integrated with the nonacademic lives of the students. The commentary observes:

Insofar as this academic approach determines the nature of the academic community it creates an environment which is strikingly different from the one in which the student expects to realize his goals. A search for objectivity necessarily involves a suspension of what might be called social factors. In the academic community, the most damning criticism which can be made of a man is that he is allowing his personality to interfere with his objectivity. The academic method is not only impersonal; ideally it is applied in a purely intellectual situation, in which social factors are reduced to a minimum. Because of the impersonal nature of academic inquiry, students will feel the need for another educational context, in which human variables—leadership, mutual responsibility, and social interaction—are present. Thus, for most, if not all, students, the academic environment must be complemented by appropriate social environment to provide them with a complete educational experience.

The authors of the commentary believe that a certain loss of contact between students and faculty stands in the way of a solution to the problem of relevance. In this view, the faculty is perceived too much in a solely academic context. Similarly, the faculty does not perceive that students come to Amherst because they hope that the education they receive will increase their ability to perform their responsible roles in society, not because they want to be junior intellectuals.

Regarding this controversy, the observer can only say that the picture of student life conveyed by the student report—as fraught with disillusionment and frustration—seems to be much overdrawn. As already suggested, the representative student would probably testify that he is pretty well satisfied with student life at Amherst, although he might register complaints about some features of that life. In particular, the "displacement of academic relevance" discussed in the Kappa Theta commentary may be a real problem, at least for a fair number. One student, in complaining about the lack of what he considered to be relevant personal involvement with subject matter, remarked that it was quite possible to have long classroom discussions of such material as, say, Paul Goodman's comments on American colleges and universities without its ever occurring to anyone to realize, "My God, it's us he's talking about."

The students seem to know what they do *not* want. They do not want paternalistic interference with their personal freedoms. They do not want institutional sponsorship of their student life. They do not want a sort of melding of the academic and nonacademic aspects to produce a "whole" student life organized around interest-oriented living groups.

In the Amherst situation, the fraternity evidently plays a crucial role in the shaping of a workable system:

It is important for us to recognize that student defense of fraternities is to a great extent conditioned by the fact that fraternities are the only place where the students can escape the heavy hand of the administration, and even there they don't always succeed. One must expect the fraternities to be staunchly defended, partly because they have certain virtues, but, more importantly, because it is inconceivable to our students that any other form of social organization will be more free.[5]

The students' role in college government

On many college campuses today there is a "student challenge to administration control." Although there are some signs that some students would like to increase the role of the students in community government, there is little to suggest that in 1965 at Amherst, the "challenge" had come in any serious way.

. As matters stood then, the students participated in various ways in community government. There is the House Management Committee, established by the Board of Trustees in 1945 and composed of one graduate and one undergraduate representative of each of the thirteen fraternities, to supervise and oversee the fraternities. The whole committee meets in Amherst several times each year; the undergraduate section of the committee meets weekly throughout the college year. The Inter-dormitory Council, made up of representatives of each of the dormitories, is concerned with various aspects of dormitory life, including such matters as visiting hours.

There is a Student Council, made up of class representatives. Each spring four seniors, three juniors, and three sophomores are elected

[5] See Henry T. Yost, Jr., "The Social Revolution on the American Campus," *Amherst Alumni News*, Summer, 1965, pp. 15–16.

for a term of one year. In October, the freshman subcouncil elects one representative to serve until the spring elections. According to the *Student Handbook,* "The Student Council acts on behalf of the Student Association in approving of athletic awards and voting of activities taxes, and acts on all occasions as the direct representative of the student body. In 1957 the Council assumed the power of trying cases involving academic dishonesty and other disciplinary problems." Section 9 of the constitution of the student government defines the powers of the council. Like many such statements, this one is somewhat ambiguous; however, potentially at least, some of its provisos would seem to confer considerable power upon the council. Thus it is provided that the council has the power to "represent the Association in all its relations with the faculty, alumni, Trustees, and other bodies, organizations, and institutions." The council may "use discretionary power in all matters requiring immediate action."

In practice, the council does not seem to be taken very seriously on the Amherst campus—at least not by the students generally. Indeed, the impression one gains from students is that student government is something of a joke. Why would this be so?

A small sample of students with whom the matter was discussed estimated that about 90 percent of the students at Amherst are quite well-satisfied with "things as they are." The situation seems to be a bit more complicated, however. One gets the impression that the prevailing mode of student life features a good bit of what might be called "lifemanship." A manifestation of this is a rather studied effort on the part of many students to "play it cool," to contrive strategies and modes of behavior designed to accommodate their own interests and activities within the existing structure of rules and regulations. If this is a correct assessment of the dominant student attitude, then the representative Amherst student stands in sharp contrast to what is frequently pictured as the essentially dissatisfied, aggressive, and authority-seeking student of today.

The reason why the representative Amherst student seems to exhibit such different characteristics may be, in part, that the Amherst environment does not generate the kinds of tensions and anxieties that are present on many campuses. This may, in turn, be traceable to the circumstance that the Amherst student lives in a highly pluralistic society. He seems to take active part in a wide variety of pursuits and interests—academic work, athletics, social life, the fraternities, the student newspaper and radio station, etc. The admissions policy at Amherst is deliberately contrived to achieve a student body with this kind of distribution of interests. In such a pluralistic community there are various ways to succeed, and this circumstance may go far to reduce tension.

Not all the students, however, share what has been described as the dominant student attitude. A significant minority, perhaps 10 percent, are what might be termed activist. They object to what they deem to be a strong element of paternalism in the environment at Amherst, and are convinced the administration of the college is a strong force for conservatism. One such student said that in his view, the greatest shock that could confront the administration of the college would be to have students involved in political demonstrations, with publicity given to these events. He felt that in the eyes of the college administration, and indeed in the eyes of the college community generally, radicalism and wildness were the worst sins.

Some insight may be provided by a brief discussion of certain events in 1965 which first reflected a more activist concern on the Amherst campus. These events centered around the dismissal from the college of a junior, otherwise in good standing, for his failure to fulfill the physical education requirement.

Several students (members of the Ad Hoc Committee on Student Life[6] and Student Council) addressed a strongly worded letter to President Calvin H. Plimpton. The letter expressed their "outrage" that the college could "callously, summarily, and unilaterally dismiss" men like the student in question "for the crime of being themselves in a way such as to harm no one and to violate only the conventional and intolerant sensibilities of others." The letter went on:

We demand the establishment of a student faculty committee to review
student tenure. We ask that the present Ad Hoc Committee on Student Life,
being the only group consisting of faculty and students now existing, be given
immediate jurisdiction in such cases until the establishment of a permanent
body for this purpose. We demand also that steps be taken to establish
a form of faculty-student government to determine College rules and procedures
in such a way that decisions will be made in terms of the individual merits
of the case, the educational consequences of the decision, and the highest
ideals, values, and aspirations of an academic community, instead of the unfair
procedures of administration and faculty politics in the enforcement of
anachronistic rules. In short, we demand immediate student representation in
matters which directly concern our educational and community life.

Responding to the letter, President Plimpton explained to the students that the dismissal in question was in no sense arbitrary, summary, or unfair. Indeed, the case had been very carefully reviewed

[6] A joint faculty-student committee brought into being to deal with certain aspects of the Student-Life Report.

by the administration of the college and by the Committee of Six.[7] He pointed to the long history and traditional status of the physical education requirement at Amherst (Amherst appears to be one of the first colleges in the country to adopt such a requirement) and expressed his opinion that it was a valuable part of the Amherst curriculum. The dismissal resulted simply from the persistent failure of the student to comply with a well-understood college regulation.

The "phys. ed." case is not so much of interest in itself as from the point of view of campus reactions to it and what these reactions say, by implication, about the community. When it was raised, a "student challenge" of this kind was a rare event on the Amherst campus, and a visitor would discover, in talking with faculty and administrators, that the physical education case was almost always the subject brought up for initial comment or question. Yet one got the impression that most of the students took the matter in stride— they were inclined simply to shrug it off. The view seemed to be, quite simply, that a student who refused to comply with such a college regulation might well expect to be dismissed. While some of the students took a different view and contemplated further action, they were aware that any further action would have to be carefully contrived to avoid a negative response from the student body as a whole.

Community government at Amherst has, however, been influenced by a proposal of the ad hoc committee. The committee proposed the creation of a permanent College Council to be made up of the Dean of Students and the Dean of Freshmen, four members of the faculty elected by the faculty, and six students, some of whom might be elected at large by the student body, others coming from existing bodies such as the Student Council, House Management Committee, etc.

The plan for the new council, which began its operation in the fall of 1967, provided that "except for the ultimate power retained by the President and the Trustees, the College Council would be the body to approve and determine policy in three areas." The first of these areas, extracurricular faculty-student activities, then was under no formal aegis. The proposal suggested that "the Council would be expected to devote a major part of its attention to imagining, initiating, carrying through, and in some cases subsidizing new possibilities for mutually interesting student-faculty activities outside the formal curriculum." The second area was the Statement of Intellectual Re-

[7] This is the executive committee of the faculty, which acts in a general advisory capacity to the President of the college on all matters of college policy.

sponsibility, which the Student Council had administered, including hearing and judging particular violations of it.[8] The Student Council was to retain these powers, but the College Council would become the body to review and make final decisions on reports, recommendations, and decisions of the Student Council—thus taking over powers exercised exclusively in the past by the Deans. Similarly, in the area of social regulations for dormitories and fraternities, the Inter-dormitory Council and House Management Committee were to retain previous administrative responsibilities, including the judging of particular violations. The College Council would become the review body and make final decisions upon reports and recommendations, thus taking over still other powers exercised by the Deans.

It was envisaged that the College Council would serve as a continuing discussion group with powers to make recommendations concerning many matters of general college interest, including a number of academic matters which lay beyond the council's own policy-making powers.[9]

One definitely stated limitation on the jurisdiction of the College Council was that "the Council would not discuss and would not make recommendations to any group on particular personnel decisions in the faculty or administration."

Whether community government is organized in this way or some other way, its effectiveness depends to an important extent upon the attitude of the student body generally. Although a relatively small group of students has been seeking a stronger student voice, it is far from clear that the representative Amherst student has really felt the need for this or indeed really wants it. There seems to be some

[8] The Statement of Intellectual Responsibility provides in part:
"The following affirmation will be printed on the back of course enrollment cards for every course; it must be signed before enrollment can be considered:
" 'I have read, understand, and accept the statement of intellectual responsibility among students at Amherst College, and agree with this principle as it relates to this course—(signed).' "
[9] This latter role and the strategic position of the College Council for dealing with issues at the forefront of concern to students, faculty, and administration have been very evident during the council's first two years of operation. The council has devoted extensive study, for example, to the question of social hours at the college, a hardy perennial among sources of student discontent, and to problems involved in providing campus facilities for visiting recruiters, an issue stirred by war-protest demonstrations against military recruiters and certain industrial representatives. The council's potential as a tension-reducing and adjudicating body was demonstrated especially on the latter issue, in which its thoughtful report, culminating in recommended procedures for maintaining an "open campus" to all visitors, was accepted by the faculty as college policy.

tension between the majority of the students and those relative few who are interested in active participation in community government. In a sense, student representatives to such a body as the College Council may have greater difficulties in their relations with their own constituents than in their relations with the other constituencies making up the council. It is a matter of great importance to the functioning of a governing body such as the College Council whether the student members of it are in a position to speak for their constituents. Greater student voice and authority in the formulation of community norms should in turn be accompanied by a reciprocal student obligation and responsibility to see that the norms are effective and that the community functions well.

Closely related is the general problem of the status of the honor principle. What might be termed a "special-purpose honor principle" operates at present on the Amherst campus through use of the Statement of Intellectual Responsibility. Thus examinations are not proctored, it being up to each student to make sure that his own behavior complies with the statement. There seems reluctance, however, among the students generally to extend the honor principle to other aspects of community life and government. In 1967, the students rejected an extension under which they would have signed an affirmation (analogous to the Intellectual Responsibility affirmation) regarding compliance with dormitory social hours. This is a matter of some interest for the future because the kinds of community government institutions which are feasible depend to an important extent on how far the students want to, or are willing to, generalize the use of the honor principle.

Amherst and curriculum reform A Wesleyan Report in 1962 pointed out:

Unless the liberal arts colleges can move into some form of advanced learning . . . they may well be doomed to gradual deterioration as finishing schools, or at best, prep schools for graduate education.

Some colleges have responded to this situation by beginning to move in the direction of university status. This approach seems clearly to have been rejected by Amherst, at least on its own campus.

Ever since 1878, when John Burgess failed to persuade his colleagues to adopt a university program, Amherst has chosen to remain a small college. Acting as a whole and through committees the faculty has opted, again and again, for interdisciplinary approaches and for an integrated liberal arts program leading to independent work and some specialization for upperclassmen. Amherst has so far chosen to resist the currents running at many universities—currents

which allow and even encourage specialization in the first or second year. "It would be easy to become a small imitation of an Ivy League university," said a senior professor, "but that's not the way Amherst is heading."[10]

As in other top-ranking liberal arts colleges, a large proportion of the graduating seniors go on to graduate education—at Amherst, something like 85 percent. In this sense, Amherst might be called a "prep school for graduate education." Amherst does not, however, view this role as one of "gradual deterioration." Indeed, some years ago, a faculty committee reporting on the needs of the college said in part:

Amherst has created a new possibility in American education—that the small liberal arts college can become a significant intellectual force—and it is the creation of this possibility that must be ranked as the College's major achievement.[11]

Although Amherst has not attempted to become a small university, it has been charged with facing the risk. A recent issue of *Amherst Reports* comments:

The charges are not new. They were made almost a century ago by men like John W. Burgess of the Class of 1867, the political scientist who was one of the founders of the Graduate School at Columbia and who predicted that the liberal college would turn either into a university or into a secondary school. Now with the vast growth of new knowledge and the accompanying fragmentation of disciplines, with the mounting professionalization of all education, and with the appearance of the teacher who is more oriented to his discipline than to general education, the predictions of academic obsolescence have become more direful, more numerous.

What, then, can a liberal college offer that isn't being offered on a bigger and better scale by every large university, or hasn't already been done long and well enough in the good high schools? Are there functions that are uniquely suited to the liberal arts college and, if so, how can they best be performed?[12]

Amherst has felt the need for adaptation to current conditions, and in the fall of 1966 instituted a new curriculum. The previous curriculum was basically one that had been designed in 1947. The central feature had been a mandatory general education core, to be taken by all students in the freshman and sophomore years.

As *Amherst Reports* notes, the 1947 curriculum implicitly defined "the educated man as a person who has some acquaintance with a small list of specified disciplines: mathematics and physics, European history, English composition, a smattering of world literature and

[10] See "The Faculty," *Amherst Reports*, vol. 2, no. 3, March, 1963, p. 17.
[11] *Ibid.*
[12] "The 1966 Curriculum" *Amherst Reports*, p. 4.

American studies." The college began to wonder, given the facts of modern intellectual life, whether this curriculum made sense. Dramatic improvements in the qualifications of entering freshmen had meant that more and more of them had been excused from the college's required program. What had been an exciting common course of study in the 1950s had become the educational core of an ever-smaller proportion of students. At the same time, there was at Amherst the conviction that the knowledge explosion, with the accompanying drive toward more specialization, made "liberal education" more important than ever before.

The new curriculum incorporates what Amherst regards as a set of procedures implying an appropriate definition of liberal education. Regarding the fundamental assumption of the new curriculum, *Amherst Reports* quotes Prof. Joseph Epstein, chairman of the Committee on Educational Policy, which drew up the new program: "The central function of the liberal college is the inculcation of a dominant, comprehensive, and valued habit of rational enquiry." Professor Epstein goes on to characterize the liberal college as one which "is first and foremost an instrument for the formation, not of a weaver or a Thomist nor a lawyer or a Platonist, but of a man for whom rationality is a habit." *Amherst Reports* sums up: "The essential element of the new program is to generate an attitude toward experience, to produce the habit of rational thought, and to leave to the participants—teachers and students—the freedom of material and style to suit their own interests and commitments."

The new curriculum abandons the old idea of an extensive mandatory core in favor of a somewhat different approach. The only required courses in the new curriculum are three interdisciplinary one-semester offerings—the three "Problems of Inquiry" courses, one each in the humanities, the social sciences, and the natural sciences. Students take all three (or under some circumstances only two) of these courses in the first two years. As the name suggests, the Problems of Inquiry courses do not attempt to cover a more or less comprehensive body of topical material, but introduce students to the methodology of the fields in question—observational techniques and regimens, procedures for formation and testing of hypotheses, etc. The methodology, of course, is conveyed in the context of what is, for each field, important topical subject matter, which may be expected to change from year to year.

In addition, the curriculum permits students to begin work in a major subject in the freshman year; it includes an independent study program, elective for students nominated by members of the faculty, which, normally in the junior or senior year, releases the independent scholars from all further college requirements and permits them to continue their studies under the guidance of one or more tutors selected by the student and a faculty committee. Exceptionally qualified students may graduate in three years; all students must demonstrate proficiency in a foreign language, satisfy specified physical education requirements, and pass a comprehensive examination in their major field to qualify for graduation.

The new curriculum followed upon a rather long period of concern with the previous curriculum, and a growing dissatisfaction. This dissatisfaction was somewhat diffuse and generalized: The curriculum had been around for a long time; the great majority of the faculty now in residence had had nothing to do with its design; perhaps the time had come for some change.

There were also particular difficulties. One has been mentioned— improvement in secondary school preparation for incoming students, as a result of which something like 50 percent of the freshmen were routed around at least some part of the old core curriculum. Another important problem was faculty attitudes toward the staff courses making up the old core. The younger faculty especially seemed to feel uncomfortable teaching these courses, reflecting perhaps the "professional" identification of modern graduate programs. They objected that the spread of material and character of the core courses made it necessary for the instructor to teach outside his field of special interest and competence. Moreover, as one member of the community remarked, it takes a real "conversion" to such courses to yield suitable and dedicated instructors for them.

The President and the Committee of Six saw to it that the problem of designing a new curriculum was put on the agenda of the Committee on Educational Policy, which then went ahead on its own to design the new curriculum and to present it to the faculty as a complete package. At this stage, some changes were made before the faculty voted to accept it.

The basic rationale for the new curriculum—inculcation of habits of rational inquiry—was provided by the Committee on Educational Policy. This rationale is presented in impressive and persuasive language, and it fits the curriculum in the sense that the curriculum appears to be a plausible way to achieve the objectives set forth. However, one gets the impression that while a majority of the faculty like the various procedures involved with the new curriculum, the faculty in general is not interested in extensive debate on the problems of overall institutional objectives, the goals of a liberal arts college, and the like. Rather, the faculty is more pragmatic, more interested in particulars.

Some members of the faculty feel that giving up the old core curriculum involved a great loss to the educational program at Amherst. They feel that these courses, which had been developed with great care and attention over the years, were really unique in educational impact, and that nothing in the new curriculum can really take their place. In addition to the merits of the particular courses constituting the old core, some people feel that it was an effective way to give the incoming students a common intellectual experience. According to this view, the shared common experience tended to intellectualize the community—tended to "put a little intellectual talk into the fraternities." However, the new Problems of Inquiry courses may not represent such a sharp break with some of the features of the old core courses as might at first be thought. These courses provide for at least some sharing of common intellectual experience, even if not on the scale provided by the old core.

Some critics of the new curriculum contend that such features as permitting early choice of a major and reducing the amount of general education tend toward specialization and professionalization in the curriculum. Its defenders argue that the basic objective of the new curriculum is the habit of rational inquiry which is not synonymous with specialization or narrow professionalization. While the new curriculum permits students to concentrate their programs somewhat more, this may be thought of as a desirable by-product which will accommodate legitimate interests and needs and which will not necessarily interfere with attainment of the basic objectives of the curriculum.

At the outset, one of the greatest difficulties with the new curriculum seems to lie with the interdisciplinary nature of the Problems of Inquiry courses—particularly, the problems of staffing them. Apparently some departments or individuals feel a reluctance to teach in this kind of interdisciplinary course, reflecting some of the same concerns which led to dissatisfaction with the previous general core courses.

To an observer, the reasons for the emphasis on interdisciplinary courses are not altogether clear. For one thing, the traditional interdisciplinary approach has now fallen into some disfavor. Further, since the student's program is multidisciplinary, one might argue that the basic rationale for the new curriculum does not require an interdisciplinary approach. The new curriculum, recognizing the explosion of knowledge as a fact of modern intellectual experience, abandons the time-honored notion that courses should be primarily intended to "cover" certain topical subject matter and makes the approach within individual courses more important than the selection of disciplines or the sequence in which they are studied. But why, if they are adequately constructed and presented, should not more conventionally topical courses in the sciences and the humanities serve the objectives implied in this program?

In one view, on the other hand, the enterprise of designing and teaching these key courses tends to condition positively the whole tone of the college, in that it brings faculty together in ways that hedge against the extremes of departmental specialization which have tended to Balkanize the modern university.

The new curriculum makes no changes in an established feature of the Amherst senior year—the Honors Program. This provides for a major project which shall take one-quarter to one-half of a student's time and credit, almost on a tutorial basis, and in the sciences shall involve original research. The program has allowed many students to do outstanding work in an independent way: Since 1962, approximately 60 percent of the seniors have embarked on an Honors Program each fall, and from 45 to 50 percent then have actually graduated with honors. Honors degrees are awarded only to those students who participate in the program; grades alone do not suffice.

There are other ways besides in which the student may work independently—in the individual reading courses now offered by most departments, as well as in the independent study program. Such emphases doubtless contribute to the high proportion of Amherst graduates going on to further study.

Hampshire College: one answer to the question of significance For some years, Amherst has been more or less continuously concerned with the question of size.[13] Thus a 1957 preliminary report issued by the Alumni Advisory Committee on Admission, discussing the issue of the size of the college, noted:

The real question is this: how can Amherst enlarge its total contribution to American society in a new era when American colleges and universities as a whole are challenged to provide more education to a far larger number of young people?[14]

A year later, the report of a faculty Committee on the Future Size

[13] See "The Question of Size," *Amherst Reports*, 1962.
[14] Cited in *ibid.*, p. 6.

of the College and Related Subjects, headed by Prof. Willard L. Thorp, seemed to provide one kind of answer to this question:

It seems obvious that Amherst cannot make any large quantitative contribution to the nation's educational problem, nor is it Amherst's obligation to service some fixed percentage, however infinitesimal, of those seeking a college education. Amherst does have a duty to perform and a contribution to make. Its duty is to use its resources efficiently and effectively. Its contribution is to provide a continuing demonstration of what quality means in the educational process. This also means that it must always be seeking and welcoming new or improved educational methods and ideas.[15]

Amherst has, in the words of the Thorp committee, been seeking and welcoming new or improved educational methods and ideas. One such area of exploration is discussed in the Report of the Committee on Cooperation to the Presidents of Amherst College, Mount Holyoke College, Smith College, and the University of Massachusetts. This committee, operating under a grant made in February, 1955, by the Fund for the Advancement of Education, was instructed to study various aspects of cooperation between those institutions and to report its findings and recommendations to the Presidents. In the introduction to the report, the committee noted:

The members of the committee accepted their assignment dutifully, but with misgivings. Could anything really be done and why? . . . But as the committee proceeded, its interest in the project grew. Moreover, a thorough-going plan of cooperation among these four institutions, if it could be devised and put into effect, might be of more than local importance. It might provide an example and indicate a pattern of action which could be successfully followed by other groups of colleges and universities, and, in particular, establishing an example of cooperation between public and private institutions might be of value at a time when the private colleges and the universities will be increasingly subject to criticism for failing to do their share in meeting the demand created by the rising tide of applicants for admission to colleges and graduate schools.

Of the various cooperative arrangements suggested by the Committee on Cooperation, perhaps the most significant is the New College Proposal.[16] In its preface, the proposal notes:

The four institutions sponsoring this report have been aware for some time of the imminent demands upon American colleges to provide space and opportunity for a vastly enlarged body of students. In an effort to expand their

15 Cited in *ibid.*, p. 8.
16 See *New College Plan: A Proposal for a Major Departure in Higher Education,* Amherst, Mass., 1958, reprinted 1965. Shannon McCune, University of Massachusetts, was chairman of the committee which originated this report and which included C. L. Barber, Amherst College, Donald Sheeham, Smith College, and Stuart M. Stoke, Mount Holyoke College.

own programs and to make better use of their resources during the past five years, they have engaged in an increasing number of educational enterprises. Last year they considered the possibility of creating a fifth institution in their general area to which they might contribute and with which they might develop new departures in educational methods and techniques.

The New College Proposal lay dormant until August, 1965, when it was announced that Hampshire College—a new four-year liberal arts institution conceived along the lines of the New Proposal—was being formed with academic support from the four colleges. The impetus for the formation of Hampshire College came from a pledge of 6 million dollars by Mr. Harold F. Johnson, an Amherst alumnus.

At present, Hampshire College has a chartered Board of Trustees (which includes the Presidents of the four supporting colleges), and has acquired about 450 acres of land located approximately equidistant from each of the cooperating colleges. Dr. Franklin Patterson has assumed the presidency, while Charles R. Longsworth, who was formerly assistant to the President at Amherst, is Vice President. A major statement of objectives and plans, has been completed. Architects have been appointed, and 1970 has been set as the time of opening.

Hampshire College is of interest from many points of view, among them the kind of response it represents on the part of the small liberal arts college to the possibility of the diminishing significance of this educational sector. On August 8, 1965, the *New York Times* editorialized in this same vein:

With few exceptions, the high-quality colleges have resisted pressures for major expansion. By letting state-supported institutions shoulder the major burden of coping with the mass demand for higher education, the private colleges inevitably incurred the risk of dwindling influence on academic and intellectual life. The Hampshire College experiment opens an avenue for such expansion, without diluting the character of existing institutions.

Insofar as Amherst is concerned, this response is especially interesting because it might not have been anticipated. A long-established and adequately financed college of Amherst's prestige might simply "stand pat." Might not such a college argue that, whatever happens to the overall size of the education establishment, its own sense of mission and of importance and significance will be amply fulfilled if it merely goes on for the next hundred years doing very well that job which it has been doing very well for the past hundred years or so?

Amherst's part in the creation of Hampshire College is an indication that the college acknowledges responsibility for the larger problems of American education. But one gets the impression that more pragmatic considerations enter in as well. There was important encouragement from the Ford Foundation's Fund for the Advancement of Education, which made the initial grant for the study. One administrator expressed the view that, in a certain sense, the colleges could not afford *not* to become involved with this project. This sort of development makes the institutions involved more visible, and can favorably affect their overall public relations and fund-raising problems. One also gains the impression that Hampshire College may have a favorable impact on faculty recruitment—at least for some of the cooperating colleges. A number of potential candidates have heard about, and are excited over, Hampshire College; the idea that they may be able to participate in this new venture may help induce them to join the staff of a participating college.

It is interesting that Hampshire College is designed to be reasonably economical and therefore perhaps a pattern that could be copied elsewhere. The original New College Proposal contemplated a student-faculty ratio of 20 to 1. More recent thinking about Hampshire College has moved in the direction of a ratio nearer 16 to 1. From the point of view of the significance of this venture for the world of education, it would seem better to continue to think in terms of the 20 to 1 ratio.

In summary, the Hampshire College enterprise may be an important key to the way in which the small liberal arts college can hope to make some general contribution—particularly if, as in this situation, it is possible to achieve a cooperative relationship with a public college or university. In addition to permitting the cooperating institutions to work with wider institutional parameters, the setting up of a new institution provides a more general kind of freedom.

Hampshire College will be designed to be free from traditional commitments regarding curriculum, alumni, departmental divisions, and other restrictions, and thus, will have a flexibility of program which will enable it to engage in experiments to determine whether costs of education can be substantially reduced without impairing quality.[17]

The commitment to college teaching

The teaching mission has traditionally been paramount in undergraduate liberal arts colleges, but professors in these colleges increasingly want to develop their own careers along the lines of research and publication followed by their university colleagues. It is said to be more and more difficult to find really first-rate instructors with the

[17] See *Amherst Alumni News*, Fall, 1965.

requisite orientation to the teaching of undergraduate students. These circumstances, it is contended, will confront the colleges with a dilemma. If the colleges maintain the traditional view of their mission, they will be unable to recruit a high-quality staff. If in order to accommodate to this problem they significantly change their mission, they will cease to be liberal arts colleges in the traditional sense of the term.

Amherst strongly emphasizes the teaching aspect of its faculty performance.

Amherst is not merely seeking physicists or economists or psychologists; it is seeking men—and women—who know their fields but who can also relate their specialities to broad areas of human understanding and who are interested in doing this with undergraduates in the general liberal arts context.

Amherst's special problem and its special strength are intimately connected. With other colleges, Amherst faces "the teacher shortage." Unlike many colleges, however, Amherst is also resisting a trend toward greater specialization and full-time research by continuing to make the classroom a central arena of the teachers' concern.

The stock-in-trade of Amherst lies in teaching.[18]

At the same time, the college places considerable emphasis upon research and publication.

While success in teaching is regarded as a prime factor for appointment to and promotion on the Amherst faculty, the College gives great weight to the continued scholarly growth of its faculty members. Research and publication is considered one of the most important indications of such growth. The College does everything within reason to encourage research and it not infrequently assists in the publication of scholarly books by its faculty members. The College further tries to cooperate in all cases where an effort is made to secure a research grant from an outside agency.[19]

Along this line, the Amherst faculty does appear to accomplish an unusual amount of high-quality research in comparison with the faculties of most liberal arts colleges. The potential dichotomy between teaching and research, which is perceived as a real problem in many colleges, should not be overstressed. In many areas, at least some professional research and writing is a necessary ingredient in the teaching process itself.

Further, the college has experienced the commonly remarked-upon shift in the way that members of the faculty identify themselves, i.e., the shift from an essentially institutional identification to an essentially professional or disciplinary identification. How does Amherst, in

[18] See "The Faculty," *Amherst Reports*, Vol. 2, No. 3, March, 1963, pp. 4–5.
[19] See *Faculty Handbook*, Amherst College, Amherst, Mass., 1964, pp. 6–7.

light of the professional pressures and its apparent accommodation to them, manage to elicit from its faculty the necessary concentration on undergraduate teaching?

One important answer lies in the matter of prestige. Is a member of the faculty who engages in little research and writing but who has a reputation as a good teacher ranked as highly on Amherst's own campus as one who engages in much research and writing and has developed a considerable professional reputation? Somewhat fragmentary evidence suggests that status ranking as between researchers and teachers has not developed as a general characteristic of the Amherst campus. One teacher expressed the opinion that the faculty community is too pluralistic to generate the kind of systematic preference ordering implied by "first-class" and "second-class" citizenship. Different groups of faculty set different values on the various kinds of academic and professional achievements.

In response to the question how Amherst has tried to maintain parity between teaching and research, one administrator replied, "By taking care visibly to reward both good teaching and good research."

Both the fact of the reward and its visibility are important, especially since there are complicating pressures from the outside. If most of the rest of the world ranks research and writing as number one and teaching as number two, how can any one small institution maintain itself as an enclave with these values reversed?

Here, Amherst's very high overall salary scale comes into play. Since Amherst is one of the ten top-salary institutions in the country, individual faculty with a genuine interest in teaching will not feel compelled to abandon these interests in favor of research and publication in order to increase their mobility and chances of higher salaries elsewhere. Even without special salary adjustments, alternatives will not be as frequently competitive as they would at a college with a lower pay scale.

Another factor may be important in maintaining the commitment to teaching in the Amherst situation—care in selecting instructors who seem to have a real commitment to teaching at the time they come. Instructors whose own undergraduate experience was in a small liberal arts college may more frequently be of this persuasion.

Nor should student influence be overlooked as a factor helping to conserve the commitment to teaching. Student expectations may be among the important motivations at work in the Amherst situation. *Amherst Reports* quotes an associate professor, himself a graduate of a liberal arts college: "The internal competition is tremendous. I spend several hours planning each lecture (of an elective course). If I am not prepared I won't have any students. No group that I know anywhere works so hard teaching as people do around here."[20] The same point might be made regarding conference and discussion groups. Of course, the problem is not only whether the instructor attracts students but whether he can live with them and with himself, day in and day out, week in and week out, in the light of their expectations, if he is not doing a good teaching job.

Yet another factor which may be of considerable importance is Amherst's participation in the cooperative four-college graduate degree program. The Ph.D. is awarded by the University of Massachusetts, but it is identified as a degree belonging to the four-college program, and the students graduating in this program have their own distinctive hood. The program is quite small, having at any one time in recent years perhaps six or seven doctoral candidates. By way of comparison, the liberal arts and sciences part of the University of Massachusetts is now producing about seventy Ph.D.s each year. The chief difference between a regular University of Massachusetts degree candidate and a four-college degree candidate is that the four-college candidate has as his thesis adviser a member of the faculty of one of the other three institutions, although he takes all or virtually all his course work in the university.

The Ph.D. program does afford some faculty the opportunity to teach graduate students. More generally, the proximity of the university and Smith and Mount Holyoke colleges gives Amherst faculty some of the benefits of membership on a university faculty. The four colleges represent, in short, a substantial intellectual community, with considerable opportunity for faculty seminars and the like.

For small liberal arts colleges which do not wish to attempt to turn themselves into little universities, cooperative Ph.D. programs of the kind described may offer one kind of solution. While a fortunate geographical location is required, a number of colleges and universities may be clustered in such a way that they could entertain this kind of program, to the colleges' advantage. In some places it might also be of considerable advantage to the cooperating universities, which could have a larger pool of faculty available to their students. While this need may be less pressing for the universities, it seems likely that the potential benefits to the colleges should make them eager to maintain such a cooperative venture as a vigorous part of their overall programs.

[20] See "The Faculty," *Amherst Reports.*

The author of the Amherst College profile was Carl M. Stevens, professor of economics at Reed College. His associate was W. Boyd Alexander, Emeritus Vice President and Dean of the Faculty at Antioch College. Acting on behalf of Amherst was Robert F. Grose, registrar and associate professor of psychology. The student observer was Stephen McCarthy of Reed College.

The extent and value of intense student-faculty give-and-take at Monteith cannot be over-emphasized. But the most critical experiment the college presents is not whether its particular approach to liberal education is good, but whether a large urban university has the capacity to cherish and nurture to excellence within itself a relatively distinctive and autonomous small college.

T WELVE years ago there was no Wayne State University; ten years ago there was no Monteith College; six years ago there were no Monteith graduates. We are here observing a young college, not just part of a university but an expression of a distinctive educational philosophy. At Monteith, the zeal of the pioneer still burns. Those who have shared in the turbulent beginning days of the college still hold the banner high and demand allegiance to it from the newcomer who has not yet shared the joys and frustrations of creating an institution from scratch.

A response to
felt needs

Monteith embodies four major ideas, stated in a document entitled "An Experimental College at Wayne State University" presented to the general Wayne community in 1958:

(1) The proposed College is an effort to impart to undergraduates, particularly those training for the professions, that common body of ideas and knowledge which every educated man should possess. The experiment will depart from common educational patterns by distributing the work in general education through the four college years. (2) The experiment is also an attempt to break down conventional patterns of spoon-feeding the undergraduate and to develop in him intellectual independence and initiative. (3) By arranging matters so that freshmen are our most expensive students and seniors are our least expensive, we believe we are proposing a novel but efficient distribution of College funds. (4) Within a large and sprawling University structure, this program will create a tightly knit intellectual milieu, an academic home for some 1000 students.

183

These four ideas were responses to certain pressures which the university was beginning to feel. Wayne had been a municipal university for the city of Detroit until 1956, when it became apparent that the municipality was unable to support the program that a large urban university must have to compete in the expanding academic arena. In the fall of 1956, Wayne University came under Michigan's state system of higher education and was rechristened Wayne State University. This shift of financial support and control brought a number of opportunities and problems. The opportunities were larger budgets which allowed new programs, new buildings, and enlarged enrollments. The problems were those of the rapidly growing "multiversity."

Regarding the first idea: As a result of the expanded funds available to it as a state university, Wayne began to speed up the process of adding doctoral programs to its curriculum. With the pressure to develop quality programs at the doctoral level came pressure down in the undergraduate curriculum for more specialized lower-cost undergraduate education—which generally meant larger class sizes —so that the fledgling Ph.D. programs could grow and thrive.

Responding to the pressure for more specialization in the liberal arts curriculum, the university proposed to create a college that would "specialize" in general education, offering a broad program of core courses. Every student in this college would take the same sequence in "Science of Society," "Natural Science," "Humanistic Studies," "Senior Colloquium," and "Senior Essay." The content of the sequences would be freshly developed each year, and within each sequence a student's program might be "tailor-made to fit his interests, present competence and potential development."[1] Further, freshmen in the college would discuss in sections of twelve, as opposed to twenty or thirty in many of the other schools on campus.

The second idea was that the new college would allow experiments, radical departures from conventional university practice. It would permit annual redesign of course content (though not calendar structure), and it would thrust freedom upon its students in unusual ways, always subject to testing and alteration. This idea was a relatively safe one, because only a small number of students, in one of Wayne's eleven colleges, would engage in the experimentation. If the experiments were good, they might be extended to other parts of the university. If they failed, the cost of failure would be small.

[1] From *This Is Monteith,* a promotional folder.

Third, with the coming of state university status came the special demands of state university budget methods. In 1958, Michigan had three major universities, and in the succeeding years, the four regional state colleges requested and received university status. Comparisons of efficiency in terms of cost of program were demanded by the Legislature so that it could examine the performance of the various universities of Michigan and allocate state funds more effectively. The third idea, on the allocation of funds, bore on these new budget requirements.

Ordinarily, teaching costs go up as the student moves from freshman to senior to graduate student; Monteith's program was to balance the cost of other programs of the university by spending more on freshmen and less at the upper levels, thereby giving the university a balanced cost program. To keep costs down, Monteith was to use the same physical facilities, the same admissions office, the same computer center, the same library, the same classrooms as the rest of Wayne State; but, since underclassmen are more numerous than upperclassmen, the overall cost per student would be higher than in many other parts of the university. (The Ford Foundation granted $700,000 in 1959 to help meet costs while the experiment proved itself.) It was argued that the experiment, like other specialized offerings, would be worth the added cost.

Another pressure-creating problem of the urban university was size: tens of thousands of students many of whom were working, few dormitories, many evening classes—no basis on which to build a sense of community within the student body. Monteith, with fewer than 4 percent of Wayne's thirty thousand students, was a response to the problem of largeness. The college was to have the best of two worlds. It was to provide breadth through its core program and yet allow depth by having its students take specialized courses in other colleges of the university. It was to combine courses taught by faculty having the clearest and purest commitment to the education of the mind and spirit with courses taught by faculty offering the sharpest focus on technical competence. It was to be a self-conscious enclave and at the same time part of an urban university. Inherent in this fourth idea is a certain amount of tension between the college and the rest of the university; this tension will appear in various guises throughout the profile.

Such were the problems and such were the ideas that emerged to solve them. Within a year after the 1958 report was presented,

Monteith College was born. It opened its doors to its first students, 314 in number, in September of 1959.[2]

With the experiment came national publicity, sociologists and educational researchers to observe the school, and some internal conflicts. For example, there was conflict within the student who had to stand with one foot in an experimental program and the other in a conventional one. To him, it must often have seemed that some of his programs and some of his teachers were preaching the gospel of breadth while others were advocating the gospel of depth. Could the average Wayne student function both ways? One student had this to say:

> Monteith provides an opportunity to get a good education, but there is no discipline here and no structure. Monteith and the Liberal Arts College people seem to have different functions and teach in different ways. The Liberal Arts College history discussion sessions were question and answer sessions too often concerned with fact. At Monteith, discussion sections covered deer hunting, the election, any subject, but with more interest in participation than in the material.
>
> Monteith however has changed me as a person. There is a solid core of ideas around here that I have picked up, but Liberal Arts has educated me and taught me how to write. My first semester at Wayne six years ago was in the Liberal Arts College. [A number of Monteith students, and Wayne students generally, take more than four years to graduate.] Then I transferred to Monteith to avoid taking English. However, I went back later because I had to learn how to write. Monteith assumed that I could write in their undisciplined program. They didn't teach me how. If you survive Monteith, you may eventually learn to write, but a lot of people drop out of Monteith because of the general confusion here. The dropout, however, may be an illusion because many of them eventually come back. My classes are different in Monteith than in Liberal Arts. What is expected of me is different. I have learned to function in both places, but the performance in each place has been up to me.

The insight and understanding that such a situation demands of students are the more remarkable when one considers the kind of students Wayne and Monteith attract. They are basically lower-class and lower-middle-class residents of the Detroit metropolitan area. The only selection at Monteith is student self-selection. Such a student population caused one observer to ask:

> How could they do it? How could a college with an unselected commuter student body attempt to offer a highly demanding, interdisciplinary, anti-

[2] Of this number, 265 were Monteith freshman students, and 49 were engineering students taking some of their general education work at Monteith.

vocational program and hope to achieve the intense effects of small elite liberal arts colleges?[3]

Midway through the fall quarter of 1965, confusion among the Monteith freshmen reached such a pitch that the chairman of the Division of the Science of Society responded with a special lecture. The time had come to restate the aims of the required unit on "The City" and to say in another and fresh way why the course proceeded as it did. Why were students confronted with conflicting views on the city, alternative forms of evidence about it, contrasting styles of studying it and describing it, and the very different problems of personal experience it presents its different observers? Why bother to consider historical studies that have been superseded? Many freshmen came to Monteith with the idea that education is learning the known answers and the proved methods; their confusion, the lecturer suggested, sprang not merely from the conflict among the ideas, data, and perspectives of the original source materials, but even more deeply from confrontation with a different idea of education. This idea is that education is a many-sided dialogue extending across time and space and through cultural barriers, that education is more a process of learning to ask better questions than one of memorizing answers, that education moves from views of the city to perspectives on man and back to insight about this man and this particular incident and this relation to a fellow citizen, that education is liberation through intellectual discourse.

It was a brilliant lecture, given in a dingy hall that could have seated twice the seventy-five students present yet spoken as directly and informally as a conversation over coffee. But I came away wondering if the confusion went still deeper. Not only were these students having their idea of education challenged; they were being challenged to spend their time in a kind of talk, thinking, and studying quite alien to what they came to college to do. This would not ensure them the income, social status, and security in life for which they had, consciously or unconsciously, bargained in offering four years of their lives to Wayne State University. Monteith was remaking their values, their very personality and self-image; they had agreed only to a face-lifting, not to a whole remodeling of themselves. The facts and course content constituting a stiff education (by their standards) were being neglected in favor of vague, troubling things like values. In addition, these people, these teachers, really were not *teaching* them. In some vague way they were suggesting that it was

[3] Quoted from Introduction, first draft of a doctoral dissertation, p. 1.

learning, not teaching, that college was all about. This guess took on reality during a talk with Ralph Dickey, a senior.

[This shift] from high school where teachers are policemen . . . and always forcing you to study into an atmosphere with most of the responsibility on yourself is quite a change. . . . In Social Science 131 I was lost—the course was set up so we fumbled for something to hold onto. We took Korean prisoners of war and looked at them from half a dozen points of view. It seemed an anarchical arrangement. They weren't telling which one was right. I expected someone to tell me who was right. . . .

. . . There were changes both in what I know and in me. It was complicated. I came meaning to go into science, maybe dentistry. I began Wayne with chemistry, biology, etc.; it was going well when I began to question why I wanted to be a dentist. I'd done well in science, seemed to enjoy it, but had chosen it because of a pamphlet in junior high about high dentist salaries— that seemed sufficient incentive. . . . By Quantitative Analysis (after two honors courses in chemistry) I decided I was wasting my time in science . . . dropped the course in mid-quarter. I was disturbed because I had to cope with many possibilities. Mother had always favored my being a doctor or dentist. I respected and wanted to please her, but she didn't understand me or my capabilities. . . . She was disturbed and long unreconciled to my being a teacher. . . .

A friend in the College of Liberal Arts complained about the setup there. He said: "Rather than teach a man how to make a living, college should teach him how to live." That's what Monteith has done for me . . . as much by the nature of the courses and the way they are taught as by the influence of those who taught.

Students   Not every senior is a Ralph Dickey. Only fifty members of the first class of two hundred sixty-five full Monteith freshmen graduated four years later in 1963.[4] By 1964, twelve more had graduated with degrees gained elsewhere in the university but with most or all of their general education from Monteith. Six more were admitted to medical school. Thirty-nine more members had graduated through the summer of 1966.

The 1962–63 seniors, studied very thoroughly by the college itself, accumulated a remarkable record. On Graduate Record Area Tests, for example, their average was at the 72d percentile nationally on the social science test, at the 74th percentile on the humanities test, and at the 78th percentile on the natural science test. On the Test of Critical Thinking sponsored by the American Council on Education, the

[4] Of the original group, 26 percent were seniors in 1962–63 (though not all those seniors graduated); 18 percent were "slowdowns," still in school but not yet seniors; and 55.5 percent had dropped out of college at least temporarily. These figures are very much like those for a comparable sample of students drawn from the Liberal Arts College—21 percent, 22 percent, and 57 percent.

1962–63 seniors advanced from an average score in 1959 of 33.52 to an average score in 1963 of 38.04; those among them who actually graduated had a 1963 average score of 40.29. Of the fifty graduates, forty have gone on to graduate school, and twenty-three have received grants or fellowships.[5]

Monteith is not an honors college. The admissions policy of the university and student self-selection determine the students that Monteith will get. Students who apply for Monteith rather than to the College of Liberal Arts, the School of Business, the School of Education, etc., are admitted on a first-come–first-served basis. Thus far, the number of entering students choosing Monteith has not been significantly larger than the number of places available. But if Monteith should some day have 800 applicants for a freshman class of 350, the college, according to present policy, would not be permitted to accumulate these applications and sift out and select the students it wanted.

The entering classes of 1959 and 1962, those on which most data are available, appear to be fairly typical subsets of the larger set of Wayne State students. Sixty-eight percent of the 1959 class lived in Detroit and another 20 percent within 50 miles of the city. Almost a third of the students had at least one parent born abroad, and 15 percent were either immigrants themselves or had parents both of whom were born abroad. Over a third came from homes where a language other than English was spoken (Russian, Polish, Yiddish, and German were the most frequent). Thirty-two percent were Protestant, with Lutherans (9 percent) forming the largest subgroup; 25 percent were Catholic and 18 percent Jewish. Less than a quarter of the fathers and an eighth of the mothers had completed college themselves. On the Wayne placement tests, Monteith students scored slightly higher than Wayne students generally on both verbal ability and quantitative ability. There is evidence that since 1962, the self-selection process has drawn somewhat more on the middle-class and somewhat less on the working-class sectors of Detroit.

If Monteith students at entrance appear to be more or less typical in everything except the fact that they choose to enroll at Monteith, they soon become distinctive. Senior student responses on the College Characteristics Index show the college to have an extraordinary

[5] Contrary to what one might expect, the students who became seniors in 1962 were only slightly more able, according to university placement tests and other measures, than the entering class as a whole. On the Test of Critical Thinking, the seniors actually had entering scores somewhat below those of the whole entering class.

intellectual climate, much closer to that of an independent liberal arts college than that of a university-associated college.[6]

One professor has defined the students in this way:

Monteith has been called a beatnik college, both by pro-beatnik and by anti-beatnik. It has a persistent, though often denied, reputation of being an honors college. The free university movement listed it as "in" (I am told, though I have not seen the document myself); this seems to be due to our "Cooperative Self-Education Program." I am also told that some people think it is a Roman Catholic college (though this would come as a shock to most of its considerable cohort of Roman Catholic students who find its style rather unfamiliar). Many people no doubt do not distinguish it from Wayne State University. This might reflect a lack of clarity, a lack of identity, even, and certainly a lack of public relations work. It also might be the consequence of a genuine pluralism and a genuine respect for individual choice.

One thing seems to be held by all Monteith students—an interest in, even fascination with, education. What is learning? What is its true value? How can it best take place? These are topics not only for the seminars and conversations, but for serious reflection.

One can detect a kind of polarity among Monteith students. At one pole is the "Monteith-Monteith" student, thoroughly committed to the college, its fashion of education, and the interests it promotes. He is verbal, an activist, interested in the here and now, interested in leadership. His weapons are his tongue and the mimeograph machine (the mimeograph might well be the symbol of Monteith). Many Monteith-Monteith students spend a good deal of time in the Student Center Building. They are the ones who control the Monteith student organizations.

The Monteith-Monteith student tends to be closely involved with the faculty—in a sense, tied to the professor. To this observer, these students seem as much dependent as independent. One student had this to say about the college:

[6] This table compares Monteith with independent liberal arts colleges and university-associated liberal arts colleges on the eight factors that make up the "intellectual climate" index on the CCI:

		Intellectual climate	
Factor	Monteith	Independent colleges	University-associated colleges
Aspiration level	3.35	2.29	−0.75
Intellectual climate	3.41	2.90	−0.92
Student dignity	3.05	2.39	−1.48
Academic climate	2.50	1.91	−0.27
Academic achievement	0.20	2.04	−1.58
Self-expression	1.80	2.17	−1.03
Nonvocational	3.60	3.16	−1.11
Work-play	−0.20	1.64	−1.94

I have taken almost half of my work in the College of Liberal Arts, but I
got the general basis of my education in Monteith. It was broader. It left the
specific courses to Liberal Arts. I believe that the Monteith work was most
beneficial to me because the quality of instruction was higher (at least I
thought so). I also worked closer with the faculty at Monteith than at Liberal
Arts. Perhaps I was "babied" more at Monteith. The faculty spent more time
with us. I would not, however, want to have a 100 per cent Monteith program
because one needs to survive in the urban anonymous world. That is a
necessary part of education so the College of Liberal Arts has kept the
"babying" from being a detriment.

Another student looked at the Monteith system as freedom and
not dependence:

At the present time I am taking a colloquium without a professor being
involved. It meets in one of the girls' apartments. It doesn't matter what we
discuss. We are trying to get an understanding of consciousness and values. We
do keep a log each session and our final log will be a projection of what
we think the next session would be. This is one of the most stimulating classes I
have ever had even though I am not sure where we are going. We are all
working from common goals to learn something. The strength in the course is
that you shouldn't accept something because someone says it's so. This
freedom is something that I like and enjoy.

It is also true that the Monteith-Monteith students often take special
courses, tutorials, and seminars at Monteith, which require substantial
amounts of independent work.

At the other pole is the student oriented both to Monteith and to
Wayne; he could be called a "Monteith-Wayne" student. He sees
himself basically as a Monteith student but takes a minimum of work
in the college. He supports the Monteith idea verbally, but is relatively uncommitted to it emotionally. Included here also are those
who simply use the Monteith-Wayne program to best advantage by
taking courses from each of the two areas without paying too much
attention to the conflicting philosophies.

**Monteith, Wayne, and
the we-they syndrome**

Monteith, as one of eleven colleges constituting Wayne State University, sits squarely in the central district of Detroit, a metropolis
of 3.5 million people. Physically, there is not much to Monteith.
Located on the edge of Wayne's sprawling campus, the college occupies three run-down former residences; two have been converted
into offices for faculty and administration; the third has been turned
over to students as a substitute student union. Because its buildings
give little focus to the college, Monteith must make its way chiefly
as an unusual combination of an idea and people who believe in it.
Wayne State University casts an imposing shadow over Monteith,

which was created by Wayne and cannot exist without it. Wayne is one of the twenty largest universities in the United States. Well over half of its more than thirty thousand students are enrolled in the College of Liberal Arts. Wayne has all the advantages and few of the disadvantages of the other great urban universities of the United States, because it is also part of a state system of higher education in a state having one of the higher per capita expenditures for such education. Also, it has all the characteristics of a state university—a separate, constitutionally established Governing Board, a system of central administration, a long-range plan for university development, a strong library, and a full program of cultural events.

Legislative appropriations for Monteith, admissions services, libraries, classrooms, health services, financial aid—all the resources of a large university—are available to the college through Wayne. Thus Monteith, unlike a free-standing private college, is protected by the university from the pressures of the marketplace. On the other hand, it is subject to all the hidden rivalries, professional jealousies, and financial infighting of a constituent college competing for its share of the finances, staff, faculty, and facilities of a major university.

Monteith is constrained in some choices by its place in the total university structure. Such decisions as building use, size of budget, enlargement of faculty, curriculum expansion, admissions policy, university rules, and calendar, for example, are Wayne, not Monteith decisions. Since allocations for future staff needs are determined among the various colleges on the basis of comparative cost studies, the total size of Monteith's faculty and staff is set by the university, although promotions and salary increases for existing faculty—within the university ranges—are decided by Monteith internally. Expenditures for the more expensive types of equipment, such as a small computer, also are determined against the requirements of the university at large.

Monteith is further constrained in terms of facilities and use of space. Given the building needs of other units of the university, such as the Medical School, there appears to be no university plan for a building for Monteith College in the next five years. (Monteith, however, is free to have its Dean seek outside funds for a building from a donor or a foundation, a pursuit in which he has been active.) Six classrooms are set apart for Monteith's special use; a few hours in lecture halls are also reserved. The classroom program is determined in the overall university schedule.

A third matter in which the university limits the freedom of Monteith is the establishment of special courses in the college to be taught as seminars in addition to the regular interdisciplinary curricular offerings. To the extent that these courses might be similar to courses already offered in the Biology or Sociology Department in the College of Liberal Arts at Wayne State, the curricular offering has to be approved by the University Council. Almost invariably, this approval is not given.[7]

While it is clear that Monteith cannot exist apart from Wayne, it is natural that dependence should breed some resentment in the college itself, or at least a desire to assert independence. One manifestation of this is what may be called the "we-they syndrome."

Monteith is still a college in search of identity. The founders of Monteith originally visualized the college as serving the general education needs of the wider university community—as being essentially a service college to Wayne. In the process of recruiting a staff, however, there came together a group of people with a different kind of vision. Their vision, in oversimplified form, was to develop a full four-year degree in general education, *drawing on* Wayne for special courses rather than *serving* Wayne with a special program.

Part of their ambition was to create a program that would bring freshmen along as fast as possible to a level where they could think, question, experiment, and interact. The Monteith faculty, convinced that freshmen in other parts of the university are less likely to be pushed in this way, feel almost obliged to point out to their students the contrast beween Monteith's expectations for them and the expectations of instructors elsewhere in the university. This sense of extraordinary expectation does foster a certain *esprit de corps* and verve which is part of the Monteith atmosphere. Sometimes it also elicits, especially from Liberal Arts College faculty, condescension and hostility in return.

A related, perhaps more basic, issue concerns the point of departure for the educational process. On the traditional campus, the faculty typically undertakes to teach subject matter and provide an atmosphere in which the student can question and ultimately decide, more or less on his own, what system of values he will carry away. To at least a significant extent, Monteith has reversed this process. The faculty attempts first to engage students in consideration of questions of value, at the same time providing a setting in which they will be encouraged to learn subject matter with increasing diligence as their search for knowledge matures. Issues such as these, real

[7] This constraint may have its brighter side as working against the proliferation of courses, an almost universal academic disease.

and imagined, have created a considerable rift between Monteith and the rest of Wayne.

Curriculum Monteith's students are all shared students, putting together courses in Monteith with courses elsewhere in the university in one of a number of combinations. Ordinarily, a student's general education work at Monteith, amounting to perhaps half his total program, is combined with electives and "major" work in another college; this may lead to a Monteith degree, a degree from one of the professional schools such as Education or Business Administration, or sometimes both. Students wishing to dispense with a conventional disciplinary major and do a larger share of their work in Monteith may take a Monteith degree in general education. A special arrangement permits engineering students to take a few courses, not more than thirty-six hours, in Monteith while pursuing a regular engineering curriculum.

A Wayne degree requires 180 quarter hours of academic work. Monteith's basic course pattern, which is spread out over all four years of the student's college experience, requires 84 hours of work at Monteith.[8] The following diagram shows the structure of this basic curriculum, indicating the amount of work required in each of the three areas of social science, natural science, and humanities, and the capstone work of the senior year:

	Freshman-year quarters			Sophomore-year quarters			Junior-year quarters			Senior-year quarters		
	1	2	3	4	5	6	7	8	9	10	11	12
4 credit hours	Science of Society						(shaded)			Senior Colloquium		(shaded)
4 credit hours	Natural Science						(shaded)			Senior Essay		
4 credit hours	(shaded)			Humanistic Studies						Senior Essay		
4 credit hours	(shaded)											

The shaded blocks of time are reserved for courses in the student's specialty or profession, for electives, or for additional work in general education.

[8] A ruling recently instituted requires freshmen to take an additional Monteith hour per quarter, for orientation and for emphasis on the considerable amount of writing required by the Monteith curriculum.

Each division has chosen a somewhat different emphasis: Natural Science stresses the historical, Science of Society the empirical, and Humanistic Studies the philosophical. The staff holds that this variety in itself indicates to the students the richness of the general approach and places on them the burden of finding links, differences, and reasons for the differences.

Essential to these Monteith sequences is a team teaching arrangement whereby each sequence meets twice a week for lectures by various members of the division staff or for dialogue between two or among several staff members. In this manner, each professor brings to the sequence his own special knowledge and skill as a teacher, as well as his own way of looking at the ideas under consideration. For the remaining two hours, the class is broken into discussion groups, twelve students with each professor. The student thus sees his professor both as a discussion leader who receives and clarifies ideas or assists with written work and as a lecturer, part of a staff, dependent upon his colleagues for the operation of the course. Some Monteith faculty believe that the close faculty cooperation demanded by this sort of teaching cannot easily be maintained if a divisional staff grows to more than twelve or fourteen members. To their mind, small size is a vital requirement for general education in the Monteith manner.

The Monteith faculty has attempted to build a framework within which discipline can speak to discipline, century to century, and idea to idea. Vice President Lawrence Chamberlain of Columbia and Prof. David Riesman of Harvard, in a 1964 report of a visit to Monteith College, wrote this:

The fields of knowledge are in flux, as everyone knows, and yet the academic disciplines by which they are organized tend to become compartments of academic vested interests even while, in many fields of knowledge, they become less and less relevant to the important issues of our time. In all the Monteith courses given by the three staffs, there is not only the effort to link fields of knowledge with each other but to tie them to major problems of contemporary society. . . . We attended, for example, one discussion class dealing with medieval philosophy and touching on Abelard, Anselm, and other thinkers; and we were impressed with the ability both of the instructor and of the class to make these writers appear relevant today—a task requiring unremitting imagination and ingenuity.

The staff-taught sequences and the Senior Colloquium and Senior Essay are not all the Monteith curriculum. Unlike many experimental general education programs, Monteith offers its staff opportunity to teach special seminars of their own design (provided they do not duplicate Liberal Arts College offerings) and in that way to keep in touch with their academic specialty and gain respite and perspective after the demands of the basic sequences. Among many others, the Monteith catalog lists these special courses: "Greek Science," "Theories of the Origin and Structure of the Universe," "Personality Theory: Identity," "Factors in the Political Economy of Underdeveloped Areas," "Art and the Philosophy of Symbolism," "Life Style and Art Style of the Enlightenment."

One innovation in the Monteith curriculum has been a program called Cooperative Self-Education, whereby a group of students may set up a course that they wish to pursue. After drawing up a syllabus and a reading list, they seek the sponsorship of a professor. The professor is not involved in teaching or attendance at the seminar that will follow, although he is responsible to the division chairman for the proposed course content. Students run the course and, together with the sponsoring professor, make the evaluations of performance. Credit is given, although only half as much as from a regular formal course with a professor. Subjects have ranged widely —"American Indians: Ojibwa," "Art and the City," "Film Language: Its History and Evolution," "Northern Student Movement," "Revolutions," "South Africa," "Teaching and Learning." Some of the courses have a definite leader or pair of leaders designated in advance; others do not. Some of them provide for lectures by students or attendance at formal conferences in the city; others are altogether discussion. Some require term papers, shorter papers, or examinations.

For some students, the freedom of these courses can provide important experiences; for others, this freedom may be limited by the tyranny of the group. One student expressed his concern about a Cooperative Self-Education course that he was in. The course, he felt, was based on the assumption that certain aspects of our society were bad, and the reading program chose books that would confirm this initial assumption. He was an enthusiastic participant in the choice of the readings; however, as the course developed, he began to feel that all the activity was intended to strengthen existing biases and that the students were unwilling to grapple with alternative points of view. He tried to make this point to the others, but without success.

Monteith offers no English composition course, preferring to have students write as part of the basic sequences. Some instructors, particularly in the Division of Humanistic Studies, are distressed at the unevenness of student writing. After having taken the sequences in Science of Society and Natural Science, some students, these instructors find, have become intellectually awakened, personally confident, and capable orally—but are still poor at expressing themselves on paper. A student who feels himself deficient in writing may enroll in an English composition course in the College of Liberal Arts as one of his Monteith electives. Monteith is not contemplating requiring a writing course, but the hour now added to freshman requirements provides more time for writing.

Through its demands on faculty and students, the Monteith curriculum sets up contrasts—tensions—of at least two kinds. First is the pull between structure and freedom. Students are expected to speak for themselves, to show initiative and independence from the very beginning. Yet the basic sequences are required of all students. They are free only within a rigid framework.

One place where student dependence upon structure has shown itself is in student government. The student organization has made repeated demands for definition of its "rights" and wants formal decisions setting forth the areas in which it can function. Until the administration complies, the students feel they cannot act. On the other hand, the administration sees no reason to make this definition and wishes the students to move ahead and take what positions they may wish to take, on the assumption that they have the right, the opportunity, and the power to influence the course of education at Monteith.

Second, there seems to be inevitable tension between commitment to the Monteith program and suppleness, willingness to keep experimenting. The college wants, and is likely to attract, faculty who like its educational ideas and the overall shape of its curriculum. Yet the task it has undertaken—a broadly intellectual education for typical city students—is an extremely complex and difficult one; it is improbable that the college will ever discover the one best way to go about it. Monteith must be a sustained opportunity rather than the embodiment of a creed.

Lawrence Chamberlain and David Riesman suggest an arrangement that might help accomplish that end:

We would think of the Monteith faculty as having the responsibility continuously to induct new faculty members who have but recently completed their graduate education, then send them on to teach in more specialized programs to which they will bring their wider horizons acquired at Monteith. This might be one way to keep the spirit of experiment alive beyond the initial years and prevent Monteith from becoming, like so many experiments, a frozen mass of congealed doctrine, rigidly defended by aging fanatics.

College structure Monteith College has a Dean, an Associate Dean, and an Executive Secretary. Its divisions—Natural Science, Science of Society, and

Humanistic Studies—have chairmen appointed by the Dean. These six officers constitute the Administrative Council of the college.

In practice, most decisions appear to be made by the divisions themselves. Within the rather broad limitations of university and college policy, each division hires its own faculty, sets its own curriculum and teaching procedures, and oversees student activities. Within the divisions, although it is perhaps premature to suggest that Monteith has developed traditions, Monteith appears to operate more by tradition than by command or consensus. A faculty recruitment process that determines a candidate's commitment to the Monteith idea helps make this method work. Whether it will be the best method in the long run is another question.

Monteith has a counseling bureau but no formal student service group such as is usually provided by a dean of men or dean of women. The function of student personnel deans is replaced by the extensive interaction between the students and faculty; the extent and value of this intense student-faculty give-and-take cannot be overemphasized. In fact, interaction with students to the extent of continuing interest in them even after their graduation could be considered the heart of the Monteith program.

The Dean of Monteith is comparable to the president of a free-standing college. His job is basically external. He is the ultimate fund-raiser, whether it be in budget negotiations with the university authorities or operating on his own to gain foundation support. He fashions the external image of the college, making speeches and telling the Monteith story. The Executive Secretary is more nearly similar to the registrar of a British university than to any comparable officer in a private liberal arts college in the United States. He is partly business manager, partly scheduler, partly housekeeper—in general, an expediter.

Faculty polarities The faculty at Monteith tend to play down the status difference between themselves and the students. Thus the Monteith catalog nowhere has a list of the faculty with their degrees and time of joining the college. Only at the beginning of the course offerings for each division is the faculty listed, and then alphabetically, without title, rank, or pedigree. The students, however, being a curious lot, want to know more about their teachers; last year they asked each member of the faculty to give a biography of himself, which they published under the title *Vita*. *Vita* is interesting reading, with the patterns of response offering considerable insight into individuals.

Some give a standard resumé, listing education, prior experience, publications, offices held, etc. Others write a three- or four-page essay explaining their philosophy of education. Still others give a brief biography beginning with childhood and attempting to answer the question, "Who am I?"

In many ways the Monteith faculty reminds one of a clannish family made up of strong-minded individuals. While they are willing to present a more or less common front to the university, there are tensions and cleavages within. One of the most significant of these polarities is that between the faculty who are mainly student-oriented and those who are more subject-matter–oriented.

Because the members of the student-oriented group see their job primarily as examining and transforming values rather than passing on subject matter, they have an unusually keen awareness of, and commitment to, the student who comes out of the Detroit urban complex, perhaps from a home where books, music, and art are unknown and even unwelcome strangers. In trying to change him, however, they are conscious of the delicacy of their job. For example, one said, "We don't want to uproot the working-class student from his background, but we are not yet sure how we can maintain continuity with this background."

The major stronghold of this group is the Science of Society Division.

The Science of Society program is empirical and nonhistorical. Heavily populated with sociologists and psychologists, the social science faculty leans toward activism and toward involvement in various projects in the metropolitan area. It is interesting that teachers from the other divisions of Monteith who are primarily committed to the student-oriented approach have sometimes switched over to the Science of Society Division.

Because of this general approach, the social science faculty may be more permissive than the faculty of the other divisions, trying to give every student a chance to do a good job and earn a good grade. They are eager for student participation and commitment.[9]

At the opposite pole are those teachers in all three divisions, but particularly in the Natural Science Division, who might be characterized as more interested in their courses than in the students. They

[9] Yet, oddly enough, the faculty in this division were not willing to give their students a part in reshaping the curriculum. Thinking they had been invited to participate, these students were baffled. So were the faculty, who thought the curriculum "sacred ground," or at least a matter about which students should do no more than make suggestions.

endeavor to teach their subject matter brilliantly, if possible, but it is then up to the students to catch on as best they can. The Natural Science Division is philosophically and historically oriented, rather than empirically, and no laboratory experience is involved. The students are expected to meet deadlines, learn material, and cover a subject.

It is interesting that a number of the students interviewed thought their best teachers were in the Natural Science Division—defining "best teacher" as someone who had taught them, competently, something interesting that they had not known before. These students did not think of their best teacher as someone who had awakened them or stimulated them or put them on the road to self-learning. This is an indication, perhaps, that the "Monteith idea"—learning to ask intelligent questions rather than merely to answer questions—is not getting across to the college's student body in toto.

Lack of communication across division lines has already been commented on; even within divisions, little attempt has been made toward governance by consensus. Most of the alliances, even between members of the same division, appear to be personal and cliquish rather than division-wide.

With all this, however, it must be said that the teachers at Monteith College in each of the divisions are competent and committed; these people would grace the faculty of practically any liberal arts college.

The future   Now that Monteith has come to the end of its probationary period and has been accepted as a regular college of the university, and now that the Ford Foundation grant has run out and the president, Clarence Hilberry, under whom Monteith began, is no longer there, the university must decide what resources will be put at Monteith's disposal and how it can ensure that this allotment is just in terms of the Monteith task and product.

As already suggested, a particularly thorny issue is the deliberately high undergraduate costs. The other parts of the university accept grudgingly the higher costs of the Medical School. The greater expense in physics and chemistry, which demand much equipment, can be rationalized if not totally accepted. But how can one justify higher cost for teaching freshman general education courses? This is the question which must be answered, not for the Monteith faculty, because they are fully persuaded already, but for the outsiders who do not share, understand, or support this high-cost education. For a time, the Monteith faculty can ease the burden by dedication and extra work, but eventually an acceptable rationale must be developed.

The college is now an ongoing, recognized member of the Wayne University group of colleges; the outlook is for continued growth in quality and programs. In view of this fact, it seems to this observer at least that Monteith might expend a bit less energy in fighting ghosts and building walls between itself and Wayne and attempt to formulate an adequate basis for coexistence. Almost certainly, different environments and treatments are needed to elicit from different groups of students the maximum growth possible for them in college. Dispute about the inferiority or superiority of liberal education in Monteith and the College of Liberal Arts should give way to efforts to find the most appropriate combination of environments for each student. It would seem that differences between Monteith and Liberal Arts should be welcomed on both sides and perhaps complemented by other distinctive undergraduate colleges or programs within the university.

These differences should not be barriers. Since the different approaches each seek education as the ultimate end, faculty exchanges, joint appointments, cooperative courses, etc., can strengthen the programs while retaining the vital differences. Of course, as newness wears away, the separateness based on differences may wear away also.

Acceptance of the value of different choices for the student within Wayne will ultimately demand accommodations in the budget. This will mean that standards of judging appropriate costs and faculty duties will have to emerge, not from direct comparisons and appraisal on a single standard, but from an analysis of what is needed to provide each variety of education its own best form. The most critical question Monteith presents is not whether its particular approach to liberal education is good, but whether a large urban university has the capacity to cherish and nurture to excellence within itself a relatively distinctive and autonomous small college.

The principal author of the profile of Monteith College was Sherrill Cleland, then Dean of Kalamazoo College. Morris Keeton, director of this study and Academic Vice President at Antioch College, was his associate. Paule Verdet, of the Science of Society Division at Monteith, was liaison for the college.

L IBERAL arts colleges have always been aware that they exist to
serve social or religious ends—by training teachers and
preachers for nineteenth-century America; more recently, by
preparing scientists, scholars, businessmen, professionals of all
sorts; by providing, say, vocational training for young women in and
around Boston, as at Simmons, or training for Evangelical missionaries
and laymen, as at Wheaton; by serving Appalachian youth or
urban minorities. But now they are being called on in addition for
the kinds of service that universities have been performing on a
large scale since World War II—advising industry, government, and
other educational institutions, conducting research under contract
from outside sponsors, administering all sorts of institutes, workshops,
foreign study programs. These services, unlike the ones colleges
have been used to performing, are generally the responsibility of
individual members of the faculty or small clusters of them, not
the whole institution. Hence they are almost certain to be disruptive,
sending faculty off campus for days or years and quite possibly
diverting their attention from students and teaching. College deans
must sometimes feel like lion tamers whose big cats are constantly
slinking off the stools and walking away.

But the alternative is isolation. Robert Nisbet,* in a 1966 paper
prepared for the American Council on Education, argues eloquently

* Of The University of California at Riverside.

for a university "in the thick of things." Now his argument can be applied with similar cogency to the liberal arts college.

<table>
<tr><td>**The professor in a new context**</td><td>*The new services asked of colleges are drastically rearranging faculty careers. Ten years ago, the typical member of a college faculty changed institutions once or twice fairly early in his career, worked his way through the ranks writing a few articles or perhaps a book en route, and finally achieved the chairmanship of his department and an influential voice in college politics. He got away from campus for professional meetings once a year and for summer vacations. If he was fortunate, the college financed a sabbatical leave two or three times during his career. He found his stimulation and his satisfaction in students, colleagues, and books.*</td></tr>
</table>

Careers of this cut are still possible, of course, and many faculty choose them. But the options are far wider now. Even in the humanities, faculty can often find support for the research or creative work they want to do. IBM needs the consulting help of logicians and linguists as well as electrical engineers. Faculty are called on to read proposals for government agencies, to work up secondary school curriculums in sociology or economics or psychology, to join geographical expeditions, to assist community planning or action groups. And each link in the network that ties the college to other institutions requires some managing, someone to oversee foreign study centers, to negotiate exchanges with universities or other colleges, to run the regional associations that seem to spring up wherever two or three presidents are gathered together. Almost any qualified member of the faculty who wants to try his hand at administration will have the chance.

This new mobility can be a great gift to the colleges if the off-campus work connects in significant ways with the students, i.e., if students can actually get in on some of the research or if faculty bring back live examples of what they are teaching and a thoroughly current understanding of what is happening elsewhere. Students are most likely to benefit from faculty off-campus interests when the college itself has a clear sense of where it is going, what it is trying to do and for whom. For example, Earlham's commitment to Japanese studies has attracted faculty interested in Japanese language, philosophy, art, music, history, and politics and has stirred those interests in faculty already at the college. A total of thirteen members of the faculty have studied in Japan or have done sufficient research to introduce Japanese materials into their teaching, and four native Japanese faculty are usually in residence in Earlham. This concentration of off-campus effort means that students are drawn into Far Eastern studies, or at least are made aware of the Far East, as they are at few other colleges. Instead of disruptively scattered energy, faculty work abroad becomes part of the curriculum.

It is too early to know what patterns will appear in the careers of college faculty when the wider range of choice is fully felt. In one pattern that is already visible, a member of the faculty will begin as a teacher but then move rather quickly to administrative work, perhaps taking his Ph.D. degree in higher education rather than a conventional discipline. In another pattern, research in a discipline may lead to consulting, planning, and development work, which will sometimes draw the person away from his original discipline into public service or into studies not yet formally recognized as disciplines. In a third pattern, members of the faculty may become increasingly interested in the process of education, devoting time to the planning of curriculums or trying new teaching devices in the schools, conceiving and promoting changes of one sort or another in colleges and universities, or conducting some variety of "institutional research."

Considering the variety of roles open to a teacher and the kinds of choices he will have to make, how should he divide his labor between being a learner himself and teaching others? between generating new knowledge and transmitting it? between designing better teaching arrangements and actually applying those arrangements himself? between direct experience in the nonacademic world and teaching the resulting knowledge? If faculty are to find the combination of jobs that seems to them most productive and rewarding, colleges will need to define assignments more flexibly than in the past—and perhaps to define their own purposes more explicitly, so that it may be clear where these purposes do and do not jibe with individual faculty ambitions. When the two can be made to pull together, students will be in for some extraordinary education.

The professor at work Discussions of faculty talent and its use often begin with talk of numbers of classes, credit hours, and students taught per week and end in pleas for greater numbers of faculty to do the same volume of work. It is true that faculty frequently work long days. Mornings and afternoons go to teaching classes, talking with students, reading papers, discussing college policy in committees and elsewhere, and

performing miscellaneous administrative, clerical, and even
janitorial duties. Reading in preparation for classes often consumes
evenings and weekends. Research or scholarly writing is likely
to come primarily during vacation periods. But neither the welfare
of individual faculty nor the significant survival of liberal arts
colleges is furthered by simply using more faculty for the same work.
Indeed, an elite college that maintains one teacher for every eight
or ten students may plausibly be accused of squandering a scarce
national resource.

The alternative is to make optimum use of this scarce resource,
to equip and support faculty so that their energies go where they
can accomplish most, to encourage the rethinking of course
conceptions, schedules, assignments, meetings with students in hopes
of finding more effective ways of inducing students to learn. Some
examples:

—Faculty at Albion College and Kalamazoo College have found
that they can comment on student papers more fully, more
quickly, and with a more personal note of concern, encouragement, or expectation if they make the comments by way of a
tape recorder. The college makes tape recorders available for
student listening. In a careful experiment at Bard, a time saving
was not realized by professors, but a marked change occurred
in standards for theme correction and in students' perception of
their learning.*

—Judson Jerome, professor of literature at Antioch College, has
taped careful, compact explications des textes to which students
may listen in the library with the text in front of them.

—Faculty who have tape-recorded class discussions and listened
to them afterward have often discovered that they sometimes
misperceive student questions in class and answer what was not
asked. A Dean of Harvard College recently described the use
of taped replays of this sort by Harvard teachers, both graduate
assistants and senior professors. He said that the most persistent
problem encountered by these able scholar-teachers is that of
learning to listen adequately to students—of learning to listen to
what they ask, hear accurately how they perceive what the
teacher has said, catch their sense of the teacher's attitude toward
them as learners, and so on.

* Harold Hodgkinson, William Walter, and Robert Coover, "Bard Corrects
Freshman Themes on Tape," *College and University Bulletin*, vol. 20, no. 10,
Mar. 1, 1968, pp. 2–3.

—Within formal associations and simply among institutions that happen to be close to each other, faculty are sharing students in the less populous subjects—classics, physics, music, non-Western languages—and even standard areas such as art, economics, and French. By transporting students a few miles from campus to campus, colleges can maintain classes of economical size and offer specialized or advanced work that otherwise would be out of the question.

—Professors Joseph Reichard at Oberlin, Aaron Everett at Antioch, and others have experimented with language classes of two or three times normal size. Classes meet as a whole for lectures and films, in individual language laboratory carrels for programmed instruction on tape, and in small groups for conversation led by native speakers or by students who have studied abroad.

—Faculty in such subjects as literature and history have combined large lecture classes with small leaderless discussion groups. They have found that with the right subject matter and the right questions presented for discussion, small groups can function well by themselves, with the instructor and upperclass assistants moving in and out of groups, contributing to discussion but not directing it.

—Large classes may effectively be taught by two faculty who approach the subject matter from different positions, as an intellectual historian and a political historian have done in a DePauw University American history course. While achieving great economy, this arrangement can also provide drama, complexity of viewpoint, and stimulation for faculty participants and students.

—At Oberlin and elsewhere, all students in introductory mathematics courses learn basic techniques of computer programming; physics, chemistry, and mathematics students then use the computer to analyze data in succeeding courses.

—At Monteith, 1966 seniors took two quarters of Senior Colloquium, as the crowning of their general education program. The task was organized this way: Three to six students agreed on a topic they wanted to discuss together and then met for two hours a week, deciding themselves on their readings and the best way to approach their common interest. They selected a member of the faculty to give them assistance if needed and to evaluate their work. At first, this teacher sat in on meetings, sometimes taking over the class, but always influencing the

discussion by his presence. Later he came only when invited—
perhaps once or twice during the quarter, maybe not at all.
—In order to give students firsthand experience with the
materials of their field, the Earlham Sociology Department has
established a "social service laboratory" and a "social action
laboratory" as part of its regular curriculum. These "laboratories"
will allow students academic credit for work with social agencies
or action groups in the Richmond area. Earlham faculty will
help make arrangements, hold regular discussions with students,
and evaluate student work partly on the basis of written reports
and logs.

These attempts to gain effectiveness in learning were largely
initiated by teachers. But these teachers had the good sense to be
concerned about reducing or holding down costs as well as about
accelerating and deepening student learning and increasing the
rewards of teaching. Often teachers assume that we can have one or
the other—efficiency or good teaching, reasonable load or lower
costs per unit of learning—but not both. In these examples, the
teachers were searching for ways to gain both quality in teaching
and a containment of costs. They often found such ways because
they were willing to think in other terms than course units and
contact hours, willing to consider freshly what learning is and how
they might help it occur.

The professor and the machine

Computers, television, tape recorders, and programmed books have
already proved their usefulness; most research shows that students
develop no great fondness for the machines but can learn some
kinds of things from them, in small doses at least, as satisfactorily
as from conventional books or live teachers. Certainly, within a few
decades we will be able to get technically excellent instruction in
almost any subject by way of television, and enormous stores of
information will be on call from computers. Some prophets conclude
from this that students of all ages will sit alone in cubicles learning
electronically. We doubt it. Social interaction will, we believe,
continue to be crucial to education.

Faculty are traditionally inclined to be puritan, believing deeply
that individual persistence and hard work will yield scholarly fruits
in their season. Perhaps the American insistence on the virtue
of self-reliance accounts in part for the almost cultish popularity
of "independent study." In actual fact, however, scholars seldom

work alone. Whether they acknowledge it or not, their brilliance is sparked by a social matrix, by colleagues close at hand or at a distance with whom they exchange ideas, questions, criticism. Laurence Barrett of Kalamazoo College writes:

Learning, even for the adult, is a social act—in many ways the most social of acts. We go to each other for stimulus, for encouragement, for information, and for evaluation; I can see myself making each of these discrete demands upon my fellow professionals in the process, say, of writing a paper on Melville. The professor in a liberal arts college can be defined as a surrogate for all of these, for he too stimulates, encourages, provides information, and evaluates. But his ultimate job is to make himself unnecessary by showing his students how to go to others for each of these functions—by introducing them into the community of scholars, as it were. Curriculum planning, if it is to be aimed at liberal education rather than simply at packing in the proper foundations for graduate work, must be sensitive to the points at which the student is ready to move away from his teacher in each of these discrete relationships, until he becomes truly independent in the sense of being inter-dependent with many people rather than with one.

Television and the computer will certainly change the complexion of learning, as the printing press changed it and as paperback books have changed it in the last twenty years. Memory will become less significant, the solving of problems more significant. Information will be ready at hand if one knows how to ask for it. But students will still need stimulation and encouragement, information and criticism, and until they are further into adulthood, the most satisfactory place to get it will be from their teachers and from other students. Faculty may find themselves performing new jobs or performing the old jobs in new ways, but they are not likely to become any less essential.

Smart fellows and distinguished scholars   *Robert A. Rosenbaum, Provost at Wesleyan University, writes:*

We sometimes receive a recommendation from a senior man at a large university that goes as follows: "Mr. X, who will receive the Ph.D. here next June, is an ideal prospect for a faculty position at Wesleyan." The full recommendation, if it were to be written, might read thus: "Mr. X is not a very smart fellow, and, although we will award him a Ph.D., we don't expect him to do much in his field subsequently. Because he is a pleasant chap, we are reluctant to believe that he is entirely devoid of talent. Perhaps, then, he is a good teacher, in which case, he's just what you should want."*

* "The Graduate School's Responsibility to Undergraduate Colleges," *Ventures,* vol. 4, no. 1, Yale Graduate School, Spring, 1966, p. 26.

College deans, faculty, and students have heard this sort of recommendation so often that it may be necessary to stress the obvious—that liberal arts colleges need "smart fellows" (highly competent teachers and scholars) as much as universities do, that it takes fully as much intelligence, good sense, and imagination to preside over undergraduates' bizarre and gaudy rites of passage as it does to initiate graduate scholars into the guild.

But it is also true that it does not take a "distinguished" faculty—as that term is defined by the academic world at large—to make a distinguished college. Though they must be bright, inventive, and increasingly competent in their specialties, not all college faculty must read papers before learned societies or publish in the quarterlies in order to help their college to distinction. A gestalt principle operates in an effective college, making the whole greater than the sum of its parts, and a college and a man may enhance each other's effectiveness in surprising ways—or prove a constant mutual annoyance and frustration.

Anyone in academic life can think of examples which illustrate this point. At a denominational college, an outspoken or abrupt member of the faculty may be considered disruptive or hard to work with, his opinions automatically discounted as radical or cantankerous. At another school, the same man may appear thoroughly sound, even conservative; he may find himself, perhaps to his own dismay, suddenly becoming a kind of elder statesman, drafting legislation and adjudicating disputes. Or a teacher who at one school is an effective dissident, a leader of the political and intellectual opposition, sought out by students and faculty, may move to another school and in effect disappear, teaching his classes but attracting little notice anywhere on campus. A person with scholarly interests and manner who draws few students and feels somewhat isolated at a small college may, at a young state university, carry great prestige and become a central figure in planning graduate programs or recruiting for his department.

This is not to imply, certainly, that each college must look for only one "right" kind of instructor for it. In a study of "What College Teachers Value in Students,"* Junius Davis found, among some more discouraging things, that of a large group of randomly selected students "it was almost impossible to find one who was not vigorously defended as infinitely desirable by at least one faculty

* Reported in College Board Review, Spring, 1965.

member." This happy situation can occur, one would guess, only when faculty values are quite as various as the students. At Monteith College, the faculty make a virtue of their differences, taking care that the students are introduced to many members of the staff and then are encouraged to work with those faculty who seem most congenial to them.

Perhaps the one ingredient essential to a fruitful matching of teacher and college is mutual respect. If an instructor pines to be at a more renowned institution and takes pleasure in reminding his students at Ball State, say, that they are not writing the kind of papers he was accustomed to read at Amherst, if he is persuaded that his students cannot learn, that they will never be interested in anything he considers valuable, that they are hopelessly conventional or materialistic or dull, it is hard to imagine that he can be of much use to the college. But if mutual respect exists, colleges can benefit from great variety in their faculties, or at least enough variety to keep resilient and self-critical.

Faculty growth All of us talk, quite properly, about student change and development and the impact of an institution on its students. But we sometimes sound as though the rest of the institution were fixed or static—a machine that prodded students or stamped them with a particular brand or a garden plot that supplied intense doses of sunlight and rain to make them grow. In fact, students are part of a human institution in which faculty and administrators also grow or shrink, become more or less authoritarian, tolerant of confusion, or adept at solving problems, become more expert in a discipline or begin to lose touch. Quite possibly, a college could be judged by the extent to which the senior faculty themselves embody the qualities or skills the college hopes to induce in its students.

In addition to the pay, equipment, and surroundings that enable faculty to function well, there are less tangible conditions—conditions affecting the amount of oxygen in the academic atmosphere— that can make the difference between productivity and enjoyment of life, on one hand, and stagnation and disgruntlement, on the other. We find these conditions to be very much like those that promote student development—familiarity and strangeness, freedom and obligation. As the interinstitutional network moves faculty across the country and abroad, strangeness—the stimulation of varied people and ideas—is becoming plentiful. Colleagues are more likely than before to be engaged in research and public affairs, and students are more widely traveled and widely read. All sorts of jobs bid for faculty time. In this situation, it is not easy to be complacent or bored.

But familiarity may be more difficult to find if it means the support of an academic home where the individual is recognized and respected, where he can afford to make mistakes and acknowledge them without jeopardizing his standing with his colleagues. It is obvious that an effective college must have a diversified faculty; nothing could be less interesting than for everybody to like and do the same. But there is a subtle and powerful tendency to establish a pecking order within colleges. The man who is highly verbal is thought a better man than the one who can picture it but not say it, or than the man who can make it but not tell about it. Something similar may happen among faculty involved with different segments of the curriculum—an upper-faculty stratum condescending to those who teach in a general studies program, for example—or among subcolleges within a university. Those of us who were study visitors to Monteith were alarmed at the hostility found between the college and the rest of the university. What entered our interviews initially as difference of opinion about facts and educational philosophies soon turned out to involve suspicion of competence (on both sides), sometimes open attacks upon motivations and integrity, and a clear controversy over the proper character and identity of university faculty. The result of situations like this one can be a displacement of effort to the politics of intrigue, a preoccupation with self-worth, and a general decline of the easy communication that stimulates cooperation, invention, and encouragement in the complex tasks of teaching. Somehow, faculty must recognize that intellectuality has many modes, which should be equally respected and cultivated, and that a one-track prestige system is sure to be deadening. Where mutual regard prevails, men may outdo themselves and show unsuspected creativity and productiveness.

The other pair of conditions that contribute oxygen to academia and keep a faculty lively are the obligation to help run the institution and see that the educational enterprise thrives and the freedom to choose one's own goals and pursue them in a congenial way. On both counts the prognostication is good. Faculty are now consulted on matters of college policy far more thoroughly than in the past, thanks partly to the efforts of the AAUP's Committee

T, partly to theories of management emphasizing the usefulness of decisions that are made not so much by people with places in a hierarchical scheme as by the people with relevant information and those who will have to carry out the decisions. Indeed, consultation is now so elaborate that deans and committeemen must sometimes long for the blissfully dictatorial manner of the college's founder. Chapter 6 deals more fully with college governance and the faculty's part in it; the point here is simply that responsibility for making the institution go can invigorate and hold faculty.

As we have seen, professors' freedom to choose the work they want most to do has expanded enormously. But this freedom cannot simply be conferred from without. A Dean at one of the Great Lakes Colleges Association schools wrote the following words in a paper prepared for the association's Faculty Council:

The year before I became an academic dean, I tried to learn from each faculty member what his own primary professional aspirations were and how he would like to further them in the upcoming year or two. At first I was surprised by the frequency with which faculty members did not know or could not articulate their aspirations. Then I asked myself the same question and compounded my surprise. Our freedom, after all, is a matter of our degree of deliberate self-direction or self-determination. Lacking self-chosen goals or lacking the deliberation that makes them operationally clear, we are not free, even though no external constraints restrict us.

Choosing goals is no easy task. Even when professors vaguely sense what they want, they may be unable to say it precisely or see how to achieve it. Yet if their greatest satisfactions come from their interest in their own particular work, everything depends on their insight in their choice of jobs. For the choice to have insight, faculty must know their own strengths and limitations, respect themselves in both these matters, and find work that will interest and challenge them and give them some continuing sense of accomplishment.

Choosing a college A dozen handbooks direct students to the college that may be "right" for them. But the teacher, even if he has a clear idea of the kind of work he wants to do and the surroundings he would like to do it in, may have little notion where to find that work and those surroundings. Indeed, the elements in an institution's atmosphere combine so subtly that an instructor, even after he has taught at a college for a year or two, may be unable to explain convincingly what holds him there or makes him uneasy and ready to move. Certainly, the differences between institutions are great for faculty as well as for students. Consider Amherst and Monteith. A member of the Amherst faculty enjoys salary, professional prestige, and general affluence comparable to that of the faculty of Harvard or Yale. An assistant professor in a natural science reports that he requested several thousand dollars worth of equipment needed for the research and teaching he wanted to do. His request was approved promptly and matter-of-factly, as though he had been asking for a new typewriter or $100 worth of chemical glassware. The location is exquisite: Faculty houses look out on hills that could make an Iowan weep. Students are as capable and articulate as any in the country, and the college values good teaching—in fact, demands it. An instructor reports that he would call off a class rather than come to it poorly prepared. A large proportion of the faculty are active scholars as well as teachers, and conditions are right for that combination: Teaching loads are as light as in most universities, libraries and research equipment are excellent, and instructors may teach graduate students in cooperation with the University of Massachusetts.

Amherst has everything that faculty conventionally hope for in a college. For a self-confident teacher strongly interested both in teaching and in research or scholarly writing, the place might well be idyllic. But we imagine that many of those who look longingly in Amherst's direction would be disappointed in the college or in themselves if they should be transplanted there. A teacher who is used to being part of a very close community might find the campus somewhat impersonal. People are busy with their own writing, traveling, and preparation of classes. An instructor may find himself further from the students than he expects. Reaction to the 1965 Student-Life Report makes it clear that many students want to keep some distance between themselves and the faculty: they do not want the faculty civilizing them after hours. Even among themselves, students preserve some distance. A visiting professor remarked that students meeting on the walks lower their eyes, like cars passing at night. Certainly the students do not "need" the faculty in the same sense that those at Berea or Morehouse or Ball State do. Though any college will be a different place to different people, our guess is that some teachers would feel, at Amherst, that they were superfluous in the promised land.

Compare the Amherst situation with Monteith. Physically,

*Monteith exists only as a group of offices and common rooms in
three brick houses on Second Avenue in Detroit, on the edge of the
Wayne campus. Its students, like other Wayne students, are largely
from working-class families within commuting distance of the
university—often first-generation Americans. Many of them hold
jobs, even full-time jobs, while they are enrolled. Though Monteith
is in the middle of the city and part of a large university, its most
conspicuous quality for the faculty is probably the closeness and
intensity of its society. In the Science of Society Division, for
example, most of the faculty have come to Monteith via the
University of Chicago and share deep convictions about education—
that it does not simply consist in the transfer of information or
skills from teacher to student, but instead is an encompassing
process of investigation and discovery that observes no formal
boundaries between one discipline and another, between what one
knows and how he acts, between instructor and student. They
believe education should draw instructor and student together into
genuine, often disturbing inquiry that may lead, not to answers,
but to further questions. This view of education, along with mutual
distrust between the college and the rest of the university, has
created at Monteith a tight enclave, an extended family.*

*None of the Monteith faculty is indifferent about what goes on
there. Disagreements among the three divisions are sometimes so
strongly felt that the college faculty simply does not meet as a
whole. This intense involvement with the college does not encourage
scholarly writing, but it does encourage extraordinary rapport with
students. At Monteith, teaching means not just planning and
preparation of classes but work with students individually and in
small groups much of the day. Far more than at most colleges, a
member of the faculty knows what problems are troubling his
students and keeps in close enough touch with them over a period
of years to see their preconceptions being tested and modified,
their competence expanding, their images of themselves and their
careers undergoing metamorphosis. The college asks an instructor to
give himself to an idea, to a group of colleagues, to his students.
It can devour him or fulfill him; it will never permit him to feel
isolated or unnecessary.*

*These sketches are oversimplified, but the point remains: An
instructor who thrives at Monteith might well find Amherst socially
and emotionally rarified. And the happy Amherst teacher would
see Monteith as a kind of perpetual group-dynamics session, leaving*

him no life or work of his own. Other colleges are quite unlike either of these.

Neither a college nor its faculty can be fully aware of what each asks of the other and what each can give. But with luck, mobility, and a modicum of self-knowledge on both sides, it should be possible to staff colleges so that faculty members are doing what seems important to them and doing it in congenial surroundings, and students are getting the respect, instruction, and concern they need.

Given faculty and students who can build a strong college, what are the critical directions that the work on curriculum and instruction should take? It is partly in search of answers to this question that we next draw on the profiles.

GODDARD

COLLEGE

*Despite the gulf between the ideal and the
reality, the existence of Goddard is basically
a philosophical commitment to an educational
ideal which de-emphasizes the importance of
knowledge and of disciplines, as such, in favor
of concentrating on the total development
of the individual.*

G ODDARD College originated as a secondary school established by a group of Universalists in 1863. Today it is a nonsectarian, accredited four-year college. The present-day character of Goddard is a direct result of a reevaluation conducted in 1937–38. Although many persons were involved in this evaluation, William Heard Kilpatrick and, through him, the thinking of John Dewey had a major role in the development of a new orientation. Royce Pitkin, who became President in 1938, has also played a major role in defining the character and philosophy of the institution.

Among the changes resulting from the restudy was a move from the city of Barre, Vermont, to an estate known as Greatwood Farms near Plainfield, Vermont. The institution, which fifteen years ago had only 100 students, is currently developing into a multicampus college; present plans call for three units, each enrolling approximately 250 students. Each unit, as now visualized, will operate in accordance with the general philosophy already developed but with somewhat different program emphases. Certain common facilities, such as the administration offices, business office, and library, will serve all campuses; these are now at Greatwood, but will eventually be centralized. Although the second unit, Northwood, started operations in the fall of 1965, the full implications of this new multicampus development are matters for future examination. In 1965 the total number of full-time students was about 450, with two-thirds of them at Greatwood.

221

The Goddard idea   To regard Goddard either as just another four-year college or as an interrelated group of colleges would be to miss much of the Goddard idea—a year-round effort to help persons of all ages learn what they need to learn. This year-round effort has three facets: (1) the undergraduate program, (2) the adult education program, and (3) a program of services.

The fundamental objective of the undergraduate program is to help students work, think, and live as independent, responsible, constructive, creative, and adult members of an interdependent society.[1] This composite objective means that the students are expected to acquire general information about the world in which they live, knowledge of themselves and of society, and specialized information and training appropriate to their individual needs and purposes. They are expected to develop abilities, attitudes, and habits of responsibility essential for living as responsible members of a cooperative and democratic community, to accept the dignity and necessity of labor, and to be aware of the need for, and learn how to engage in, creative thinking. The four-year bachelor of arts degree is based on the liberal arts as a foundation for sound vocational choice.

The college program itself involves:

1. The relating of subject matter to the changing concerns, problems, and needs of present-day society and its members.

2. Studies in small groups where students and teachers work together, and independent study by individual students working with the assistance and guidance of teachers.

3. Definition of a student's program and his progress in terms of his own purposes. The program is developed in conference with faculty counselors and is revised from time to time as changes are indicated.

4. Use of learning situations in the wider community away from the college, where students must accept and carry adult responsibilities and meet standards of professional performance.

5. Work and study in the United States or abroad during the winter months of January and February, and possible work, study, or travel during the summer months of July and August.

6. Participation in the responsibilities of community government.

7. Participation in the planning, operation, and supervision of the work necessary to the operation of the college. (There is no pay for this work, but fees are adjusted to student resources to the extent that the limited college budget and donations permit.)

8. A college-wide program of research and experimentation.

[1] The Goddard Bulletin, 1964–65, p. 6.

The adult education program includes important conferences for educators. In recent years, for example, the Current Educational Issues Conference has brought together annually nearly one hundred teachers and educational administrators who work on a central problem in modern education; the Conference on Education in the Behavioral Sciences has examined the applications of various findings from researches in human behavior; and the Conference on Psychoanalytic Concepts in Education has considered the use of psychiatric and psychoanalytic insights in increasing the effectiveness of educational programs. During the summer, the Goddard Music and Art Center attracts amateur musicians and artists from all parts of the country.

The Canadian-American Seminar for Management is a short residential adult school for business executives from Canada and the United States. Expert consultants present information and ideas about the economic, social, political, and cultural relationships between the two countries for discussion by the members of the seminar; several days of the sessions are spent in Ottawa and Washington. The aim is better understanding of each country by influential persons in the other.

Goddard College also has an adult degree program which makes it possible for persons who left college without graduating to work toward a Goddard bachelor of arts degree. This program alternates two-week resident seminars, held in February and August, with six-month periods of individually planned independent study. The program is open to persons who have completed at least one year of satisfactory college work, have been out of college for at least five years, and are at least twenty-six years old. Recent enrollment has been well over one hundred.

The services provided to the area by the college help to meet local, state, national, and international needs. They include a Plainfield nursing kindergarten and a northern New England educational resources project; a Vermont community development project was begun, but recently has been relatively inactive. A few students have participated extensively in these projects as parts of their educational or off-campus work experience.

At Goddard, knowledge has value only as it is related to understanding and solving problems. The student learns through engaging in a wide variety of experiences; thus formal distinctions between course work and other types of learning experiences become meaningless. The individual must come to accept the responsibility for understanding and dealing effectively with his own problems and those of society. The college not only must encourage such behavior in the student; it must itself exhibit such behavior. Thus the concern of Goddard College with adult education programs and with services demonstrates acceptance by the administration (and possibly by the faculty) of the values implied in the objectives stated for students.

Ideally, adult and undergraduate programs should frequently interact; students may be included in the conferences, either helping to organize them or attending those which bear upon their studies. Members of the faculty may take part in some of the community service activities. Thus adult education and services are expected to extend the academic life into the larger community and, in the process, provide new dimensions for classroom teaching, learning, and counseling. The adult program also functions as a model, making visible to students the ways in which knowledge and other educational resources can effectively be employed in dealing with the world beyond the campus.

While many of the faculty and students seem to be relatively untouched by these programs, some surveys made by the college indicate that almost all those who graduate have at some time or another engaged in studies or field projects in the programs.

The physical setting Inevitably, the site, the physical plant, and the environment contribute to the forging of any community. The Greatwood Farms estate, in itself a functional though not an especially well-kept campus, is set in lovely Vermont hills. New buildings have been added and old ones remodeled, but a sense of informality and earthiness remains. Whether because of indifference, stringent finances, or commitment to student labor, maintenance is inadequate, and the potential charm of the campus suffers thereby.

Classroom, laboratory, and office furnishings are sparse and worn; some are decrepit. Lighting is makeshift, as exemplified by a fluorescent fixture hung by wires from nails driven into the ceiling beams of a beautifully paneled room. Dirt walkways provide a rural air but do not make for clean floors. In the past, student pets freely wandered in and out of classrooms and residence halls; pets are no longer permitted.

Such an environment contributes to informality and perhaps to a sense of a community in which people and ideas are much more important than surroundings. It may also encourage or excuse the untidy, unkempt, and unshaven appearance of many of the students.

Certainly, with the muddy walkways, those who go barefooted in wet weather have a good excuse.

The President's very pleasant office is in a structure that was originally a silo, proving that such facilities can be made attractive as well as functional. Most of the ideas ruminated upon at this rural experimental college appropriately come out of this silo. Perhaps the combination of life and learning for which the college stands is symbolized aptly and jointly by the President in the silo and drama in the Haybarn Theater (unfortunately, "haybarn" is all too descriptive of the inadequacies of the theater). Whether this sort of environment is really essential to the character of the institution and whether it will be retained on the new Northwood campus remains to be determined. The buildings on this new campus are unpretentious and suitable to the terrain, but something of the Greatwood look will certainly have been lost, for the new campus has neither a silo nor a haybarn.

The educational ingredients One searches the Goddard catalog in vain to find courses and departments. Learning at Goddard is expected to occur in relation to a question or problem of concern to the learner; possible problems and questions are discussed under such headings as

1. Human Behavior
2. Societies
3. Cultures and Languages
4. Physical Sciences and Mathematics
5. Biological Sciences
6. The Arts
7. Education and Community
8. American Society
9. English Language Studies

The discussions under these headings promise a variety of learning experiences—group courses, independent studies, field experiences, work experiences, study abroad—and mention a large number of learning aids and resources, among which are included the faculty. Traditional areas of study are suggested by the use of subject-matter terminology, but no program of required fields and sequences of courses is anywhere evident. Instead, individual programs are developed in advisory meetings of students and teachers.

The first-year student usually takes three group courses which are scheduled for large blocks of time, varying from 1-1/2 hours to half a day. Some of these group courses have only two, three, or four enrollees, but a "large" class of thirty to forty-five students is not uncommon. The time block includes seminar meetings, directed activities, individual consultation, and other activities as decided upon by the instructor and students.

The experiences of the first two years are built around broad problems and are expected to encourage self-examination and self-development, as well as to acquaint the students with the available resources for learning and the techniques for using them. Students in the Senior Division, for which the student must apply and present a tentative program, engage in more advanced and specialized work and have greater independence of effort. In the final year, at least half of the student's work is devoted to a project determined through consultation and carried out under supervision of a member of the faculty. As already noted, students are also encouraged to participate in community service projects and attend the various conferences sponsored by the college.

During January and February of each year, the student is required to find an off-campus job. Conceivably, this work experience may be an extension of some on-campus educational experience or a career exploration. More practically, many students need to seek a job with at least modest pay.

For advanced students, relationships between independent study and nonresident work experience may provide great flexibility. While the college takes some responsibility in planning with the student the work experience to be sought and requires some follow-up evaluation, in large measure the student is on his own.

In addition to his studies, the student at Goddard is expected to contribute to community government and to the general community welfare, and to spend 120 hours per semester in helping with the maintenance and operation of the community, through such jobs as working on the kitchen staff, working in the Learning Resources Center, gardening, and operating the PBX. While in themselves such jobs are hardly to be justified in terms of the contributions they can make to a student's academic development, at Goddard, there is another justification: The total individual being the focus of concern, the involvement, cooperation with others, and sense of contribution to community welfare that come from a job, regardless of its content, are considered important.

Students also participate in the government of the community and in the planning and execution of the entertainment and cultural programs of the college. This participation is viewed as an essential part of the program in encouraging maturation of the student, acceptance of responsibility, awareness of the need for cooperation with others, and the development of ability to cooperate effectively. However, Goddard's use of the town meeting, including faculty, students, and administrative officers, although it apparently proved workable with a student group of 100 or fewer, no longer operates effectively with a student body two to three times that size on each of the two campuses.

Goddard College had about one thousand applicants for the fall term, 1965. The intent is to admit students who understand the unusual ways of the college and who have sufficient independence and maturity to profit from them. However, the freedom from traditional procedures is apparently no more an element of attraction to students than the small size of the institution, the close relationships between students and teachers, and the location.

The great majority of the students are from public schools rather than private, but the number from private schools has been increasing. Most of the students are drawn from a fairly high socioeconomic level, although approximately 45 percent receive financial aid, ranging from $100 to $1,900 in tuition adjustment or from $100 to $1,000 in loans. Goddard students come mainly from New England, New York, and Pennsylvania, but a few come from other sections of the country, and a few from abroad.

Freshman men have somewhat higher scores on the Scholastic Aptitude Test than freshman women, on both the verbal (median for men 573, for women 554) and the mathematics sections (median for men 510, for women 477). Something about the type of students attracted to Goddard is indicated by the fact that the median mathematics score for men is well below the median verbal score.

The college is sufficiently distinctive to ensure that any prospective teacher who seeks a job there does so because of what Goddard offers and perhaps because he has been dissatisfied with the other colleges or universities he has previously known. Certainly the catalog and other materials make it clear that Goddard is not an institution demanding research or satisfied with teaching that is largely confined to lectures or discussions covering content. The narrow-discipline, content-oriented teacher is not sought, and he would be most unhappy at Goddard should he get there. The relatively low turnover among the faculty indicates effective selection, whether natural or otherwise. From 1963 to 1966, faculty size increased from thirty-nine to fifty-seven; in the same period, loss of faculty was only two, three, or four persons a year.

The 1964–1965 Goddard catalog listed forty-seven persons on the faculty and administrative staff. Of these, thirteen had the doctor's degree, twenty the master's degree, and eleven the baccalaureate, and three were without degrees. Many of those with a master's degree had had years of additional study, and some have since acquired or will ultimately acquire the doctorate. Thirteen of the faculty had degrees—or at least significant study—in foreign universities, and another five had foreign job experience. This is not uncommon in colleges and universities on the Eastern seaboard, but it says something for the character of a college located near a small Vermont town that it either seeks out or attracts individuals with foreign experience or education in their background. Another interesting and significant fact about the Goddard faculty is that many members—thirty out of forty-nine in 1964–65—have had vocational experience in the nonacademic world.

It is perfectly obvious that to remain at Goddard, a member of the faculty must like students and enjoy interacting with them. The enrollment in the group courses depends largely upon the extent to which the instructor can attract students, for there are no requirements, and students feel free to withdraw from, or walk out of, a course at any time if they find it boring. (The college could well take boredom as a sign of poor teaching and attempt to correct it.) At Goddard, clearly, the faculty are expected to listen to students. "However incomplete, however fumbling" a statement made by a student may be, it expresses "his own needs, questions, unsurenesses, and attempts to make sense out of his life." Students are more important than subject matter. Community problems also are more important than subject matter. Hence the teacher at Goddard must be interested in students and in problems; subject-matter competence is not enough. Regardless of his field, a member of the Goddard faculty must be something of a psychologist—and something of a sociologist and political scientist as well.

Plainfield is removed by its rural setting from the major centers of learning and culture. While such places as Boston and Montreal are accessible by car, they are not immediately available for stimulation. Thus the teacher who goes to Goddard has turned off from the main highways of life and has, in effect, accepted Goddard as the better alternative. Some of the Goddard faculty could perhaps successfully compete on any university faculty, but most, if not all, would be misfits in such a milieu because of their broad interdisciplinary approach and their lack of competitive drive. For the person who wishes to read, to talk, to work closely with students, and to contemplate, Goddard is a good place. Most of the faculty seem to find it so.

With the development of two (soon to be three) campuses, the administrative structure of the college is undergoing some change. Mere examination of this structure as presented in the catalog raises some questions; discussions with the administrators raise more. In a small institution with informal relationships and easy exchange on a first-name basis among not only the administrative officers themselves but the students and the faculty, it is perhaps unnecessary to draw organization charts and develop clear lines of authority and responsibility. The role of the President is central; in addition, each campus will have a Dean charged with the responsibility for its operation. The college also has a provost (who is a business officer), a director of educational experimentation, and a coordinator of evaluation. Administrative titles generally suggest a confusing overlap, although the areas of responsibility seem adequately distinguishable to the individuals concerned.

Certain names recur in the administrative roster. Undoubtedly the presence of family combinations, particularly at the administrative level, gives rise to a central influence group which, despite all the extensive signs of democracy, may considerably dominate the development of the institution. Some newer members of the faculty appear to suspect and resent this.

Rules and restraints are held to a minimum. Goddard has no grades; formal regulations, including curricular requirements, are few. In a sense, of course, this very absence of specific rules constitutes a severe set of restraints, as is evidenced by the difficulties that many students have in adjusting to such a situation. Some simply cannot do so.

The ideal and the reality Much is made at Goddard College of the fact that it is an experimental program, which is under continuing evaluation. The term "experimental" is, of course, widely misused in talking about innovations in education. Seldom indeed is any program "experimental" in the sense that it can be meaningfully compared and contrasted with other, traditional programs. Furthermore, any innovation of any depth usually is accompanied by a commitment and even a missionary zeal that views evaluation only as a means of demonstrating how good the program is—or, at best, as a means of checking up on parts, or on interrelationships of parts, of the program. In a program which is truly unique and idealistic, a defensiveness is all too liable to develop which causes evaluation to be viewed as an intrusion and an unwarranted expression of skepticism.

Something of this is evident at Goddard. Even so, evaluation—

both unsystematic and highly subjective, on the one hand, and systematic and as objective as possible, on the other hand—is an essential and ever-present element in the Goddard approach.

Goddard has developed a pattern of education which is definitely apart from the mainstream of American higher education and which therefore requires for its success both a type of student and a type of teacher that are not easily found. Neither the secondary schools which turn out the prospective students nor the universities which turn out the prospective teachers are concerned with cultivating the characteristics and aspirations essential to the Goddard ideal.

The cost of a year's education at Goddard, including board and tuition, is $3,100 (1965–1966). As already noted, some 45 percent of the students receive aid, but the majority come from a fairly high socioeconomic level. Goddard cannot cater simply to those students who most desire to have its particular type of program, but must select from among its prospects those who are also capable of paying the fees—a respect in which the institution is not atypical. However, its program is so very different from the program of most colleges that it is doubtful whether, even with all the materials provided, the freshman coming to Goddard has much idea of what he has selected other than a small college.

For example, he finds that rules and restraints are held to a minimum. Goddard has never had grades; formal regulations, including curricular requirements, are few. In a sense, of course, this very absence of specific rules constitutes a severe set of restraints, as is evidenced by the difficulties that many students have in adjusting to such a situation. Some simply cannot do so. One member of the faculty characterized Goddard as a natural-selection process weeding out those who are incapable of self-direction and self-discipline and retaining those who are truly independent.

(It would be unfair to leave the impression that rules are avoided entirely. If one may judge from limited observation, the few rules that exist are lamely enforced, and then only when viewed as necessary to the preservation of Goddard ideals. Thus students *must* seek a job during the two-month winter interim. Attendance in group courses is to be checked and reported, including, specifically and curiously, the last class.)

With transfer students, coming to Goddard is another story. These students have had experiences unsatisfactory either to themselves or to the institution they attended or both, and they are seeking something different. For many of these students, the freedom at Goddard is a positive attraction. Approximately one-third of the students are transfers from other colleges, and somewhat fewer than half the students who enter as freshmen remain to graduate, a figure which accords roughly with the national statistics.

Yet the complete success of a program at an institution like Goddard depends on finding students who will remain at the institution for the full four years, for in a program which is a sequentially organized, cumulative, integrated experience, students who drop out after a year or two or transfer in after a year or two cannot realize the full benefits. Furthermore, this inflow and outflow of students inevitably disturbs the educational climate and the interrelationships among those students who stay the entire period. Relatively few students receive the full educational impact that was originally intended. In recognition of this, Goddard does insist that transfers, regardless of prior years of study, put in one semester at Goddard before admission to the Senior Division.

The Goddard program is strongest in the humanities and the social sciences; whatever the quality of instruction in mathematics and science may be, it is largely elementary. The usual range of courses, the equipment, and the staff necessary for a strong science program are clearly lacking. The deficiencies, in turn, mean that relatively few students interested in science and mathematics are attracted to the institution, so that the character of the student body is biased in the direction of the humanities and social sciences. Furthermore, since going to Goddard involves in some sense a withdrawal from the larger society to one which is smaller and widely different from what can be found elsewhere, introspection characterizes much of the thinking there.

It is inevitable that a college of this kind will attract a certain number of misfits. Some are persons who wish to go to an expensive, elite institution but, incapable of qualifying for other institutions, end up at Goddard. Others have been irritated by lockstep experiences elsewhere but are incapable of responding with appropriate responsibility to the freedom Goddard offers. A few students take the unusual freedom as license; others take it as an opportunity to sink back into lethargy.

In discussion, students do not appear to be highly concerned about national and international issues, nor do they exhibit an interest in precise expression or exact knowledge. What seems to be the pervasive student concern at Goddard is the personal impact of each event or experience, without much sensing or caring about the significance of that event or experience in the lives of others or in the history of humankind generally. Every issue becomes quickly a personal and/or philosophical issue, and too often is grappled with at a relatively naïve level.

Both students and faculty have been attracted to Goddard by the small size of the institution. Indeed, one of the common complaints at this stage is that Goddard is becoming so large that people are losing contact with one another.[2] A three-campus pattern will inevitably strain further the enlarged family type of experience which earlier students, faculty, and administrators at Goddard seem to have prized so much. The new faculty that have been added to the staff at a fairly rapid rate in recent years have tended to question the basic preconceptions of the college. There are pressures toward a more traditional or conventional approach to education. Even now, some older members of the faculty transferring to the new campus are delighted to break away from what they see as a tendency on the original campus toward departmentalization.

Yet increased size can bring increased resources and facilities not readily supplied to a very small institution. It can also offer more choices in associations among students, in major interests, and in cultural experiences. Whether what is lost by increase in size is as important educationally as some things that may be gained by it is difficult to assess.

Regarding rules, the fact that the New England town-meeting pattern becomes increasingly ineffective as the college grows larger poses problems in developing acceptable norms and policies governing behavior. More rules seem to become necessary, but if students are to develop personal responsibility, why should rules be imposed upon them? So it appears to the students; in a recent episode, for example, students demanded unrestricted (twenty-four-hour) intervisitation between men and women in residence halls. In response, faculty and administrative officers point to the necessity of developing some kinds of statements of acceptable behavior patterns if the educational character of the institution and the mutually beneficial character of the college community are to be preserved. The clearer and more rigorous the educational outcomes required, the more likely that some specific procedures for ensuring these outcomes will need to be spelled out. The larger the group, the greater the need for spelling out acceptable behavior. However, a contrary ten-

[2] The size during the spring semester of 1966 was 298 at Greatwood, 131 at Northwood, 18 part-time students, and 120 in the adult degree program. The college thus had 429 students on campus, or 567 students counting everyone enrolled.

dency is also at work; each campus insists on the right to make its own rules.

Evaluation of student achievement Who is to be the final judge of whether a student is making satisfactory progress or has attained a level of development warranting the bachelor's degree? Goddard puts great emphasis on student self-evaluation; thus it may be difficult to demonstrate to a student that despite his own satisfaction with his progress, his achievements are inadequate.

Several factors are at work to encourage or even force a student to accept some responsibility for his contributions to group courses and to maintain acceptable standards of achievement. The small classes do not permit an individual to "goof off" without detection by the instructor. Fellow students, too, can and do register displeasure. Confrontations between instructor and student concerning group courses or independent study provide another setting in which the student's weaknesses may be frankly faced. The Junior and Senior Division Committees review the performance of each student each semester, and the student whose work is inadequate may be warned or dismissed. He may also be required to spend an additional semester, although he never repeats one.

These factors probably have more to do with keeping up standards of performance than does the central record file which has replaced the grades discarded at Goddard—but this file is not unimportant. In it are accumulated the regular self-evaluation reports of the student, instructor reactions to these, work-experience-evaluation reports, papers, correspondence, and almost everything else on paper that has to do with the student's experience while at Goddard College. For making a judgment on a student's tenure or for writing a letter of appraisal about a graduate, these records are indispensable. These confidential records also provide unusually detailed information for the researcher who desires to study what has happened to individual students over a period of time. With appropriate provision for anonymity, the records of a number of recent graduates were examined in some detail.

Student and instructor comments regarding values achieved from courses make interesting reading, for they often focus on personal and developmental considerations which are far afield from the course itself. Thus there is emphasis on improvement in developing ideas and seeing meanings, on sense of personal achievement, on improvement in self-expression. Such comments as "Builds house of many windows" and "Hasn't learned to throw the hay high and let it fall into heaps in her mind" suggest how far from usual considerations of content these evaluations may be. It is difficult to decide from the instructor's comments just how well or how poorly a student has performed. Several instructors frankly admitted that these written evaluations were meaningless and that they themselves would not write highly critical comments for the record, although they never hesitated in communicating critical comments orally to the student. Some members of the faculty have expressed dissatisfaction with these evaluations, but no satisfactory alternative has yet been found.

The central records also include student reports of plans and accomplishments in group study, independent study, and work experiences. In one unusual but not altogether atypical case, a student proposed to examine mathematics in the cultural setting by reading about mathematics in music and studying chess, among other experiences. The study led, according to the student, to a perception of the relationship of mathematics to economics, philosophy, religion, and painting. Suspicion of superficiality is hard to avoid when such a report is examined, although the end result may have been no worse than some general education survey courses offered in other colleges.

In practice, at Goddard as elsewhere, independent study may not be as independent as one is led to believe. Although the catalog says students meet with study advisers infrequently, examination of records showed that some students met with advisers once a week or more often. Others apparently suffer from a lack of guidance. Students frequently planned overly comprehensive studies and then modified their plans in order to reduce the work load. Sometimes objectives were completely revised. One student commented on this in an interview by saying that a common way to get out of writing a planned paper when time got tight was to submit an annotated bibliography. It is a bit surprising, though perhaps defensible, to find a student receiving credit for a student leadership activity and also performing a critical examination of his role as independent study. Although the student seemed to have carried on the activity pretty much as he would have otherwise, he received recognition for two independent study projects. But despite these negative or doubtful aspects—or perhaps even, in part, because of them—most students do seem to develop some capability for independent study.

The off-campus work experience—at least to an outsider more

accustomed to an Antioch College pattern of work and study—leaves something to be desired. The seven-week period is ordinarily too short for a really worthwhile job experience. Some students prevail on friends and relatives to provide a task which meets the requirement, whether income-producing or not. Some jobs that are reported, such as assisting father's secretary or working in a relative's home, sound a little artificial. One student, in contrast, had a succession of highly significant experiences closely related to his educational goals. Most were somewhere in between. The majority of a group of twenty-seven students who responded to a questionnaire reported having found paid full-time jobs. Faculty, however, do not appear especially interested in this phase of the student's experience: Some reported semiseriously that to them, the most significant element of this seven-week period was the freedom from interruption by students! Although students gripe about the difficulty of finding worthwhile jobs with reasonable pay, they seem generally to favor the off-campus work program as an opportunity to break away from the rigors of academic life and exercise complete independence. Greater assistance by the college in locating suitable jobs would materially improve this facet of the student experience.

The students have difficulty in seeing on-campus work assignments—dishwashing, sweeping floors, campus cleanup and the like—as "a worthwhile educational experience," although some apparently enjoy the activities as a break in the routine of study, and some report acquiring new attitudes and useful skills. One recurring student gripe is that some students shirk responsibility, thus increasing the burden of the conscientious. An appropriate retort in the spirit of Goddard is that "this is life." Clearly, the appearance of the campus does suffer from the dependence on student labor, and one may wonder if it does not to some extent confirm students in, or habituate them to, disorder.

Goddard places great emphasis on the maturation of the individual. A study of student development made by the college suggests that a group of Goddard students, as appraised by the faculty, did increase in "goal directedness, personal stability and integration, venturing, resourcefulness and organization, full involvement, motivation and persistence, and interdependence." Such development is consistent with Goddard goals and indicates that the student experiences have had, at least in some measure, the desired effects.

Mean scores of Goddard students on the Graduate Record Area Tests show successive and significant increases in social science, humanities, and physical science achievement. On the basis of national senior norms, the performance from the freshman to the senior year improved from roughly the 50th to the 70th percentile. In science, the improvement was from approximately the 45th to the 60th percentile. Recent senior means are higher than those attained earlier.

The papers produced by Goddard seniors demonstrate that these students have learned to express themselves, to use library and other resources, and generally to carry out and report on a program of independent study. One other indication of the quality of education received is that approximately one-half of Goddard graduates go on to graduate study. Thus such evidence as is available indicates that the academic progress of Goddard students is at least as great as that occurring in many other colleges. Academic progress has not been stultified by the attention given to total personal development.

The relevance of Goddard

Goddard is a notable experiment. It certainly has been blessed with unusual leadership and vision. It appears to provide for some students a highly significant educational experience, and it certainly constitutes a haven for a certain type of teacher who is interested in broad reading and discussion and in working with young people in patterns not acceptable in most of our colleges and universities in this country. Goddard provides a different kind of education from that of most institutions, and there exist no common symbols or means of evaluating the outcomes of a Goddard education in comparison with the results achieved by more traditional institutions. One can be critical about what happens at Goddard, but to say that an institution fails to some extent in attaining its ideal is not essentially damaging, since most institutions and most people do fail to attain their ideals. The most difficult task is to attempt to appraise Goddard in terms which the institution itself would accept as relevant to what it is trying to accomplish. Although these goals can be and have been stated in reasonably meaningful words, the fact remains that to evaluate the impact on students is a task which neither Goddard nor any other institution has successfully achieved. Despite the gulf, then, between the ideal and the reality at Goddard, the existence of the college is based on a philosophical commitment to an educational ideal which deemphasizes the importance of knowledge and of disciplines as such in favor of concentrating on the total development of the individual. For students interested in the arts, humanities, and social sciences, the program appears to be effective. The program is relatively ineffective in attracting or developing students interested in the sciences.

What lessons can other colleges learn from Goddard? One clearly is that it is hard to find a faculty that can take the broad point of view of higher education required in an instrumentalist-oriented institution such as Goddard. Clearly, faculty can be found that are interested in students and interested in ideas in a nondepartmental way, but many of these faculty are not much interested in off-campus work experiences, community service, and other aspects of the educational program which in the philosophy of the institution are of equal importance. Second, the difficulties Goddard has encountered in recent years as its enrollment has grown suggest that the integrated experience which was originally planned may quickly become almost impossible of achievement beyond the point at which every person—student, teacher, and administrator—can be well-acquainted. Third, some doubts must be registered on just how effective an off-campus work experience can be unless a great deal more time and energy are expended in its planning and supervision than has been possible thus far at Goddard College.

As a fourth consideration, despite every intent to have a wide variety of interrelated educational experiences, it is apparently difficult even in a small institution to have all these planned in an integrated, cumulative way. One starts from the fact that a minority of the students have the full four-year experience. Beyond this, both students and faculty have interests which inevitably emphasize some facets of the program more than others, to the point where integration is neglected.

Fifth, it is clear that this program depends upon dedicated and enthusiastic leadership and on the ability of this leadership to infect at least a majority of the faculty and students with the philosophical point of view to which the institution is committed. It seems quite likely that the character of the institution may be markedly altered by change in leadership, by increase in size beyond some critical point at which all can be infected with the Goddard point of view, or possibly even by a crystallization of the point of view in a way that caricatures the former ideal, preserving the appearance without preserving the spirit.

Sixth, perhaps one of the most interesting departures from standard practice at Goddard is the attempt to develop several campuses in the same pattern with some common resources. Some of our large universities, with enrollments reaching to twenty thousand and thirty thousand, have been starting at the other end of the scale to develop small experimental liberal arts colleges on their campuses in an attempt to bring back to the university, at least for some of the students, an approximation of the small-college experience. At Goddard, we have a small college deliberately proliferating itself in an attempt to extend to a larger number of students an unusual pattern of small-college experience and achieve something of the advantages and economies of a slightly larger enterprise. The experiences of both, starting from these opposite extremes, should be worth studying. It will be of particular interest to observe what may happen at Goddard as it expands, for many liberal arts colleges with enrollments from eight hundred to two thousand have already found that some of the prized advantages of the small liberal arts college have somehow been lost. Thus the expansion at Goddard may have much long-run exemplary significance for American higher education. As for Goddard itself, in undertaking this development, the college demonstrates conclusively that it does retain its innovative character; for it is quite possible that expansion will greatly modify the original Goddard ideal.

Paul L. Dressel, Assistant Provost and director of institutional research at Michigan State University, bore the chief responsibility for the profile of Goddard College. Associated with him was W. Boyd Alexander, Emeritus Vice President and Dean of the Faculty at Antioch College; George Beecher, director of educational experimentation, was Goddard's representative. The two student observers were Carol Dressel of Michigan State University and Barbara Tuttle of Antioch.

RIPON
COLLEGE

The faculty at Ripon emphasize solid, certified academic achievement for themselves and for their students. Students generally consider it their business to learn what the professor has to teach them, not to debate or to introduce new information or new lines of argument into the discussion.

R IPON is a Wisconsin community of six thousand, located about 80 miles northwest of Milwaukee and 160 miles from Chicago. It came into being in 1844 as Ceresco (after the goddess of the harvest), a Fourierist settlement. This effort at social reform in the Fourier fashion broke up in 1850, and Ceresco was superseded by the municipality of Ripon.

Experiment with forms of human association did not end with the collapse of the Fourier community: In 1854, Ripon gave birth to the Republican party (a claim not exclusive to Ripon). The town has thus had an interesting past as the scene of events of some consequence in the drama of history. At present, it is a quiet town in an agricultural setting, with a modest industrial development.

Conservatism   Unlike the town, Ripon College, founded in 1862, has never been experimental; with the exception of Wheaton, it has probably been the most consistently conservative of the colleges described in this volume. Its conservatism appears first in the faculty's emphasis on solid, certified academic achievement for themselves and for their students. Sixty-five percent of the regular full-time faculty (exclusive of those in military science) have earned doctorates, and for the most part at excellent graduate schools. The college was granted a Phi Beta Kappa chapter in 1952, and points to this as "the highest formal accreditation a college or university can receive." Students are able

243

academically. The median score of the freshman class on the verbal section of the Scholastic Aptitude Test has risen from 446 in 1956 to 474 in 1958 to 544 in 1965; the median scores on the mathematical section for the same years were 484, 505, and 571. In 1957–58, 40 percent of the freshmen were graduated in the top quarter of their high school classes. By 1965, this percentage had risen to 55. And both the students and their instructors are likely to measure their growth in college largely in terms of grades or progress toward graduate school. In the last five years, 43 percent of the graduating classes have gone on to graduate or professional schools.

The distribution of Ripon students among major fields is unusual and appears to reflect, not an academic, but a social and political conservatism. By far the most important major is economics: From 1960 to 1965, 118 students of the total of 635 were graduated with majors in that department. The second most popular discipline is history, with 89 student majors during the same five years. Next are biology with 60 majors, mathematics with 51, psychology with 43, and chemistry with 41. English, which in many colleges is the most heavily populated major, ranks seventh at Ripon. Political science has graduated only 3 or 4 majors a year.

Data collected on the Educational Testing Service's College Student Questionnaire from a sample of 110 freshmen who entered in the fall of 1965 suggest that Ripon's own influence tends to move students toward careers in business and the academic disciplines. Of the students reporting that they intended to go on to graduate or professional school, the largest groups at the beginning of the year were those looking toward law (18 percent), education (13 percent), and medicine (12 percent). By the end of the year, these percentages had shrunk to 12, 10, and 7 percent respectively, while the number naming business had risen from 9 to 20 percent, and the number naming graduate work in a discipline had risen from 26 to 34 percent.

In the classroom, students generally consider it their business to learn what the professor has to teach them, not to debate or to introduce new information or new lines of argument into the discussion.

The Ripon curriculum has resisted change. The college has never added a Department of Sociology, feeling it wiser policy to strengthen existing departments than to divert resources to a study the academic credentials of which may still be suspect. In 1965–66, the faculty did vote to adopt a new format for the curriculum—a "four-four" plan whereby students take just four courses at a time, each one carrying four hours of credit. This plan encourages greater depth in the study of each subject and requires some reorganization of course content. But the new format was adopted only after months of heated discussion (faculty meetings often lasting from four o'clock in the afternoon until ten in the evening with a break for dinner), discussion so intense at times as to generate bitter controversy and disrupt faculty relationships of long standing.[1]

In 1965–66, the college required all men to take two years of military science (ROTC). When the four-four curriculum went into effect, this requirement was reduced to one year. Apparently students have objected to the ROTC requirement, but the objection has been neither widespread nor based on a fundamental distrust of a military unit on campus. A student columnist in the Ripon newspaper, *College Days,* wrote in April, 1966:

Ripon is called a liberal arts college for a very good reason. In our four
years here, we are supposedly to take courses which will introduce us to all
available fields. Unfortunately for some, this entails requirements to force
the students to expose themselves to what is offered. The science major who
rebels against taking philosophy or music and the drama major who rebels
against taking military science are at the wrong college. . . . No area of
our liberal arts education can be minimized, especially military science. Unfortunately, "The arts of free men" must include that of defense and we would
be foolish, indeed, to ignore this.

In their social and political behavior, too, students are conservative. Twice a week students dress up for dinner, and in between they generally keep themselves clean and combed. Clothing stores, jewelers, cleaners, and florists advertise regularly in the student newspaper. Women's dormitory hours are enforced, and visiting between men and women in their rooms is not permitted except on special occasions. In a straw vote taken at the time of the 1964 presidential election, the students gave Barry Goldwater a slight margin over Lyndon Johnson.

Under the headline *"We Shall Overcome* Just Not Our Song," *College Days* reported the results of a 100-student poll it had conducted in College Commons during lunch hour. To the question, "In your opinion, does the Northern college student have an obligation to participate in Southern civil rights protests and demonstrations?" 88 percent answered "No," 8 percent "Yes." Closer to home, the questionnaire asked, "If you had learned that Negroes were being denied their civil rights in your own state, would you

---

[1] A study of the faculty-meeting minutes of this period suggests that the major issues were more procedural and political than substantive. Were department interests adequately represented? Were departments losing their share of required student time?

participate in an organized protest?" Sixty-four percent said "No," 20 percent "Yes." But 56 percent said they would sign a petition of protest to their governor. Only 28 percent resolutely declined to do anything.

Causes? The sources of this conservatism and the mechanisms by which it is perpetuated are less clear than one might suppose. There is nothing comparable to Wheaton's doctrinal stand ensuring that Ripon will continue to draw students and faculty who hold certain beliefs in common. People on campus have offered a number of explanations for the college's prevailing ethos, none of which seems altogether satisfactory by itself.

The location, it has been suggested, may have something to do with the college's tone. Although one can get to Milwaukee or Chicago in a few hours, the activity of both students and faculty is centered mostly within the Ripon community, town and college. Certainly they do not feel the immediate press of urban problems or social movements as people at Morehouse do. As a countermeasure, however, the college takes steps to be sure it does not become isolated: A guest professor program brings to the campus each year ten outstanding scholars and artists, who usually spend a week there teaching classes. The External Affairs Commission of the Student Senate annually sponsors a series of lectures. In 1965–66 the topic was DeGaulle and France; in 1964–65 the lectures were on Vietnam; the year before that, Norman Thomas, Russell Kirk, Clarence Manion, and others lectured on political philosophy. Furthermore, it is easy to think of colleges quite different from Ripon in tone that are at least as remote from urban centers: Goddard, students say, can be reached only by dogsled during four months of the year.

A more likely source of campus ethos is the background of the students themselves. As the Ripon Dean of Men has speculated:

Many students come from very nice suburbs and derive their values from these. The attitudes that these people pick up—compulsive, aggressive, striving, country club sophistications—a certain kind of house, a certain kind of status—come from the suburbs. . . . A student will come into my office and say, "I've gone to Hinsdale High School in Chicago and—oh, I'm so tired of all the superficiality. People are such snobs, everybody's trying to get ahead. You have to have a certain kind of car. Oh, I'm so tired of all this." The student comes to Ripon and says this in all honesty. And yet when he makes specific decisions—what he'll study—he's still influenced by the fact that he's lived in Hinsdale for 18 years. . . . A few of the people from middle class suburbs go

into the Peace Corps. So apparently we soften a little bit of this practicality and increase awareness.

Data collected on the College Student Questionnaire from a sample of 110 freshmen as they entered in August, 1965, require one to qualify the suburban stereotype somewhat. Twenty-four percent of this sample came from suburbs of all kinds—a trifle fewer, actually, than the 27 percent of suburban students in the Educational Testing Service's comparison group, made up of students from all kinds of institutions. The largest single group, 27 percent, came from cities of ten thousand to fifty thousand population. The students' parents were reasonably affluent, if the students' reports were accurate: Half the families earned between $10,000 and $20,000 a year; 27 percent earned less than $10,000, and 17 percent earned more than $20,000. Sixty-nine percent of the students came from Protestant homes, 19 percent from Catholic; there was only one Jewish family represented in the sample. There was no Negro family, though there are a few Negroes on campus. Apparently the students' families were generally stable: Only 2 percent of the students reported their parents divorced or separated, and 75 percent saw their fathers as the chief source of child-training authority in the family.

In their attitudes, the students were somewhat less conservative than their parents. Sixty-eight percent of their parents, the students say, were inclined toward the Republican party, but 55 percent of the students described their own political viewpoint as fairly or very liberal. On questions of specific policy they stayed fairly close to the ETS comparison group, sometimes favoring a more liberal position, sometimes a more conservative one. Seventy-seven percent were concerned about the extent of poverty in the United States, and 50 percent believed the government should step up efforts for universal medical care. On the other hand, 72 percent thought labor unions did more harm than good, and 81 percent felt the decision to drop the bomb on Hiroshima was right. A third of them said they probably or definitely planned to join the Peace Corps or VISTA.[2]

What seems to emerge here is a picture of students from fairly well-to-do, fairly conservative backgrounds, but students who come with no one clearly defined or coherent set of attitudes. If there is a distinct flavor to the campus, it must emanate in considerable part from local institutions and permanent members of the community.

[2] By the end of their freshman year, the students' attitudes had altered somewhat, but not consistently in one direction.

Probably the most important institutions within the college are the eight fraternities and five sororities, all but two of them affiliated with national organizations. With one exception (a local fraternity), fraternity groups are assigned quarters in college-owned dormitories and houses—for example, Sigma Alpha Epsilon, Theta Chi, and a group of independents in North Hall; Sigma Chi, Delta Upsilon, and independents in South Hall; all sorority as well as independent women in Johnson and Bartlett halls. All students take their meals in Pickard Commons. About 85 percent of the students belong to Greek organizations, the percentage being slightly higher for women than for men.

In 1965–66, the effect of fraternities on the campus was the subject of a good deal of debate, stimulated particularly by the Ripon newspaper, which took polls, interviewed students, faculty, housemothers, and Deans, and invited editorial comment on all sides of the issue. According to one *College Days* poll, two-thirds of the respondents felt that fraternities and sororities at Ripon College "establish an atmosphere conducive to the personal development of their members"; 25 percent felt they do not establish such an atmosphere, and 9 percent were undecided. This appears to be a rather strong endorsement of the system, especially since 30 percent of those polled were independents. But to another question, "Do you think fraternities and sororities at Ripon College establish an atmosphere conducive to the intellectual development of their members?" Only one-third answered "Yes"; 52 percent said "No," and 15 percent were undecided.

Some students, inside the fraternities as well as outside, argue that the Greek system encourages conformity to a somewhat limited set of expectations—that a student dress well, get acceptable grades, and demonstrate a kind of social "cool." A *College Days* poll asked freshmen women to rank eight factors that might influence their choice of the boy they would most like to go out with. "Social poise" ranked at the top of the list, ahead even of "what I myself think of him." However, the women placed "the fraternity he belongs to" at the bottom of the list.

The fraternities are also often charged with indifference to intellectual, political, or academic issues. The Dean of the College is emphatic on this point:

I'm convinced the fraternities and sororities have a harmful effect on campus. . . . I think they give a lot of lip service to scholarship by having study classes and trophies and so forth, but I don't think they have any particular interest in these things. They're more concerned with parties, the

Watertower [the City of Ripon watertower near the South Woods], and the Spot [a restaurant and beer parlor in town], and this is what they encourage.

A fraternity man replies:

The fact that on Ripon's campus the independents have a higher grade point [than the Greeks] does not suggest any obvious superiority; it rather says that fraternities consider other qualities as desirable as scholarship alone, recognizing the worth of the individual as consisting in more than that single criterion.

Whatever may be the justice of these debates, the fraternities and sororities do certainly create groups, freshmen and upperclassmen together, that become important to many of the people in them. They afford many students a sense of belonging, of having been chosen. They also, to date, have had an essentially conservative influence on the campus.

Some would argue that the extremely conservative political and social views held by Fred O. Pinkham, who completed a ten-year term as President of the College in 1966, have inevitably had much to do with setting the tone of the institution. And yet the President did not identify himself closely with the faculty. He defined his task as providing the funds for increased salaries and general institutional development. He was disappointed that the faculty did not, in his view, respond to this encouragement with imaginative proposals for improving the educational program. The President's role, as he saw it, did not include active leadership in educational matters, at least in the ongoing college program. (He did take the initiative in suggesting some major developments—for example, a junior college branch to be located adjacent to the campus which would emphasize education in the fine arts—but in these as in other matters, the President did not share his thinking with the faculty.)

Politically, the Ripon faculty considers itself more liberal, on the whole, than the student body. Educationally, however, it contributes to the pervasive conservatism. Since Ripon (like many liberal arts colleges) cannot draw faculty because of a religious position or affiliation, a commitment to an unusual educational philosophy, or a link with a minority group or a distinctive region of the country, it is appropriate to ask how it is that the college attracts and holds a well-trained faculty. Salaries are competitive, having increased markedly in the last few years.[3] Teaching loads are generally twelve

3 For 1965–66, a median nine-month salary of $13,300, plus benefits, was reported for the twenty-four professors; $10,550 was reported for the sixteen associate professors, $7,933 for the twenty-six assistant professors, and $6,900 for the fourteen instructors. For all ranks the median was $9,800, the lowest salary being $6,500 and the highest $15,300.

hours. Beyond salaries, what draws these people? Certainly the attraction varies from person to person, but many of the Ripon faculty must welcome the opportunity to teach and carry on scholarly work at their own pace, without feeling a frantic need to get their work into print. Most of them publish essays or articles from time to time and take part in community groups and scholarly organizations; a few of them publish significantly and are widely known and respected in the scholarly world.

In the quietness of their scholarly pursuits and their general avoidance of academic pressures, the Ripon faculty are much like the faculties of other colleges described here (Oberlin and Amherst being striking exceptions). But unlike some of the others, they eschew another kind of turmoil as well, the turmoil that comes from constantly reconsidering the kinds of growth a college ought to be encouraging in its students and periodically trying new devices to stimulate that growth. This sort of experimentation may well be wasteful; surely it is unsettling. With exceptions noted later, the Ripon faculty seem willing to take it for granted that their business is with academic achievement and that that achievement can be adequately measured by grades, Graduate Record Examinations, and admission to graduate school.[4]

The winds of change May a college not pride itself on being thoroughly conservative educationally and socially, on developing its students' moral and intellectual powers within a traditional, tested framework? Is not the worship of change—the conviction that something new must always be happening, the compulsion to be where the action is—a piece of American idolatry that a college can well afford to shun? So it would seem. But either because the American impulse to change is too strong to be resisted or because some elements in the Ripon pattern are genuinely inimical to liberal education, a number of people at the college—administrators, faculty, and especially students—are dissatisfied with things as they are.

It is difficult to tell just how widespread this concern is, but conversations with students and faculty suggest that it is not limited to

---

[4] The Ripon faculty, like many others, has been prolific in producing rewards that are meted out on the basis of grade averages—Phi Beta Kappa, Honors Society, Dean's List, permission to have a car on campus, and graduation in its various gradations of glory from magna cum laude through "department honors" down to "also graduated."

a small minority. According to the aggressive and intentionally provocative *College Days*, students deplore many things: Course work and life outside of class are separate spheres, and issues discussed in class are not carried beyond the classroom door; who was most recently pinned and by whom is a more important topic than Vietnam; bright, alert, imaginative freshmen fall victim to the social pressures for conformity; everyone is bored—there is nothing to do on a date but go to the Spot or the Watertower; "it's not cool" to earn good grades or be concerned with important problems of the day or talk about things intellectual outside of class; there is no challenge at Ripon. These criticisms of the Ripon atmosphere cannot be read as an objective description of what Ripon is like, but they are a fairly sure indication that change is coming. Indeed, considerable change has already occurred.

Campus tone emanates from two sources, the formal instructional program and the "informal curriculum," the activities that go on outside of class. At Ripon, both are changing. In the formal program, the adoption of the four-four plan is a real change. Another is the residential instruction program, in which five groups of about a dozen freshmen take a considerable portion of their classwork in the halls where they live—an attempt to "reduce the artificial barrier between the students' social and academic lives." Beyond this, the greatest innovation comes by way of the Associated Colleges of the Midwest, ten private colleges in Minnesota, Wisconsin, Illinois, and Iowa that have banded together to provide economies and educational opportunities which would be beyond their individual reach. ACM programs include the Wilderness Field Station, which makes possible summer research in biology and geology in the canoe country of far northern Minnesota; the Newberry Library Seminar in the Humanities, which brings together students, faculty, and scholars of international reputation to work for a term or longer in Chicago's Newberry Library; the Argonne Semester, which enables students and faculty to work alongside staff physicists, chemists, and biologists in the Atomic Energy Commission's Argonne National Laboratories; the Urban Semester, in which students live in Chicago, teach as interns in the Chicago public schools, and do seminar work in urban problems; field studies in Central America, providing opportunities for research in a great variety of academic areas; and the cooperative program that sends teachers, graduates, and some students to Cuttington College in Liberia. These activities do not involve large numbers of Ripon students at any one time, but their influence is bound to permeate the campus and may be expected to increase as existing programs are further developed and new ones introduced.

The more significant impulse toward change in campus tone, however, will probably come, not from the formal instructional program, but from the informal curriculum. A striking instance of the way student and faculty energy can be channeled for change is the establishment of the Brand Rex Coffee House (the name comes from telephone-company reels, used for tabletops, manufactured by the Brand Rex Company). The idea of starting a coffee house came out of conversations among students and faculty about the need for a place independent of the college where they could meet for informal intellectual and artistic exchanges, for the free discussion of topics which might be of interest or importance to the college community. The legal entity is a nonprofit corporation headed by a five-man board of directors (all faculty); the actual operation is in the hands of a student committee, which is responsible for upkeep, menu, and program.

During the first semester of its existence, Brand Rex put on plays, folk-singing performances, hootenannies, concert recitals, and forums for the discussion of such questions as "Does the Northern college student have an obligation to participate in the Southern civil rights movement?" "Does Ripon College have a satisfactory intellectual atmosphere?" and "Fraternities and sororities—a real issue?" Attendance at these events has varied from as few as twenty students to ninety for the discussion of fraternities and sororities. So far, the coffee house has not become the preserve of any one group but has provided a locus for all-campus discussion and debate.

The influence of Brand Rex is augmented by the college newspaper, revitalized under vigorous student leadership. At the time of the Brand Rex debate on fraternities, the newspaper ran a special 12-page issue, with 8 pages devoted to interviews, polls, columns, pictures, editorials, cartoons, and reports of panel discussions, all having to do with fraternities and the campus atmosphere. Similarly, the paper has helped to keep the campus in touch with other parts of the world. One issue in September carried long reports from a student who had spent the previous year at the University of Swansea in Wales and a student who had spent the summer studying archeology and digging in England, a political column by a student studying at the Newberry Library, and an analysis of Kenyan politics by a Ripon student from Kenya. Consistently the paper has been a stimulating influence, reporting campus news competently and creating its own news from time to time.

The newspaper, along with the campus radio station, has helped to stir interest in other extraclass programs—the External Affairs Lectures, the Film Classics, the Fine Arts Series, the music recitals, the play productions, and the guest professor program. In the spring of 1966, students on their own initiative produced *Point of Order,* the documentary drama based on the 1954 Army-McCarthy hearings. The campus received it enthusiastically.

Though *College Days* finds "*We Shall Overcome* Just Not Our Song," Ripon has recently become engaged in several programs with civil rights overtones—an Upward Bound program, the Biloxi service project, and the Tougaloo exchange. The Upward Bound program, initiated in the summer of 1965, attempts to identify and help young people with high academic potential who have been deprived of the opportunity to develop their talents. Directed by the College chaplain, the program brought to the campus thirty-two boys, most of them of American Indian descent and about half of them from Menominee County in Wisconsin. Some eighteen Ripon staff members and several students, including a student of mixed Indian and Negro ancestry who transferred to Ripon from Tougaloo, worked with the boys in one capacity or another. The group is expected to return in future summers, accompanied by additional groups.

Each spring since 1962, eight to twenty-five students have contributed a week's work to the Back Bay Mission in Biloxi, Mississippi. This volunteer service has given them an opportunity to see the social problems of the area and to become exposed to Mississippians of varying views and various stations in life. Friendships made during this project have led to an exchange program with Tougaloo College, a predominantly Negro college near Jackson, Mississippi. Beginning in 1964, groups of eight to fifteen Ripon students have spent a week each spring at Tougaloo, and Tougaloo students, in turn, have spent a week at Ripon. A semester exchange between the two institutions, which sends two students each way, was begun in 1965.

A Ripon student's report to the campus paper on the attempt of the integrated group to observe the Mississippi State Legislature in session gives a sense of the impact that the Tougaloo visit must have had on the Northern students:

The eight Ripon students who spent the first week of their Spring Vacation as exchange students at Tougaloo College did not observe the Mississippi State Legislature in session.

This was despite the hour-long effort of Professor James Bowditch [who accompanied the group to Tougaloo] to persuade nine members of the House of Representatives to sign passes for them to be seated in the gallery. All-white groups were seen to be admitted without these passes. . . .

Typical answers by the Representatives to the request were: "I'm too busy." "I've already signed my quota of passes for the day." "I'm new here and don't know the procedure." "I'd like to, but I just can't." . . .

Barred from observing the House, the Ripon students inspected the statue of former Senator Theodore Bilbo, the leading racist of all times, in the Capitol rotunda along with two large portraits of the two Mississippi girls who became Miss Americas in recent years.

What is ahead? In ways such as these, change is coming to Ripon. But what of the future? What sense of direction or purpose will guide change at Ripon in the next decade or two? A formal statement of college purpose reads this way:

Ripon is committed to the philosophy that the liberal arts offer the richest foundation for the intellectual, cultural, and spiritual growth necessary for a happy and productive life. This aim is best attained, Ripon believes, in a small, coeducational, residential institution.

While the statement is explicit on some points—Ripon will offer liberal arts education, as opposed, presumably, to highly technical or strictly vocational training; it will continue to be small, residential, and coeducational—it is not altogether clear on the kinds of students the college hopes to enroll and the kinds of development it hopes to encourage in them. Some members of the faculty regret, rather wistfully, that no person or event in the college's past has managed to stamp it with an unmistakable character.

Within limits, it may be possible to abstract purposes from present practice. Not long ago Ripon served mainly a Wisconsin student body; now it is more generally Midwestern and becoming increasingly national. In 1952–53, nearly 60 percent of the students were from Wisconsin; in 1962–63, one-third; in the fall of 1965, one-quarter. In 1965–66, about a fifth of the students came from the northeastern United States. While the student body has become more diverse geographically, rising tuition has probably made it more homogeneous economically and socially. The Tougaloo exchange is one sign that the college hopes to increase the economic and cultural diversity of the student body, and the faculty and administration have spoken of the need for larger financial-aid funds so that a balance among socioeconomic levels may be preserved or restored. (In fact, the financial-aid budget for freshmen entering in the fall of 1967 was doubled.) How this intention will fare in competition with other aims—for example, the aim of attracting students of high academic achievement—remains to be seen.

Aside from being predominantly Midwestern and coming from families that are somewhat more affluent than average, the Ripon students appear to be very much like the majority of American college students—not very sure of their social and economic convictions, eager to do well but rather pliable, willing to adapt to the situation they find themselves in. What does the college hope will happen to these students while they are at Ripon? Evidently, it would like to see them master the language and the techniques of the traditional disciplines so that they can begin to use these like professionals; it would like to see them have some acquaintance with a variety of fields—physics and history, drama and military science; it would like to see them become part of a rather formal, continuing group of students of their own sex in fraternities, sororities, or dormitory sections. Beyond these purposes (and others subsidiary to them), a fourth purpose seems to be emerging, if Brand Rex, Tougaloo, the newspaper, the ACM Urban Semester are any indication: The college would like to see its students confront difficult issues, worry through them in the crossfire of contradictory opinions, and arrive at some convictions they are willing to defend and to act on.

If this fourth aim becomes more central to the college, the place may be transformed. Students may become more inclined to challenge their instructors, to debate in class; instructors may find themselves preparing somewhat differently for class sessions and being evaluated differently by students. Faculty may give more formal recognition to the questioning, inventive, sometimes mistaken student. The student definition of "cool" may even change, according greater status to concern and commitment and less to social poise.

The adoption of the four-four plan has proved that the faculty, given time, can agree on basic modifications of the curriculum, modifications that entail overhaul of the graduation requirements and reorganization of individual courses. But this crack in tradition's dike does not mean the college will be inundated with curricular change. A decision was reached to add a Department of Anthropology and Sociology, beginning with one faculty member in 1967, and a second in 1968. Other changes will come gradually when faculty are ready to conceive and think them through, and carry them out. (A "Concepts and Methods of Science" course for non-science majors was introduced a few years ago at the urging of the President, who heard of a similar course being offered elsewhere. Neither students nor faculty considered the course successful, and at the end of the 1965–66 academic year it was dropped.) The most promising source of curricular change, or so it would seem to one looking in from the outside, is the Associated Colleges of the Midwest; in fact, awareness of change at other ACM colleges was important in moving Ripon to adopt the four-four plan. Though the faculty have not so far been notably enthusiastic about ACM off-campus programs, they might find it natural to develop at Ripon programs of African studies, Renaissance studies, or studies of urban problems that could connect with the ACM programs in Liberia, at the Newberry Library, or in the Chicago schools.

More rapid change will probably come, as it did in 1965–66, in the informal curriculum. Brand Rex and *College Days* may help to provoke self-examination and social concern in other quarters. Since Ripon has no summer school, the college might broaden its world greatly by helping students to find unusually demanding work or work in unfamiliar surroundings during the summer—service assignments in this country and abroad, jobs in the middle of Washington or New York or Atlanta, work following the fruit harvest up the West Coast. Fraternities themselves might become places where students argue out the issues closest to them and where some movements for social or political action find a nucleus of support.

But none of this is likely to happen automatically. In colleges that do not already have strong traditions of student initiative—and even in colleges that do—sustained and successful student activity requires continuing encouragement, counsel, and sometimes money from the adult community. Brand Rex sprang from student *and faculty* effort; it was the faculty who raised the money and formed the legal corporation. A member of the faculty encouraged the student production of *Point of Order* and acted in it. *College Days* and the radio station both benefit from regular faculty advice. A member of the faculty accompanies the Ripon group to Tougaloo. If the college intends to use the informal curriculum to help educate its students, as it has begun to do, it will need to attract more faculty who find satisfaction in working informally with students, and it will need to write this instruction into its budget.

For its new President, Ripon has chosen the former Dean of Students at Oberlin, Bernard S. Adams. He will find Ripon a different place from Oberlin. But Oberlin's experience may be relevant to Ripon in one way: Oberlin has demonstrated that a college can be *selectively* conservative, fostering a strongly traditional academic program alongside political and social liberalism and vigorous student activism. Ripon cannot and should not imitate Oberlin. But it might well look for the mixture of tradition and change that can best nourish in its particular students the growth that it calls liberal education.

Principal author of the Ripon profile was Norman Burns, executive secretary, North Central Association of Colleges and Secondary Schools, and professor of education, University of Chicago. His associate was Albert B. Stewart, professor of physics at Antioch College; Robert P. Ashley, Dean, served Ripon as liaison. The student observers, both of Berea College, were Nancy Sue Van Zant and Doug Jessee. This description, except for specifically noted later dates, refers to 1965–66.

CHAPTER 5

THE MEANING OF

A COLLEGE EDUCATION

THE most baffling task of our study has been to gain some insight into the curriculums and instructional methods of liberal arts colleges and the ideas that underlie them. We knew from the beginning that at best, these insights would be limited. Our difficulty has been to clear even a few openings in this tangled thicket of theory and practice. In a liberal arts institution, what should a college education mean?

As we have considered the problems encountered by the deans, faculty, and students in the colleges visited during this period, two kinds of need have come to seem most pressing—one a need for further clarity about the concept of a college education, and the other a need for an approach to the management of curriculum and instruction that will more readily implement this concept than present approaches. On the first count, the clarification of concept, we have been forced to wrestle with definitions of liberal education. On the second, an approach to managing enterprises of liberal education, three elements of approach (treated more fully in Chapter 6 and elsewhere) have emerged as offering promise: It would seem advisable to (1) seek educational impact through freer and more autonomous functioning of faculty and students rather than more prescribed curriculums and teaching arrangements, (2) increase the specialization of functions among institutions of *higher education, and (3) view the campus as home base in an educational network of enriched opportunity. To make these considerations concrete, the latter part of this chapter treats four specific curricular problems: the alleged encroachment on liberal arts territory by high school programs and graduate training; the difficulty of reconciling coherence in a curriculum with faculty and student autonomy; the question of a curriculum's "relevance"; and the place of science in a liberal arts college.*

Concept of a college education

During the 1965 meeting of the thirty educators who were to prepare the college profiles in this volume, these inevitable questions arose: "What is a liberal education?" "What criteria will we use to decide whether a college is providing a good liberal education?" At that time we considered some definitions, decided not to take a "creedal position," and warned ourselves against overhastily applying the ideal of liberal education prevalent in one college to the judgment of another college; but we agreed that a laissez faire acceptance of anything and everything called liberal education would be a disservice. During our work, judgment has gradually crystallized, at least among the staff, regarding some of the key elements in a definition of the ideal. At the same time, we have begun to understand why it is so difficult to arrive at a conception of liberal education that everyone will accept. If one looks at definitions of liberal education (in college catalogs, for instance), it becomes clear that they do have half a dozen ideas in common; the phrase "liberal education" does convey definite and discernible meaning. But it also becomes clear that the key terms in these definitions must often be variable terms, properly referring to different specifics when applied in different times and places. Let us illustrate this by looking at some common elements in definitions of liberal education.

First of all, every definition of liberal education that we have seen puts major emphasis on the cultivation of intellect. However, "intellect" is a complex idea, and particular colleges will not put equal weight on each of its component meanings and ramifications. Ripon, for example, is likely to think of the prime intellectual task as the assimilation of ideas developed and refined over centuries of human thought. Monteith and Goddard are more likely to define it as the cultivation of analytic skills and habits or as the ability to make imaginative and powerful syntheses of ideas. Similarly, the intellectual development of students entering college varies widely from group to group and from individual to individual. As long as all gentlemen's sons who were admitted to Oxford had about the same upbringing and school background, differences may have been viewed as unfortunate deviations attributable to negligence or depravity. But today the differences in students' backgrounds and training are painfully apparent, and no college, in good conscience, can simply dismiss the resulting problems as an unlucky result of laziness or bad schooling. If liberal education means development of the intellect, it must acknowledge that intellect will come in many forms and stages of ripeness.

To complicate matters further, the notion of mind—or intellect— is itself culture-bound, even subculture-bound. Our understanding of human intelligence is only beginning to be illuminated by really scientific investigation, and our ideas about how to develop and use the mind are being radically altered by changes in technology and pedagogy. Colleges and researchers are beginning to rediscover that some people have intuitive, imaginative, or manipulative intelligence that cannot be measured by the tests currently in vogue. As colleges find ways to recognize and encourage these less "legitimized" forms of intellection, the substance of liberal education may become more diverse than it is now—without neglect or betrayal of its dedication to reason and the mind.

Second, nearly every definition of liberal education encourages the student to use "independent judgment" or "critical thought." It is immediately clear that these terms will have different content in different settings. Implicitly or explicitly, these critical activities are to be applied not only to questions of what is but also to questions of what ought to be or what is ideal. Even those who think that their ideology or religion already reveals this ideal expect that a liberal education will enable a student to grasp this meaning more accurately than before and to apply it more appropriately. Independent judgment and critical thought are achieved through the student's doubting and examining what is commonly believed among his peers or within his social class or nation. And no matter how sure the founding church or the president and trustees may be about the "true values" one should emerge with at the end of this process, the professors and students find, once they have embarked on it, that a force has been set loose which does not stop with the approved conclusions. Thus liberal education's commitment to independent judgment and critical thought works havoc with any attempt to specify in advance their outcomes in moral conviction.

Moreover, since the judgments to be improved are those of different students from different backgrounds who are doubting different conventions and traditions, the specific subject matter of the inquiry will vary from college to college and person to person. This variance need be confusing only if misconstrued. If one tries to make an exhaustive catalog of the content of liberal education, he faces an infinitely elaborate task. If he applies the finding as a working rule—a guide question—his task is simplified. He asks, "What are the matters, in this setting and with these students, to which critical judgment can best be applied to ensure that the students will acquire a habit of independent and rigorous thinking?"

As a third and closely related point, many definitions of liberal education speak of liberating the individual—permitting him to see the world from other perspectives as well as from those he inherits from his family, his peer groups, his political or religious affiliates, his country. Sometimes this liberation is put in Rousseau-like terms—enabling the youth to "fulfill himself," to "become a man." Former Dean Truman of Columbia University says that liberal education must "release a man's mind from those conditions that make him intellectually and morally servile." This element of definition is clear and meaningful. Yet its terms must vary. The limitations of perspective with which a Ripon student is burdened may be entirely different from those that encumber a Goddard student. And within a given college, the backgrounds of individual students will subject them to extremely varied forms of servility and call for equally varied prescriptions for liberation. Further, the idea of "liberation" or "fulfillment" or "servility" takes on a precise meaning only in a larger moral or intellectual context. One cannot argue from the idea to a single absolute application of it.

A liberal education, fourth, has an integrating function as well as a critical and freeing one. In part, at least, it liberates one from ideas and conditions to which he would otherwise be in bondage by evoking in him an integrated view of the world which can serve him as an inner guide. Often this integration is spoken of as the acquisition of a religious or moral perspective or the finding of meaning in life. As we indicated in Chapter 2, we believe that providing conditions in which this sort of integration can occur is indeed part of a college's job, and these conditions may include the institution's enforcing commitments of its own; ethical neutralism does not strike us as a necessary or admirable institutional stance. Until a student begins to develop a coherent set of attitudes, ideas, and beliefs, he will be at sea emotionally, and he will lack a framework for remembering, comparing, and sorting out information intellectually. Yet none of the profile colleges, not even Wheaton, would or should undertake to impose a single integrating system on individual students. Though a college may make known some of the principles that give its actions coherence, for an individual student this coherence must be integral to his own life, developed largely from within.

In our own view, a college can best assist with this integration in three ways: by acknowledging and defending the assumptions that underlie its own practices, and even by sometimes taking positions on public issues; by providing occasions, in class and out, for students to state positions, defend them, modify them, and restate them without risking ridicule; and by seeing to it that students become more than casually acquainted with the faculty and other students, so that they can perceive and judge for themselves the web of habits, opinions, and ideas that give pattern to another person's thought. This last point deserves special emphasis. The preoccupation with "subjects" in college may have led us to undervalue the role of the individual teacher as exemplar and mentor in the development of a framework in which facts and experiences can become meaningful and useful for the student. One hopes that teachers may themselves illustrate what we wish for in the student—a transplanting of knowledge into a whole life. But even negative examples can be of enormous assistance to students in search of a workable pattern of attitudes and ideas.

A fifth element of a liberal education often follows from the fourth. If a student has an integrated attitude toward himself and the world, he will be better-equipped to serve his society. Whether the means and practices of social service should be part of the curriculum (as the Earlham Sociology Department is now making them) is a matter of much dispute. And certainly people in the profile colleges would not immediately agree on what constitutes social service. Is it teaching? occupational therapy? Evangelism? civil rights activities? competent work in business or industry? campaigning for peace? But even the Hutchinses profess that training of the intellect is preeminently a preparation for public service and citizenship, which are proper ends of liberal education.

We have devoted this space to defining the aims of liberal education, not to haggle over semantics, but to show why we suggest a particular approach to the designing of a curriculum. We are convinced, first, that liberal education cannot be defined as a given set of subjects to be studied or books to be read. Even if the *liberal arts could once be encompassed by the Trivium and the Quadrivium, that day is long dead. But we do not therefore conclude that the terms are useless or meaningless. David Truman puts the matter this way:*

Today we encounter difficulty in listing the liberal arts, and not merely because the quantity of knowledge is so great and its forms so numerous. The difficulty is at least as much that the liberal presumption concerning any set of subjects is so uncertain. . . . Why? I submit that it is because we forget too readily that a liberal education is an experience that is philosophical, in the broadest sense, and that the particular subjects do not so much contain this quality as provide jointly a possible means of approaching it. . . . The liberal arts, then, include those subjects that can most readily be taught so as to produce an understanding of the modes of thought, the grounds of knowledge, and their interrelations, established and to be discovered.*

The manner in which a subject is taught is thus crucial to its functioning as one of the liberal arts.

The approach we suggest would begin simply with a setting aside of all dogmas except commitment to the aims that remain constant in liberal education. The next step would be to take a fresh look at the variables that affect the achievement of those aims at a specific college—the background and intellectual habits of students; the interests and training of the faculty; resources such as money, buildings, and equipment; location; the institution's religious, political, or intellectual traditions; and its social context. With this yarn and dye as its raw materials, a college must weave a course of study that serves its students and bears the college's distinctive shades and patterns.

The profiles and the preceding chapters give glimpses of ways in which a curriculum may reflect the distinctive character of a college and the people in it. Here, we would like to address four curricular problems that have troubled liberal arts colleges in recent years and will very likely continue to do so. We do not pretend to solve the problems, but we can indicate how they could be approached, given our convictions and biases.

Problem: the squeeze *According to Jacques Barzun† and other observers, the traditional territory of the liberal arts college is being threatened from two directions. The secondary schools, on one side, are invading the*

* National Conference on Higher Education of the Association for Higher Education, Mar. 14, 1966.
† In his address at the convocation celebrating the first year of Hofstra's existence as a university, Dec. 11, 1963.

subject matter that used to be the province of the first two years of college, by teaching freshman- or sophomore-level history, composition, foreign languages, literature, and mathematics. At the same time, the preparation for professions invades the college curriculum from above, introducing more and more specialized instruction in high-energy physics, topology, Near Eastern politics, linguistics, and so on. Eventually the two invaders may meet, Barzun argues, leaving no legitimate function for the liberal arts college. Barzun does not approve this development, but he seeks to understand it as the consequence of our society's drives.

If liberal education were a matter of mastering certain set topics, a specified bundle of facts and ideas, then this education might indeed be taken over by secondary schools, leaving post-high school education to the specialists. But if liberal education consists instead in the development of intellectual skills, attitudes, habits of mind, ways of looking at the world and arriving at judgments about it, then it clearly must be part of all education beginning before nursery school and running beyond graduate school. It aims at no set end point.* In the past few years, secondary schools have unquestionably introduced their students to more intricate ideas than before, asked them to read more sophisticated books, invited them to make more complex judgments. But nowhere in our observation of the profile colleges did we sense that the need for college-level liberal education has been lessened by this improvement in the high schools. Knowledge increases at an appalling rate, and social and scientific problems become more tangled and baffling. It seems

* The liberal arts colleges themselves have contributed, we believe, to a misunderstanding of liberal education by seeming to equate it with certain elementary courses, either interdisciplinary general education courses or beginning courses in the various disciplines. As we have indicated, we believe liberal education can occur in fourth-grade arithmetic or in mathematical logic, in the reading of fairy tales or the analysis of *Finnegans Wake*, provided they are taught with at least one eye on the development of widely applicable intellectual skills or the clarification of personal attitudes. As a practical matter, we contend that it is a mistake to encourage or require students to take a great many elementary courses during their freshman and sophomore years. If colleges can spread nonspecialized work over the whole of a student's career, these benefits, we predict, will follow: The college will seize immediately upon the student's enthusiasm for the field of study where his major interest lies instead of asking him to wait until his second or third year to get into the material that especially attracts him; nonspecialized work will be seen as a natural, continuing part of education rather than as a barrier of "requirements" that must be surmounted before one can get to more satisfying studies; and the nonspecialized work, by appearing on the junior and senior level as well as earlier, may be more sophisticated and more rewarding for both students and faculty than the nonmajor work most colleges now offer.

unlikely that the nation can get an adequate supply of men who can deal with those problems with intellectual versatility, incisiveness, and poise—and with a sure sense of the ground they stand on. No institution can guarantee to produce such men, but colleges that make this sort of education their deliberate aim are not likely to lack a job to do. Insofar as high schools suppose that their students are incapable of liberal education and graduate schools suppose that their students need no more of it, the colleges have a mission not only to discover better ways of achieving it but also to evangelize, preaching the need for it throughout all the years of schooling.

Problem: coherence and autonomy If one agrees that liberal education need not be tied to any given body of subject matter—indeed, that its subject matter must vary with the abilities, backgrounds, and interests of students—a college still needs some principle of organization in its curriculum, some pattern to guide a student's studies. A number of colleges have introduced coherence by way of interdisciplinary core courses— required of all students in their first or second year. It is difficult to generalize about the success of this plan. The core course in humanities at Berea draws almost universal praise. But Amherst's experience is perhaps more representative. There, the required subject-matter-oriented core curriculum began to chafe both students and faculty, especially as it came to be taught by faculty who had not been party to formulating it; it has now been replaced by a curriculum that aims to inculcate "habits of rational inquiry," partly through three Problems of Inquiry courses—one in the sciences, one in the social sciences, and one in the humanities—in which the specific content may change from year to year.

Defenders of the core curriculum, at Amherst and elsewhere, argue that it does much to create an intellectual community by giving students a "common intellectual experience." The argument on this point seems to us still unresolved. Is a common intellectual experience essential to the most fruitful out-of-class discussion and to an atmosphere of liberal learning? Do students who take the same courses actually have a common experience? Amherst has reduced the number of required courses and attempted to ensure a shared experience of probing inquiry throughout the general education curriculum. This may well provide the vocabulary for meaningful discourse among students with varied information and interests, possibly producing greater controversy, mutual instruction, and motivation to learn than would a more monolithic program.

The new Amherst curriculum exemplifies what appears to be the current tendency to look to methodology for the thread of coherence in a curriculum. Theodore Schultz, for example, emphasizes methods of analyzing and solving problems and the ability to keep on learning as the most lasting of education's fruits. In order of decreasing obsolescence and increasing durability he lists (1) vocational and job skills; (2) knowledge of principles and theories; (3) ability to solve problems and develop analytic tools; (4) ability to keep on learning. "Fleeting facts memorized for examination, debate, or other special occasion" he does not even bother to list.*

Similarly, a report by Daniel Bell for Columbia University unequivocally embraces methodology as the organizing principle in liberal education. The indispensable element in undergraduate education, according to Bell, is continuous, increasingly sophisticated training in the methods of the natural sciences, the social sciences, and the humanities. The first he characterizes as sequential, proceeding from axioms to theorems, from hypotheses to deducible consequences, and from simpler to more complex ideas. He argues that the social sciences work by means of linkages, the understanding of linked contexts within a social system, and that the humanities use a "concentric" methodology in which one returns again and again for ever-enlarging meanings to a few major themes such as the nature of tragedy and the discovery of self.

Even if one concedes that Bell's analysis, or a more elaborate one, can make sense of the methods of the disciplines, it does not necessarily follow, of course, that sophisticated acquaintance with these methods can be equated with liberal education. Henry David Aiken, for example, objects:

Now a concerted understanding of methods of inquiry, while it may serve for integrating the scholarly activities of the academic man, may still leave him, even as an intellectual being, a complete shambles. . . . What we must return to . . . is the Socratic assumption that an integrated mind, fully awake to its own more ultimate concerns and aware of its own human possibilities, is,

---

* Cited by Theodore O. Yntema in *Education: Some Neglected Opportunities,* University of Chicago, Graduate School of Business, Selected Papers, no. 11, Mar. 20, 1964, p. 2.

While concurring in a general way with Schultz's observation, we are inclined to emphasize a demurrer which he also accepts. With no facts, fleeting though they may be, a student could not appreciate the meaning or utility of principles or develop his analytic skills and habits of learning. If he learns only those facts that are immediately useful, he misses learning how to select relevant information in a complex unsolved problem. If too much time is spent on skills, facts, theories, or principles—in short, on any one of the essentials—the highest priorities in his education may elude him.

at all stages of its educational development, more than an intra-cranial meeting place for the disciplining of disciplines.*

Given adequate teachers and sufficient collaboration among them, however, a college could well mount a superior liberal education program on Bell's framework: If the teachers exemplified in their own thought and action an integration that goes beyond the "disciplining of disciplines," they could help supply the omissions that Aiken identifies.

If conceiving a rational and coherent curriculum is difficult, executing it is much more difficult. Curriculum planners often act as if teachers were—or ought to be—standard interchangeable parts. Some colleges not only offer a Swarthmore curriculum to students a standard deviation and a half away from Swarthmore's students on the aptitude scales but also try to adopt programs that it would take a Harvard faculty to teach, with a faculty lacking two-thirds of the specializations and competences of Harvard's. One can as easily waste money by mistaking the skills, knowledge, and versatility of the faculty as by failing to start with students where they are.

Further, equally competent faculty may teach in strikingly different ways, and their different ways of teaching, though each is effective and appropriate to students, may be far from interchangeable from their own points of view. Good teachers differ on every conceivable variable—their preference for lecture, discussion, or individual conference; the kinds of tasks they like to set for students; the extent of uncertainty they feel comfortable with in subject matter and class procedures; the extent to which they consider it proper to make known their own opinions, experiences, and perplexities; the balance they strike between encouragement and criticism of students; the latitude they allow for expression of emotion or connecting of subject matter to immediate student concerns; their ways of evaluating student performance; and their choice of particular subject matter, even when the boundaries of the subject are conventional, as in American government or seventeenth-century English literature. We have no doubt that faculty teach best when they themselves are intensely interested in their subject, when they are free to devise or adopt an approach congenial to them, and when they feel successful in what they are doing rather

* "The American University," p. 13 of a mimeographed reprint from *The New York Review*, 1966, with permission.

than superfluous or inept or out of place. Faculty are capable of tremendous development if they feel accepted as well as challenged, confident that their best work will not be disparaged or prohibited because it fails to coincide exactly with customary procedures. For the curriculum, this means that whatever rationale gives order to a student's studies, the pattern must be loose enough to allow a teacher to grow toward excellence in his own individual, even idiosyncratic fashion.

In these days when educational change is rapid, any well-conceived curriculum will have openings in it where members of the faculty, or groups of them, may insert offerings that depart in small or large ways from a college's traditional expectations for a "course." The curricular arrangements, of course, will vary. Some colleges may choose to establish an "experimental curriculum" where courses may be offered temporarily without the imprimatur of catalog listing and the formal endorsement of the faculty; other colleges may simply see to it that the catalog shows a liberal sprinkling of "problems" or "seminar" courses that can accommodate unusual instruction of nonspecialized students as well as upperclass majors; still others may set aside a sizable portion of the curriculum—the whole freshman year, a senior quarter, a winter intersession each year—for instruction that differs from the usual course pattern.

Whatever the arrangement, there should be room for faculty to offer studies that depend primarily on field work even for beginning students, studies in which students define their own aims and come to the faculty for guidance and evaluation, studies that cross disciplines in odd ways—seventeenth-century science and literature; the social geography of three Indiana counties; the idea of mind considered from the point of view of physiology, psychology, philosophy, and computer science; game theory and the dynamics of conflict resolution. It is highly unlikely that whole college faculties will find a single kind of educational experiment congenial and manageable. But every college will do well to develop an atmosphere that encourages groups of faculty, after an appropriate show of reasons and plans, to try out new means of instruction. "An appropriate show of reasons and plans" need not make the whole faculty feel they would like to teach in this new way; it need only show that the proposers have formulated their aims with reasonable clarity and have foreseen and taken account of difficulties that may arise. The professional competence of the proposers should be viewed as settled, just as would be that of any member of the faculty with continuing appointment conventionally performing his academic tasks. With the respect and encouragement of their colleagues, faculty experimenters can put their own imagination and enthusiasm to work for educational ends and can extend rather dramatically the whole faculty's awareness of instructional practices that might complement or replace traditional ones.

Problem: relevance The air is filled, these days, with charges that the college curriculum is "irrelevant"; typically, the charges do not specify what it should be relevant to, or why. Some critics mean that studies should bear directly on the pressing social problems of poverty, civil rights, international war, overpopulation, and the like. Others mean that the curriculum should cater to urgent preoccupations of students— methods of "consciousness expansion," response to the draft, religious doubts, job security and advancement, or social problems of the sort already mentioned. Other critics mean that often courses are so centered on a professor's specialization that they fail to appeal to student interest, to meet social need, or to provide liberal education.

Each of these criticisms has force, but none holds much promise of reforming the curriculum forthwith. Society's problems do not stand ready-formulated in clean abstraction; often one can reach them only through past events or through a forest of economic, political, and cultural habits and institutions. Similarly, a direct focus on student interests is liable to be frustrating to students themselves, since it rarely penetrates to the remoter sources of their curiosity or discontent. And avoidance of the professors' specializations will drain away professors' enthusiasms and waste a part of their special competence. In what sense, then, can a college expect its curriculum to be "relevant"?

We find it reasonable to expect studies to start, for the most part, where students' interests are, provided that the studies then lead to outcomes which competent teachers will find worthy. We would not by any means abandon the curriculum to student preferences; indeed, many students have little idea where their preferences lie. But we think that when students join faculty in the choice of starting points and basic questions, the result can be an increased sense of relevance and a quickening of learning. Since education in college is a long process, with frequent renewals and fresh starts, with daily and weekly reconsiderations of direction and meaning, we need some natural, not too elaborate devices to allow students to take part continuously in the initiation and planning of their studies.

The use of student initiative is probably one key to Goddard College's success. Paul Dressel, author of the Goddard profile, makes clear his uneasiness, even dismay, over Goddard's abandonment of practices that usually mark a strong undergraduate college. Yet he acknowledges that the best evidence we can muster shows students doing exceptionally well on the ultimate tests of learning achieved. We do not argue that every college should rush to emulate Goddard. Monteith gets its impact in a different way, offending some of the fundamental wants and expectations of students but sustaining the active participation of a majority by close student-faculty relations and other means. The point is that where students have a say in the ends and means of their learning, education is likely to move with increased zeal and better-chosen aims.

If this is so, what methods are at hand for engaging students in the planning of their studies? Present experiments range from student-run "free universities" through formal inclusion of students on curriculum and educational policies committees to informal influence exerted in a dozen different ways. We see only a modest utility, in the long run, for "free universities"—i.e., programs organized outside of universities and managed wholly by students or by faculty they recruit and pay. These ventures may encourage variety in an excessively uniform array of teaching strategies or in a constricted choice of subject matters. They may provide a safe testing ground for high-risk curricular innovations. But "free universities" are often hopelessly inefficient and disorganized or consume inordinate amounts of student and faculty time in clerical and administrative work. More important, some tend to separate students from faculty influence and competence, thereby making the "free university" as irrelevant, perhaps, as the lectures it was intended to displace.

How can students, then, participate effectively in curriculum making? Student-initiated courses, running alongside regular studies, are one way: Monteith's seminars, planned by students and run with only nominal faculty assistance, have proved tumultuous but unquestionably educational, judging by student logs. By asking each seminar to arrange for a member of the faculty to evaluate its work, Monteith has illustrated one solution to the most difficult problem attendant on student-initiated courses—devising a plan for *evaluation that will appear convincing to the faculty and fair to the students.*

Almost every one of the profile colleges has accepted students as members of college committees. Whether students vote or do not vote, whether they are a majority or a minority, whether the committees are standing or temporary—these specific arrangements are less important than the quality of rapport between student and faculty committeemen. Probably any arrangement can yield good results if the participants combine mutual respect with determination to make the most of the special perspectives and competences of each of them.

Quite possibly, the most significant student influence on curriculum will come informally, outside of official college structures. In the colleges depicted here, because of their size and atmosphere, students regularly make their judgments felt through steering committees for courses, through organization of particular class activities, through assisting teachers in courses, and through simple comments to instructors on the merits and defects of certain teaching procedures. Sometimes the informal student voice is amplified impressively, as in the Oberlin Student Congress. Sometimes, as in Ripon's Brand Rex Coffee House, the comment is implicit rather than explicit, the students (with faculty assistance) creating occasions for the kind of instruction they feel to be in short supply in the curriculum.

Problem: science and the liberal arts college*

On our visits to college campuses we found some teachers and administrators who had lost their confidence in their ability to continue to provide effective science instruction for their students and some who were convinced that their college was destined to make a smaller and smaller contribution to the education of American scientists. It is not surprising that there should be misgivings and hesitancies about the future of science in the liberal arts colleges. The mounting cost of instruction and research, the continuing exponential growth of science with increasing competition for science faculty, and the public identification of science with big science and of big science with big institutions strongly supported by federal funds all seem to lead to the conclusion that the action is elsewhere. Some of the colleges have noted a recent decrease in the numbers of entering

* This section is primarily the work of Albert Stewart.

students identifying science as a career and attribute this decrease to the greater attraction of the institutes of technology and large universities for students who judge that the place to study science is a place that engages in big science.

It is conceivable that the colleges might, as a response to these alarms, concentrate on science for the general student, encouraging those students who want to extend their science studies to transfer to a university or to accept a longer period of preparation. We did not find any colleges with developed science departments seriously considering this kind of concentration. Faculties prefer to do what they think they do well, and there is a strong feeling in the colleges that existing science programs for the non-science major are inadequate and ineffective. Wherever we interviewed science professors, we found them dissatisfied with their efforts to convey to nonscientists the depth of understanding of science that is necessary for the citizens of a country like ours, shaped by the ideology and the products of science. A number of colleges studied—Monteith, Ripon, Earlham, Amherst—had tried or were trying one or another approach in which initial hope had been high. But again and again we encountered a frank admission that things had not gone nearly as well as they had hoped.

Science instruction for the general student is difficult to do in any setting; we are convinced it is impossible to do well without a strong program for science majors. This judgment is based not only on the difficulty of getting competent science faculty without majors for them to teach, a serious problem in itself, but also on the recognition that students learn a great deal from other students in many ways that elude the formal curriculum. An effective program in science for future teachers, poets, lawyers, mothers, and fathers requires students intensely interested in the various sciences to serve as examples of the compelling attractions of science and to contribute to the campus discourse.

There seems to be no way for the liberal arts college to escape the necessity to provide effective science programs for both majors and nonmajors. Are the colleges losing their effectiveness in preparing students for careers in science, or can they face their continued obligations with self-confidence based on current accomplishment? An important source of the fear of decreasing effectiveness could be identified, ironically, as a result of the efforts of friends of the liberal arts colleges to dramatize the needs of these colleges for science support. Thus one widely publicized report, "Physics in the Four-year College,"* concludes from a study of 600 four-year colleges that offer a physics major, but no Ph.D. degrees, that "the Ph.D.-granting institutions are three times as effective in producing bachelor degree graduates who ultimately receive a doctorate degree in physics as the non-Ph.D.-granting institutions."

The evidence we gathered during the course of this study indicates that it is flatly wrong to accept these figures as representing a failure of liberal arts colleges to provide undergraduate preparation for future scientists. Instead, the evidence indicates that there are many colleges that have been increasing their contribution to the undergraduate education of professional scientists much more rapidly than the universities. For example, the ten most productive university colleges (in science Ph.D.s) have been compared with some associations of colleges† chosen without advance knowledge of their productivity of graduates who go on to earn a doctorate in science. A comparison of the percentage of graduates going on to science doctorates in the decade of the 1950s with the percentage doing so in the first half of the 1960s shows that in the associations of free-standing colleges, the number of students going on for science doctorates increased more rapidly, without exception, than did college enrollments; the opposite was true for the university colleges.‡

The most remarkable observation to be made about these figures on the colleges is the large increase in the numbers of their graduates going on to the Ph.D. in the biological sciences. Here, it seems to us, there is real reason for hope that the liberal arts college can be quickly responsive to both the needs of society and the increased excitement in the active fields of biochemistry and microbiology. It would be useful to uncover the most important factors that have led to this adaptive response by the liberal arts colleges. Whether the biological sciences are seen as more humane, more relevant, better-taught, or more accessible than the physical sciences we do not know. Whatever the reasons, many liberal arts colleges have become increasingly productive as sources of future biological scientists.

* Report of the Committee on Physics Faculties in College (COPFIC), American Institute of Physics, Publication R–187, New York, December, 1965.
† The Great Lakes Colleges Association, the Associated Colleges of the Midwest, the Central States College Association, and three smaller groups: Amherst, Mount Holyoke, Smith; Bryn Mawr, Haverford, Swarthmore; Pomona, Occidental, Redlands, and Whittier.
‡ See Appendix C.

We think that inordinate damage to higher education has resulted from false inferences from studies such as the COPFIC study,* partly because they have supported the shaping of national policy on the assumption that no free-standing college represents an efficient investment in the education of scientists, partly because they are having the effects of deflecting students with strong science interests from seeking admission to liberal arts colleges and deterring scientists from seeking teaching positions in the colleges. In short, prophecies that the colleges are becoming poor places to study science may be self-fulfilling, preventing the colleges from doing what they are well-suited to accomplish.

We do not think that the colleges will be able to provide effective science instruction for all their students, nonmajors as well as majors, without a revolution in their conception of the ends of science education. Most of those concerned about current indications that large numbers of students are turning away from science and being strongly attracted by activities that are humanistic and expressive are mindful of the scientific and engineering manpower needs of the country. They think of science education as a pipeline, with teachers and instructional resources devoted to engendering an adequate flow of scientists to keep the economy going.† But this model misrepresents the science education needs of our society. Even those whose concern is focused on the productivity of scientists and technicians are coming to believe that without some under-standing of the nature of scientific research by legislators, managers, and citizens generally, much important and necessary science may

* There are a number of sources of the apparent discrepancy between the conclusions of the COPFIC study and the study reported here covering all science fields, biological as well as physical. First, physics seems to be unusual among the sciences in the extent to which future Ph.D.s are now doing their undergraduate work in the institutes of technology. In addition, there is a nationwide decline in the number of students earning a bachelor's degree in physics. It is also true that many of the institutions in the associations referred to above do enjoy conspicuous advantages—selectivity in the choice of students, strong financial position, ability to draw competent faculty, access (on campus and off) to equipment, and laboratory experiences helpful in advanced studies in science. But even when all the colleges in one state (Ohio) were compared with the Ph.D.-granting institutions in the same state, the colleges increased their productivity more than the undergraduate divisions of the universities, although the increase was not as great as in the association colleges.
† The science manpower needs of the country are not easily ascertained. There is a pressing need for studies, such as the one begun in 1968 by the American Institute of Physics, to learn how scientists are actually used. We do not know whether we need more scientists or whether technicians and craftsmen are in short supply.

wither for lack of support. On a broader basis, it is inconceivable that a culture so influenced by both the fruits and the ideas of science as ours can remain healthy (or be restored to health) without a broadly dispersed understanding of the possibilities and limitations of science.

From this point of view, the main educational task in science for the colleges and universities is the education of the general student. Secondarily the colleges should provide the opportunity for students to develop as scientists (and as science teachers) to the point where they can continue their graduate studies or enter special programs. We would do much better to think of science education as an irrigation system, with students carried various distances along the course of science education. The postdoctoral students who drip out near the far end of the line should not be seen as the justification for constructing the distribution system.

It is all very well to call for a revolution, but who will man the barricades? Many, perhaps most, science professors find it extraordinarily difficult to sustain their own interest in teaching general students. To a much greater extent than teachers in the humanities and social sciences they find themselves restrained by the sequential conceptions of their subjects from talking about the problems they themselves are working to solve. Also, research competes strongly for the science teacher's time and interest, partly because such research is so frequently productive and engrossing, partly because research productivity is the key to advancement. Science faculties in the colleges we studied were largely free from administrative pressures for research productivity, but many science teachers felt the necessity to do research in order to keep alive in their field and to gain some recognition in their profession. These factors make science faculties predominantly concerned with the teaching of students who will major in their field, secondarily with students majoring in related sciences, and only as a poor third are they willing to develop the bit of a scientist present in all of us that needs to be recognized and nourished.

Where can the colleges find professors to do the difficult job of making science accessible in appropriate measure to all their students? We know that a few well-qualified science professors are already at work developing programs to meet these needs; the task is not entirely without appeal. If we accept that there is a need for all students to become involved in some way with ongoing scientific work and to get to know men and women engaged in such work, it is clear that the colleges must engage the services of *scientists and technicians outside their own full-time faculty. If the talents of a variety of specialists can be engaged to teach part time, introducing students to the problems that engage them professionally, colleges may open some new avenues to the education of both non-science and science majors.**

In the matter of science teaching, the problems of free-standing colleges are very similar to those of university-based colleges. Both types of institutions have yet to devise sufficiently effective ways of associating research and teaching activities. By constantly evaluating our experiences with science education in many settings, we can hope to learn how to provide a range of science education that fits the needs of the society.

* See Gerald Holton, "Science for the Non-Scientist: Criteria for College Programs," *Teachers College Record,* 64, March, 1963, pp. 497–509. Reprinted in Hoopes, *Science in the College Curriculum,* Report of a Conference Sponsored by Oakland University and Supported by a Grant from the National Science Foundation, May 24–26, 1962, Rochester, Mich., 1963, p. 35.

EARLHAM
COLLEGE

*"There is that of God in every man." From this
comes Quaker pacifism and belief in the
supreme value of every individual. It seems to
lead, at Earlham, to a concern for the individual
student which the students certainly feel and
which even a casual visitor could hardly overlook.
Other aspects of life in the Earlham community
probably stem from this principle—emphasis on
freedom of thought and expression, concern for
service to others, and a minimizing of hierarchical
distinctions.*

O UTSIDE the Friends Meeting House at Earlham College stands a statue of Mary Dyer, a Quaker woman who was hanged for her religious convictions on Boston Common in 1660. However her witness may resemble that of contemporary Earlham, the statue is a reminder that Quaker principles are important in the life of the college and that they may sometimes conflict with values espoused by the rest of society.

A coeducational college of liberal arts,[1] Earlham enrolled a little over one thousand students in 1966. Present policy is to maintain about that size, although financial and other pressures may force the college slowly to grow. The ratio of men to women among its students is maintained at about 3 to 2.

The campus is located on the outskirts of Richmond, Indiana, a city with a population of about forty-four thousand. The campus proper covers about 90 acres, but since the college owns several hundred adjacent acres, space is no problem. Physically the college appears prosperous, but it is by no means ornate; "Quaker sim-

---

[1] The Earlham School of Religion, offering graduate courses leading to the M.A. and B.D. degrees, is also affiliated with Earlham College. The Eastern Indiana Center of Earlham College and Indiana University, offering chiefly college credit courses at the freshman and sophomore levels, some adult education, and a few upperclass and graduate courses, uses the Earlham plant and is an interesting example of a twenty-year cooperative venture between a private college and a state university. The center may acquire its own campus. Purdue and Ball State Universities have now joined in the work of the Center.

283

plicity" sets the tone. The buildings are in good repair, and the grounds are kept extraordinarily neat.

Earlham has an endowment of about 7 million dollars. Faculty salaries are fairly good; life at Earlham being as pleasant as it is, the college is able to recruit good teachers and is successful in retaining most of those whom it wants to keep.

Earlham's history and the Quaker roots

Earlham had its beginning in the concern of members of Indiana Yearly Meeting for the education of their young people. It opened in 1847 as Friends Boarding School, with students on both the secondary and college levels. In 1859, the name was changed to Earlham College. In 1881, Western Yearly Meeting became a joint sponsor.[2]

The Society of Friends has always emphasized the liberal arts, including science; it has stressed religious studies, the development of the spiritual side of life, and service to society, but not the professional training of ministers so common in nineteenth-century church colleges. This interpretation of religious and educational responsibility has been a continuing theme at Earlham.

From its founding until 1900, Earlham was primarily concerned with serving Midwestern Quakers and other residents of eastern Indiana. Enrollment increased to over three hundred; several buildings were built, and several hundred acres of land were acquired. In general, however, Earlham was a modest, regional, and somewhat parochial institution during the first period of its history.

The second period can be regarded as extending from 1900 to 1946. Earlham drew more and more of its students from other regions, and the proportion of non-Quakers rose. When the enrollment reached about five hundred students, more than half of them were not Quakers. Furthermore, non-Quakers were appointed to the faculty. The years of depression and of both world wars brought financial stringency and policies of caution to cope with the assorted difficulties. As a matter of conscience, the faculty decided not to seek a military unit during World War II, preferring to cut their own salaries substantially.

The third era dates from 1946, when Thomas E. Jones, a Quaker and a graduate of Earlham, became President and undertook a major renovation of the college's plant, program, and staff. He communi-

[2] The first few paragraphs of this historical sketch are condensed and paraphrased from *A Profile of Earlham College*, prepared by Earlham in 1961 for the Ford Foundation.

cated to the entire college a conviction that Earlham was on the threshold of an era of increasingly significant service to the world. When he retired in 1958, the college chose as his successor Landrum Bolling, another Quaker, not an alumnus but a member of Earlham's faculty in the Department of Political Science.

In this postwar period, Earlham was at first flooded with students as war veterans returned, and then went through a period when it was difficult to find enough qualified applicants to fill the college. In recent years it has had to turn away three for each one accepted. It is hard to predict whether the college will choose to become highly intellectual and competitive, like Reed, Oberlin, and Swarthmore, for example, or decide that it has moved far enough in that direction and should place more emphasis on other aspects of the development of young people. Increased academic emphasis would be a natural outcome of highly qualified students and an intellectually able faculty with professional drive, unless this could be altered by a deliberately fostered sense of mission of a different kind.

Earlham as a Quaker college As a Quaker college, Earlham differs markedly, but sometimes in rather subtle ways, from either a nondenominational college or a college related to a different sect. Faculty, administrators, Trustees, alumni, the various publics with an interest in Earlham, and most students recognize that its Quaker tradition makes it distinctive. But there is not, nor is there likely to be, widespread agreement on the details of this distinctiveness. And there are some students who feel, perhaps because they have little experience on which to base comparisons, that the Quaker tradition makes little difference.

In terms of numbers—fewer than a quarter of a million throughout the world—Quakers are a minority group, but they have made an appreciable impact. Quakers have no formal creed. Many hold beliefs that are indistinguishable from those of the Evangelical Christian sects; some, even, are Fundamentalists. Others hold views far from those of orthodox Christianity, views much like those of Unitarians. It is even possible to find agnostics who have been accepted into membership. In fact, the very freedom from dogma in Quakerism makes it attractive to many intellectuals.

Quakers are often regarded as rather Puritanical, a description that would have been much more nearly justified three or four generations ago than it is today. There was a time when most Quakers were opposed to smoking and drinking and to artistic expression such as music, art, dancing, and the theater. This early view that participation in the arts is sinful may be partly responsible for the fact that several Quaker colleges, including Earlham, are particularly strong in the natural sciences. It is more likely that this strength arose because there has always been a practical element in Quakerism and because, excepting the Puritanical ideas just mentioned, Quakers have usually accepted the wholeness of life as an important principle. Furthermore, lacking fixed dogma, Quakerism was less troubled than many other religious groups by conflict between religious belief and scientific ideas (although Earlham did have a small share of such troubles several decades ago).

One theological statement is central to Quaker belief—namely, "There is that of God in every man." From this comes Quaker pacifism and belief in the supreme value of every individual. It seems to lead, at Earlham, to a concern for the individual student which the students certainly feel and which even a casual visitor could hardly overlook. Other aspects of life in the Earlham community probably stem from this principle—emphasis on freedom of thought and expression, concern for service to others, and a minimizing of hierarchical distinctions.

At least twelve of the twenty-three members of Earlham's Board of Trustees must be Quakers from Indiana and Western Yearly Meetings; outside of this, there is no requirement for membership in the Society of Friends. Although Earlham has never had a non-Quaker President, neither that office nor any other at Earlham must be filled by a Quaker. About half of the present faculty and administration are Friends. Some preference is undoubtedly given to Friends when appointments to the faculty are made. Even without this, though, the proportion of Friends on the Earlham faculty would be relatively high, since they are more likely than others to seek positions there and to remain even though opportunities may beckon elsewhere. Also, some non-Friends who come to Earlham subsequently join a meeting and so swell the proportion of Friends there.

About a quarter of the students are Friends, and a good many more have attended Friends schools. Earlham intends to maintain a fairly high proportion of Quakers in the student body. The policy is to admit first those Quaker applicants who seem to have the ability to succeed at Earlham (that is, to earn a C average and thus be able to graduate) and then to make selections from among the other applicants until all the available spaces are filled. Preference in admissions is thus given to Quakers, especially to those from the Midwest; they are also given some preference in the award of scholarships.

As far as financial support is concerned, Earlham receives only about $15,000 a year from the two yearly meetings that own it and no regular financial support from any other Friends group. However, substantial contributions are received from many Friends as individuals.

In spite of its Quakerism, a student can go to Earlham for four years and escape practically all formal religious study or worship. There are no required courses in religion, and by exercising his options, a student can avoid religious convocations. Whether he can escape the influence of religion is altogether another matter.

While Quakerism is rightly regarded as a pacifist religion, there are many Friends who are not pacifists, and even among Friends there is much disagreement about the pacifist position. Furthermore, Friends seldom try to impose their views on others. Earlham College thus has no official position on pacifism. It is characterized, as are many other colleges, Quaker and otherwise, by a strong concern for international understanding. At Earlham, this shows itself in the curriculum and also in lecture series (the annual Institute of Foreign Affairs), institutional projects (foreign study programs, a Kenya education project), and the involvement of several members of the faculty in international educational and cultural programs.

To help us judge the Quaker impact, we asked that the first students to meet with us on our first visit to Earlham should be a group of freshmen. We wanted their initial impressions of the college (the time was mid-October), when these impressions could be compared most realistically with their expectations. The group consisted of four young men and four young women. Only one, a girl who had attended a Friends school, was a Quaker; thus Friends were underrepresented in the group.

We asked them to tell us in what ways they saw Earlham as a Quaker college. They agreed that the most important characteristic they saw was a sense of community. Other student groups, members of the faculty, and individual students gave the same response. Whether or not a sense of community is characteristically Quaker, it is undoubtedly a vital part of Earlham.

Students like the quality of personal relationships. "There is a lot of extra helpfulness about people" and "People here have a real concern for me" were typical comments. One girl said, "This is a community where dissension and agreement can live together."

There were criticisms. One freshman had "wanted a place where religion would be important; there are not as many people interested in religion as I wanted." Another was unhappy because Earlham pacifism seemed too weak to him; others, of course, would find it too strong for their tastes. They were impressed, however, with the absence of dogma. One of them said, "Quakers let you do your own choosing. They aren't people who force anything on you; you can make up your own mind.... Quakers set the basis; you do the thinking."

On the second visit four months later, and again by design, we met with the same group of freshmen. They were a little less impressed with the strength of the Quaker influence and with the sense of community, but on the whole their initial impressions had been confirmed.

Upperclass students, although probably more realistic and possibly more cynical than the freshmen, generally agreed with them that the Quaker influence is real and subtle, and on the whole a force for good. However, some students question whether, in its typically Quaker search for consensus, Earlham may fail to take a sufficiently firm stand. Others object that failure to reach consensus seems to be used as an excuse for inaction. This is particularly irritating to political activists, who find Earlham frustrating. They are not punished for their rebellions; they are just driven wild by the attitude of sweet reasonableness.

Among the faculty, a few of the older members are somewhat fearful that current pressures will cause a decline in Quaker influence; some of them feel that this has happened already. The faculty accepts the Quaker influence as a distinctive characteristic of Earlham; most of the faculty, Friends and non-Friends alike, regard this as good. Newcomers find some features (especially faculty meetings without votes) a bit surprising, but in general they like what they find—respect for diversity, concern for the individual, sense of community, search for consensus.

What are the attitudes of Earlham's constituency and of the city of Richmond to Earlham's Quakerism? Among Friends, there are not only differences of opinion but different ways of worshipping—in "pastoral" (programmed) and in "silent" (unprogrammed) meetings. The pastoral meetings (many of whose members, and especially those from rural areas, tend to be politically, socially, and theologically conservative) are largely located in the Midwest. Eastern meetings, as well as some meetings in other areas, are unprogrammed; their members, mostly living in urban or suburban areas, are on the whole more liberally inclined, especially in theological and social matters. Although Earlham is owned by two Midwestern yearly meetings, much of the Earlham community leans toward Quakerism of the liberal Eastern variety—and this, of course, has in it the seeds of trouble. Today, the relation of the owning meetings to the college is a little like that of a conservative parent to a progressive child— affection and some pride, bewilderment and even some dismay, with occasional clashes of will.

While town-gown relationships, between the college and the city of Richmond, are in general quite good, they have been badly strained at times, especially during World War II. The surrounding community is fairly conservative, and the college has sometimes been subjected to a good deal of criticism regarding pacifism, free speech for Communists, student demonstrations, and college involvement in civil rights causes. More recently, the chief complaints of the town have had to do with student appearance—beards, long hair—and with interracial dating.

The idea of community Earlham is, to a remarkable extent, a society of peers. Hierarchical distinctions are at a minimum; different people have different talents and are given different jobs to do, but rank in itself is relatively unimportant. Administrators do not necessarily receive higher salaries than teachers; no member of the administration other than the President is paid more than the most highly paid teacher. When a teacher joins the administrative staff, he is not thought of as being elevated; he has merely changed his job.

Titles are seldom used. Without making a fetish of it, members of the community, students and faculty, often follow the traditional Quaker practice (rapidly becoming obsolete) of using full names— Landrum Bolling, for example, instead of President Bolling or even Mr. Bolling.

Earlham, like most other Quaker colleges, has no fraternities, and their absence undoubtedly contributes to the sense of a single community. The Quaker belief in "that of God in every man" is inconsistent with the idea of exclusiveness inherent in the fraternity system, and Quaker preference for openness is opposed to the elements of secrecy that are sometimes associated with it. Since Earlham students themselves would probably not tolerate the establishment of fraternities, the question is unlikely to arise, but if it did, faculty, administration, and Trustees and surely the alumni as well, would be united in their opposition.

Aside from separation of men and women in the dormitories, there are no systematic devices to generate distinctions in matters of student housing. One possible exception should be mentioned: The college has purchased houses on two streets which frame a corner of the campus as these houses have come on the market, and uses them for overflow dormitories. These residences now serve about 150 students; they tend to be preferred by those who want a little more freedom than ordinary dormitory life affords, and especially by those who have returned from study abroad. Removing these students from the mainstream of Earlham life runs counter to the idea of community, but the once active discussion within the faculty about whether these houses should be replaced by new on-campus dormitories has died down.

Eating patterns may have particular significance for developing a sense of community, for eating is quite literally vital and has certain overtones associated with the sacred. At Earlham, the symbolism of "breaking bread together" is reinforced by the few moments of silence—Quaker grace—before the sit-down meals. Students eat together in a single dining area. Breakfast, lunch, and Friday, Saturday, and Sunday evening meals are cafeteria style; weekday dinners are sit-down, family-style affairs. This arrangement helps foster an atmosphere often absent from college life, though there are sporadic student protests against the system.

As in other institutions, a good deal of informal faculty business is conducted at lunch, in an area adjoining the student dining room where members of the faculty and administration often eat. Some students resent the separation, feeling that the sense of community would be strengthened if the faculty ate with them more often.

The younger faculty, many of whom have a more conventionally professional orientation than some of their elders, may chafe a bit under the burden of trying to be teachers, scholars, and members of an integrated community all at the same time. On the whole, though, the sense of community has much the same effect on the faculty as it does on the students. They like it and appreciate it. They soon learn how things are done at Earlham, and since most of them approve, they behave as expected. Furthermore, the community is good to them; they and their families are accepted promptly, and they soon feel a part of things.

It would be a mistake to conclude that life at Earlham is insufferably bland. The normal tensions that exist among scholars, reinforced by the view that every person has a right to his own individuality, are quite sufficient to prevent any such outcome. Things are stirred up much of the time, but usually the stir arises from genuine issues of importance to Earlham as an effective college community, not from personal hostilities.

The structure of the government of Earlham can be indicated on an organization chart that looks much like the charts of other colleges. The Trustees have ultimate authority, the President reports to the Trustees, certain other people report to the President, and so on. But no organization chart can convey an idea of how decisions at Earlham are really made and how college business is carried out. One is almost tempted to say that it is all done with mirrors—but not quite. The Trustees fulfill their appropriate functions; the President is really the President, who makes the executive decisions after a process of consultation and consideration that is at once informal and inescapable; the faculty make decisions in areas where power to act has been delegated to them; decisions involving details of operation are made by persons to whom authority has been delegated. But in matters of policy, decision making occurs by consensus. This process helps to make the idea of community a concrete reality and at the same time is a consequence of it.

Decision making by consensus entails certain problems. It is slow, sometimes exceedingly slow, as people tug and haul while they work toward a common agreement. But there are advantages too. The diffusion of authority tends to blunt the sharp edge of conflict; it works against polarization and against civil wars. A second and perhaps more important advantage may not be so apparent. If Quaker thought emphasizes "that of God in every man," it also recognizes man's frailties. Through all Quaker thinking there is a thread of empathy that precludes wholesale condemnation of others and stresses what each man has in common with his fellows, including communal responsibility. This is clearly symbolized in the American Friends Service Committee and in the impulse to service that is part of the Friends' tradition. The diffusion of responsibility fits perfectly with Quaker recognition that men's destinies are intertwined and that responsibility is in reality shared whether one recognizes it or not.

A corollary of this pattern is an administrative style that is relatively informal and loosely defined. Limits of authority and responsibility may be blurred. This means, not that nobody is responsible, but that everybody is invited to share in various phases of responsibility. On most matters of educational policy, where the faculty has the responsibility, the actual decision is taken in faculty meetings. But issues often travel a long, hard road before they get there, and in the process a great deal of faculty time is consumed.

Earlham has two kinds of faculty meetings—"seminars" and "business meetings." Seminars are for the discussion of issues, including specific proposals; it is only at business meetings that formal action can be taken. Complex issues are rarely brought to a business meeting for action without previous discussion in a seminar. A committee will work on an idea until it is in good enough shape for wider discussion and will then ask the Seminar Committee to put it on the agenda for a seminar, where it will be thoroughly discussed before being sent on to a business meeting or back to the first committee for revision or decent burial. Consensus, even on a fairly controversial issue, is thus often achieved in effect before the business meeting at which formal action is taken.

New proposals at Earlham can be initiated by anybody. Part of the splendid anarchy of the Earlham system is that ideas can get a hearing in a great variety of ways; it takes more than procedural technicalities to stop a proposal that has appeal. Sooner or later, a good idea will be taken up by a committee and will eventually find its way to a faculty meeting.

On occasion, summer workshops are used for the initiation of proposals. Also, each fall before college opens, there is a faculty retreat at which orientation of new faculty is combined with discussion of important issues. Some of the ideas considered at a retreat are assigned to committees for further discussion. Some proposals will be adopted, some will be modified, and some will drop quietly out of sight. Those that are not dropped will be presented in due course to a faculty seminar and, if all goes well, to a business meeting for formal action.

The faculty meetings themselves are conducted by "Quaker procedure" rather than by parliamentary rules. Votes are not taken; instead, issues are decided by the "sense of the meeting." An issue is presented for decision, all those who want to express themselves on it have their say, and when it is obvious that consensus has been reached, the presiding officer so announces, the decision is minuted, and then action is taken.

Silence does not necessarily signify agreement. If someone disagrees but knows that he is alone or nearly so, he may remain silent. Often such a person will state his disagreement and his reasons but add openly or imply that since others do not seem to share his views, he will not press his objections.

On an issue where opinions differ sharply, discussion sometimes brings substantial agreement; if it does not, no action is taken at that meeting. A determined few can almost always block action under Quaker procedure; for this reason, people must, and usually do, act responsibly when this procedure is being used. In a sense, the primary objective is the reaching of consensus, rather than bringing about the victory of a particular point of view: the concepts of victory and defeat are irrelevant.

In making the system work, the skill of the presiding officer is vital. He must be able to sense the right moment to announce that consensus has been reached—that is, the moment when the weight of opinion is heavy enough so that a statement of the consensus will be recognized by all as just. He must be able to judge accurately when he should rule that no consensus is possible and when he should allow the debate to continue if there is some chance that a consensus will emerge. He should not allow one or two diehards to block action; on the other hand, he should not rule that consensus has been reached when there is still an intelligent minority position that has not been adequately answered. In the hands of a good presiding officer, this system can often avoid the "tyranny of the majority."

At Earlham, the presiding officer at faculty meetings is neither the President nor the Dean, but the Clerk of the Faculty. He has the assistance of a recording clerk, who serves as secretary. These people are chosen by the faculty after being nominated by the Nominating Committee. The person presiding over any meeting has some power; at an Earlham faculty meeting, the Clerk of the Faculty has power (and responsibility) of an unusual kind, since he decides, somewhat subjectively, what a given decision is. Selection for this position would suggest that the Clerk's colleagues regard him as firm, fair, and courageous.

By not presiding, the President gives up some power. However, if he were the presiding officer, he could not properly express his views as freely as he can from the floor.

Student community We might define a true community as one in which all members have an appropriate share in making decisions. Faculty and administration share in decision making at Earlham, but the role of students is much less clear. The section on "Government" in the Earlham catalog includes the following: "Since the College is a student-faculty community, the central campus governing agency, the Earlham Senate, has both faculty and student representation. . . . Senate consists of about 30 students and six faculty members. . . . All student organizations are responsible to Senate." It is logical, in view of the stress on community, to include both faculty and students. The effect seems to be, however, that faculty are involved in the affairs of students without corresponding involvement of students in other affairs. The impression left on our observers, both faculty and student, is that Senate is actually weak and disorganized.

Earlham has an Honor Code that seems to work well in spite of certain confusions surrounding it. The catalog reads as follows: "Under the Honor Code, if any student knows of academic dishonesty he is obligated to take action in the matter, either by talking directly with the student involved or with the professor of the class. Primary responsibility for the maintenance of honesty in academic work rests with Earlham students." This statement conflicts in part with a similar statement in the *Faculty Handbook,* which is more explicit about the responsibility of the student.

Faculty take it for granted that students will not cheat. The students receive little formal indoctrination into the Honor System, and the faculty even less. Lack of careful instructions to freshmen about their responsibilities under the system is a risk, but perhaps the student was right who said, "The best shock treatment is for a freshman to be handed an examination, take it out, and do it." The simplest explanation may be the best: "There is a feeling of trust on the campus; so you don't cheat."

Earlham students with social concerns are more likely to try to reform society than to rebel against it. They prefer positive action to negative protest. (This is in part attributable to the sense of community; demonstrations for unpopular causes—and few bother to demonstrate for popular ones—are cautiously undertaken lest they bring the community into disrepute.) And they like to promote discussion. Student initiative at Earlham provides opportunity for discussion and dissent on Vietnam, on civil rights, and on methods of education at Earlham. But it has also produced action; it has stimulated an Upward Bound program for deprived young people with high academic potential and raised funds for a Kenya work camp, to name two of many examples.

The liberal approach that is responsible for most such activity is not unchallenged. A very small but vigorous Conservative Club sponsors conservative speakers, programs, and discussions. The confrontation of differing views is facilitated and encouraged by the Opinion Board on which both students and faculty can post their opinions publicly. Located in the path of heavy traffic in the administration building and only a few steps from the mailboxes, the Opinion Board is a free forum, a kind of courthouse square.

The college newspaper and the college radio station also serve as outlets for opinion and hence for the dissemination of a variety of views. However, the Opinion Board has advantages. Provocative statements made over the air or printed in the paper have a way of irritating the surrounding community, and even at a college that scrupulously avoids censorship, editors and station managers are sensitive to the outside criticism their words visit upon the school. Being a medium for exchange of ideas within the college, the Opinion Board affords a somewhat freer forum.

Scholastic aptitudes and student goals Not everything happening at Earlham can be traced to Quaker predilection. Indeed, some changes—greater scholastic aptitude among students, a more diverse and cosmopolitan program and staff, greater emphasis on academic and professional training—may be moving the college away from its distinctive Quakerism and closer to the most demanding of its nonsectarian sister institutions.

On the evidence of College Board tests, required of all applicants since 1959, it is clear that the intellectual competence of Earlham's entering students has been rising. According to some Earlham people whose experience goes back that far, the sharpest increase in quality occurred about a decade ago, before College Board scores were available for all students. The few objective data that exist support these old-timers in their judgment that Earlham students today are considerably more able than those of a decade and more ago.

Scores on Graduate Record Examinations are another indicator of quality. Again, they should not be taken too seriously, but since thirteen departments at Earlham require them of all senior majors, the scores here may mean more than at colleges where only a self-selected few take the tests. The median GRE score at Earlham was close to 560 each year from 1959 to 1962 inclusive. Each year since then it has risen appreciably; in 1965 it was 633 for men, 608 for women.

The most striking change in the intellectual quality of Earlham students is suggested by the proportion of admitted freshmen who graduate four years later. Of those admitted in 1957, 35.4 percent graduated in 1961. In the next four years this proportion rose steadily: 49.8 percent of the original class graduated in 1962, 50.3 percent in 1963, 57.1 percent in 1964. By 1965, the figure had risen to 63.1 percent.

About half of Earlham graduates currently go on to graduate and professional schools—47 percent in 1963, 46 percent in 1964, and

53 percent in 1965. Business was the choice of 16 percent in 1963, 19 percent in 1964, and 22 percent in 1965. Social service—a broad category including such activities as social work, the Peace Corps, and VISTA—attracted 10 percent, 9 percent, and 7 percent in those three years, respectively. Teaching, without preliminary graduate training, was chosen by 23 percent, 22 percent, and 15 percent. Civil service and military service together accounted for most of the remainder.

The student body is much more heterogeneous and cosmopolitan than it used to be, although more than a third of the graduates of the class of 1963, a rather typical class, listed the state of Indiana as home,[3] and enough more from Ohio to bring the number from these two states to more than half of the total. Those who graduated represented twenty-one states, the District of Columbia, Canada, and Ceylon. Normally, entering students come from thirty or more states, the District of Columbia, and from two to eight foreign countries. An increasing number of applicants have been admitted from the Eastern seaboard in the past twenty years.

In terms of economic, racial, and religious backgrounds, the Earlham student body is homogeneous compared with a university in a large city. But compared with many other small colleges, it is fairly diverse. In each of the last four years, fifteen or more religious sects were represented by ten or more students each in the Earlham student body. White, Anglo-Saxon Protestants predominate, as one might expect. Quakers constitute the largest single group; as noted earlier, about a fourth of the students are Quakers. Other Protestant denominations taken together constitute about three-fifths, leaving less than fifteen percent for all others—Catholics, Jews, other non-Christians, and those with no religious affiliation at all. If any change is occurring, it involves a slight decline in the proportion of Quakers, thus giving more diversity to the community.

There are a few students from Asia and a few from Africa. The number of Negro Americans is slowly increasing; seventeen entered the class of 1970, and thirteen were admitted with the class of 1971. As in many other colleges, the small size of the Negro population is not a result of current racial discrimination on the college's part; the cost simply tends to keep many Negroes out, and Negroes who have both the money and the ability for Earlham often prefer to go to an institution that is better-known.

[3] Some came from other states as freshmen but listed Richmond as home by graduation.

Faculty: head and heart Like the student body, Earlham's faculty is capable and increasingly diverse. In 1965–66, 60 percent of the total teaching faculty held earned doctor's degrees; and if one excludes members of departments like Physical Education and the Fine Arts, where the doctorate is not often expected, the proportion is 70 percent. Several members of the faculty who do not yet hold the doctorate are active candidates for it, and will soon complete that work. (But three of the most honored and effective teachers at Earlham have no advanced degrees, and one of these, a full professor, does not have even a bachelor's degree.) In 1964–65 and 1965–66, Earlham faculty published at least ten books on subjects as various as William Faulkner, Old Colony Mennonites, electrostatics, the Old Testament, chemical energy, and a new China policy. Of more than thirty articles during the same period, about half are in the sciences or mathematics.

The diversity of Earlham's faculty is worth noting. Five out of twenty new faculty in the fall of 1965 were from abroad—two from Japan, one from China, one from Hong Kong (a Britisher), and one from Ceylon. The eighty-seven members of the teaching faculty (including six on sabbatical leave as well as their temporary replacements) took their undergraduate work at sixty-seven different institutions.

The faculty is relatively young. Only six 1965–66 faculty were at Earlham before 1946; less than a quarter came before 1950; between 40 and 50 percent had been at Earlham less than five years. The fact that most of the newcomers are recently trained—and also well-trained—means that if most of them remain (as they probably will), there is little danger that Earlham will soon be out of date. And these young scholars may well help the college to academic distinction.

But academic distinction is not the college's only goal. President Bolling writes:

> The most crucial need of our troubled contemporary society is not academic achievement per se, is not professional competence per se. It is for men and women who can and will assume leadership roles, who have the combination of competence and a high sense of moral and social responsibility. . . .
>
> If Modern Man is not able to make it, it will not be because of a shortage of Ph.D.'s or of high-level colleges with selective admissions and tough grading patterns. It will be because too few of our educational institutions, maybe none of them, did an effective job of hitching competence and will to noble moral and social purposes.

Curriculum and innovation Because of its self-conscious concern for the social and moral as well as the intellectual, Earlham prefers to emphasize *educational* excellence rather than a more narrowly defined *academic* excellence. In practice, this means attention to teaching (in two consecutive years, 1965 and 1966, two different members of the Earlham faculty won awards from the Danforth Foundation for outstanding teaching) and constant experimentation with new instructional programs. Some of the most important of these—the international programs, for instance—can be seen as a direct outgrowth of the college's sense of social responsibility. But any proposal that promises to stimulate learning will get a hearing. The 1965 summer workshop, for example, considered proposals to substitute area examinations for conventional degree requirements, to make the curriculum more flexible, to offer a freshman-year program without conventional courses, to adopt a new calendar, to integrate "service" and "field" work with academic work, and to institute a School of Public Affairs and a School of Community Services. During our visits to the campus we heard discussion of additional proposals—some very tentative but some quite serious—including a proposed program for a master of arts in teaching and the elimination of academic ranks and titles.

A few of Earlham's innovations might be considered briefly here. We have mentioned its twenty-year experiment in cooperating with Indiana University in the operation of the Eastern Indiana Center. Earlham was among the first of American colleges to adopt the "three-three" plan—an academic calendar that divides the normal academic year into three equal terms of about eleven weeks each, in each of which the student takes three courses. This arrangement eliminates the "lame-duck session" after Christmas, which is a major drawback of the conventional semester system, and has the further advantage of reducing the fragmentation of student interest that results when a student takes four or five courses at once.

Earlham, along with one or two other colleges, took the lead in creating the Great Lakes Colleges Association, composed of Albion, Antioch, Denison, DePauw, Earlham, Hope, Kalamazoo, Kenyon, Oberlin, Ohio Wesleyan, Wabash, and Wooster. Within the association there is some exchange of students and faculty, and a large number of projects, great and small, are undertaken by the group which would be impossible for one member college alone. Thus the association makes available five languages not normally included in undergraduate college curriculums and study of their related cultures. Antioch is responsible for Portuguese, Kenyon for Arabic, Wooster for Hindi, Oberlin and Wabash for Chinese, and Earlham for Japanese. Each of these colleges has affiliates overseas. In general, this adds to the range of education available to all students in

GLCA colleges; in particular, it means that Earlham students have unusual opportunities for contacts with Japanese language and culture.

Although non-Western studies are becoming so common that they can hardly be regarded now as an innovation, Earlham was in the forefront of the movement to introduce them into the liberal arts college curriculum. Because of President Bolling's own experience as a foreign correspondent and as teacher of international politics at Earlham before he became President, one of his first acts after he took office in 1958 was to press hard for an expansion of Earlham's participation in foreign study. With Antioch, Earlham began a co-operative program in Asian studies in 1959, choosing the Far East because competent specialists were available in that area. Subsequently, cooperation has extended to all the members of GLCA. There is not a full Department of Japanese at Earlham, but Japanese language through an advanced level is available there, and courses are offered in Japanese history, Chinese history, Far Eastern geography, calligraphy, and Asian religions. The college has developed library resources for Far Eastern studies, including a file of the *Japan Times*.

In addition to a specialist in Japanese studies on its permanent staff and frequent visitors from Japan, Earlham has other persons on the faculty with competence in non-Western studies. In 1965–66, at least thirteen members of the faculty had worked or studied in the Far East. Additional faculty are gaining such competence, since Earlham encourages them, through a GLCA program of grants and through its own leaves of absence and financial support, to pursue scholarly interests in non-Western lands. Courses dealing wholly or in part with non-Western areas are now offered or planned in several departments, including Art, Drama, History, Political Science, and Religion.

Closely related to Earlham's interest in non-Western studies is a program of off-campus study. Students are encouraged to spend a term or more abroad or at one of several approved centers in this country, usually in supervised groups. For example, students can study at universities in Bogotá, Colombia; in Beirut, Lebanon; in Tokyo, Japan; or in Guanajuato, Mexico, as part of the GLCA program. Students interested in psychology, sociology, and family relations may study for a term at the Merrill-Palmer Institute in Detroit. Others may attend the Hoover Institution on War, Revolution, and Peace at Stanford. A group of students usually goes for the winter term to Washington, D.C., where they may study in an environment obviously rich for people with interests in politics or the arts. Students travel and study in France, Austria, Germany, England, Italy, or the Scandinavian countries, each group under the leadership of one of the Earlham faculty, usually for a summer and one academic term. In the course of their college careers, about 40 percent of Earlham's students study off campus, either in this country or abroad. Since the cost is little more than that for an equivalent period at Earlham, students need not forgo this experience because of expense.

Our student observers from Berea reported their belief that aside from the considerable opportunities that Earlham offers for independent study, the most important part of the Earlham program is off-campus study, especially study abroad. They felt that those who had been abroad had gained tremendously in sophistication and in maturity and brought back new insights and new points of view that had their effect even on those who stayed at home.

One result, of course, is that not all is peaceful. Students who have lived relatively free lives in Paris or in Washington feel especially confined by the restrictions on personal freedom which Earlham, like most other colleges, imposes—restrictions such as hours for women to return to the dormitories and no liquor on campus.

Many of Earlham's courses are fairly conventional, but at least one department, Chemistry, has experimented with new methods with consequences that have extended far beyond the Earlham campus. A few details may be of interest: In the fall of 1956, members of the Chemistry Department initiated plans for revision of the four-year chemistry curriculum. By chance these plans came to the attention of some chemistry teachers who were organizing a conference on teaching high school chemistry. Professor Lawrence Strong of Earlham was invited to the conference, and out of this developed a new kind of high school course, with chemical bonding as its central theme. Earlham subsequently became the headquarters of the Chemical Bond Approach project, received supporting grants of more than a million dollars from the National Science Foundation, and for several years carried an expanded staff to help write a textbook and workbooks and try them out in hundreds of schools before their publication for nationwide use.

The future of Earlham Change at Earlham has not stopped. President Bolling is dissatisfied with much of American education, and a good many of the faculty share his view that an important part of Earlham's mission should be the development and testing of new ideas. During the academic year

1965–66, freshman seminars were introduced, a new physical science course was approved, and upperclass students were allowed to schedule one upper-division course each term outside their major field on a "pass or fail" basis, with consent of the major adviser. Other changes, some of which have already been approved by the faculty, will undoubtedly be in effect by the time this profile is published.

As a Quaker college, Earlham has a particular concern for service, and ideas for future change reflect this. The faculty has approved the addition of the proposed program leading to the degree of master of arts in teaching; and it is significant that the first "guinea pig" participant, a graduate of the class of 1965, could spend one year of the two-year program as an apprentice teacher at a high school in Kenya, where Earlham has special experience and interests. In the winter of 1966, Earlham received news of a grant to support a year's additional training for ten or twelve high school physics teachers—Negroes who lost their jobs because of the closing of segregated schools.

Such changes at Earlham have been deliberately undertaken and can be controlled. There are other kinds of changes, some very welcome and others much less so, over which Earlham's control is doubtful. Some challenges to Earlham's values result from extension of the effective boundaries of its campus beyond Richmond to the world. Others stem from improvement in the average quality of Earlham students, improvement that results from better education in the secondary schools and from Earlham's ability to be more selective as more applications are received. Strong students make demands on a college which are different from those of weaker students. Along with better-prepared students at Earlham goes a better faculty—better to the extent that an improved salary scale and a favorable public impression of the college make it possible for Earlham to compete successfully for new teachers, often teachers headed for impressive achievement in their own academic disciplines.

Some people connected with Earlham fear that although brighter students and a more highly competent faculty tend to produce graduates better-qualified for further intellectual pursuits, something else may be lost. Everett Wilson, a member of the study staff who helped collect information for the Earlham profile, defines the danger in this way:

If anything distinguishes Earlham as a Quaker college it is something of the heart, not of the head. It's an expressive rather than an instrumental emphasis. I don't mean to suggest that there is an unbridgeable gulf between these polarities. A degree of attentive support and concern for the individual may promote the more instrumental concerns of scholarship. And scholarship itself may justify heartfelt commitments.

But this is to speak at the individual or psychological level. At the group level there is reason to suggest an inverse relationship between heart and head. My thesis, then, is that for Earlham as for any other organization, expressive interests and instrumental emphases vary inversely. As Earlham is increasingly implicated in the outside world, commitments of heart and soul should be weakened. And as these commitments are weakened, so will the faculty's concern for the general, coherent growth of the individual student be weakened. One outcome is that the boundary lines between Earlham and other good, small liberal arts colleges may be obscured. This will render Grinnell, Earlham, Antioch, Oberlin, Reed, and Haverford indistinguishable from one another in their corporate character—in the distribution of their social, cultural, scholarly, religious, political beliefs and behaviors.

To the author, the fears seem exaggerated. Certainly, Earlham will continue to change—it has too much momentum to stop. But the people there have a commitment to the intangibles that are characteristic of Earlham's education at its best; as long as they continue to attract others who feel as they do, there seems little likelihood that Earlham will lose its vital core. In liberal education there must always be the element of integration, some coherent if complex unity built from the thoughtful articulation of various experiences. A major contributor to this kind of unity at Earlham would seem to be its enduring Quaker tradition.

The Earlham profile was written by William E. Cadbury, Jr., then Dean and now director of the Postbaccalaureate Fellowship Program at Haverford College. His associate was Everett K. Wilson, then professor of sociology at Antioch College and now professor of sociology, University of North Carolina. Joseph E. Elmore, Vice President for Academic Affairs and Dean at Earlham, was Earlham's representative. Two students from Berea College served as student observers— Mike Clark and Carol Ann Van Zant.

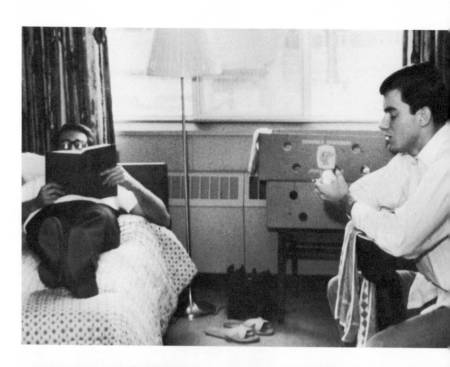

*The most interesting aspect of the College of
St. Thomas is the way in which it is responding
to a problem common to all Catholic institutions
of higher education today—how to move from
a taken-for-granted Catholicism and a conventional
curriculum to an experience for students that
is genuinely stimulating and that uses
Catholicism as a catalyst in the process.*

WHY are they here? "Because St. Thomas is a good men's college, a Catholic college, and it's near home." This was the consensus of the majority of students, 98.6 percent of whom are Catholics. Over half of them live in the twin cities, and two-thirds in the state of Minnesota; almost another fourth come from the nearby states of Illinois, Wisconsin, and Iowa. The college has long been known in the upper Midwest as a good men's college. The Ford Foundation in 1962 testified to this effect by making a 1.5 million dollar challenge grant to St. Thomas, up to that time one of only three Catholic higher institutions to receive such a grant. Its sister institution, the College of St. Catherine, not much more than a mile away on the same street in the city of St. Paul, got one the following year. This double recognition seems to indicate that the Roman Catholic population of Minneapolis and St. Paul, which constitutes about one-fourth of the million and a half metropolitan total, has been well-served by its church colleges.

St. Thomas's remarkably homogeneous student body, coming mostly from middle- and upper-middle-class Catholic families, does not experience the stimulating influence of different subcultures. This seems to account for the prevailing atmosphere of agreeable conformity, with distinctly less conflict, controversy, and debate than prevails today on many American campuses. The most interesting aspect of the college is the way it is responding to a problem more or less common to all Catholic institutions of higher education today—how to move from a taken-for-granted Catholicism and a conventional curriculum to an experience for students that is genuinely stimulating and that uses Catholicism as a catalyst in the educational process. In its search for the answers, this college must take into account two major determinants—its role as not only a Catholic but a diocesan institution and the fact that it is operating in a locale where the competition for students is keen.

The diocesan tie and Catholic aims

St. Thomas's reason for being has changed radically since 1885, when Archbishop John Ireland founded the St. Thomas Seminary. "The college of St. Thomas," says the 1963 Report of the Liberal Arts Committee, "owes its origin to circumstances similar to those that brought into being the first American colleges in colonial New England, *viz.*, the need of an educated clergy native to the soil which was to be their field of labor." Today, when the education of lay students is paramount, continues the report, the faculty see three distinctive elements of a Catholic college: "(1) The College should provide an environment of which Catholic worship and other religious activities are an integral part and in which standards of morality are Christian, (2) theology and the philosophic sciences are integral parts of a liberal education in a Catholic college, and (3) a Catholic standard of judgment is brought to bear on topics which coincide with the subjects of divine revelation." The report maintains that "the third element is, of course, in no way prejudicial to the objectivity of knowledge, but rather presumes such objectivity as a condition."

In its first decade, the seminary served as the nucleus for four educational enterprises—a high school, a college, a minor seminary, and a major seminary. The college performed a double role as minor seminary and college, with both a theological and a classical curriculum. In 1894, the major seminary for the training of priests was separated from St. Thomas; the minor seminary was moved away in 1923. The St. Thomas Military Academy (the high school) and the college continued to live together until 1965, when the academy moved. The college now has to itself the 45-acre campus on Summit Avenue in St. Paul, midway between the downtown districts of St. Paul and Minneapolis.

Following World War I, the college embarked on an expansion that proved to be beyond its powers. From 1919 to 1923, six schools were established—Commerce, Education, Law, Music, Engineering, and SLA (Science, Literature, and the Arts). In 1929, the top-heavy little empire collapsed. The Fathers of the Holy Cross were invited to take over the college for a period of five years. Five of the schools were absorbed into the college; the Law School was terminated in 1933.

The Fathers of the Holy Cross reorganized the curriculum of the college to bring it closer to its original liberal arts goals and to incorporate "those changes brought about by the rapid development of the physical sciences, [and] by the emphasis placed on the social sciences." The curriculum was organized in five divisions—Language and Literature, Science and Mathematics, History and the Social Sciences, Philosophy and Religion, and the Fine Arts. In 1931, Education became a sixth division, and Business Administration was joined with History and the Social Sciences. The curriculum still rests on this foundation.

In 1933, the archdiocese decided to reclaim the college from the Congregation of the Holy Cross, marking St. Thomas as one of the very few locally controlled Catholic colleges. Only 14 of the 148 dioceses in the United States operate full four-year colleges.[1] Until 1966, almost all other Catholic institutions of higher education were operated and controlled by Catholic orders of priests, monks, brothers, or nuns.[2] The relationship with the archdiocese constitutes an unusual element of strength and local support. However, the college's responsibility to its local clientele carries with it certain limitations on the freedom to develop into a regional or national institution.

The college neighbors St. Thomas must also be understood in terms of its immediate college neighbors, which influence both admissions policies and financial situation.

The twin cities contain one of the largest college and university complexes in the United States. The University of Minnesota has its main campus in Minneapolis and its Agricultural College on a cam-

---

[1] Earl J. McGrath and Gerald E. Dupont, The Society of Saint Edmund, *The Future Governance of Catholic Higher Education in The United States,* Institute of Higher Education, Teachers College, Columbia University, New York, 1966.

[2] Until 1966, the following statement was true: "There are approximately 250 four-year Catholic colleges which admit lay students. Of this number only one is nationally sponsored by the Church at large. . . . No Catholic college is operated exclusively under lay control although two of the diocesan colleges are staffed and administered by laymen." (Edward V. Stanford, O.S.A., *A Guide to Catholic College Administration,* The Newman Press, Westminster, Md., 1965, p. viii.)

Recently the pressures (ecumenical and otherwise) on the Catholic colleges and universities have brought several of them under lay control—e.g., the University of Notre Dame, St. Louis University, and Webster College. Webster, under Miss Jacqueline Grennan, formerly Sister Jacqueline of the Sisters of Loretto, has gone farthest in this direction.

pus in St. Paul; a branch of its Liberal Arts College is to be established on the St. Paul campus in the near future. The university, with 40,000 students and a faculty in the thousands, offers a tremendous variety of programs of undergraduate and graduate study. In addition, it is one of the great research centers of the country. Because its tuition, substantially subsidized by public taxation, is less than half that of St. Thomas, the university offers stern competition on economic grounds, not only to St. Thomas but to all the private colleges in the area. By 1970, the state will also have in operation four community colleges in the metropolitan area.

Among the private institutions, the College of St. Thomas has just over 1,800 full-time undergraduate students, all men. Counting graduate students, the total was 2,159 for 1966–67.

The College of St. Catherine has a student body of about 1,500. There are five other private liberal arts colleges in the twin cities, with enrollments running from 900 to 1,500. Twelve other colleges are in the area, seven private and five public, most of them within a radius of 100 miles. This represents a tremendous concentration of college and university students—about 50,000 in the twin cities and another 30,000 in the area. Three-fourths of the total attend public institutions, which is not far off the national average.

St. Thomas feels keenly the competition of the public institutions. To compete successfully, it must maintain and even increase its reputation for quality. The main competitive strength of St. Thomas, however, is its Catholic affiliation and the emphasis on Catholic beliefs, which help to shape its curriculum as well as its value system.

The students In one sense, there are two student bodies on the St. Thomas campus. Almost one-half the students are "day hops," or "brown baggers," who live at home within commuting distance. On campus only in the daytime, they are less involved in, and dependent on, campus affairs and social life, and their hangouts are not the same. The dormitory residents and the out-of-town students who live near the campus eat at the college dining room in Murray Hall. The locals pick up luncheon snacks at the coffee shop and rarely enter a dormitory.

At the same time, it would be hard to find a more homogeneous group than the students who go to St. Thomas. German and Irish names predominate, along with much smaller numbers of English, Slavic, Italian, and Scandinavian. Mixed as this ancestry may be, the students have been assimilated thoroughly into the regional sub-culture. While Chicago and Milwaukee are sending increasing num-bers of students, this gradual widening of the area represented will do little to dilute the present homogeneity, except for the unlikely possibility of a big drop in the percentage of Catholics.

The local students come to St. Thomas mainly from St. Thomas Academy and four Catholic high schools; a minority come from public high schools. The academy and Cretin High School in St. Paul each contributes nearly one-half of its top-half students to St. Thomas; the others send smaller but considerable numbers. The two strong forces pulling local students away from St. Thomas are the university and the desire of many students to go away to college.

A sample of 130 freshmen in November of 1965 revealed some significant facts about their social and educational status. Half of their fathers were professionals or proprietors, and only one-fifth were unskilled or semiskilled workers. Half of their parents had in-comes over $10,000 per year, 18 percent over $20,000 per year. About 40 percent of the fathers and 25 percent of the mothers held college degrees. As would be expected in a Catholic group, almost all the parents were living together. This is a differentiating factor of considerable significance: In the majority of non-Catholic colleges, many students come from separated families, a group which usually contains a higher percentage of the emotionally unstable than the rest of the student body. Three-fourths of the St. Thomas freshmen expected to do graduate work, and 40 percent looked ahead to a doctorate.

The academic ability of the freshman class in 1965, as measured by the College Entrance Examination Board verbal and mathematical aptitude tests, was almost exactly average. The scores were 500 on the verbal and 534.95 on the mathematical. The 1964 scores were almost as high and represented a significant rise of about 25 points from 1963.

Despite the faculty's expressed policy of limiting admissions to the top 60 percent in high school rank or its equivalent, 19 percent were in the bottom 40 percent and 10 percent scored below 400 on the verbal aptitude test. These weaker entrants account for the major part of the near 50 percent of dropouts and complicate the teaching problem in the freshman and sophomore years.

Figures collected July 6, 1965, showed that 47 percent of the 1965 seniors were going to graduate school. This figure does not include all who will eventually go. A quarter were going to law school, and 15 percent to medicine and dentistry, with 60 percent going to a wide variety of other graduate work. The percentage of this general group has been rising.

The large number of business administration–accounting majors, few of whom go to graduate school, acts as a brake on graduate school percentage. These men constitute about a fourth of all majors in the college and about 35 percent of the 1965 graduates.

About two-thirds of the nonbusiness majors go to graduate school. The physical sciences and mathematics, which enlist another fourth of the majors, send the largest percentage on to graduate and professional schools, a fact that testifies to St. Thomas's reputation for strength in the sciences. The social sciences have another fourth. Because business, the physical sciences, and the social sciences are all "strong fourths," the humanities majors, including history, come to about 18 percent. This distribution checks with the opinions of our two student observers that there is a prevalence of mundane and practical goals, particularly among the business majors—even though they are required to take the same program of liberal studies as all other students.

St. Thomas does not require Graduate Record Examinations except for honors candidates. Therefore it is difficult to make direct comparison of academic achievement as measured by these tests. In 1966, only 22 students, 8 percent of the graduating class of 269, were graduated with honors. A 3.25 grade-point average is required for consideration. Candidates then take special written and oral examinations, and their Graduate Record Examinations are taken into account. Only half the 1966 St. Thomas honors group ranked in the top 16 percent on the Graduate Record tests of general education; 14 of them were in the top 16 percent in verbal and mathematical aptitude. For several years, St. Thomas produced two, three, or four Woodrow Wilson scholars annually.

For a variety of reasons, probably, the tone of student intellectual life on the campus does not seem very compelling. The student observers on the study team reported a lack of informal coffee-table discussion of academic or contemporary social topics. An appreciable number of students deplored the comparative absence in their courses of reference to contemporary topics. Both of the observers (men) believe that the presence of women students would stimulate intellectual discussion. While the College Bookstore shelves contained a wide range of interesting books, the students' own bookshelves, though well-filled, seemed to contain mainly textbooks and closely course-related books.

Students' attitudes toward the academic program are respectful;

while they think the faculty set high and sometimes harsh standards, the modal attitude is acceptant and conforming. When asked for self-criticism, some of the best students used the term "passive" to describe their intellectual posture.

When asked about the lack of much exciting intellectual conversation on campus, the students gave several reasons: (1) their basic agreement on fundamental beliefs, (2) their homogeneity in general, (3) the dispersion of so many students to their homes, and (4) a lack of contemporary relevance of many courses. They illustrated their point on homogeneity by stating that their most interesting discussions usually took place with the graduate students in education, people of more maturity and different background, some of whom were not Catholics.

A number of faculty took strong exception to the criticism about the lack of contemporary material in courses. For example, a non-Catholic economics professor made the point that he brought the papal encyclical *Pacem in Terris* immediately to his class for study and discussion. The religious director told of making the reports of the Vatican Council available at once to students.

Student initiative brought about a campus conference on Vietnam which was very well-attended. Another group, at serious financial risk, arranged to bring the Minneapolis Symphony Orchestra to the campus for an open-air concert. The student observers, though impressed by this evidence of student interest and initiative in intellectual and cultural affairs, considered them more the exception than the rule.

Though the majority of St. Thomas men come from prosperous families, the pressure for upward social mobility and materialistic goals emerges clearly in serious conversation with students. One might say that the "ods" (other-directed) outnumber the "ids" (inner-directed) by a wide margin. The faculty's training and experience somewhat exceed the academic potential of the student body as a whole, though the high mortality of the first two years leaves upperclassmen who are more nearly worthy of the faculty's steel.

The fact that half the students are locals has had implications for campus leadership, since residence is a considerable factor in determining the extent of a student's participation and leadership in campus life. In the fall of 1967, the dormitory population was 43 percent of the student body, with out-of-town freshmen and sophomores the large majority, though 195 juniors and 50 seniors were "living in." Out-of-town freshmen and sophomores have little contact with the large number of upperclassmen who live outside, and this does not prepare them well for campus leadership. Yet, because they are not town boys and do not look to their homes, churches, and high school friends for social life, they are more likely than town students to become leaders as upperclassmen. Most of the campus leaders are thus upperclassmen, once dormitory residents, who now live "in digs" in the vicinity of the college.

Partly as a result of this situation, student government is not a strong force at St. Thomas, but it had been gaining in influence, especially in the 1965–67 period. There is an All-College Council which runs student affairs and plays an advisory role in student discipline cases. In the wake of a controversy about the abolition of student credit at the bookstore, the ACC recommended that students be consulted on any decision of the administration concerning student life or activity on campus. Msgr. Terrence J. Murphy, then Executive Vice President, met this proposal halfway. The upshot was the unprecedented appointment of students to the Administrative Committee (made up of top administrators and department heads) and to the committee planning the new dormitory. A student committee was established to work on a plan, with the Dean's cooperation, for student evaluation of courses and professors.

Both in student government and out of it, however, campus leaders seem disposed to cooperate with the administration and agree with it on important questions. A good many of the leaders are in the Tiger Club, a self-perpetuating upperclass organization limited to twenty members, which some students feel "runs practically everything." This does not appear to be strictly true, but it is true that the total number of leaders is small. It might fairly be said that students have more power and more opportunities to participate in, and influence, college affairs than they use.

The responsibility for the enforcement of standards of campus behavior falls upon the Dean of Students. His power and influence are widely felt and discussed. However, students have due-process rights when brought before the faculty-elected Discipline Committee by the Dean, and the committee has the final authority on severe sanctions. The student observers, one of whom was from a Catholic college, were surprised, amused, and even a bit shocked by some of the current rules and standards, to which they applied such pejorative terms as "picayune" and "Mickey Mouse." Freshmen are required to be in their rooms studying from 7 to 9 P.M., and there are curfew hours, progressively relaxed for upperclassmen, in the dormitories. The supervision of the dormitories, largely populated by freshmen and sophomores from out of town, comes from above by a system of faculty proctors and "assistant deans." The latter are older students who sometimes find themselves embarrassed by their dual roles.

The American student revolt so much in the public eye in the mid-sixties is conspicuous by its absence at St. Thomas. Students describe the administration as liberal and fair though firm. They accept its "benevolent paternalism" with only mild objections to the "Now, my good boy" attitude of the Dean of Students and some faculty proctors.

There is no boy-girl socializing of any importance on the campus, where girls were not often seen until 1965–66, though student exchanges between St. Thomas and St. Catherine had been going on for more than a decade. By 1965–66, however, about fifty girls from St. Catherine were taking courses on the campus, and forty St. Thomas boys were traveling to the St. Catherine campus to attend classes. Probably the girls have not tarried long at St. Thomas because there have been no adequate social facilities.[3] Dating patterns and social relationships differ markedly from those on a coeducational campus. Dates occur off campus and have to be arranged in advance rather than impromptu and informally. At St. Thomas, this leads to steady dating. Often a student first meets a girl through a blind date arranged by another couple. St. Thomas boys date many St. Catherine girls and attend formal functions there in large numbers. Many of the locals find their dates in their home districts, where they have most of their social life.

Under these circumstances, it is hardly surprising that the student observers encountered very little mention of sex problems on campus. Their analysis was that boy-girl relationships take place "somewhere else," which occasions little campus gossip or comment. The all-male atmosphere and the paucity of social space seemed to account for this "peculiar" state of affairs. One of the student observers felt drinking was a prevalent and serious problem; but he praised the college for enforcing the legal restrictions on drinking rather than "hypocritically winking" at them. His observation (and this was confirmed by other information) was that marijuana and LSD had not invaded the St. Thomas campus.

Intercollegiate athletics is a unifying force of considerable strength. St. Thomas belongs to the eight-college Minnesota Intercollegiate Athletic Conference, in which its teams compete very successfully.

[3] Now that the two colleges have synchronized their calendars and the number of student exchanges is rising, more informal boy-girl socializing will probably occur.

Regarding the problem of campus parochialism, several activities which could help to mitigate this are already under way. St. Thomas, St. Catherine, Hamline University, and Macalester College have had a student and faculty exchange program for fourteen years. While it has not functioned vigorously in recent times, it does exist as a potential for strengthening all four institutions. For example, a foundation-aided program of area studies has sponsored for several years an annual cooperative course in one of five areas—Russia, Africa, Latin America, the Middle East, and the Far East—and the six-semester-hour course is taught by four teachers, including the coordinator, from the four colleges and is open to qualified upperclassmen from all of them. The four colleges have recently extended their exchanges by opening all their courses without charge to any student whom his own college recommends.

St. Thomas and St. Catherine especially see promise in this exchange program and are moving to strengthen it. Bus service between the two campuses began in 1966–67. In the spring of 1967, the faculties of St. Thomas and St. Catherine voted to allow their students to take majors not offered by one college at the other. This action opens up a number of new majors for St. Thomas men, including art, elementary education, medical technology, and even nursing; new majors for St. Catherine's girls will be available in journalism, physics, and business administration. The two colleges have for the first time signed a joint contract in a minor business matter involving the production of ID cards.

Another possibility, as yet unexplored, for widening the student's intellectual horizons might be the vigorous promotion of student and faculty exchange with more colleges, Catholic and non-Catholic, both at home and abroad. One gambit might be exchange with Catholic colleges in other cultures—for example, Laval University in French Canada and one of the Latin American universities, such as the Pontificia Universidad Javeriana at Bogotá.

The faculty The greatest single strength of St. Thomas is its relatively stable faculty of 101 full-time teachers (1965–66), of whom 43 have doctor's degrees. The North Central Association average of doctorates for its four-year colleges, when last computed, was 35 percent. The national average is about 26 percent.

There are twenty-six part-time teachers, three of whom have the highest degree. Only two of the faculty are women. The proportion of Catholics on the faculty, though high (84 percent), is less than among the students (98.6 percent). Although about 60 percent of the faculty are graduates of Catholic institutions, fewer than half of the doctor's degrees are from Catholic universities. Furthermore, the degrees come from widely scattered institutions.

Only twenty-three of the full-time lay faculty are St. Thomas alumni, five of whom are full professors. Fewer than half of the priests are St. Thomas graduates. By way of contrast, the administration has a larger proportion of alumni: In 1965–66, three of the five chief administrators, including the President, were alumni. Thus inbreeding does not seem to be a major problem in the teaching faculty, though it may be in the administration.

Salaries are comparatively low at St. Thomas, and many of the faculty have training and experience which they could sell in a much higher money market. One department head recounted a number of offers of substantially higher salary, and several other teachers mentioned the resisted temptation of higher salaries elsewhere. Such people choose to come to St. Thomas and to stay because they prefer a Catholic college to a secular one. Higher salaries at the lower ranks (AAUP indexes A and B for instructor and assistant professor) are doubtless helpful in obtaining, if not retaining, new faculty. Those that stay seem to do so because they are happy about their teaching, because they have a decisive influence over academic affairs, and because they find the atmosphere pleasant and in harmony with their religion.

Still, these factors do not dispose of the problem. The AAUP rated the St. Thomas 1965–66 salaries as D for average full-time compensation (including the fringe benefits of retirement and insurance) and D for average salary. The figures given represented gains over the previous year of 7.7 percent and 5 percent. Compared with its Catholic competition, St. Thomas shows up reasonably well, in the upper fourth of thirty colleges which made reports to the AAUP and comparable to the lowest third of sixteen universities. But it compares poorly with the non-Catholic private colleges in its own state.

Before 1966, teaching loads were approximately twelve hours per week, under the average for the North Central Association, although loads in many colleges in the North Central and elsewhere ran well below this figure. With most of the courses now meeting four hours per week, members of the faculty teach only three courses per semester, and their number of simultaneous preparations has been reduced. The student-faculty ratio of about 17 to 1 is higher than in most liberal arts colleges, though it is less than the 20 to 1 figure recommended by Ruml and Morrison.[4] Many classes for freshmen and sophomores go to 40 or more; most of the junior and senior courses are much smaller.

Where the teaching load takes a toll is in the limit it places on scholarly studies and production. The faculty accepts teaching as the paramount task and willingly devotes a major proportion of time to it. Inquiry among 80 percent of the faculty disclosed that scholarly research and writing are more the exception than the rule. True, the present faculty has produced fifteen books and many articles, but this represents total lifetime output—a low level of scholarly production when measured against the productiveness of superior liberal arts faculties.

The teaching we encountered, though conventional, was competent. The lecture method was the main instrument of instruction, according to observers' reports and the testimony of students. There was little visible evidence of experimentation in teaching methods, although some teachers seemed to make considerable use of the audio-visual materials in the library. Experimentation, though by no means a sure sign of superior teaching, does indicate an active search for its improvement. St. Thomas teachers probably can find little time for it.

Student judgment of the teaching at St. Thomas was on the whole quite positive, even though the students singled out certain stars and poor teachers. Only one department, Theology, was criticized as a whole for uninspired teaching. Most students reported that teachers are accessible for counseling and discussion; only a few of teachers were described as "teaching and running." Some concern was expressed about large classes and the difficulty of getting to know faculty well. In student opinion, the standards set by the faculty were severe.

Some members of the faculty take part in local politics and run for office. In fact, the last three unsuccessful candidates for mayor of St. Paul were members of the St. Thomas faculty. The newly elected mayor, a St. Thomas honor graduate, formerly taught at the St. Thomas Academy. The 1966 elections placed six alumni, including one professor, in the State Senate of Minnesota and eight alumni and one former professor in the House of Representatives. Senator Eugene McCarthy was on the St. Thomas faculty, teaching sociology and economics from 1946 to 1949.

[4] Beardsley Ruml and Donald H. Morrison, *Memo to a College Trustee*, McGraw-Hill Book Company, New York, 1959.

The feeling of the local AAUP chapter seems to be that St. Thomas faculty have little to complain about except salaries and teaching loads. And they do not complain much about either one. They accept the limited time for research and writing as an institutional necessity; the administration, in fact, was praised for "leaving us free to teach." The AAUP chapter sees its most valuable function as an *agent provocateur* of faculty discussion rather than of protest.

Academic freedom and faculty legislative power are taken for granted, but when one probes into the matter, they are clearly a deep source of faculty satisfaction. Members of the faculty are not required, as they are in some religious institutions, to sign a pledge to respect any dogma of the church. However, one memorable faculty meeting attended by the observers, in which the required courses in theology were being discussed, made it evident that the majority of faculty, including those in such mundane subjects as business administration, showed deep concern for the teachings of the church and the value system it stands for.

The curriculum Like most liberal arts colleges, St. Thomas has moved gradually but steadily into fields of study preparatory to business and professional careers. It has retained its liberal arts goals, though the strictly classical content of the curriculum has been greatly modified. Today, the teaching of Greek and Latin occupies only a little more than the full time of one member of the faculty.

During the presidency of Bishop James P. Shannon, from 1956 to 1966, graduate study for classroom teachers and school service personnel was added as a public service beyond the liberal arts boundaries. Bishop Shannon felt strongly the college's obligation to the church and to the community to provide graduate teacher training because there is no other Catholic institution performing this function in the upper Midwest.

As a similar public service, Bishop Shannon several years ago created a Management Center which offers "the business community of the Upper Midwest" formal courses, seminars, and conferences on business management; it is affiliated with the Industrial Relations Center of the University of Chicago. By decision of the faculty, the center is conducted parallel with, but not as an integral part of, the college. It offers no college credit.

Bishop Shannon was also instrumental in initiating a Department of Journalism in the college, regarding journalism as a legitimate major field for a liberal arts college because it requires literacy in dealing with intellectual matters over a wide front. The St. Thomas journalism curriculum emphasizes intellectual content more than technical proficiency.

In 1962–63, the college carried on one of its periodic curriculum reviews, under the aegis of the Liberal Arts Committee, which proposed some changes. The Curriculum Committee then worked on the proposal a year and a half, and the faculty accepted it in principle in 1965. The St. Thomas academic program, like that of most liberal arts colleges, entails a distribution of required general courses over the humanities, social and natural sciences, and a major field of study. The review resulted in a thorough but not revolutionary revision, which widened and enriched the liberal education program.

The extensive required courses in religion and philosophy, more than one-fifth of the general education total, were continued with only minor modifications. Added requirements included a course in art, a second course in literature, a third course in science or mathematics, and two years of a foreign language. A major change reduced the number of courses taken at one time by a student and correspondingly the number that a member of the faculty must teach. Departments were required to reconstruct their offerings to meet present and foreseen needs, to prune away unnecessary courses, and to arrange them into larger units of study. The Liberal Arts Committee recommended raising admissions standards and requiring the College Entrance Examination Board tests, including English composition and one other subject. Its report emphasized the need for changing the approach of freshman courses and for advanced placement of able freshmen.

Before the process of curricular revision was completed, virtually every member of the faculty had taken some part. The administrative leadership in the long campaign, which required sixty meetings of the Curriculum Committee, came from the Dean of the College.[5]

A central problem in the curriculum of St. Thomas is the role of Catholic theology—particularly, how it is to become an active catalyst in the educational process. The importance that the college and the faculty place on instruction in Catholic theology is shown by the

[5] One of St. Thomas's strengths has been the consistency and integrity of academic administration over a period of two decades by the Dean of the College. A veteran member of the St. Thomas faculty emphasized this point strongly because he knows of other Catholic institutions where "the opposite has produced very grave disaffection." In 1967 further changes in the curriculum were made, reducing required courses for the degree from thirty-six to thirty-two, and reducing the English, philosophy, and theology requirements by one course each.

requirement that all students take four theology courses, over 10 percent of the entire general education curriculum. In addition, three courses in philosophy are required.

With students, the theology courses have long been the most unpopular group in the curriculum: Such terms as "dull" and "rote" were freely used in describing them. The students claim that they do not object to required instruction in Catholic theology (on the contrary, they came expecting it), but they maintain that it could and should be made more stimulating, more interesting, more rigorous, and more relevant to contemporary life. All members of the faculty seem to be aware of this negative student response to the theology courses.

Two Catholic members of teaching orders were among the observers, and made a point of looking into this problem. The senior observer, a priest who visited St. Thomas twice and had many conversations with the priests, lay faculty, and students, thought that one of the main reasons for the students' negative opinion of the theology courses was what he called "pastoralism." He believes that students tend to accept the theological teaching as "baptized rationalizations" handed down to them with pastoral authority rather than as intellectual material for critical examination. The other observer, a nun, who attended two classes in theology, agreed with this view. She reported that in one of the courses, particularly, interesting and challenging questions were raised but there was not a single student response.

With this basic attitude on the part of the students, it would appear that the teaching has not successfully come to grips with the situation. That the faculty are deeply concerned was made quite clear by a warm debate over the theology curriculum during the curriculum-revision process described earlier. The Curriculum Committee approved only the first two courses of a seventeen-course program the Theology Department had proposed and referred the balance of it back to the department for further consideration. The department vigorously defended its proposals, but the faculty voted to uphold the Curriculum Committee. The vote was very close, after debate in which many members of the faculty, from a variety of disciplines, took part. One result of this split decision was to convince lay faculty that their power of academic decision extended even into the realm of theology. In the spring of 1967, the Theology Department presented a new proposal composed of only nine courses, which was passed by the faculty without discussion.

In further mitigation of student feeling concerning the theology requirements, the Liberal Arts Committee recommended that in the new curriculum, beginning in 1966–67, students should be allowed to substitute an approved related course for one of the advanced theology courses. The recommendation did not pass, but a year later the theology requirement was reduced by one course.

In addition to credit courses in religion, the college provides ample opportunities for religious observance. It does not, however, require attendance at religious services.

The physical and financial resources

In conducting the search for its "identity," St. Thomas has certain resources—physical, financial, and human—at its command.

The physical plant of the college, well-distributed over the 45-acre campus, serves its needs in excellent fashion.

The 1.6 million dollar O'Shaughnessy Library, built in 1959 to house a total of over 150,000 volumes, already holds over 125,000 books and 750 periodical series. It is a magnificently spacious and functional building which meets both faculty and student needs for books and periodicals, audio-visual materials and projection, study and seminar space, and special collections. The private studies for faculty are very popular.

Also recently constructed are the Murray Hall student union, at a cost of 2.3 million dollars, of which about 1.8 million dollars was provided by government loans, and the 300-bed Dowling Hall, financed mainly by a government loan of 1.2 million dollars. The two main academic buildings, Aquinas and Albert Magnus halls, average about twenty-seven years in age but are in excellent condition. The classrooms and laboratories are well-furnished and -equipped. There is a large and well-equipped physical education building, and the extensive athletic fields have stands for 6,500 spectators.

Another dormitory of 240-bed capacity is being erected on the site of two recently demolished academy buildings, and will increase the total dormitory capacity to 800 men, over 40 percent of the full-time enrollment. A government loan is expected to provide most of the capital cost.

With the exception of added dormitory space, which may be needed if the trend to admit more students from a distance continues, the college could stand fast on the present plant.

In terms of needs, however, the college's financial resources are more modest than its physical assets—an almost standard pattern in Catholic colleges. Like St. Thomas, many with imposing plants operate on very tight budgets and low faculty salary scales.

The operating income of the college for 1965–66 was over $3.5

million, including a conservatively stated amount of $125,000 of contributed services from the twenty-six priests in the administration and faculty.[6] The auxiliary services—dining, dormitory, and bookstore—constituted over one-fourth of the total. Excluding the income from auxiliary services, the net educational income was thus about $2.5 million. Tuition and fees supplied about 78 percent of this amount, which is in the tuition-policy zone of most private colleges. Only $177,000 came from endowment, or about 7 percent of the educational budget. The "living endowment" of contributed services amounted to 5 percent. Annual operating gifts contributed $125,000 or about 5 percent. The remaining 5 percent came from miscellaneous but fairly stable sources of income.

In the decade of President Shannon (1956–66), major fund-raising efforts produced over $8.5 million, including the Ford $1.5 million. Under his leadership, the Ford match was made in three years and three times over, rather than the required double match. When the financial smoke clears, the college's endowment should amount to about $5 million, which should produce at least $200,000 of annual income. The $750,000 raised by certain parishes was contributed to the endowment to provide scholarships for teacher preparation. The *Catholic Digest*, with a capital value of almost $750,000, was also turned over to college ownership in the recent Ford matching campaign. A $5 million endowment is still modest, however, and even if the $200,000 per year income is directed largely to increasing faculty salaries, these will still need to be raised, in the next decade, by much more than the additional income will finance.

The annual gifts seem to be far below the potential, in view of the Catholic good will for St. Thomas in the twin cities. Indeed, one of the most important assets of the college would appear to be the general respect in which it is held locally. Because a great many of

[6] The archdiocese makes no annual contribution to the college's operating budget, although after World War II it built and presented to the college a new science hall at a cost of over $1 million. The influence and support of the archbishop has been a constant and important factor in all the college's fund-raising efforts—for example, a $750,000 scholarship fund given by parishes in the archdiocese, and the provision of funds as a "friendly creditor" at crucial periods when otherwise the college would have had to seek bank loans. The assignment by the archbishop of the twenty-six priests to the college staff is an especially valuable current contribution, because these priests stay permanently or for long periods with the college and are allowed leaves for travel and study. Their scholarly training slightly exceeds the lay faculty's as measured by advanced degrees. They form the nucleus of the faculty from which to date the Presidents and Deans have developed; the three strong leaders of the last thirty-three years, their chief administrative assistants, and some of the most distinguished professors have been priests of the archdiocese.

St. Thomas's graduates teach, practice professions, and hold important business and industrial positions and political office there, the college's alumni can and do give it support, not only by financial gifts but also by public advocacy and personal service. The financial gifts are, on occasion, substantial. Thus one alumnus has given the college two important buildings, and when the college carried on its Ford matching campaign, many of these men took an active part. An additional strong source of support is the large body of students and their parents who live in the twin cities. Yet more aggressive fund-raising efforts on the local scene might produce operating funds to strengthen the college's program and salary structure.

Governance and relations with the Church

The human resource of leadership and governance constitutes an important element in any institution's dynamics. At St. Thomas, this factor is one of the Church's key contributions.

The college has been fortunate in having three strong Presidents in the period from 1933 to 1966. Msgr. James H. Moynihan led it through the difficult depression and war years, from 1933 to 1944. He held fast to the classical ideal but adhered to the new divisional organization that was created in 1929 by the Fathers of the Holy Cross.

Father Vincent J. Flynn (1944–56) was the first President of St. Thomas to have done graduate work in a secular university; his Ph.D. in English was taken at the University of Chicago. He exercised his leadership far beyond the bounds of Catholic education and in 1949 served as president of the Association of American Colleges.

Within the college, he encouraged much greater faculty participation in governance. He appointed a faculty committee to prepare a faculty organization plan and to formalize and codify the academic powers which he had encouraged the faculty to assume. The faculty was given the power, subject to the veto of the President, to decide upon changes in the curriculum, requirements for graduation, tenure standards for students, student discipline policies, and all other faculty-student relationships. An Academic Council was established, with six elected faculty as members plus the President (without vote) and the Dean, to advise the President on "faculty rank and tenure and other matters he refers to it."

Bishop James P. Shannon, who became President in 1956 following Father Flynn, earned a Ph.D. in American studies at Yale University, and was appointed a bishop in 1966. He, too, was recognized as a leader in college administration by election to head the Association of American Colleges, in 1966. While his financial leadership was outstanding, one of his major contributions to St. Thomas was probably his furtherance not only of lay faculty but of lay control.

Bishop Shannon was succeeded as President in May, 1966, by Msgr. Terrence J. Murphy, formerly Executive Vice President. It is significant that the faculty was consulted and was influential in the election of the last three Presidents. The archbishop, as Chairman of the Board, polled the faculty before the election of President Flynn, and in the recent change Archbishop Binz consulted with the Academic Council and secured its approval before nominating Monsignor Murphy.

Monsignor Murphy is the first President to have had experience in administration. He took his training for the priesthood at St. Paul, the archdiocesan seminary and, after eight years as a parish priest, joined the St. Thomas faculty in 1954. Choosing political science as his academic discipline, he completed a master's degree at the University of Minnesota and a doctor's degree at Georgetown University. In 1962, he left the teaching staff to become Executive Vice President.

The college's first problem in its relations with the Church is its admissions policy, which is growing steadily more selective. First, the faculty, having already raised the standards to limit admission to the top 60 percent of the high school class, will raise them in the near future to the top half. Second, the spreading reputation of the college is bringing more students from a distance to its door.

Even now, the college must deny admission to students from its own diocese who do not meet the admissions standards. As the threshold rises, more and more local students will be turned away. This may create serious strains in the college's relationship with the archdiocese, not because the rejected applicants will be unable to enter an institution of higher education, but because there will be no Catholic college in the area for them. The question which the college must confront is whether it has an obligation to these students, who want and need some form of post-high school education. One alternative would be to add a two-year associate in arts program with terminal vocational courses. Another might be to start a separate Catholic junior college in the archdiocese. Otherwise a large number of local Catholic boys who need such a program will enter the open doors of the secular community colleges, which the archdiocese may not view as desirable. The upper limit of enrollment which President Murphy foresees is twenty-five hundred. Beyond that figure, he thinks, the physical plant would have to be enlarged substantially at great expense.

A deeper dilemma, not only for St. Thomas but for the Roman Catholic Church, concerns the trend toward secularizing Catholic institutions, or at least placing them under lay control. The time is approaching when the Church in the United States will need to give careful consideration to its college and university policy on lay participation in governance. Many Catholic institutions have grown so rapidly that the number of lay faculty far exceeds the number of religious faculty. Except for the seminaries, the church institutions of higher education are increasingly oriented to science, scholarship, and the lay world. Some of them play important roles in their local economies. In the past few years, and particularly since the first convocation of Pope John's Ecumenical Council, there have been signs of unrest, even of revolt, in Catholic college faculties. Catholic students, too, have voiced their concern about college governance: In August, 1963, the National Federation of Catholic College Students at its convention (which met, incidentally, at Minneapolis) censured the Catholic University of America for refusing to allow four prominent Catholic theologians to speak there. On all sides, pressures are mounting for increased faculty and lay Trustee control of Catholic colleges.

While these pressures are being yielded to in some measure, the statesmen of the Church, in doing so, are probably uneasily aware of the history of the Protestant colleges that spread over the country in the first half of the nineteenth century. At first completely controlled by their churches and usually presided over by ministers, many of these colleges have in the last hundred years severed their church connections. Those that remain connected range from church control that is still almost complete to only the most nominal relationship. Many colleges have almost had independence thrust upon them by the inability of their churches to give them substantial financial support. While there have been other reasons for the growing gap, finances have certainly been a major one. This same problem confronts the Catholics, because the church has had to let its colleges forage for themselves to build their buildings and pay their faculties.

Historically, the Catholic college in this country has been controlled by a religious order, and its Board of Trustees consists of members of the religious community. The president gets his directions from the board, of which he is usually a member. No laymen are involved, though there may be an advisory board of influential laymen from the local area. No better system of isolation from the ongoing world could be devised.

St. Thomas is one of many Catholic institutions that are aware of this self-imposed handicap; indeed, St. Thomas presents an interesting case study in moving toward more lay control. Of its eighteen Board members, thirteen are laymen. The five priests include the archbishop, as Chairman, and the President of the college, who is president of the legal corporation. The other three priests on the Board are monsignors of the Church from the archdiocese. The non-clerics, while laymen, are by no means "lay figures" in the sense of being meekly complaisant. They take active roles in policy discussion and decision; among them are some of the strongest supporters and most energetic workers for the college.

It is noteworthy that in the academic year 1966–67, two prominent Catholic universities, Notre Dame and St. Louis, turned control over to boards with a majority of lay Trustees. These moves, which are attributed to the liberalizing influence of the Vatican Council, may be the beginning of a general movement to lay control. They may also ensure, to some extent, against possible constitutional objections to government aid such as were recently sustained by the U.S. Supreme Court in the so-called "Maryland case," in which the Maryland Supreme Court refused to permit the State Legislature to make grants to three church-controlled colleges.

Separation from the church is neither contemplated nor possible for St. Thomas. It must find a way to make its religious instruction vital and stimulating enough to attract and hold bright young Catholics. Perhaps it can fairly be said that up to now, St. Thomas has done a better job of preserving doctrine than of communicating it vitally.

The shape of the future

The future of St. Thomas rests on the fairly solid foundations of its long-established reputation, its special appeal to Catholic boys, and its recently demonstrated ability to raise funds, mainly capital, from its clientele. Because the growing competition of low-tuition state colleges puts conservative limits on its own tuition charges, the college will increasingly need to secure substantial current contributions. In the last three decades, however, the College of St. Thomas has faced new issues in higher education with a foresight and courage that have made it a bellwether among Catholic colleges. Its leadership, its governance, and its opportunities in the populous and progressive twin cities should enable the St. Thomas of the future to stand out with a clear identity and to continue as a pioneer Catholic college.

The St. Thomas profile was written by W. Boyd Alexander, Emeritus Vice President and Dean of the Faculty of Antioch College. His associate was Edward J. Drummond, S.J., vice president of the Medical Center, St. Louis University. Acting on behalf of St. Thomas was the Rev. Henri Dulac, then chairman of the Department of Philosophy and now director of development. The student observers were William May of St. Louis University and Elliott Long of Antioch College.

P RIVATE colleges cannot give leadership in American higher
education unless they encourage and exemplify able leadership
within their own precincts. In both universities and free-standing
colleges, the obstacles to effective leadership are vast. But if a
college can create the conditions in which leadership flourishes, it
will be able to recruit the leaders it needs. Indeed, potential
leaders will seek it out.

What are the conditions for effective leadership? Who will the
leaders be? How can a college best use them?

Who will lead *The leaders we wish for the colleges will not all be presidents,*
at what? *trustees, or administrative officers. We speak of leaders in a broad
sense, including faculty, students, alumni, and members of a larger
community who can play a substantial part in shaping the future of
a college; for we see many colleges as requiring a diffuse, decen-
tralized, multifaceted type of leadership. Even though some colleges
may arise and thrive for a time under thoroughly autocratic or
hierarchical leadership, these patterns will become more and more
exceptional.*

*Why do we suppose that leadership will change in the direction
of decentralization? Research on management suggests that a
bureaucratic or autocratic pattern of governance works best where
the task is simple and unchanging and where the activities making it*

up require little individual judgment or special knowledge. However, as the functions of an organization become so complex and so changing that they require large proportions of highly educated personnel and constant adjustments in the productive processes, it becomes essential to give increasing autonomy to the individual worker. Continuous communication up, down, and sideways begins to be essential to keeping tasks clear and methods of work effective. Commitment to the organization's being and purposes begins to be crucial to efficiency; long-range organizational health requires a morale built on more than a sense of being well cared for. This is not to say that organizations will be anarchic or aimless. But they will reach decisions more by consultation than edict, and the esteem in which individuals are held will depend more on their own ability and judgment than on their place in the administrative hierarchy.*

When these findings are applied to higher education, it seems inescapable that the dominant styles of leadership will change radically within a decade or two and that the change will bring about new and more autonomous roles for faculty, students, "friends in the community," and administrative officers. One can see this already happening in the profile colleges. St. Thomas has moved gradually toward lay control, which means greater autonomy for the administrative officers and for the institution as a whole. Goddard has established a second campus, Northwood, which has its own faculty and student body and makes many of its own academic and social plans, though it shares administration and some facilities with the Greatwood campus. Since the profiles were written, Oberlin and Earlham have both adopted new administrative structures, parceling out some of their academic deans' duties to faculty who continue to teach part time. Fully two-thirds of the profile colleges are becoming seriously engaged in associations, unions, centers, or collaborative enterprises of one sort or another. This means that individual faculty, administrators, and even students perform jobs for the association from time to time and bring back ideas,

---

* These generalizations are not without exceptions. For example, individuals who have a high need to be dependent upon others will require more direction even in complex and changing tasks; but at the same time one function of leadership among such workers is to teach them to become less dependent in order that the work of the organization may better succeed. Also, some subfunctions of the college will be of the routine or unchanging type that is best-managed in a highly directive way. Perhaps, too, a college can afford and enjoy a highly democratic process on only a limited number of questions at a time; to achieve this end, it will have to permit other matters to be run more arbitrarily.

experience, and money from outside the college, again undercutting conventionally hierarchical patterns of government. In virtually every one of the profile colleges, students are seeking greater influence in college policy decisions—and getting it, through mechanisms that range from student-faculty-Trustee retreats at Wheaton to the campaigning of a so-called "Student Liberation Front" at Morehouse.

Leading in the choice of mission

The significant choices of mission discussed in Chapter 2 will not come easily. Usually such choices are not a matter of selecting from among clearly defined and available alternatives, but of imagining those alternatives and creating the conditions in which they represent feasible choices. A primary task of leadership— among students and faculty as well as among constituency and trustees—will be the achievement of this self-definition.

Hardly any contemporary college is in a position to rest content with its current articulation of its mission. The words "articulation of its mission" are used advisedly: A college may have a sense of its functions that is quite accurate and perceptive without having expressed this insight in a form that can clarify college programs, inspire cooperation within the college, and draw support from its public. Or a college may have a well-articulated purpose that fitted an earlier time and different circumstances. The rapidity of change today requires a college constantly to reconsider what it should be doing and how it might be getting it done. As we argued in Chapters 2 and 5, this reconsideration is essential because, though liberal education is an abiding and definite aspiration, its implications and applications change with the circumstances of men.

In urging colleges to articulate their missions, we do not wish to oversimplify. We are persuaded that college mission or purpose can best be thought of as a cluster of functions, some of them having to do with the development of students, some with service to a further constituency, some with the pursuit of certain intellectual, religious, or social convictions. No college will have a single mission only. Further, while many of the college's functions can be and should be deliberately chosen, other functions may remain latent, fulfilled more or less inadvertently. Not many faculty prize their colleges and universities because of their usefulness in providing an ideal setting for the delay of marriage and for effective matchmaking or because of their ability to get individuals of different and potentially hostile subcultures within America to appreciate each other and to work together. Yet these unadvertised functions may be among the major contributions of higher education to the strength and productivity of our society.

More than that, some elements in a college's purpose may be (or appear to be) at odds with other elements—vocational preparation versus more liberal explorations at Simmons, "pastoral" theology versus theological debate at St. Thomas. As we attempted to show in Chapter 2 and in some of the profiles, these cross-purposes may stimulate a college, provided the people that hold them also hold other aims and attitudes in common. For these reasons we do not propose that a college's mission be set down in clear and unambiguous prose to which faculty, administration, trustees, and students shall subscribe. Words are not always reliable bearers of meaning: The focus on a verbal formulation of purpose can end in agreement about words among people who differ in intent or in disagreement about words among people who seek fundamentally congruent ends. The game of trying to formulate a single, wholly acceptable statement of purpose often requires more energy than it is worth.

An approach that is likely to be more fruitful is a running discussion of college purposes in the context of specific decisions, a continuous and multipronged process of self-criticism. As a college adds new faculty or drops old programs, as it replaces key administrative officers, as it undertakes to set admissions policies, decide on its proper size, establish new relationships with other institutions, or raise money, it will do well to think repeatedly about its aims—what students it wants to serve and how, what intellectual explorations it is particularly equipped to make, what ideas it would like to stand for.

A variety of arrangements can further this process of self-criticism and reconsideration of purposes. In the 1950s, college self-studies were first enormously popular and then came under a cloud of doubt. The difficulty with many of the early self-studies was not the intended self-scrutiny, but their prodigal use of time and money and their frequent failure to reach conclusions relevant to immediate college decisions. To get a sanction for replacing an incompetent department chairman, a college does not need to perform a whole institutional self-study. On the other hand, one cannot intelligently debate the functions of the Department of Sociology in an urban college without studying the social changes occurring in the city.

A part of the plan of the Union for Research and Experimentation in *Higher Education,* of which Goddard and Monteith are members, is that each of its colleges should set up an office of "research" (largely examination of the college's ongoing programs) and development. This policy means a regular investment on the order of 2 percent of the total budget and personnel of the college. In the colleges which are the most successful of the group in evaluating their own programs, however, this office functions, not primarily as a mechanism for centralized planning, but as a stimulator of evaluation and planning throughout the institution. Among a staff of fewer than two hundred, for example, as many as 20 percent within a single year have obtained modest financial support for projects ranging from the preparation of a single multimedia presentation to something as far-reaching as reformulating the functions of a department and recasting the requirements to be fulfilled by students majoring there with different postgraduate objectives. Cumulatively, this sort of research and development can contribute substantially to a college's awareness of its mission and its imaginativeness in carrying out this mission.

A second important mechanism of self-scrutiny is the review committee or task group. There was a time when colleges could be expected to have a fairly standard set of permanent committees to take care of the business of the day and to prepare for plenary faculty meeting whatever required the approval of the full faculty. Although our study found a few fairly standard committees under variable nomenclature, there was widespread use of ad hoc subcommittees, study groups, visiting consultants, and staff task groups, to question present practice and propose improvements. Colleges making regular and substantial curricular changes often separated the work of a "curriculum committee"—to approve minor changes and to interpret the applications of going policy— from that of an "educational policy committee," whose business is to question going policy and to propose program and policy changes. The use of ad hoc "visiting committees" or "review committees" to monitor the quality of work of departments or of special programs is beginning to be regarded as normal, and an occasional college has scheduled annual reviews, sometimes combining internal with external criticism, of a substantial proportion of its educational program. In this arrangement, the academic dean becomes less the architect of administrative position on issues of educational development and more the supervisor of the process of arriving at sound decisions. A cadre of senior faculty—or of young faculty and even students—may emerge as those with the detachment and judiciousness and colleague support to chair these influential efforts at self-criticism within the institution.

Third, the reexamination of college mission can take place indirectly as individuals or departments or programs within the college compete for scarce resources—either resources of the college itself or resources it might attract from foundations or government. Groups pressing for new programs or expansion of old ones can reasonably be expected to argue their case from what they understand to be the college's purposes. For example, when President Bolling and others began pushing for foreign study and other off-campus experience for Earlham students, they argued that the college could not accomplish its mission if it confined itself and its students to southern Indiana; partly because of its Quaker convictions, it must be responsive to human problems and human experience in every quarter of the world. When the argument proved persuasive and off-campus programs were adopted, world involvement became an even more significant part of the college's definition of purpose.

Similarly, individuals may be expected to relate their own plans to college purposes, thereby clarifying both. We suspect that the strong college of the future will invest considerable talent from among its faculty and administrative leaders in assisting other faculty to think through their own ambitions as teachers, scholars, or creative artists and to consider how they and the college can support each other in improvement. Under one guise or another, a number of colleges already do this. Some department chairmen and deans ask faculty periodically to indicate the work they hope to be giving particular attention to in the next year or so, and to suggest ways in which the college can assist them or special ways in which that work might be of value to the college.

Often, the seeking of outside grants provides an occasion for reexamination of the aims of individuals and of the college. Administrators sometimes talk as though this were simply a policing job—seeing to it that individual projects are budgeted so that they do not become an expense to the institution. Certainly a college is obliged to say no to projects that will divert substantial money and energy away from its central purposes. But, more important, discussion of individual projects with the dean or with a faculty panel can sometimes lead to a fresh formulation of college purposes or to a redirection of some projects so that they mesh with college aims at the same time that they advance the careers of their proponents. Thus a scientist who makes a breakthrough in synthesis of a scarce organic compound may ask support for continuing research which the easy availability of the synthesized compound makes possible for the first time. Through such research, he can contribute to learning among undergraduates and colleagues and involve them in both his methodological and his conceptual work. Or he may treat this research as an entirely separate matter, leading to a dilution of his work as teacher and member of the college community. A sociologist can similarly make his research on the inner city either a diversion from his teaching or an enhancement of the relevance and impact of that teaching.

In these ways and others, the question of a college's mission can be kept before the faculty and staff and kept relevant to decisions. But that does not mean that a clearly articulated consensus will automatically emerge. Disagreements may be genuine and deep. More than that, articulation of mission may be difficult because it calls for essential change. Americans are adept at relabeling and repackaging the same old cereal; they are as resistant as the next people to changing a basic recipe. Highly verbal Americans, such as professors and students, are particularly adept at delaying decisions to make a basic change and at averting the change after it is resolved upon—and all this honestly and with good reasons. "The wrong change is proposed." "The idea is good, but it won't work as expected." "The idea is good, but you can't do it without destroying the quality of what we are already doing." "There is not enough time to get ready." "There are problems in it that we do not know how to resolve." Sometimes the critics of change are right. To find out when and how and yet to get on with the choices, a college must invest in faculty and administrative leaders who can deal with emerging facts and forces, not by strong-arming them, but by listening, questioning, considering and reconsidering—and finally by deciding.

Communication as a concern of college leaders

A second major preoccupation of leadership in the strong college of the future will be communication. As Warren Bennis and other students of organizational dynamics affirm, enterprises are best able to deal with complex and changing problems when their governance is more than ordinarily democratic and human. More specifically, five qualities characterize this mode of management: (1) full and free communication, regardless of rank and power, (2) a reliance on consensus, rather than on the more customary forms of coercion or compromise, to manage conflict, (3) the idea that influence is based on technical competence and knowledge rather than on personal whim or prerogatives of power, (4) an atmosphere that permits and even encourages emotional expression as well as task-oriented acts, and (5) a basically human bias, one which accepts the inevitability of conflict between the organization and the individual but which is willing to cope with and mediate this conflict on rational grounds. Bennis continues: "Changes along these dimensions are being promoted widely in American industry. Most important, for our analysis, is what we believe to be the reason for these changes: Democracy becomes a functional necessity whenever a social system is competing for survival under conditions of chronic change."* This is precisely the challenge facing private colleges. "Curiously enough," according to Bennis, "universities have been stubbornly resistant to democratization, far more so than most other institutions." Private colleges may seize an advantage here and demonstrate that they can make this change in style of management more readily than the more complex public institutions.

These ideas provide a context for three suggestions about communications as a vehicle for strength in our colleges-to-be. First, colleges should be more open to the expression of emotion than they have been in the past. It is fashionable in collegiate controversy to chide the opposition for the unconstructive, emotional, and logically irrelevant tone of its discourse. Often a substantively sound criticism is rejected because the ground rules of unemotionalism and strict logical relevance have been violated. Yet often the most cogent and significant criticism comes from people so frustrated by the long neglect of their concerns that they no longer have the patience to be gentlemanly. The idea that intellectuals are, or ought to be, less emotional than other mortals is highly suspect. Some studies correlating verbal aptitude with impulsiveness and unconventionality of behavior suggest, in fact, that intellectuals have more than their share of these manifestations of emotion. Perhaps the ability to feel strongly about ideas is one of the virtues of the intellectual community and, if we can but harness it, a potential strength for society. If so, we must within colleges try to learn how it can be used. An administration that is willing to take student outbursts and faculty resistance as signs of important ideas dressed in high emotion will indeed buy new problems aplenty, but it may also tap energies for construction of a substantial future. An

* Warren Bennis, *Changing Organizations*, McGraw-Hill Book Company, New York, 1966, p. 19.

emotional broadside loosed at the dean's curricular policy may actually signal that he is viewed as too domineering; whether or not he is, it may be important to get the question into the open for resolution.

A second suggestion we would press regarding communication bears upon consensus and resolution of conflict. As practiced in an institution like Earlham, with its long tradition of consensus seeking, consensus is utterly different from unanimity. Given the sharp minds, high emotions, diverse interests and competences, and ready tongues of intellectuals, a college that waits upon unanimity will waste vast amounts of time. This point is well-understood in Quaker meetings that have effective experience in consensus seeking. One learns in such a meeting not to make an "issue of conscience" out of every dissent he feels, and the clerk (chairman) learns to incorporate elements of minority concern into the majority resolutions in order to accord respect as well as give influence to every contender.

We are not arguing that a formal commitment to consensus is appropriate to every college. Some may permit themselves a formal vote whenever the chairman senses that action is essential, unanimity will not be achieved, and the minority is not ready to yield. This pattern is preferable to formal consensus in a community without experience in consensus and without developed skill in knowing when individual concern should give way to majority judgment. In other colleges, a tradition of hierarchical prerogative may have important meaning. Thus in selecting a new President, the College of St. Thomas may achieve the effect of consensus while preserving the form of election by the Board of Trustees, of which the archbishop is the Chairman. The archbishop manages this by consulting the faculty and others, with a quality of listening no different from that of the best Quaker clerks. Good listening, after all, was not invented by George Fox.

Whatever the vehicle and mechanisms, we are convinced that the extraction of maximum insight and understanding and performance from college communities of the future will require increasing use of consensus in governance. And that increase will occur more through good communication and listening than through the further elaboration and formalization of committees and councils, which may become so complex and cumbersome as to be self-defeating.

Our third suggestion about communications concerns what is relevant to decision making and whose voice ought be to heard. We have already opened the door to the communication of feelings as germane. This means that good management in a college goes beyond the cognitive. Let us now mention four kinds of relevant contribution the members of a college community may bring to the making of a decision: (1) representation of a special interest, (2) a report from a particular perspective, (3) testimony based on special competence, and (4) commitment achieved by participating in the making of the decision, with resultant effect upon the productivity of the decision. These are not mutually exclusive categories; for example, with sufficient ingenuity, one could derive all of them from the idea of diverse competence. But the rubrics may be helpful in remembering the variety of people who may legitimately contribute to the solving of a college problem.

If a college intends, for example, to review its foreign study programs and make whatever changes seem called for in its policies and operation, a number of people must be heard—students who have been abroad and others planning to go abroad, faculty with conflicting views about the primary values of foreign study and how they can best be obtained, administrators whose work is affected by the foreign program (financial-aids officer, registrar, departmental chairmen, business manager, etc.), faculty with whom students study abroad or who evaluate academic work done abroad. Each of these witnesses could supply different information and opinions when representing his personal interests as they are affected by foreign study, his perspective as an observer of students while they are abroad and after they return, and his special competence to judge the probable effects of proposed changes. Moreover, the cost of proposed programs will have to justify itself in competition with needs elsewhere in the institution. Clearly, if in such a context a decision is to be well-informed and to win the support of the people who must make it work, it cannot be made simply by administrative fiat or by a faculty committee alone or by a quick pooling of votes in faculty meeting. It will require skillful leadership from a number of people, leadership that can look far for information and opinion and yet not become immobilized by a bombardment of facts, logic, and impassioned convictions.

The product: a best buy? Third, college leaders will give increasing thought to their colleges' "productivity"—the results they are achieving and the relation of college costs to those results. If there is a single urgent and unanswered charge on this score, it is that the private colleges are elite enclaves, overspending scarce social resources which might *better be used through public channels to serve a larger, more representative population. This charge is difficult to refute or to substantiate, because one cannot yet hold up educational results to be conclusively weighed and measured. Much less can one compare, with any confidence, the education a student acquires at one college with that he might have acquired at another.*

Still, we are inclined to agree with the critics: A college should go out of business unless it offers or has a strong prospect of offering a sound "buy" to its students and other constituents. In one sense, all the chapters in this book have dealt with effectiveness and efficiency in colleges. But we will stress here four courses of action that should come often to the minds of college leaders as they husband resources and measure effects against expenses: Colleges as a group should diversify their "products" and their services even while attending to the common task of liberal education; by discarding the notion that it must be a self-sufficient entity and by forging a variety of links with other institutions and among various programs of its own, a college may improve its quality and hold down its costs; colleges should attempt to release the energies that lie in intrinsic student motivation; and colleges should invest substantially in discovering what results they are achieving and at what cost, and should then communicate these findings to the public.

1. In Chapter 2 and again in Chapter 7, we emphasize the need in America for highly diverse colleges and universities. The richness of life in a society, we argue, depends upon its capacity to combine order and justice with passionately defended differences among individuals and groups. There is a danger that education, along with radio and television, may erode these differences until all of us talk like NBC or think like the state university. This need not be the result: Education can lend variety and texture to a society rather than sameness, but only if the institutions of education are aware of their distinctive characters and take pride in them.

An Earlham may be costlier than a competing state college, cheaper than an elite private college, and a better buy than either of the others for a student who shares the Earlham ideal of liberal education. We are not suggesting that merely any religious or philosophical contrivance will do as justification for a separate college and a big investment of means. Decadence, primitivism, and irresponsibility can infect religions and philosophies as well as the institutions that embody them. Given this reservation, however, we believe that private colleges can help keep society awake and self-critical by extending the variety of world views available to student choice.

This variety will encompass other differences. Educational philosophies diverge on many grounds. Faculty and students who have no quarrel with the aspirations of a "multiversity" may nevertheless prefer a Goddard-like setting in which greater informality and spontaneity are possible. To some individuals, this feature of college may be of critical importance, well worth a considerable price in the lost benefits of "scale." Again we must ask—without necessarily being ready to answer here and now—whether the university, in order to reduce costs and serve large numbers, sacrifices effectiveness in changing student values and making the most of individual competence. Similarly, we ask whether the college fails to correct weaknesses in its students as it accommodates their temperamental styles. Both kinds of institution have responsibility for reasonable control of costs and assurance of quality. How to discharge that responsibility well is still uncertain enough to warrant a number of ventures that test the issues in practice and thus produce evidence which will eventually enable us to see more certainly what diversity in aim and method is frivolous or wasteful and what is of genuine value.

2. Whatever face a college decides to wear, it will need to balance its budget, getting as much education, research, and service as it can out of each dollar. Several principles of management seem to us to offer college leaders unusual leverage in improving results with modest means. All of them fit with the conception of a college as a home base, providing access to the experiences students and faculty need, within a nationwide or even worldwide network. Let us illustrate with examples of multiple use of programs, people, and equipment, the purchase of services from other institutions at a fraction of the cost, and the encouraging of new symbiotic arrangements.

The use of the same activity for more than one educational purpose is a familiar practice that could be much more widely applied. It may produce two or three benefits for little more than the price of one. Many colleges draw on public schools to provide practice teaching opportunities for undergraduates; or a college may set up a laboratory school to teach undergraduates, to train master's students in education, to do research on learning, and to provide schooling for children. Going a step further, the Associated Colleges of the Midwest and the Chicago school system are collaborating in a program that incorporates practice teaching in

schools ranging from the ghetto to the suburb, city school experience
for faculty, study of problems and policies of urban education, and
discussion of urban sociology with some of the best-informed
people in the city. A joint ACM program with Cuttington College in
Liberia provides a similarly mixed bundle of benefits to that college
(which, incidentally, has acquired a library of forty-six thousand
volumes through this relationship) and to ACM students, faculty, and
recent graduates. A theater that mixes workshop plays—student-
produced and even student-written—amateur performances open
to the public, and professional performances with supporting casts
of students, faculty, and townspeople can fill a community's need for
good drama and serve as a richer laboratory for instruction than a
college could afford on its own. Virtually all the profile colleges
recognize and support social and political action by students—
tutoring, community-center or mental-hospital work, campaigning for
local or national candidates. The work in itself needs to be done,
but more than that, the firsthand introduction to slums, to mental
illness, to ward politics, can often make studies more vivid and
show students how to link learning and action. Finally, Goddard
and other colleges of the Union for Research and Experimentation in
Higher Education have operated a beachhead on one of the smaller
Hawaiian Islands, where students and faculty will spend a year
studying the island's demography, politics, art, education, etc., and
helping the local government to plan and establish a community
college—a rather dashing example of field studies combined with
service.

Frequently a college or university in a given geographical area
will have a program in rare languages or in a costly branch of
science, a program of field research in the social sciences, or some
other rather specialized educational service by virtue of government
or foundation support. This special program may be underused,
since its purpose is to introduce opportunities hitherto missing and
to develop interest in its subject. If other users are charged the full
unsubsidized unit cost, the price may be prohibitive. But if, in
the stages of developing cooperation, other institutions are charged
only incremental costs, usage may increase until the unit cost
becomes bearable, and the supplying institution may be in better
position to command able faculty and to provide strong supporting
staff. Some institutions—such as the Newberry Library and the Argonne
National Laboratories, which regularly receive students and faculty
from ACM colleges—consider it part of their public obligation to
share their extraordinary resources with people in a position to

benefit from them. At the profile colleges, this sort of sharing occurs most often within formal associations—sharing of specialized courses by Morehouse and other members of the Atlanta Center and by St. Thomas and St. Catherine, sharing of graduate teaching talent by Amherst and the Connecticut Valley group, sharing of foreign study centers, field stations, language programs, and off-campus research, study, and action projects by the Associated Colleges of the Midwest, the Great Lakes Colleges Association, and the Union for Research and Experimentation in Higher Education.

Within a college, improvements of program or additions to staff often occur with little synchronization or symbiosis among these developments. A computer may be installed because a progressive college should have a computer, but the training of programmers and the development of instructional uses that would make the computer of really substantial help may come about only as an afterthought. Sometimes financial support is proffered to colleges in a way that fosters this uneven and wasteful kind of development, as when the earmarking of the grant explicitly excludes uses that would "compromise" a pure research effort or some other special purpose. Sometimes the most productive and efficient collaboration in program development may be of a type that links unlikely partners—biology with philosophy rather than chemistry, research with public service rather than with graduate study, postdoctoral with undergraduate teaching rather than with graduate study, etc. We expect that in the future, colleges will be more ingenious in discovering symbiotic relations among people, programs, and institutions.

3. If there is a single greatest untapped source of efficiency and productivity in learning, it lies in the energy that might be released if colleges could rely less on extrinsic inducements to learning and more on the interests, convictions, and ambitions that can move students from within. Though many people have argued that grades, credits, and degrees are irrelevant paraphernalia, only a few colleges have begun to test the implications of this idea for contemporary undergraduate instruction. Even rather modest experiments disclose that students are under much greater compulsion in their studies than has been commonly suspected. "Cram," "book it," and other campus terms and phrases suggest that getting grades does not correlate well with learning what either students or faculty consider genuinely important. The great objection to relaxing external sanctions in favor of the inherent appeals of learning has been that students are not mature enough to put the emphasis

in the right place if left to their own choices. To provide a campus climate and a system of studies that will encourage good choices is a challenge yet to be met by American higher education. This problem, of great intrinsic interest for educational theory and practice, has preoccupied such colleges as Goddard and Antioch in recent years and has underlain much of the interest in the Free University movement. As the colleges progress in solving this problem, they will also be gaining ground in the stewardship of resources for learning.

4. Finally, college climates, the directions in which colleges push their students, the changes that occur in students' attitudes, skills, knowledge—these have become the object of a large-scale research effort in recent years. We are convinced that successively more sophisticated tests along the lines of the College Characteristics Index (and a shorter version of it, the College and University Environment Scales), the College Student Questionnaire, the Omnibus Personality Inventory, the Graduate Record Area and Advanced Tests, will prove more and more illuminating and provocative for college leaders. But a college should not rely exclusively on even widely used, thoroughly tested instruments like these—nor expect too much from them. A college that embarks on an institutional testing program with the hope of discovering what really happens to its students and exactly where the flaws lie in its own character is sure to be disappointed. Though tests and questionnaires can help greatly, they cannot supplant individual observation and judgment.

Further, the most effective means of sizing up the results of a college activity may be something much more modest and impromptu than a "testing program." For example, students from another campus—or, better, several other campuses—can sometimes make trenchant comments on the quality of student life after a visit of only a few days. Often a simple canvass of student and faculty opinion on a particular question—the effect of comprehensive examinations, for example, or senior theses or noncredit courses—can produce considerably more information than any one person could lay hands on before. If a college is considering alternative architectural schemes for new dormitory space, it may learn a great deal simply by taping conversations with students now living in several kinds of quarters—in a large dormitory, in a college-owned house near campus, in a private apartment. Students and faculty are notoriously willing to talk, and for some purposes they can be heard more satisfactorily through interviews or recorded discussions or open-ended questions than through professionally prepared questionnaires. In short, colleges will neglect their obligations if they do not use devices of all kinds, scientific and impressionistic, to learn as accurately as possible what their programs are accomplishing.

Institutional design A fourth area of concern for college leaders, that of institutional design, encompasses many of the others. People think it almost self-evident today that a house or an academic building should have a design produced by someone knowledgeable in making a building serve the uses the client intends. It does not strike them as self-evident that a college can or should be similarly designed. Or rather they may think that there is not much to such a design: Just provide academic freedom, an able faculty, and good students, and the rest will follow.

This view, attractive in its simplicity, is unfortunately naïve. It implies, first of all, that the classroom is the prime vehicle of learning. The study staff does not condone any disparagement of classroom work. But college is, or can well be, a complete environment for its students; and the design of that environment can determine whether there is a ghost of a chance of accomplishing what the teacher in the classroom is striving to bring about. In a college where fun is king, where students are primarily income producers, and where name faculty are used to draw funds and clientele rather than to be the teachers of committed students, the most conscientious and able teacher is bound to be ineffectual. In a college where the faculty talk to classes about freedom but keep students on a short rein outside the classroom, it is merely wishful to hope for a surge of creative and autonomous thinking on the students' part. If the surge occurs, it will probably be in revolt against faculty and administration and on issues other than those the authorities would have chosen.

A factor to be reckoned with in the intelligent design of colleges will be their relations with accrediting bodies. The accrediting association is, of course, created by the colleges and the professors to further their ideals. The trouble is in the ideals and in the tendency to overstress some at the expense of distinctive purpose and inclusive aspirations. The aspiration to educate generalists is often construed as inimical to the division and specialization of labor within the college; in fact, the best-educated generalist is more likely to emerge from the cooperation of many highly competent persons whose efforts are coordinated by someone especially skilled in that task of integration than from each professor's trying to be all things to each student. Often, too, a criterion of quality that was once useful and is still sound for some conditions is applied out of context. For example, for many years, accrediting examiners viewed a high ratio of faculty salaries to total budget as a mark of strength in a college, without reference to how this was accomplished. Small colleges that looked good on this index frequently did so by affording negligible secretarial help, technician assistance, and administrative support—conditions which implied the use of faculty time for duties other than those for which faculty members were best-qualified or most efficiently employed.

For many colleges in the next decade, the most delicate problem in overall design may follow from the very changes we have been reporting and promoting—new combinations of careers for faculty, greater independence in student conduct, greater movement of faculty and students out from the college and back to it. These trends appear to endanger the qualities that have been most valued in small colleges—their sense of personal concern for each individual, their sense of orderliness and integration of effort, and their sense of rootedness and stability. Colleges cannot afford to lose these qualities, especially when universities are trying to reduce their mass to a more personal scale and reestablish a sense of wholeness within subcommunities. We are not altogether pessimistic on the score of cohesion. We were surprised to find, in each of the profile colleges, a remarkably strong identification with the place, in spite of already increased mobility and the supposed drift toward professional as opposed to institutional loyalty. And some of the trends we foresee—such as wider participation in decisions, clearer and more imaginative choice of purposes, more open exchange of feelings and ideas—may do much to hold college communities together even though the people who belong to them will not always stay home.

The problem of institutional design is crucial enough and complex enough to deserve the continual and primary attention of college leaders. Different colleges will resolve it in different ways. (And some, failing to solve it, will scatter their people and loyalties in a hundred directions.) In the long run, however, few colleges will be able to keep their wholeness in the old way, holding faculty and students securely within the walls as though no change had occurred. Those that succeed will almost surely do so with the help of able leaders drawn from a variety of quarters. They will be leaders who can work with the complexity, confusion, and uncertainty of an increasingly democratic, competent, and diversified college community. They will be able to tolerate a struggle for purpose that cannot be captured in simple statements or reduced to completely deliberate choice. They will search for more responsible ways to use public resources and press for new modes of educational quality. They will, as a group, prize diversity of outlook and function as the way to further their common purpose of liberal education, believing truly that this achievement will be their crucial contribution to a society which enriches its life through the interplay of liberty and mutual concern.

BALL STATE UNIVERSITY,
THE COLLEGE OF
LIBERAL ARTS

*The College of Liberal Arts at Ball State
University is an idea, not a physical presence. It
is the genius of Ball State to mix on campus a fine
range of vocational interests and motives. In the
process, the industrial arts major has the chance
to learn as much about Gibbon as the history
major about electronics or interior decorating.*

D RIVING west on Riverside in Muncie, Indiana (Robert and Helen Lynd's Middletown), a visitor will see much that is new. The small teachers' college of Middletown has multiplied several times over and is still growing fast. To the right, near New York Avenue, are the nine-story East and West Studebaker Halls of Ball State University; beyond them is a new health center; nearby is the handsome Noyer complex of men's and women's residence halls. At the corner of Riverside and McKinley is the great Emens Auditorium, first opened in March, 1964, as a joint achievement of Ball State and the Muncie community.

The liberal arts treatment If the visitor were to accost a passerby and ask, "Can you direct me to the College of Sciences and Humanities?" or "Which of all these new buildings will be the liberal arts college?" the first response would be likely to be a puzzled frown. The liberal arts college is an idea, not a physical presence. Although some major subdivisions of the university, such as the unborn College of Architecture, may become fairly well-entrenched in a single location, there is no general feeling that it is necessary or even desirable to have complete concentration. Thus the campus structures continue to be subject-oriented; there is an English building, a music building, a temporary sociology building, for instance, and a new political science and mathematics building is going up. Still more new buildings are on the drawing board, but to date there is nothing about the layout of departmental facilities and laboratories that physically defines liberal arts perimeters.

In minimizing separate centers and keeping the administration building a major focal point for all students, Ball State has developed a uniquely complex administrative strategy. One analogy is to a single factory handling a wide range of products, without one assembly for trucks and another for sports cars; one system takes care of everything. As seniors signing up for their final quarter's work, an education student, a prelaw student, an industrial arts major, and a professional musician might all meet in the administration building on any given day of the preceding quarter. A liberal arts student at Ball State would understand very well that his liberal arts college is not a place, but a virtually invisible controlling principle, a "manufacturer's specification," less obvious and more complex in operation than either a typical private liberal arts college or a completely self-contained unit in a great university system.

Rebirth of a university Some reasons for the complex patterns of Ball State lie in its background as both a public and a private institution. Founded in 1898 as Eastern Indiana Normal University, the school had three successive identities prior to 1918—Palmer University, Indiana Normal School, and Muncie Normal Institution. In 1918, the Ball brothers of Muncie, a prominent industrial family, purchased the campus and buildings of the Muncie Normal Institution and donated them to the state of Indiana. The property was placed under custody of the Trustees of Indiana State Normal School at Terre Haute, and for a time the Muncie school was called Indiana State Normal School, Eastern Division. In 1922, the title of Ball Teachers College was added. In 1929, with its separation from the state school, the school became known as Ball State Teachers College, and it kept that name until 1965. On February 8, 1965, it again became a university.

While changes over the years may have made the place more heterogeneous, few of the original shaping influences have been lost in the process. With the redesignation of Ball State as a university, some long-time observers felt that institutional "self-actualization" had taken place. That its latest development is only a fulfillment of the real genius of the school is suggested in various ways in recent publicity: "It [Ball State] has from the beginning been a multiple-purpose institution serving the needs of students for general education and liberal and applied arts on a regional basis." Today, these multiple purposes are aided by local, state, and federal funds, working independently as well as in extraordinary combinations. The university has been gaining at the rate of some twelve hundred students per year, in response to the needs of its community as well as to the specific vocational and preprofessional interests of students. Yet it still bears the name of generous benefactors, as do some private colleges. The institution attracts some interest in its unusual combination of initial support from private funds and later support from state funds. The working out of its liberal arts role in this elaborate context merits attention.

About eight years ago, when enrollments still totaled less than six thousand but were increasing each year by about 10 percent, inner fermentation for change began to take tangible form in the faculty Long-range Planning Committee. By then Ball State Teachers College had solidly established its graduate programs. It had awarded well over five hundred master's degrees since 1934 and had founded two cooperative doctoral programs. (In the next eight years it was to increase tenfold the number of master's degrees and grant nearly thirty doctorates of its own.) Despite its obvious experience in graduate training, however, the college operated an almost monolithic departmental system. Only fourteen departments existed:

Air Science	Music
Art	Physical Education
Education, Psychology, and	English
Special Education	Foreign Language
Business Education	Mathematics
Home Economics	Science
Industrial Arts	Social Science
Library Science	

In general, these names conformed to the teacher licensing pattern. To get some feeling for the implications, one may put pencil to paper: If the typical student took 36 courses during his four undergraduate years, he would average 2-1/2 courses per department. Thus he would tend to have much in common with his fellow undergraduates; he would be likely to know many of the same teachers and to have read many of the same books. Take away some of the special-interest subjects, the practical or vocational courses that reach only limited numbers, and there remain about eight liberal arts departments. Among these, the chances are that there would be even higher average enrollments. For a student body in which some 80 percent of the senior class achieved teacher certification, such an academic structure had obvious convenience, in that the fulfilling of general requirements would be almost automatic. Yet the pattern of uniformity might, on some shoulders, rest a little heavily.

In time, a kind of fission took place, with three divisions assuming form—Education, Fine and Applied Arts, and Science and Humanities. Later a Division of Business was established. Originally the Science and Humanities Division consisted of just five departments—English, Foreign Language, Mathematics, Science, and Social Science.

Some present alignments that otherwise might appear improbable can be explained by the fact that each department could choose which division it would join. Eventually, divisions became colleges; when this happened, the departments tended to remain where they had first lodged themselves. The Department of Physical Education, for example, which had first elected to be in the Division of Fine and Applied Arts, now remains in the College of Fine and Applied Arts (though it has become in its own right the Division of Physical Education and Athletics). In the College of Fine and Applied Arts one may find other unexpected combinations also—Aerospace Studies, Industrial Education and Technology, Art, Music, and Nursing, for instance—which can perhaps only be accounted for by the same interesting principle of "departmental free election."

Now there are twenty-nine departments in place of the original fourteen. The Science Department has split into five individual natural science departments, Social Science has divided itself into three departments, Speech has grown out of English, and so on. In the year 1962 the Indiana Legislature authorized the establishment of a College of Architecture, and the time for Ball State's rebirth as a university had nearly arrived. During 1965 the five colleges enrolled nearly nine thousand undergraduates and well over two thousand graduate students. The faculty numbered nearly five hundred, and had to delegate most of its legislative business to a senate.

The new curriculums Departmental self-determination at Ball State has helped to produce an operational pattern that seems closer to English common law than to systematic codification. What someone once perhaps almost casually decided tends to become hardened into precedent—with unpredictable (and sometimes felicitous) consequences. The very fact that the College of Sciences and Humanities could grow up out of a consortium of departments that simply decided to work together may be maddening to some systematic academic minds. The college thus formed lacks a Department of Fine Arts, among other things. It has no offering of its own in psychology. For physical education it must refer students to another college. In short, it is not a self-sufficient entity, it is not a logical entity, and it is not a historical entity. It may not be a permanent entity either, but a symbiotic type of creature having mutually useful survival relationships with the other colleges. At the moment, it is neither capable of, nor interested in, a self-contained curriculum. The result, as pointed out earlier, is that the liberal arts college is not a place but a concept—a set of forces and specifications at work.

The complexity of academic patterns at Ball State justifies the curricular adviser scheduling system. Curricular advisers are members of the instructional staff whose full-time assignment is to work out academic programs with students, meeting a specified number daily by appointment. By means of the advisers, who interpret regulations, approve changes in programs, help with vocational plans, and so on, registration becomes a continuous process. Ball State never has any long registration queues. As soon as a student has his adviser's OK, he is signed up for the next quarter. In addition to his curricular adviser, whom he meets in the administration building some time each quarter, a student also may have a major adviser, a member of the regular faculty whose duty is to guide within the field of specialization.

Some observers evaluate the curricular advising system as an administrative superfluity, though a convenience to students and to the faculty. However, because the "single processing line" at Ball State is so very complex, a "special processing plan" for each student may be a sufficiently efficient way to proceed. Every student's academic route, moreover, takes him outside his own college. At its best, the adviser system expresses a philosophy beyond that which has formed any single college, division, or department; it may represent grand reconciliations that collectively act as a liberalizing force.

According to options now available, students have two great choices to make: They must select a curriculum and a major. Lesser decisions will follow, but the Rubicon and its main tributary will have been crossed. It is a special feature of Ball State University that the choice of curriculum determines whether a student shall be classified liberal arts or something else. The "something elses" at the moment are general arts, professional arts, and teacher education; with liberal arts, these make four curriculums in all.[1]

Curriculum is officially described at Ball State as "a pattern of studies leading to a degree," and it is "characterized by three components—general education, specialization, and electives." All curriculums require 186 quarter hours for graduation. Everyone completes a block of 75 hours in general education, with the requirements distributed among social and behavioral science, humanities, and the natural sciences. Ranges of the three curricular components are as follows:

General education (limited electives), 75 distribution hours, plus 6

hours physical education

Specialization (major), 48 to 96 hours

Unlimited electives, 0 to 57 (or more) hours

Within a curriculum, the "major denotes the student's specific specialization." It may consist either of "a cluster of courses in a single subject" or "courses in several fields related by their contribution to professional preparation." A few examples will illustrate some of the possibilities.

Because some 80 percent of Ball State students on the average still meet teaching requirements, one may surmise that most students are not excessively burdened by free choice and decision making. But there is a more varied pattern of schedules than once existed, now that there are twice the number of departments, and the free electives could exceed 73 hours for some curriculums. If curricular advisers did not help to balance things up, students might begin asking why Ball State academic programs offer such extremes in freedom and rigidity. What is impressive is that in the midst of rapid expansion in numbers of students and uneven relaxation of curricular restrictions upon them, the institution can remain so unruffled and apparently free from growing pains. Almost the worst that students will be likely to mutter about their university is that the quiet hand of paternalism pats gently here and pushes there, so that students are controlled and scarcely know it.

[1] In addition to the role they play in the four-year programs, the university's general studies programs include two-year curriculums in such vocational fields as printing technology, secretarial skills, and so on.

The students Ball State University now has some eleven thousand students. Stop
one of these students in passing and ask a question; the chances are
you will find yourself vis-à-vis the red-blooded mid-American youth
in his—or her—most attractive manifestation. If the student is male,
the odds against a beard are very high indeed. The appearance of the
student, male or female, will be clean, moderately well-groomed,
natural—so natural, in fact, that you may discover you are silently
asking yourself "Is anything wrong? There must be something
unwholesome about being so wholesome."

A campus sociologist generalizes that the Ball State student body
is an "upwardly mobile" group, from a "fairly thin cultural matrix."
A great many of the students, in fact, are first-generation college
students. About 71 percent of the fathers did not go beyond high
school, and 75 percent of the mothers did not. About 5 percent of
the parents had completed work beyond the bachelor's degree. The
students do not, characteristically, come from bookish homes. Patterns of parental occupations show increasing numbers of managerial,
proprietary, and professional vocations. The median family income
is about $10,000.

Some other salient features of the student body may be noted.
Geographically, the students represent a highly homogeneous group.
All but about 6 percent of the undergraduates are Indiana residents.
(Some twenty foreign countries are now represented in the student
body, however, and some thirty states.) Densely populated areas of
northern Indiana, such as the Gary region, are closer to Ball State
than to Indiana University, and contribute many students. Close to
Muncie, within a radius of 75 miles, are some two and a quarter
million persons, half of whom live in the urban centers of Indianap-
olis, Fort Wayne, Richmond, Anderson, New Castle, Marion, and
Kokomo. Most Ball Staters travel somewhat less than 100 miles from
home. In consequence, the university gets the sobriquet of "suitcase
school." At the start of every weekend, there is an exodus, and on
Sunday nights the crowd comes trooping back for another five-day
week. (However, there may not be nearly so many weekend pil-
grimages as people commonly suppose. A study made in 1965 of
454 undergraduates revealed that although 78 percent believed a large
portion of noncommuting students left campus on weekends, 80
percent of the same people reported that they left campus three
weekends or fewer per quarter.)

Though the cities near Muncie send their share of students, it is
significant that almost half the 1964–65 freshmen came from high

school classes of fewer than two hundred. More than three-fourths of them were in the top half of their class, but their Scholastic Aptitude Test scores were below 500 for both sexes, on both the verbal and the quantitative tests. During the 1962–65 period, the incoming-student averages have risen substantially, however, and one young Ball State professor declares with passion that the scores have been misleadingly low. In maintaining that the student body has a high potential uncaptured by College Entrance Examination Board statistics, he claims that a combination of non-English backgrounds (parents who are first-generation American), rural ignorance of the techniques of one-upmanship, and general lack of "test motivation" has produced unjust or untrustworthy information. Naturally, the university can boast of some top-scoring students, but these are believed to be mostly the children of professional men from city locations. If Ball State's country people could have had similar opportunities, Ball State SAT data would be transformed, or so the argument runs. This teacher is not alone in his belief, and the very existence of such fiercely protective faculty feeling for the students may say something important about the institution.

The student visitors to the Ball State campus for the present study felt that Ball State freshmen are far more individualized than the seniors. "Selective retention" (the university's right to refuse certain students permission to continue), for one thing, operates in favor of uniformity, and so do the voluntary transfers to and from the upper classes. The university admits all graduates from an accredited or commissioned secondary school who have "unquestioned good character, satisfactory health, and willingness to abide by the regulations," except that non-Indiana graduates from the lower half of their classes are not eligible. Thus there is bound to be a considerable range of aptitude in newly admitted classes, particularly during the winter and spring quarters (during those periods are admitted, "on warning," Indiana students who were low in their high school classes). Undoubtedly the policy of selective retention operates as a necessary pruning force. However, it is not clear that the bright nonconformists tend to drop out or transfer at the end of the sophomore year. Our student observers reported many comments indicating that standards were getting higher and that the university might be attracting as many bright transfer students as it was losing.

Granted that the Ball State students may come to look alike and that the appearance is attractive, the question arises of what internal differences and polarities exist among them. To a casual observer, looking over the crowd during the morning coffee hour at the cafeteria, the patterns are as natural and unstructured as can be. But a knowledgeable student can quickly enough disabuse him of that impression. In the center section, it will be pointed out, sit the "Greeks." To the north are commuters, and to the south are resident independent students. A section of Negro commuters tends to form itself to the northwest. And the lines between these elements can be drawn fairly sharply.

What about the resident-commuter situation? About 15 percent of the students are commuters, and some 25 percent live in off-campus housing. That these persons do not mix readily into the campus population was the conclusion of the student visitors. Resident students tend not to go off campus very often or very far (relatively few, for example, take in Muncie movies). If the commuters and off-campus people want to get acquainted with the university crowd, they must come to Ball State; a kind of social "check-valve system" tends to keep the flow going one way only, if at all.

A sign of possible two-way interest, however, was the recent flurry of general excitement over off-campus residence problems, with some dormitory students joining in the demand for university support of a stronger "open housing" policy (a policy that landlords cannot refuse a student on pain of removal from the university's approved list). The episodes, which finally consisted of little more than a few heated verbal and written exchanges, also suggest somewhat ominously that potential stresses and fracture lines do exist in the seemingly homogeneous student body.

The Negro enrollment in the university does not seem representative of local or statewide census counts. Those living in the dormitories find Ball State to be a pleasant place, but the resident group tends to be relatively well-to-do. The more financially handicapped Negro students cannot afford to live in the residence halls, and in the absence of a firm "open housing" policy, the off-campus housing available to them is across town, where most of the Negroes live. If they had the money to maintain automobiles for easy commuting, they could afford to live on campus. Thus they tend to be caught in a vicious circle of insufficient financing, which also affects their ability to participate in campus affairs.

A sturdy WASP element flourishes at Ball State, but northern Indiana provides a growing share of southern European stock, predominantly Catholic. The right (or wrong) campus issue could dramatize differences between these groups which, at the moment, are peaceable.

Divisions between Greeks and "barbarians" naturally exist, and it would appear, with a minimum of friction. Sororities do not have separate houses; certain residential-hall suites are set aside for them within the main dormitories. The fraternities house themselves in their own off-campus units. In all, affiliated students account for about 15 percent of the student body, though most independent students assume this figure to be much greater.

One reason the fraternities and sororities are thought to have more members than they actually do is that for years they have modestly and efficiently "run things." In the spring of 1965, for example, possessing fewer than 1,500 votes of their own, they continued in control of Student Senate, Judicial Board, and class offices, besides interfraternity positions. Their political organization is United Student Association, a party whose initials have obvious public relations appeal.

However, in the next election, a new organization, one that combined Greeks and independents on its slate, opposed the all-Greek roster of the USA party. Faced with the difficult problem of coping with the USA initials, the new group came up with UPP—University Political Party. The party leaders aimed at fairly limited objectives; they hoped to place a minimum of two candidates and build for the future. Instead, they made almost a clean sweep. The tone of their campaign was set by the motto "Action, not apathy." Some sense of their willingness to challenge "the establishment" is conveyed by two items from their platform: One calls for extension of women's dormitory hours, and one seeks a restatement of policy on expulsion, after labeling the present rule "ambiguous." (The rule in question is the "right to refuse" declaration implied in "selective retention," indicating that the university may exercise this right in denying continued attendance to a student when "convinced that the student lacks the personal qualities, professional characteristics, general health, and scholastic attainments essential for success.")

Prior to the "upset" elections, the student observers had the strong impression that the main personal factor setting Greeks apart was interest in organization. "Students who want to 'do things,' participate in organizations and all that, have their chance through the Greek structure. The ones who remain independent just aren't aggressive, or don't care." It now appears that they care more than anyone had supposed.

Student experience   Aside from the commercial possibilities of the late teen-ager's capacity to enjoy food, there is not much profit in Muncie in the entertainment of students. Centripetal forces at Ball State exceed the centrifugal ones to the extent that, as everyone says, students hardly ever get off campus. There are "things going," in fact, that draw people from town rather than toward town.

Emens Auditorium is a new vital center. A considerable acoustical achievement (one local musician calls it a miracle), generally acclaimed as a triumph of the German consultant, Heinrich Keilholz, the 3,600-seat hall and the small experimental theater adjoining it have proved adaptable to a varied series of offerings. During the 1965–66 school year, the schedule included several dramas—for example, Broadway theater as well as the National Players doing Shakespeare and Molière, the opera *Rigoletto* (in the smaller theater), several concerts, a contemporary dance program, Helen Hayes, and a number of public figures such as Ted Sorensen, Senators John Sherman Cooper and Gale W. McGee, and Murray Levin.

The award-winning campus paper, the *Ball State News,* is a lively source of stimulation. There is multiple staffing, in that different groups take over the paper on different days of the week, with naturally resulting competition. Columnists flourish; so does the "We Get Letters" corner; all the parts of a full-fledged paper are visible, including cartoons, editorials, syndicated features, and so on. Local events tend to crowd out national and international reports, but the result—a sense that any number of exciting things are happening right on campus—tends to work against apathy, and may be worth the risk of provincialism.

The impact of public events does reach students through the kinds of speakers brought to campus. In addition, many other cultural forces are at work. As already suggested, music and drama are flourishing, and so is art; and no student escapes their influence. Even beyond these, industrial arts, ROTC, and the vocational program bring a variety of practical interests that provide gardens and workshops around the base of the ivory tower—aerospace studies, interior decorating, woodwork, graphic arts, printing and nursing, for example. Against the charge that Ball State students tend to get more "typed" as they move toward the upper classes, the counterargument can be made that as they progress, their range of experience expands. They encounter students from all walks of life before they leave the campus, and they certainly become more sophisticated. On February 2, 1966, the *Ball State News* printed an interview with a well-known popular singer whose appearance on campus had been celebrated in advance with laudatory, if not reverential, publicity. The event was reported in straightforward fashion, along with stories on a Nobel prize winner's forthcoming lecture, a spread on the Bennington College Dance Group, which was shortly to appear on campus, an item on the Muncie Inter-Relations Council, several other stories on music (including an announcement on *The Fantasticks*), and an announcement on Religious Emphasis Week. The interview, between staff members of the paper and the visiting great man, was a masterpiece of taxidermic technique, in demonstrating the lineaments of a stuffed shirt. The following is a typical quotation: "I love college audiences. It's very stimulating for me to perform for young people— people who are young in mind. There's something about school, something about fraternity and what have you, the brotherhood of man and all that sort of triteness, that stimulates me to be very, if nothing, very sincere and very truthful in my performance."

Some possible effects The most valuable effects of Ball State on its students may be a combined function of its size and its "single processing line" system. In describing the past as "a man speaking to men" but one with "more enthusiasm and tenderness, who has a greater knowledge of human nature, and a more comprehensive soul" than other men, Wordsworth suggested one of such effect. This outcome is one of becoming a person "who rejoices more than other men in the spirit of life that is in him . . . [with] a disposition to be affected more than other men by absent things as if they were present. . . ." A graduate who has been helped by college to become such a person will have acquired there "a greater readiness and power in expressing what he thinks and feels, and especially those thoughts and feelings which . . . arise in him without immediate external excitement." It may well be that Ball State has some success in producing this effect.

Another key effect emerges from the presence of strong professional and vocational interests. Vocational and professional concerns abound at Ball State, and they are growing in strength. There are those persons at the university who openly say that a paradox has produced liberal arts at Ball State: "You keep pushing the professional schools, and you *keep* pushing them. First thing you know, if you have enough vocational and professional activity, you somehow have liberal arts also, as a precious by-product." Will a direct quest for the liberal arts really attain them, or can they flourish only in a non-liberal arts setting? At any rate, it is the genius of Ball State to mix on campus a fine range of vocational interests and motives, and in the process the industrial arts major has the chance to learn as much about Gibbon as the history major has the chance to learn about electronics or interior decorating. Liberal arts colleges, conceivably, may come to recognize such mixing and stretching as one good method for producing "Renaissance men," and better than some of the methods they have tried out.

Yet a third effect is signaled by symptoms of internal stress at Ball State University in some of the administrative opinions about what must be done with its teacher's college background. In sorting out his aspirations for the institution, one administrative leader urged Ball State "never to lose the teacher education flavor as we expand." Another wrote, "We are limited by the teacher's college image Ball State University has presented for so long. This is a distinct handicap." As one whose natural sympathies originally favored the second point of view, I found myself changing sides. The university's tradition of training teachers may not necessarily be a limiting factor, but the very opposite. In the course of mulling over the problem, the image of the clerk of Oxenford came to mind as an ideal bookish man who could never be charged with pedantry, for "Gladly wolde he lerne and gladly teche." There is something about the way the two processes go hand in hand that improves both. Robert Frost observed that you read poem A the better to read poem B the better to read poem C the better to read poem A. It may be that you teach the better to learn the better to teach the better to learn, and anyone who tries to sort out the two processes may be just destroying them.

Ball State has a great tradition as a teacher's college. It may have an even brighter liberal arts prospect as a teacher-learner college. The force of tradition is apparent in—for example—a long, three-column autobiographical story in the *Ball State News* on what it is really like to do practice teaching. This is an article for that 80 percent of students who qualify themselves to teach, and it deals with the way in which learning becomes authentic for them. It may not stretch much above the somewhat folksy statements that "liberal arts" people enjoy making fun of, but it is an authentic record of the way a perhaps mediocre student became better as a teacher than she ever supposed she might be.

After four weeks of working night and day to prepare lessons, correct papers, keep up with the classes, and getting no apparent response from the students, I wondered what in the world other student teachers had done to have such wonderful, rewarding experiences as they had said they had.

No one ever told me teachers had to study also—I thought they knew everything before they started teaching!

It is hard to imagine the counterpart of this communication at the strictly liberal arts college; but the strictly liberal arts college may be the loser.

Its size, its traditions in education, its "variety in unity"—these factors make Ball State University a most effective educational center at this moment. Will the effective moment pass as the institution grows larger? This remains to be seen. In the meanwhile, liberal arts colleges would do well to study the specifications of this small university and be ready to adopt some of them.

Edward K. Williams, Dean of Westminster College, was the principal author of the profile of the Liberal Arts College of Ball State University; his associate was W. Boyd Alexander, Emeritus Vice President and Dean of the Faculty of Antioch College. Richard W. Burckhardt, Vice President for Instructional Affairs and Dean of Faculties at Ball State, was the liaison with the college. The student observers were Margaret Hall of William Woods College and Melvin Hall of Westminster.

MOREHOUSE
COLLEGE

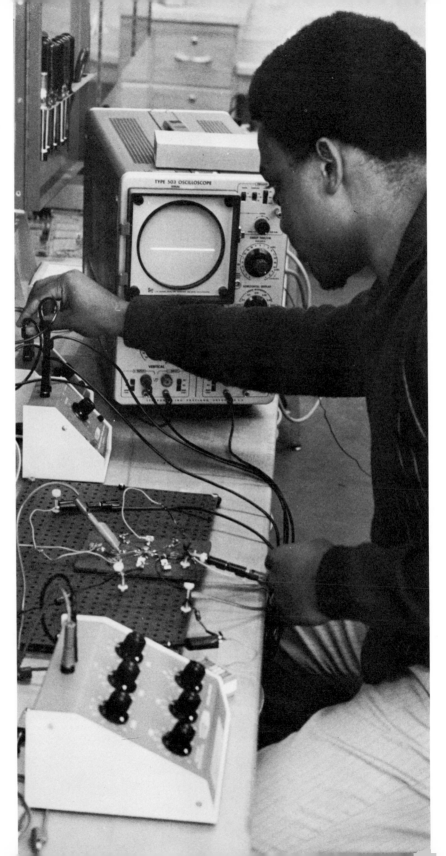

Every member of the Morehouse community, regardless of his age, has a stake in unlocking the shackles of the American Negro. The students want to be in white America but not necessarily of it. They want to be able to enjoy Bach without being ashamed of "chittlin' culture."

S TUDY of the institution today known as Morehouse College[1] reveals how deep a meaning a liberal arts college can come to have for its faculty and students. That the meaning has spread beyond Morehouse's own campus to the country at large through Martin Luther King[2] and countless other men, both living and dead, is no accident of history though perhaps one of its ironies. For Morehouse as a college for Negro men in the Deep South has survived all the indignities that man's inhumanity to man could devise and has transmuted them into ways of peace to enable its students "as citizens to furnish a quality of leadership that will be constructive and far-seeing." This, of course, is the college at its noblest and does not deny its weaknesses—its moments of boastfulness, its perhaps undue emphasis on the Protestant ethic of success, its aping of the white world's fraternities and football queens. But then, as one student observer astutely remarked, since when has suffering always brought wisdom?

One wonders what the seal of the college might have been in 1867, when the parent Augusta Bible Institute was founded, if designed with what has been called "twenty-twenty hindsight." Would

[1] The college took this name in 1913 to commemorate the efforts of the longtime corresponding secretary of the American Home Baptist Society; before that it was called successively the Augusta Bible Institute, the Atlanta Baptist Seminary, and the Atlanta Baptist College.
[2] A.B., Morehouse, 1948; L.H.D., 1957.

369

the institute, for instance, have reached into the pool of Negro experience to take a line from a spiritual—"Let my people go"? Or perhaps "Feed-a my sheep"? Such a question suggests the levels of irony and ambiguity at which a sensitive Negro American must live today. However, the seal as originally designed (by New Englanders) has its own ironic comment to make on Morehouse today as well as yesterday—a refulgent sun rising behind massive clouds, with the Latin text of Genesis 1:3, "And there was light." Circumscribing this is a double circle within which are printed the words, "Morehouse College, Georgia."

Evolving purposes In 1961 and 1962, Morehouse students and students of the other Negro colleges in Atlanta were living under the threat of violence that lurked in the wake of their civil rights picketings (which after months and several hundred jailings desegregated lunch counters and stores in Atlanta). This was all the more poignant because from the beginning, the college has tried to ensure that its graduates would fill positions of responsibility and respect in society at large. At first this meant, for the students, concentrating on the academic program that provided liberal training for ministers, missionaries, and teachers. More recently it meant picketing Rich's in Atlanta and organizing demonstrations of sympathy for the Selma Negroes—and preparing to take positions in IBM or General Motors, to serve as federal judges or state senators, or to become scholars and college presidents. Former President Benjamin Mays said to the class of 1966 that Morehouse never releases a Morehouse man from the obligation "to do whatever he does so well that no other man could do it better." This is more than platform rhetoric; one of the deliberate aims of the college has been to persuade its students that they can amount to something—indeed, that they must. Several of the brochures that Morehouse issues to prospective students carry the words "Motivation, Scholarship, Integrity, Success" (with "Success" occupying a position of honor at the end) and state succinctly what the college has been trying to do since 1867—"build men."

In 1867, when the Augusta Bible Institute was established by the Baptist Home Missionary Society of New York City, it was no more than a grade school offering training at night in the basement of a church for an adult student body of thirty-eight desperately poor freed slaves, whose aim was to equip themselves for religious ministry to their people.

For twelve years in Augusta, the institute struggled against almost insuperable odds—a shifting student body, an almost total lack of funds, and a scarcity of teachers, most of them white, who were not only ostracized by the white community but frequently threatened with physical danger. Even so, by 1879 the institute had enrolled 245 men, 150 of whom were preparing themselves for the ministry. It was the curriculum, however, that showed how far the institute had come. Though there were still courses at the elementary level, the curriculum included algebra, geometry, physiology, botany, Latin, and New Testament Greek.

In spite of these gains, it was clear that the institute would find greater opportunities in Atlanta, which was the center of the South's industrialization. And so in 1879 the institute moved to Atlanta, as the Atlanta Baptist Seminary.

At least three factors in its survival call for special mention, since they still characterize the Morehouse of today. The first of these was the quality of its biracial leadership and faculty. The three men who served as Presidents of the institution during its first thirty-six years were white men of unusual character, broadly and liberally educated as well as religiously committed, who were able to rally financial support from both Negro and white associations of Baptists.

The second factor began to operate in strength after the seminary found, in 1880, its second and final site in Atlanta. With that move there emerged the *esprit de corps* that has always distinguished Morehouse. To some extent, it was the psychology of the enclave. On the other hand, Morehouse has never seen its mission as a provincial one; the task it adopted was the development of its students' minds and talents not only for their own sakes but for the sake of society as well.

The third factor involved was the policy of appointing qualified alumni to the Morehouse faculty as these persons became available through advanced training. Fortunately, the appointments were never so many that the institution became inbred; and from its beginning in Augusta, it was always firmly committed to the principle of a liberal education. This commitment was later to be of the utmost importance for the future of Morehouse College when it was caught up in a national debate between Booker T. Washington and W. E. B. DuBois regarding the appropriateness, for Negroes, of a liberal arts education.

By 1897, the curriculum started at the high school level (the Academy), rather than grade school, and ended at the baccalaureate level. While the average age of the students was still high, the fact that boys of fourteen now sat side by side with men of thirty or forty was an indication of the increased opportunities that Negroes had won for themselves.

In 1897, the bylaws were changed to make the Board of Trustees a biracial body consisting of seven white men and four Negroes. The basic reason for the change was the growing consciousness on the part of the Negroes of the need for a governing hand in their own affairs. When in 1919 a biracial Commission on Interracial Cooperation was established in Atlanta to try to meet the racial unrest unleashed by the return of Negro veterans of World War I, John Hope, then President of Morehouse, was one of its most influential members; he was later (in 1932) to become the commission's first Negro president.

One of the important conclusions the college drew from its experiences as early as 1897 was that it must link itself with other institutions in order to strengthen and conserve its own resources. The work in theology, such as it was, was limited to a two-year sequence in the main curriculum; men interested in further theological training were urged to enroll at Richmond Theological Seminary. The normal course, or teacher's course, was conducted jointly with Spelman Seminary, a school for Negro women, which moved next door to Morehouse in 1888, when the Rockefeller family began to support the women's school. The Morehouse decision to work so closely with other institutions resulted in the containment of the curriculum within reasonable limits, the conservation of resources generally, and the strengthening of ties with Spelman.

Practically every major event in the life of Morehouse has been accompanied or followed by a local or national manifestation of racial tension. On the accession of John Hope, the first Negro to hold the office,[3] to the presidency of the college, the most sensational riot in the history of the South broke out, in September, 1906, two weeks before the opening of the academic year. After the riot, it was uncertain whether the college could open. But it did, and what began as a trickle of students in late September swelled to a flood by December.

[3] Hope was unlike his predecessors in office in many respects; he was not a minister, for instance. Interestingly, he could not have been distinguished from them by his color. Born in Augusta in 1868, he was the son of a Scotsman and his octoroon wife. When he graduated from Brown in 1894, widely heralded in Providence as a Negro and as the class orator, people who came to hear him on Class Day complained that they had been misled: "After all, he was only a white boy." Interestingly enough, a representative of another minority group in education graduated in the same class with Hope—Mary E. Woolley, later the President of Mount Holyoke College and the first woman to receive a bachelor's degree from Brown.

Almost as his first act in office, Hope allied himself openly with the meeting of the radical Niagara Movement at Harper's Ferry in 1906, an act that in the time of wider publicity and Senator Joseph McCarthy might have caused Hope to be ousted from his job. In 1910, when money was not forthcoming for another desperately needed classroom building, he successfully sought the aid of Booker T. Washington, whose philosophy of industrial education had won national sources of financial aid but had brought Hope and Washington into open conflict. In 1929, after twenty-three years as President of Morehouse, Hope left it to accept the presidency of a reconstituted and relocated Atlanta University as the first step toward realizing the vision of a great University Center with graduate and professional schools for Negroes. It was the vision of no one man or institution; it would not, for instance, have taken shape without the energizing support of the General Education Board and the Laura Spelman Rockefeller Fund. But it was Morehouse that led the way for the formal contract of alliance with Spelman and Atlanta University, whereby Atlanta University gave over all its undergraduate work and Morehouse and Spelman all aspirations they might have had for graduate curriculums.

In 1929, when the formal contract of the Atlanta University system was signed, only Spelman and Morehouse were physically contiguous, but today the University Center—an affiliation of six undergraduate, graduate, and professional schools—is a closely planned mosaic of campuses. Morris Brown College moved in 1932 from the northeast section of Atlanta to occupy the former site and buildings of the old Atlanta University. The Atlanta School of Social Work became an integral part of the new university in 1932. In 1941, Clark College came from South Atlanta. The sixth campus is that of the Interdenominational Theological Center, which combines into one institution the Gammon Theological Seminary, the School of Religion of Morehouse, Turner Theological Center of Morris Brown, and the Phillips School of Theology of Lane College, Jackson, Tennessee.

The city From the highest point on the Morehouse campus, the belfry of Harkness Hall, one looks down on Atlanta, sprawling out in the valley below, its famous Peachtree Street running from south to north, with each successive accretion of suburbs manifesting the phenomenal growth of the city in the last ten years. The city can with justice call itself the pacesetter of the Southeast, for in the last twenty years its growth has reflected the change in Georgia from a predominantly agricultural economy to one based on industry. In 1940, more than two out of five jobs in the state were related to agriculture; today only 7 percent of the population remains in farming as a full-time occupation. The men and women and their children who used to farm Georgia's land have moved to the towns and the cities.

Atlanta has grown in area and population; it has likewise grown in wealth and urbanity. But the support that has made Morehouse one of the most distinguished Negro colleges in the country has not come from Atlanta.

Atlanta is well aware of Morehouse; how could it be otherwise when two Morehouse graduates sued the Atlanta Transit System, won their case, and were instrumental in abolishing segregation on the buses in Atlanta? The city knows the college well, but has not taken it to its heart. During the ninety years that Morehouse has existed in the city, Atlanta has not put so much as $1 million into the colleges that have for a century borne the cost of educating a large part of its Negro population. The awakening of conscience that has come with the civil rights movement has not led to a significant rise in financial contributions. When the Rockefeller Brothers Fund a few years ago proposed a gift of $250,000 to Morehouse, Spelman, Clark, and Morris Brown if the four colleges could raise $500,000 to match it, they were able to raise only $360,000 in Atlanta, and most of that came from foundations. One of the difficulties was the inability to get really influential citizens in the community to head the campaign. Atlanta thinks of Emory and Agnes Scott as its responsibility, but not the Negro colleges, which it sees essentially as Northern imports that the Northerners can support. Even so, though the $360,000 was a small sum, it represents much more than could have been secured ten years earlier.

The students A college's purposes make sense only in relation to the students it deals with. The Oberlin ethos, which tries to wring some education out of every waking hour, is fitting for the Oberlin students, many of whom have been around the schoolroom all their lives. It would prove suffocating to the average Morehouse student. Conversely, Morehouse's insistence that its students must do well in whatever occupation they enter, must succeed beyond any ordinary expectation, would be pointless at Oberlin or Amherst, whose students can scarcely avoid success.

Who, then, are the Morehouse students? Geographically, Georgia contributes the largest group, with Alabama and Florida next. Then come South Carolina, North Carolina, Louisiana, and Mississippi. In short, the majority of the students have their homes in the Deep South, with about one-half of the young men from Georgia (half of those from Atlanta) and about one-tenth from Alabama. But it is interesting to see that in the last five or six years there has been an increase in students from New England, the Northeast, the Middle West, and even from California—the most significant increases being from Michigan and New York, Detroit and New York City especially. In the academic year 1965–66, thirty-one of the fifty states were represented, as well as five foreign countries—young men sent by the African Scholarship Program for American Universities from the Congo (two students), Kenya, Nigeria, Southern Rhodesia, and Zambia. Morehouse can now also expect one or two white students each year. In June, 1966, Morehouse graduated its first white student; in addition to the A.B. degree, he and three of his Negro classmates received Woodrow Wilson fellowships.

Why do the students choose Morehouse over other institutions? A very large number come because of the prestige Morehouse enjoys in all fields, and in the sciences in particular. Since most of them come from the South and have been educated in segregated schools, it is not surprising for them to choose a Negro college. In these schools, many of them have been taught by Morehouse alumni; or they have encountered alumni in their communities. It is estimated that 40 to 50 percent of the students who come to Morehouse have been influenced to do so by Morehouse alumni, either directly or by example.

Where a choice between a Negro and a white institution is possible, many undoubtedly choose Morehouse because they feel more at home socially in a Negro college. One student who transferred to Morehouse from a large university in the Middle West said that there were eighteen Negro men enrolled in the university and only two Negro women; his social life was practically nonexistent. Another transfer student had had a taste of the kind of treatment that breaking the color line in a college in the South brought with it: He frequently had to dodge bricks on his way to and from the campus, and police patrol cars followed him home for his protection. His father lost his job and had to move to another town; his aunt, a schoolteacher, was also forced to leave.

A third transfer student, this one from Detroit, came because he was interested in finding out what the Negro heritage in the South actually is. He felt that Negroes in Detroit are a post-1940 phenomenon and lack historical identity with the city. He discovered that in

Atlanta the Negro feels a certain kinship with the very air he breathes and that his roots are deeper and more stabilizing there. He discovered:

Family structures are more pronounced and community life more complete. Not only is there characteristically Negro crime, religious charlatanism and neighborhood deterioration; there is also a characteristically Negro academic community, business community, social community, political community. In short, one can associate his blackness with something besides the twentieth-century "urban problem."

The same Detroit student had an academic reason in addition to the sociological; he is a singer and had met at a singing contest the former chairman of the Music Department at Morehouse.

I think that I was at first fascinated by him as a person. For example, the fact that he had studied violin with Siegfried Gerhard and others in Berlin in 1913 was to me extraordinary. I had not previously imagined that such training could possibly have been a part of any Negro's experience before Roland Hayes and Marian Anderson. Inevitably his many years in Atlanta at Morehouse formed part of his conversation. This is really the main reason I wanted to spend at least a year at Morehouse. This is my third year. Morehouse certainly isn't paradise but it has shaped a lot of my thinking since I first came in 1963.

In view of the many sociological studies that have stressed Negro broken families and their matrifocal pattern, it is significant that a majority of the Morehouse students come from homes which are unbroken and which have a strong religious background, usually Baptist or Methodist. The average income of the families is between $3,000 and $5,000, but the scale ranges from less than $3,000 to $25,000. There are many young men whose parents hold blue-collar jobs, but where both parents work, one or both are usually employed in white-collar positions. The mothers of many students are teachers.

The class of 1969 was the first group of Morehouse students required to take the College Board Scholastic Aptitude verbal and mathematical tests. What the results revealed might have been assumed anyway—namely, that the segregated schools from which the majority of the students come do an inferior job. On the verbal tests, scores ranged from 610 to 200, with a mean of 375; on the mathematics test they ranged from 640 to 240, with a mean of 405. Undoubtedly the most glaring deficiencies are in the fields of English composition and reading. The SAT test scores alone are not reliable indicators of Morehouse students' basic intelligence, but they can be of immense importance prognostically when they are correlated with material that the Morehouse Reading Center has accumulated in its testing and remedial work with freshmen over a period of twenty years or more. While the median SAT verbal and mathematical scores are probably the lowest of the twelve colleges examined in this study, it would be far from safe to conclude that Morehouse members of the class of 1969 are the least intelligent. One has only to look at the alumni records to become cautious; for example, of the nineteen hundred Negroes who up to 1965 had earned academic doctor's degrees in this country and abroad, one out of every eighteen had received his bachelor's degree at Morehouse.

Since more than 50 percent of the entering students test below the college freshman level in reading skills, the Reading Center has developed a program to help bring them up to the point where they can begin to function at the level of their native intelligence. For some who are severely handicapped, however, it means a postponement of courses in mathematics and the sciences for a year. About 50 percent of the graduates, therefore, require five years in college rather than four, especially if summer schools are included. Well over half of the entering students never reach graduation, a very large number withdrawing between the freshman and sophomore years. The number of students dropped at the end of each year is startling, as is the number of freshmen who are put on probation. This situation is the major reason for the college's insistence on a general education program covering mathematics, science, humanities, and social sciences; this program is an attempt to rectify the poor level of students' preparation.

While many private colleges have become more selective in the last five or ten years, Morehouse, paradoxically because of the success of the civil rights movement, has become somewhat less so. Large foundations are giving money to predominantly white colleges and universities for Negro scholarships, but they have not made corresponding grants to recruit white students to Morehouse and other predominantly Negro institutions—which tend, quite understandably, to resent the loss of some of their best students as a result of foundation-financed raids.

Though it would be a mistake to assume that every dropout represents failure on the part of the college or the student, Morehouse wants its share of the best-prepared and most highly motivated students as well as those who are not so well-prepared but who will, with the kind of help Morehouse is experienced in giving, make the grade. And it is taking steps to get them. Through large gifts, the college has been able to increase its scholarship grants from $60,000 in 1962–63 to $155,810 in 1967–68, though much of this is earmarked money that will be expended within a relatively short time.

If Morehouse can correlate the materials from its own abundant files in the Reading Center with the College Board scores, it will be in a better position than ever before to formulate realistic criteria for winnowing applicants for admission. Finally, the college might expand its application list by increasing the number of early-admission students: Since 1951 it has admitted at least two hundred of these bright young men coming from the tenth or eleventh grades. Such an increase would seem appropriate, considering the poor quality of instruction in many, if not most, segregated high schools.

From its beginnings, part of the mission of the college has been to take youth whose potential powers and talents have been obscured by educational, social, and economic circumstances and to offer them an education that would challenge them to stretch their powers to their fullest extent. The vocational ambitions of Morehouse students and the careers of their predecessors attest to the college's success in this mission.

A good half of the student body expect to go on to graduate school, with interests centering on medicine, law, engineering, and business, in that order. Since Morehouse in all that it has to say about itself and its graduates is especially vocal about the alumni who have earned doctor's degrees, it is not surprising that the college attracts many who are interested in graduate study. The big difference between the Morehouse freshman today and the freshman of thirty years ago vis-à-vis graduate work is the present relative openness of vocational or professional choices. Thus the Morehouse student graduating in 1935 might have been interested in law, but the chances of succeeding in practice were so poor that he would undoubtedly have chosen another field, perhaps education.

Morehouse graduates of the 1920s and 1930s have especially distinguished themselves in the fields of higher education and the ministry. The pulpits of large churches for Negroes in many of the biggest cities in the country are occupied by Morehouse men. Nineteen Negro colleges have had, or now have, Morehouse graduates as Presidents, with Howard University in Washington, D.C., leading off with two successive Morehouse alumni as Presidents. Of the eighty-five senior colleges in the United States which are predominantly Negro, fifteen—or one out of every six—have had a Morehouse man as President.

But the times are changing. Out of the 240 students in the class of 1969 who answered a study question about their vocational choices, only 19 preferred work in education, as compared with 54 who hoped for work with a corporation, 32 for public or private research,

56 for their own professional offices, and 48 for work with the government. These students want adequate salaries, but they still rank prospects of above-average income far below the satisfactions that they want from their work—the opportunity of helping others, working with people rather than things, and freedom to be creative and original. If history is any indication, they will achieve much of what they aim for.

Student life The attitudes of Morehouse students are complex, sometimes contradictory. Partly, they want both the inward reality and the outward signs of poise, social competence, success American style. The students speak of their own "snobbishness" and claim that you can distinguish a Morehouse man (like a Spelman woman) at 100 yards by the way he carries himself.

To anyone who comes from a college where the activists have been distinguished by jeans and long hair, the appearance of the Morehouse students presents a mild shock. They could almost serve as sartorial models for college students anywhere. Beards, once a rarity, are becoming somewhat more common since the black power movement, but the students are still attentive to dress. The college encourages this correctness: At freshman orientation, the Dean instructs the new Morehouse men in the proprieties of dress, speech, and manners. When the members of the class of 1969 were asked to characterize themselves, they chose the word "nonconformist" as the *least* descriptive of themselves.

One gets the impression that Morehouse students are sought out by Atlanta Negro society, that there is no lack of parties to go to over weekends. And they are apparently successful in "turning out" (taking the most attractive girls from) the Clark and Morris Brown campuses, to the chagrin of their fellows at those colleges. Morehouse itself offers a full calendar of special lectures, concerts, entertainment, and all the activities that accompany athletic events. There is a fairly extensive "informal curriculum" of forums and "speakouts" (meetings at which students are encouraged to get up and discuss topics freely).

Even so, for Morehouse as well as for the other associated colleges in the University Center, the extracurricular life could be greatly improved by a student union. When one is erected, with its program supported by intensified counseling services (including psychiatric aid), Morehouse will be able to stretch itself socially in a way that it cannot now do.

Activism at home Morehouse students' determination to succeed is tempered by a strong admixture of activism and idealism. But the Morehouse idealism differs from the idealism on other campuses in ways that are important, though somewhat difficult to sort out. There are few overtones of dissent with the international policies of the United States; up to 1966, for instance, there had been no Vietnam demonstrations. Morehouse idealism might be best described in contrasts. It is social rather than political, national rather than international, and local rather than national. The Morehouse man today is consciously ambiguous and skeptical, as could be expected from the present racial situation in the United States. Like Hotspur, he wants to be shown. "I can call spirits from the vasty deep," said Glendower. "But will they come?" was Hotspur's rejoinder.

That the most thoughtful of the students have in the last four years become increasingly vocal about their dissatisfactions with certain aspects of their college life is clearly evident in their publications and in their requests ("demands" would be too strong a word) for the abolition of some college rules that smack of a too vigilant paternalism—requests for greater freedom and greater trust in which to achieve maturity.

It is interesting to speculate on what has created an apparent rift between the students and the college. In most colleges today, the academic community is divided into at least two subcultures—that of the administration (inclusive of most members of the faculty) and that of the students. But the rift at Morehouse is something more, as well as something less. It is something more in that it breaks apart members of the Morehouse community who have a common stake in unlocking the shackles of the American Negro; it is something less in that the students, in spite of their experiences in picketing and in civil rights demonstrations, had not by 1966 strongly voiced their dissatisfactions with the college. In all probability, the rift began to open after the civil rights demonstrations in 1961–62. For the students, a number of things went down together with the Jericho walls of segregation—among them, tolerance of the remnants of the paternalism that had perhaps once been necessary but that today is inconsistent with the social sophistication of most Morehouse students.

When President Mays was asked whether Morehouse students had confronted the college with a demand for a hand in its governance, his answer was no. He pointed out that there had recently been some agitation on the part of a group called the Student Liberation Front to relax the rules on compulsory chapel and similar matters; after some negotiations, the issues had been dealt with satisfactorily by a student-faculty committee.[4]

This incident, however, may be taken as illustrative of a continuing process of student protest. The dissatisfaction with outmoded traditions and with the college's inclination to think of students as not very responsible minors has apparently spread to include almost every aspect of the college program, from social matters to the curriculum. In essence, what a great many students hope for is a thoroughgoing examination of all aspects of the college. As in most colleges which are experiencing the same phenomenon, the students want a hand in the survey.

If Morehouse students are to have a voice in college affairs, it seems unlikely that the formal student government will transmit that voice. Today's student government at Morehouse takes charge of some large social activities, such as homecoming and recreation night. The student court deals with such minor offenses as cutting in on the cafeteria line and unbecoming behavior. But all serious offenses—such as drinking that has got out of control, possession of firearms (this is a fairly widespread practice), and stealing—go immediately to an Advisory Committee made up of students and faculty.

Student publications may provide a more effective platform for student opinion. In view of a great deal of cheating, students, with the support of members of the faculty, have agitated for an academic Honor System in all their publications; *The Catalyst,* a magazine that began in the 1964–65 academic year, probably presented the students' arguments best. *The Catalyst* is noteworthy as a product of the joint efforts of students throughout the University Center, though the number of articles written by Spelman and Morehouse students makes it look as if these two colleges produced it.[5]

Of the two leading articles in the first issue of *The Catalyst* which deal with the Honor System, the first is probably the more generally representative of the student body. The second sounds as if it were written against the background of condemnation of the American economic system and bourgeois values; however, its last sentence veers off into a theological position more nearly consistent with

---

[4] The Student Liberation Front, some of the leaders of which were included on the committee, seems spontaneously to have disappeared once the matter was cleared; the chief result of the committee's work was to cut compulsory chapel attendance from six days a week to three. Since then, the compulsory chapel requirement has been reduced even further.

[5] Since this time, *The Catalyst* has become a literary magazine rather than a journal of opinion.

Martin Luther King's Southern Christian Leadership Conference than with SNCC (Student Nonviolent Coordinating Committee) theories. Both articles are representative of the widespread feeling against what the students consider Morehouse's traditionalism and paternalism.

The first article starts thus:

I am convinced that any honor system at Morehouse College would be both good and workable. It would be good because it would make students more responsible. Ever since I have been at Morehouse students have complained that they were treated as children, or at most, as high school students not screened by the entrance requirements that colleges require. The new elevation of the student to adult status will bring with it a new view of self and of the responsibility that every "self" must assume in a system where there is equality in the distribution of responsibility.

The second article, which hints that the college stands for the secondhand values of the "black bourgeoisie" (a phrase used by the Negro sociologist E. Franklin Frazier), ends with these words:

But before Morehouse can achieve a revolution in honor, Morehouse itself must be honorable. She must be a champion for what is right and what is honorable not only on the campus but in the community, not only in the community but in the state, not only in the state, but throughout the nation. She must be willing to jeopardize her traditional respectability, renounce her middle class silence, and openly support that which is moral, ethical, and honorable.

To imply that all the students at Morehouse are actively concerned with social and college problems would present a false picture of the college population. It is as diverse as that on most campuses, and many of the groups are more taken up with their own interests than with reforming the college. There are the fraternity groups, for instance, which have some prestige but evidently cause no heartache on the part of those who are excluded. While there are no fraternity houses, the members do go around together. The pledges march to dinner in single file, stand at attention in front of the tables at which the fraternities sit, and shout in unison, "Good afternoon, big brothers." No one outside the fraternities pays much attention to this.

Other groups form themselves around athletics, the glee club, and the political activists. Easily the most thoughtful of the student groups collects at Canterbury House, a semireligious center independent of the college, which offers a meeting house for group discussion at almost any hour of the day or night. Interesting people from inside and outside the Atlanta University Center come there to speak on a variety of issues. Most of the students who frequent Canterbury

House have such interests as folk music, cinema, or writing; among them are also the most active students politically.

The student body is a subculture that is intensely conscious of being Negro. This is true not so much from a political point of view (though there are undoubtedly some Black Panthers and nationalists among the activists) as from a cultural point of view; there is a concentration on what the Negro heritage, both here and in Africa, has to offer to the United States. The language of the student subculture is an argot which in all likelihood has been adopted from Southern Negro dialect ("soul" and "brother" are right out of a Baptist past) with overtones of Harlem; one introduction to it might be Claude Brown's *Manchild in the Promised Land*. To immerse oneself in the argot is to begin to feel like a modern-day Negro and to begin to think like one. This is of vital importance to most, if not all, of the students in their developing pride in what the Negro has to offer his country—and, what he has offered. The students have an intense interest in the blues and in rock and roll, precisely because of the Negro origin of this music.

The situation of Negro students creates strange contrasts. A member of the Morehouse faculty expressed amazement that Spelman girls had picketed in Atlanta—"Spelman, an imitation of Agnes Scott, which is an imitation of a New England nunnery! On campus they are proper and conservative. But in opposition to a common suppression they can become radical."

Similarly, Morehouse students, on their way to becoming leaders, must feel very sharply the conflict that separates Roy Wilkins from Stokely Carmichael—on one hand, the desire to get out of the ghetto and enjoy a share of America's wealth and privilege; on the other hand, the impulse to damn the whites who have handed out humiliation for over two hundred years. In one form or another this debate pervades much of the talk in bull sessions and forums, discussions in faculty houses. The students dissociate themselves from an older generation of Negroes, whom they see as middle class, imitative, ashamed of their negritude, and willing to be judged by white criteria. Students want instead to be *in* white America but not necessarily *of* it. They want to be able to enjoy Bach without being ashamed of "chitlin culture." They want to encompass both societies, to become genuinely Afro-American.

Faculty It is not hard to see how Morehouse has been able to keep a capable faculty though salaries have been relatively low, opportunities for research limited, and offices crowded. A faculty position at Morehouse carries prestige throughout the Negro community, and members of the faculty have enjoyed the esteem, sometimes almost the veneration, of their students. The faculty are themselves proof that what the students hope for is not impossible, that a Negro can earn a Ph.D. degree and become a professor.

A look at the distribution of the Morehouse faculty among the various teaching groups reveals some interesting facts. In the first place, there is a very heavy concentration of numbers at the professorial level. This is significant, because in its professorial group, a college has many of those who have devoted their entire lives to its service and have made major sacrifices for it. Most of them can be expected to be approaching their sixties, and many of them will be on the point of retirement. So it is at Morehouse. In May, 1966, more than half of the twenty-one professors out of a faculty total of sixty-one were in their late fifties or early sixties, with only two or three in their early forties. The group contains most of the chairmen of departments. Some of them have come up the long, hard way to their doctor's degrees, taking perhaps ten or twenty years to finish the requirements. Within the period from 1966 to 1971, if sixty-five is taken as the age of retirement, the college will have to replace at least nine or ten of them; the retirement of President Mays also helps to explain the unease with which the senior members of the faculty face the problems of the future.[6]

The faculty at Morehouse has always been catholic in terms of race, sex, and religion. While the professorial group is almost exclusively Negro and male, the concentration is not the result of design. The history of individual tenure at the college shows that Negro faculty have been more likely to stay at the college than white, whose tenure averages no more than four or five years. Since ten of the full professors received their bachelor's degrees from Morehouse (an appointment policy that, born of necessity, goes back to the very beginning of the institution), the most powerful group in the college tends to look back to the past for guidance. And since the memories of many of them go back to the Academy and to the days when Morehouse and the old undergraduate Atlanta University were competitors and Spelman was a loved colleague but weak in curriculum,

[6] Dr. Mays retired on June 30, 1967, to become President Emeritus; he was succeeded by Hugh M. Gloster, a Morehouse alumnus and former Dean of the Faculty at Hampton Institute.

it is not surprising that they tend to be a somewhat conservative group in terms of planning for the future and the pace of change.

The rest of the faculty is rather unevenly distributed (as of 1965–66), with eight holding the rank of associate professor, twenty-one the rank of assistant professor, and eleven the rank of instructor. In the associate professor group there are two white men and one woman. In the assistant professor and instructor groups there are almost as many whites as there are Negroes, and a fairly large number of women. Former President Mays said, "The college has been segregated but never segregating."

Close to two-thirds of the faculty hold the doctor's degree, and many of the remaining third are on the verge of completing degree requirements. There is a heavy concentration of doctorates in the professorial group, and a fairly high number of the associate and assistant professors are also Ph.D.s. In recent years, Emory has supplied Morehouse with a number of young men and women who either are completing their doctoral work or have completed it and are embarking on teaching for the first time. The tone of the faculty is scholarly, but their published output is limited.

The austerity that in the past has marked the Morehouse program still prevails: Financial limitations still demand sacrifices from both faculty and students. Faculty office space is in short supply, to say the least. In September, 1966, however, a new building for modern foreign languages, physics, and mathematics provided fifteen additional offices. The entire faculty was dependent on the services of only two typists and whatever student help happened to be available. Teaching loads have been progressively reduced in the last few years, until now the average is a little over ten hours; the college aims at an average of nine hours. The salaries, though substantially increased from 1961 to 1966, are still below the AAUP norms.

The college does all it can to help teachers complete their doctor's degrees or engage in research or writing by granting leaves of absence with some pay, ranging from one-fourth to full pay for a year's leave of absence. In 1961–62, there were two such leaves; in 1962–63, three; in 1964–65, four. The generosity of the Chairman of the Board of Trustees provided each year not only stipends for six juniors to travel and study in Europe but also two faculty fellowships for the same purpose.

No one enters Morehouse either as a student or as a member of the faculty without knowing what will be demanded from him as a member of the Morehouse community. The thing that undoubtedly brings many teachers to the campus is the promise of participating in an enterprise that is marked at its best by a sense of expectation and of desire for intellectual and social betterment. However, this kind of purpose is more easily lived with in the short term than over the long haul, and it is little wonder that there is considerable mobility in the ranks below the professorial level. At the end of the 1965–66 academic year, the college had to withstand twelve retirements and resignations, with half of the resignations unexpected. The twelve who left represented the highest turnover the college had experienced in twenty-five years.

Administration In a recently published book, *The Predominantly Negro Colleges and Universities,* Earl McGrath has observed that in Negro colleges the president plays a dominant if not patriarchal role. While Benjamin Mays would have been a dominant personality in any group, it is probably more accurate to ascribe the relative weakness of his administrative machinery less to the dominance of the President than to too great a reliance on informal practices that were effective ten years ago when the total enrollment was somewhere in the neighborhood of six hundred. At that time, the President himself could be at the center of discussion concerning faculty appointments, promotions, tenure, teaching assignments, curriculum, student admissions, regulations governing student conduct, budget allocations, even very small ones, and many other details of the college's management. This very personal administrative structure (if it can be called a structure) is no longer adequate now that the college has grown and demands on the President's time have multiplied. Today he must spend far more energy than before on money-raising, long-range planning, and educational obligations off campus. Morehouse has developed no satisfactory substitute for the President's immediate direction of college affairs; among the faculty, communication languishes and rumors fly.[7]

What of the powers of the Dean? At Morehouse the position of Academic Dean was not set up until 1912, and the office has never had clearly defined responsibility for academic departments; this

[7] For the last eight years, with the blessing of the President, a council of departmental chairmen has moved in to strengthen communication among the various departments, meeting more or less regularly once a month. But while the council serves a useful function in getting the chairmen to talk among themselves, its powers, if any, are inadequately defined. The Academic Dean is a member of the council, but he does not chair it.

responsibility has been reserved for the President. Delegation of greater authority to the Dean seems imperative in the future, along with other administrative changes.

Curriculum and the Atlanta Center
The present curriculum includes an almost overwhelming number of required courses, many of them interdepartmental. This curriculum goes back to 1950, though its liberal arts roots reach back to the very beginnings of the college and to the famous debate of John Hope with Booker T. Washington regarding the objectives of education for Negroes. Except for the heavy dependence on the required courses in general education, the curriculum could not be distinguished from that of most other colleges. Unlike Berea's, for instance, it makes little attempt to touch regional or ethnic interests, though with the aid of some money from the Ford Foundation, the college within the last few years has introduced three two-term sequences of area studies in China, India, and Africa.

In recent years, several changes in the curriculum have come from two groups of faculty and the Dean, who have attended summer workshop conferences sponsored by the Danforth Foundation. As a result of the first Danforth team's recommendations in 1960, a departmental Honors Program was inaugurated, as well as comprehensive examinations. The second Danforth team (1964) put the entire program of the college under its microscope, designating the following four areas it wished to consider:

1. Factors in instituting an effective, creative college Honors Program, and a preregistration system.

2. Special programs, especially in freshman English, designed to help the underprepared student.

3. Strengthening of the curriculum in science and in social science.

4. Strengthening of vital areas of student life, teaching, faculty security, and a few other phases of Morehouse's program of liberal arts and science education.

Specific curricular recommendations were made—changes in the required course in biology, as well as changes in the interdepartmental course in the social sciences.[8] A major portion of the team's

[8] The social science course was retained for a while even though, as the coordinator admits, there was "evidence that the course had been a profound disillusionment for some freshmen—perhaps among them some of the most perceptive—[who] see the lack of substance of the lectures as being symptomatic of intellectual sterility at Morehouse." It has now been dropped and replaced by a required history course.

report analyzed the reasons for student cheating and recommended the introduction of an Honor System. It is unfortunate that the recommendation was not implemented before the student agitation which came along a half year later. The report is as striking in its sense of urgency as in the scope of its recommendations.

More important than the modification of particular courses or programs, however, is increased sharing of offerings among members of the Atlanta University Center. Morehouse, for example, offers only one course in fine arts, depending on Spelman for the rest of its art curriculum. Similarly, Spelman sends its students to Morehouse for much of their work in science. A glance at the Morehouse catalog will give some sense of the interdependence along the center schools. In education and psychology, Morehouse lists twenty-two courses of its own, seventeen Atlanta University courses, six Spelman courses, and three Clark courses. In economics and business, the catalog lists almost three times as many courses from Atlanta University as from Morehouse itself. In French, Morehouse offers a year course each in elementary, intermediate, and advanced French. Beyond that, students may go to Spelman for a sophomore-level survey of French literature, to Clark for a junior-level conversation course, to Morris Brown for a senior course in methods of teaching foreign languages, or to Atlanta University for graduate-level courses in seventeenth-century French literature. Not all departments have put much effort into balancing their strengths with those of other colleges in the group. However, collaboration has begun.

Since Morehouse is very much aware of its past, its special character, and its prestige, the faculty are wary of any collaboration that threatens to absorb Morehouse into the University Center or divest it of its identity. And the other colleges may be fearful of domination by Morehouse. Recent talk of merging certain departments at Morehouse and Spelman caused uneasiness on both sides. Yet the advantages of sharing teachers, facilities, and administrative arrangements are so evident that the colleges will almost surely move closer together, even if gradually and reluctantly.

Students' reactions to their programs One gains the impression from reading students' comments on their academic programs that on the whole, the teaching effort is lower-geared than a great many entering students expect it to be. If it is, this would be understandable in view of the number of marginal students who are being given the chance to prove themselves. One consequence is that Morehouse students, at least in their first two years, probably are not led into as much independent work and outside reading as students at many of the other colleges represented in this volume. The 1964 Danforth team's report to the faculty confirms this: "Greater effort must be exerted to improve the quality of students being admitted to Morehouse College. This process should also be accompanied by a more challenging teaching and student response so as to create a more dynamic and intellectual atmosphere on this campus."

The college has what many publicly supported institutions have—an upwardly mobile student body. What makes for exhilarating teaching in such situations (and this is certainly true at Morehouse for many teachers) is the response that can be measured in terms of expanded thought and deepened values. A student observer noted one such experience in a voluntary class meeting held in the home of a young assistant professor one evening: "You can see the honest efforts of boys with poor diction, Southern accents, poor grammar, but good minds, just lapping up the care and the nurture Morehouse is giving them. . . ."

The future At the close of the academic year 1966–67, Morehouse rounded out its first century. No one can doubt the truth of former President Mays's assertion that few institutions have done so much with so little and so few. One could wish that the recent gains in civil rights and opportunities for Negroes had cleared away most of the problems with which Morehouse has had to struggle during its entire history. Instead, the expanded opportunities, while easing some problems, have created others.

President Mays had said that a realistic goal for funds with which to celebrate Morehouse's centennial anniversary would be 11,140,000 dollars, with the major portion providing a new academic building for humanities and social sciences, expanded space for biology and chemistry, an endowment for salaries (7 million dollars), and another for scholarships (2 million dollars). But even that large sum would not provide for a student union or for some of the other physical needs. If these were added, the 11,140,000 dollars might go up another million and a half.

Where is the money to come from? Undoubtedly a great deal will come from the federal government, especially funds for buildings and for scholarships and loans. While the Trustees and the president are wary of state aid, it can be expected, as Frank Bowles has predicted,[9] that such aid also will come eventually and fully, though not without strong and violent resistance at first. It might be hoped that Georgia would be as much a pacesetter here as it has been in industry. It could also be hoped that Atlanta itself would open its treasury, which must be as ample as any in the South. The city should be generous, if only in acknowledgment of the long-standing contribution Morehouse and the other members of the Atlanta University Center have made in the education of Atlanta's Negro citizens.

But the crucial decisions on which Morehouse's future hangs are not the financial ones. In the past, the college's purpose has been to prepare Negro students for real accomplishment, partly by academic training but equally by convincing them that they can do a job as well as any man. Many people and ideas have worked together to create this conviction—the alumni, who, as the students are frequently reminded, have recorded imposing achievements; the faculty, who offer daily proof that a man can be free, self-respecting, willing to speak his mind; Benjamin Mays, with his confidence, his national reputation, his pride in the college; and the idea of "the Morehouse man."[10] This has been an appropriate purpose, and the college has pursued it with admirable success.

For many students, this is still exactly the stance the college should take. But for others, the boosting of confidence and the coaching in correct behavior are no longer necessary. (One student said, "I hope the new President will be affluent so he won't assume all the students come right out of the hills and need to have their edges sharpened.") They or their friends have organized and carried out civil rights demonstrations. Some of them have been jailed. All of them have heard the Black Muslim message that the Negro is not *equal* to the white man, but *superior*. They know that Negroes all over the country are moving up—filling important jobs, moving into expensive neighborhoods, earning graduate degrees. The talk about the accomplishments of Morehouse graduates, though still inspiring, no doubt, is beginning to have a provincial ring. The idea of the

---

[9] "What's Ahead for Our Negro Colleges?" *College Board Review*, Fall, 1965.
[10] "The Morehouse man," according to somewhat irreverent students, honors his elders even if it means completely submerging his own desires, attends church on Sunday and chapel every day though he may know little about religious issues, and goes to concerts and stays whether they are any good or not. He is a good student, not a radical or a drinker. He dresses well and knows how to handle himself in any situation. He aims always to be the best even in insignificant jobs. To an outsider, it sounds very much like the program that has produced results for generations of American Protestants.

Morehouse man, though it still has great force, is less compelling than it once was. ("When someone calls me a Morehouse man," one student said, "I feel like I'm in chains.")

Neither the increased self-respect that has come with the civil rights movement nor even the integration of the college itself will change the character of the Morehouse student body overnight. (As former President Mays pointed out, many *white* Southern students will be poorly prepared for college for many years yet.) But gradually students will come better-prepared and more sophisticated. And as this happens, they will be less tolerant of such inconveniences as breakfast served from 6:30 to 7, though classes do not begin until 8, of requirements like consistent class attendance that seem to them unnecessary, of teaching that moves too slowly or demands too little. And faculty, if they are like their colleagues elsewhere, will become less attached to Morehouse as a tradition and a cause and more eager to get on with their own work, with the help of an efficient administration and adequate space and equipment. Unless the college can gradually reinterpret its purpose in terms more relevant for today and implement that purpose efficiently, it may become insular and out of date, losing some of its most vigorous students and faculty.

Fortunately, many people are ready to see Morehouse move out from the enclave and become a major force in the region and the nation. Benjamin Mays has described, more clearly than any other person in the Atlanta Center, the vision that may animate the second century of Morehouse history. He sees the college working closely with the other schools in the center to create a great university specializing in interracial and intercultural studies, "an example of democracy in education in the heart of the South." Unlike any predominantly white university, the Atlanta Center can look forward to becoming genuinely interracial: Both its students and its faculty will be drawn from all races and from all nations; its curriculum, which will transcend race and single cultures, will nevertheless be firmly founded on the experience of the Negro American.

In his book *The Burden of Southern History,* C. Vann Woodward discusses the profound lessons the Southern heritage of poverty and defeat has to offer America today when it is dealing with nations that are newly emerging from subjugation. Without the counterpoise of the Southern experience, our history as a nation dangerously isolates us from the common experience of other countries; we tend to deceive ourselves by a legend of national innocence and of freedom from frustration and defeat. As Woodward points out:

America desperately needs historians who have learned that virtue has never been defined by national or regional boundaries and that morality and rectitude are not the monopolies of factions or parties. Such historians must have a rare combination of detachment and sympathy, and they must have established some measure of immunity from the fevers and prejudices of their own times, particularly those bred of nationalism, with all its myths and pretensions, and those born of hysteria that closes the mind to new ideas of all kinds. America might find such historians anywhere within her borders, North as well as South. But surely some of them might reasonably be expected to arise from that region where it is a matter of common knowledge that history has happened to their people in their part of the world.[11]

And where, it might be asked, could such history better be taught, such self-knowledge better be found, than in the colleges of the Atlanta Center? Thus their mission becomes national as well as international and racial as well as nonracial in a way that is possible to no other university in the United States, not even Howard. No other institution has the location, the participation in the tragedy of Southern history, the detachment that has come from the participation, and the long-time plan for just such a mission. For this mission was implied in the matrix of all the successive affiliations—of Morehouse with Spelman, of Morehouse and Spelman with Atlanta University, and then of those three with the others, Gammon and Clark and Morris Brown. Herein lie the new-old ethos and the "ampler aether" for which the Morehouse student body is ready and for which the Morehouse faculty is rather cautiously making curricular plans.

The Morehouse College profile was the work of Elizabeth Geen, then Dean and Vice President of Goucher College; her associate was Conrad Hilberry, associate director of this study and professor of English at Kalamazoo College. Melvin D. Kennedy, professor of History at Morehouse, was college representative. Randall Evans of Monteith College was the student observer.

---

[11] C. Vann Woodward, *The Burden of Southern History*, Louisiana State University Press, Baton Rouge, La., 1960, pp. 190–191.

A hostile environment can prevent America's private colleges from being the social asset they could become. The danger is not that our society will deliberately seek an end to private colleges, but that it will drift into a condition inimical to their vigorous survival. Trends in sources of support and in access to students suggest that the public universities are gaining a monopolistic hold on both the means of education and the college clientele. Unchecked, these trends could prove as unhealthful for public higher education as for private. For, as in other types of enterprise, monopoly unrestrained by either competition or monitoring by higher authority is likely to go slack and unproductive. Since higher education does not lend itself easily to monitoring by political or other authority (in fact, this kind of interference stifles the freedom essential to teaching and learning), the need is urgent to establish conditions that will promote competition among colleges and universities. We stress the need for such competition at the very time when on other counts these institutions should be developing an extensive and integral network of cooperation.

Previous chapters dealt with matters to which an array of approaches, reflecting institutional differences, might be taken. This chapter will urge the creation of a context in which both public and private institutions can serve American society energetically and

393

effectively. To this end, we offer a series of recommendations which deal with a common body of public policy.

The context we are recommending should comprise the following elements of public policy and program:

First, the federal government should commit itself to a policy of equal access, for every eligible person, to the kind of higher education most suited to the development of his talents and his capacity for serving society. Every adult who is interested and qualified should be encouraged to complete the equivalent of an undergraduate liberal education, along with whatever other post-high school training or education he may need.

Second, to implement this commitment, vigorous effort must be made to improve the matching of students to colleges and programs.

Third, as part of the concern for quality in higher education, there should be federal policy that undergraduate education, in a wide variety of forms, represents an essential investment in the strength, productivity, and enrichment of the life of our times. This policy implies encouragement of the continuing emergence of colleges with highly diverse missions—colleges standing for a wide range of philosophical, cultural, religious, and educational orientations—which nevertheless incorporate effectively in their objectives and programs a concern for liberal education. Implementing this policy will require a system of financing higher education that increases individual freedom and institutional autonomy, assures a steady and substantial growth in the quality of higher education, and does both at a manageable level of cost.

Fourth, although the differences between public and private institutions may become less marked than they are now as federal support to higher education increases, the basic distinction in source of control should be preserved.

Fifth, so that the costs of strengthening undergraduate education may be held within manageable bounds, colleges should be given incentives to explore patterns of interinstitutional cooperation and division of labor that will make for efficiency and give students access to learning opportunities outside their home colleges. Colleges should also be encouraged to test ways in which the social and economic utility of the activities of higher education can help to pay for the teaching involved. Some colleges may depart from the model of the entirely separate, free-standing undergraduate college without prejudice to the continuing usefulness of a major body of free-standing institutions. Such experiments may include, for example, linking of colleges and elementary or secondary schools, combining of undergraduate education of late adolescents with adult education, collaboration of colleges with industries or government agencies in work-study programs, and college acceptance of subcontracts for production of services or goods where this productive effort serves also as a teaching laboratory.

Sixth, if this set of policies is to be of real service to the community, the whole endeavor must be conceived and implemented in a way that stresses freedom, public accountability, and genuine productivity on the part of those who teach and those who learn.

Let us consider each of these proposed elements of policy in order to explore its implications and something of the complexities of its application to present conditions.

Equal access to higher education   The idea that every citizen should have equal access to the kind of higher education he can effectively use is by now widely accepted, at least in the abstract. As often happens with ideals, however, we find ourselves differing on interpretation and application.

Specifically, what major needs for higher education must be met if the ideal of equal access is to be even approximately achieved? There are not only the people who now miss higher education altogether, but people who fail to get the kind of education that would be right for them.

What groups need college education but do not now get it? Every normal adult is capable of some furthering of his liberal education as we have defined that objective. Moreover, whether he himself wants it or not, his society is increasingly dependent on his having it. The more complex, populated, and fluid our culture becomes, the more critical it becomes to enlist the intelligence and understanding of every possible adult in dealing with the questions troubling our communities, institutions, and nation. Among the categories of people now missing higher education and especially deserving consideration are these:

1   Late adolescents from Negro, Indian, Puerto Rican, Appalachian, and other minorities who are "educationally disadvantaged" at the normal age for college. It is not right to say to them, "Go back to high school." At their age and in their circumstances, it would be preferable for them to be in "college"—either present-day colleges with adapted programs or new institutions designed specifically to fit their needs.

2   Late adolescents from every social and economic stratum of American society (and perhaps from other societies as well) who

need a change from the book-oriented and teacher-dominated curriculum of their earlier schools to an experience-oriented and problem-oriented one. In such a curriculum, public service, Peace Corps service, VISTA volunteering, foreign service in the work of the church, work in civil rights agencies, or other productive experience may be used as the stimulus and occasion for instruction. These youths may not need this type of study for their entire college fare; for some, more of it and for others, less of it may suffice. Experiments might be tried in which this activity is not called college at all and neither credits nor degrees are awarded; in other experiments, a more conservative approach might be taken to ensure that learning worthy of "academic credit"—whatever the qualified faculty consider this term to mean—will be achieved.

3   Adults whose earlier education stopped short of college, whose college education lacked the elements of inquiry and reevaluation inherent in a thorough liberal education, or whose inquiring has not persisted since college—people who need continuing education, credit or noncredit, with or without the prospect of a degree, with liberal learning as its focus. Church education programs for adults and programs such as those offered by the League of Women Voters sometimes meet this kind of need, but not for many people and not always effectively. This group would include adults with baccalaureate or even graduate degrees who have an interest in continuing liberal education.

4   Adults who did not complete high school and who may lack some of the traditional prerequisites for college but who are ready for the kind of exploration of ideas and evaluation of ideals and practices that typify a good liberal education at college level. Supplying these needs might well be combined with meeting the needs of the first group of late adolescents listed above.

5   Adults from abroad who want to be introduced to the meaning and problems of American civilization. This work will doubtless best be done as nondegree work when it is short term and not focused on a particular professional need. In some areas, however, such as teacher education, there may be need for a longer degree program at the master's level which can be ideally met by a liberal arts college in ways that have already been pioneered on some campuses.

6   University-age youth of other lands who want a general education complement to their university or career training.

7   Normally qualified youth who today do not attend college

because they cannot (or think they cannot) afford it or because they fear they will not be admitted to a suitable college.

While this list is not exhaustive, it indicates the range of needs we think important. The list is stated in terms of the "students" who should be served. If it were stated in terms of society's interest in having these people in college, it might focus on the need for a twentieth-century urban equivalent of the Morrill Act. It would surely reflect the need for transition into a single world society as distinct from a nineteenth-century society of nations. It would deal with the distinctive role of science in the late twentieth century and thus with the urgent need for widespread citizen understanding of the impact of this role upon the ideals and activities of our time. It would take into account the ways in which religious and other traditional sources of social ethics have been displaced by new wellsprings of values in contemporary life and would consider how the cogency and vitality of ideals for these times can be sustained.

Looking at the needs from society's point of view bears upon the other half of the problem of access: What are the kinds of learning or curriculums which contemporary students could well use but cannot readily find? Again, let us list some types of students whose needs remain unfilled:

1   Students whose talent is not of the traditionally verbal or mathematical type, but artistic, manipulative, entrepreneurial, or the like, and who need a curriculum and setting for learning in which they can start with these aptitudes and grow into an understanding of, and skill in, other modes of thought and apprehension.

2   Students whose drives are of the "collegiate" (fun-oriented) or "vocational" sort and who are now in colleges that either deny altogether or downgrade the opportunity to approach liberal education from within these orientations.

3   Students motivated primarily by social concerns, who cannot see the relevance to these concerns of curriculums as now organized and taught.

4   Students for whom the present pace of academic studies is too rapid or too rigidly scheduled, yet who are fully capable of the depth and quality of understanding typically expected for a baccalaureate program if they can get it at their own pace.

5   Students who are misplaced in terms of the climate and values of the college they attend—in particular, students who need to be part of a more integrated subcommunity within the university or college.

6   *Students for whom quite different mixes of learning methods than are now available would be more effective—less lecturing, less reliance upon class discussions, more use of programmed supplements or tutoring or research participation or apprenticeship.*

Again our list is merely illustrative. It is sufficiently fundamental and massive, nonetheless, to make it clear that the unmet needs call for more than minor adjustments or patching of the old system. To respond adequately to needs of these kinds and magnitudes will require a fundamental reshaping of American collegiate education.

The matching of students and colleges

Our observations and reflection during this study have convinced us (as specialists in the work have long felt) that the traditional criteria for college admissions are often defective, either for estimating the potential of the individual student to make something significant of the college experience or for producing the mixture of students and student cultures that would best further the college's purposes. We have no remedies to prescribe, but we did try out, during the study, two kinds of "probe" that might contribute to a better overall system of matching. Both approaches assumed that better matching could occur if colleges were to disclose more openly what they are and want to become and if students were to state more frankly their interests, limitations, and needs. Present competition among high school graduates to get into certain colleges and among colleges to get a certain type of student works against this openness on both sides. Our two probes were the publication of uncensored college profiles done by sympathetic, competent, but unattached outsiders and the gathering of materials for a short film of similar intent but with allowance for the demands and capabilities of that medium. There are substantial hazards and limitations to each of these devices, and neither is of great use unless supplemented by procedures that go much beyond it. For example, it is not very likely that a written profile of a particular college will be read by prospective students who would be suited to it or by those who ought to read and decide against applying. Filmed profiles, which in ten to twenty minutes can show a good deal about the people, attitudes, and educational programs on a given campus, might have a better chance of reaching their audience. But it would be a large undertaking to produce such unbiased films on a nationwide basis, and while they might be promoted and used by the colleges if they were indeed unbiased, they also might not. The costs of both types of profiles, written and filmed, seem to us modest in relation to their prospective utility, but admissions departments of most colleges would find it a major break with tradition to incorporate these aids into their kit of tools for recruiting and selecting students. Arrangements within associations of colleges have demonstrated that even strong colleges can gain recruiting power through collaboration without surrendering the advantages of competition in rendering a good service. Perhaps these consortia can more readily test new approaches to matching of students and colleges than can any other single agency.*

A policy on federal and state financing of higher education

Given a catalog of needs, how can priorities be established for those changes to be undertaken first and for the financing of the effort? Until recently, there was no federal policy on undergraduate education; or, to put it another way around, such federal policy as existed was to support undergraduate education only if and as it served some other end of federal policy. In view of the difficulties reported by both private and public colleges in obtaining the financial support they need from existing sources, we think that only a major reshaping of the financing of undergraduate education will be adequate. We believe no single change in the present patterns of support would produce the desired support; rather, a complex of additions and amendments to present methods of financing is needed.

Former President Grayson Kirk of Columbia University stated in 1967 that Columbia's prospective deficit in the operating budget for 1967–68 would be 2 million dollars. This figure, he stated, is not a freak of temporary or one-time circumstances, but the end result of a long-time trend, in which the deficit left by inadequate tuitions has finally exceeded the capacity of endowment income and special gifts to close the gap. He stated that Columbia's problem is not unique, and in fact is smaller than that of many colleges of less resources. In the public universities, where deficits may not be incurred even to accept increased numbers or to maintain quality, the symptoms of underfunding take a different form— normally, the undermanning of courses at the lower-division level,

* A most notable recent experiment is the adoption by the Associated Colleges of the Midwest, in 1967, of a "single admissions method" whereby students may apply to any or all of the ten colleges in preferential order by filing a single application form.

the assigning of less qualified personnel to teach them simply out of lack of other means, and the flunking out of large numbers of students who with different instruction and counseling might succeed.

We think that a sound resolution of these complex problems, in which funding interacts with the quality, type, and quantity of undergraduate educational services, will require many minds and much time. We here recommend only a few essential steps as a beginning of that endeavor.

One essential step is a recognition that the federal government should support undergraduate education in its own right. The reasons are obvious. The provision of full and equal educational opportunity at this level represents a direct investment in the strength and productivity of the nation and the enrichment of its life. The cost cannot now be met by the funds available to public universities or, for private institutions, by the means to which they have had access. While we recommend concomitant changes to improve the yield of some of these other sources of funds, we cannot see that the possible increases would come anywhere near being sufficient. In the paragraphs which follow, we suggest elements of the federal policy we would recommend.

A first element of this federal policy is to guarantee or underwrite the individual's access to the higher education he aspires to get, provided he can gain acceptance at a recognized institution offering this education. The financial arrangements we propose would enable a student, at some cost to himself (which he could finance in part by borrowing), to attend the college he chooses for the program he can get admitted to, even if he requires assistance with living costs as well as with tuition and fees. In a working paper prepared for the study, Christopher Jencks and a study group proposed a federal guarantee of loans which would make this policy feasible.* In September, 1967, the Panel on Educational Innovation of the President's Science Advisory Committee, headed by Dr. Jerrold R. Zacharias, made a similar proposal for what it called an Educational Opportunity Bank.† If taken as the one and only pattern for student financial aid, we think the proposal has undesirable and probably unworkable limitations. But if viewed as one of a set

* "Federal Scholarships for Undergraduates," Study of the Future of Liberal Arts Colleges Working Paper no. 19, Jan. 3, 1967. It is presented as Appendix D of this volume.
† Educational Opportunity Bank, A Report of the Panel on Educational Innovation to the U.S. Commissioner of Education, the Director of the National Science Foundation, and the Special Assistant to the President for Science and Technology, 1967.

of many ways of paying for higher education, we believe that its inherent dangers and inequities can be balanced to make it an extremely helpful addition to the arsenal of means.

The principle of this proposal is that, upon certification of his admission to a recognized program, the student is eligible for an insured loan which he will pay off later by a tax upon his income, the tax being set as a percentage of his net taxable income (as calculated by the laws in effect at the time of taxing) for each $1,000 of loan incurred. By this arrangement, a student would pay in proportion to the economic yield his opportunity, ability, and education provided. It would not make a more expensive education as cheap as a less expensive one for the student but would make it equally accessible if he were willing to incur the tax liability. Since a person would undertake such an obligation only because of some supposed benefit worth the difference, such a loan program would put pressure on the colleges that claim especially good results to make clear what those results are and how they justify the costs charged.

The loan program could probably be made wholly self-financing; or it could give preferential treatment to some categories of disadvantaged students whom the Congress wished especially to aid. Similarly, if the federal government wished to attract students to certain types of programs in order to meet manpower shortages, the loan program could contain partial "forgiveness" provisions that would have that effect. This loan program might initially be financed and any needed subsidies provided jointly by private and federal sources, much as the national endowments in the arts and humanities are being funded.

A second element of financial aid should be provided, either as an independent program of outright grants or as a variation on the loan program. This aid should go both to economically disadvantaged students and to students undertaking programs for which incentives must be offered to offset unattractive occupational conditions— e.g., programs for teachers in the inner city (where pay and working conditions are often inadequate to draw the needed quality and quantity of staff), for community development work in transition urban areas (where the novelty of the occupation calls for special incentives to individuals and for encouragement of new curriculums in the colleges, probably at the master's level), and for forms of national service that should not be subject to compulsion.

A sensible national policy on financial aid would probably include an increase of state programs already tested in some regions, where students may obtain state grants and low-interest loans to attend private colleges or to undertake high-fee programs at state institutions. For students attending private colleges, the amounts of these loans and grants are set so that they require a smaller outlay of state funds than if the student took the same programs in a state university. At the same time, the programs have the effect of encouraging the private colleges to compete with state institutions, on terms that are essentially favorable to the state institutions but still provide incentive to improve quality.

In a comprehensive public policy on financing higher education, programs of direct financial aid to students should be complemented by programs for general institutional support and by grants and contracts for specific educational projects of importance to the public. The reasons, in social policy, for providing general institutional support are at least three: (1) it is in the public interest that students should be well-educated; (2) it is in the public interest not to weigh individuals down with excessive debt that might hinder their later choice of the careers most beneficial to themselves and society; and (3) it is in the public interest to sustain effective competition among public and private colleges.

Support of special projects is essential to gain needed program changes. Writing in The New Republic, Christopher Jencks assesses the sources of educational change in this way: "The system of education which dominates today's universities, while far less narrow than a century ago, is still largely irrelevant to the interest and needs of many undergraduates. The possibilities of internal reform are meager. Change, if it is to come at all, will depend on outsiders brandishing checkbooks and working with creative minorities on campus."* Jencks estimates the need in earmarked project and institution-building money at magnitudes of 50 million dollars in federal money in a beginning year, rising to 20 to 30 percent of the nation's overall expenditure for college instruction, which would come to a figure in the neighborhood of 1 billion dollars a year. This level of funding—if it were not to be a fiasco of waste and confusion—would require guiding ideas comparable to those of the Morrill Act, as well as means of implementation suited similarly to the circumstances of today. Developing these ideas and these means could well absorb major foundation and private gifts in the next decade, in addition to such exploratory and experimental funds as the federal government and the state governments can

* Oct. 23, 1965, p. 21.

decide to invest in the guidance of their own future expenditures.

As an aid to this work, it would be in the interests of public policy for all colleges to ascertain and state the full costs of their programs per student served, as accurately as seems reasonable in view of the difficulties and costs of making such estimates. Students and parents would thus understand the true costs of the service being received, relative costs and benefits of public and private colleges could be compared as a step toward holding both types more accountable for the management of their resources, and finally, more rational procedures could be devised for determining how these true costs can best be paid. At present, tuition and fees are put at a figure well below direct instructional costs, and even a statement of full costs normally does not include any capital costs.

Essential to implementing such a policy of federal investment in undergraduate colleges will be a more sophisticated understanding of what services are deserving of support from federal sources and which colleges are best-equipped to render them. An example will clarify this need. The National Science Foundation has operated, in part, on the policy that its function is to increase and upgrade research productivity in selected sciences. Such research has a clear utility for both national defense and national economic productivity, and hence for national survival in a rapidly developing world. Administratively, the Foundation has conceived its task as mainly one of fostering a greater number, quality, and variety of Ph.D.s in these sciences.* If the task of preparing such Ph.D.s can be thought of as a pipeline, then the Foundation's job has been to increase the flow at the end of the pipeline. It has been interested in undergraduate education, during this phase of its development, only as it might increase the flow and quality of research doctorates in science. Yet such a policy is not likely to increase the nation's research productivity in sciences as rapidly as would a policy of providing a more sophisticated array of support activities, taking into account the logistics of science research. Research requires technicians, science writers, teachers of science at many levels, and many kinds of personnel besides prospective research doctors. An "irrigation system" serving the whole area to be cultivated would be much more productive than a "single stream" of doctors of science.

Finally, it is critically important to implement national policy in such a way that the freedom of the institution may be preserved. If

* These sciences are designated currently (1969) by a list of 88 specific disciplines in the biological sciences, chemistry, engineering, earth sciences, mathematics, physics, selected interdisciplinary sciences, and "multiple" or other sciences.

financial policy emphasizes earmarking funds in minute detail and preauditing expenditures line by line and voucher by voucher, freedom can suffer greatly, whether this authoritarian procedure is applied by the federal government, the states, private foundations, individual donors, or boards of trustees. Nor is a policy of laissez faire giveaway to any and all likely to work any better. Our recommendations require a concerted effort to reach a few critical understandings about objectives, a method of keeping these under review and revision, and procedures of accountability which permit postauditing of performance and the award of new responsibility on the basis of potential estimated from past performance and quality of present thinking and planning. The freedom we regard as essential applies equally to private and public colleges.

Public-private competition

On grounds of both college self-interest and public interest, we strongly oppose policies that would make life easy for the administrators of either public or private colleges. At the moment, this danger appears unimaginably remote, but it is conceivable that precedents could be set now which might lead, by small steps, to this result. We favor a system in which there is competition in the efficient performance of services, with a variety of checks on performance and enough funds to permit experimentation and responsible mistakes without encouraging waste and incompetence. On such high-sounding principles we can hardly expect argument, but how can they be made to work? We have proposed some first steps: fuller disclosure of the realities and the potential of each institution and its programs; financial-aid policies that, by emphasizing individual choice for prospective students, give each student some voice as to what college is aided; competitive application for state, federal, and foundation support; and public reporting on programs completed and in progress.

To supplement these measures, we urge that there continue to be substantial differentiation between the control and support patterns of so-called "private" and so-called "public" colleges. What do "public" and "private" mean when applied to colleges and universities? What is actually private about a private college today? And what would be lost if private colleges closed or were turned over to public control?

Three things would be lost—something of the variety of ways in which the governing boards of colleges are chosen and organized, something of the variety of patterns of financial support for colleges, and as a consequence of the first two, a considerable measure of the flexibility and responsiveness of the American system of higher education to changing needs.

Sources of income do not distinguish a private institution of higher education as simply as they once did. On the one hand, member universities of the Committee on Interinstitutional Cooperation (which includes the Big Ten and the University of Chicago) call themselves "publicly assisted universities" because some of them in recent years have obtained more than half of their annual operating budget from sources other than state appropriations (fees, tuitions, foundation grants, alumni gifts, and federal funds). On the other hand, a few major private universities have been drawing substantially on both state and federal funds, as much as 35 to 55 percent of total operating budget coming in some years from public sources. Few, if any, private free-standing colleges—that is, colleges not part of a doctorate-granting university—approach this level of dependence upon public funds; but this difference stems less from their "privateness" than from their emphasis on under-graduate instruction, since federal support for higher education has gone first to graduate schools and research and is only beginning to reach into the exclusively undergraduate institutions.

This is not to imply, however, that private institutions cannot be distinguished from public ones in their sources of support today. Most significantly, for undergraduate instruction, public colleges draw their major support from direct appropriations by state legislatures (with a few exceptions, such as the sovereign-owned and -operated U.S. Air Force Academy), whereas private colleges generally depend upon their own endowment and tuitions for upwards of 70 percent of the instructional budget; generally 65 to 85 percent of this budget comes from tuitions alone. In states where legislative committees or superboards or executive bureaus control major portions of the budget on a line appropriation or authorization-to-expend basis, this difference is of great potential significance. While neither type of institution is altogether slave or free, the two types are liable to quite different sets of external influences.

In the last five years, the federal government has increased dramatically its contribution to students' college costs and to certain direct expenses of colleges—costs of buildings, research, program innovation, strengthening of weak institutions, equipment for improving instruction in sciences, faculty fellowships in the arts and humanities, programs in languages, attracting students into areas important to national defense, etc. Except where there were constitutional impediments, these programs have not taken into account whether the institution receiving the help is public or private, basing support instead on the institution's ability to make effective use of it. If this trend continues, there may come to be greater divergence between source of control and source of support, with some "private" colleges—especially those serving disadvantaged students and those experimenting with new educational ideas—meeting much of their instructional expense from public funds.

If all colleges are linked in an elaborate network of learning opportunities, if all have various forms of federal and state aid, if all make tuition charges at least in the form of fees, and if all are public in the sense that they must account to society for the effective and reasonably efficient use of their scarce resources—given all of these "ifs," does the "private-public" distinction make sense any more? There is, we think, still a most important difference. It is the difference between a board of control responsible to a publicly elected official or legislature and a board of control that answers only to its charter and to electors named therein. Governed by different mechanisms, these boards will account to different publics or different representatives of the public interest. We think the experience of three centuries has shown that the competition of interests and ideas implied in this arrangement is more likely to yield healthy institutions than is the adoption of any one ideology or dominating interest, no matter how persuasive or full of good will it might be.

At present, the proportion of students being educated in private colleges is declining. Perhaps it will continue to decline; the provisions we advocate will allow this trend to take its own course as experience determines how various public objectives can best be accomplished. Thus we recommend against trying to determine as an explicit policy matter that the proportion of students educated under private auspices shall either rise or fall.

Efficiency, interdependence, and college policy

Cooperation among colleges appears to be almost universally accepted now as an efficient way of enriching college programs and sometimes as a way of actually reducing instructional costs. Eight of the profile colleges belong to associations of colleges with ambitious and varied plans for collaboration—Morehouse to the Atlanta University Center, Amherst to the Connecticut Valley group, Ripon to the Associated Colleges of the Midwest, Oberlin and

Earlham to the Great Lakes Colleges Association, St. Thomas to a group of four St. Paul, Minnesota, colleges (with closest ties to the College of St. Catherine), Goddard and Monteith to the Union for Research and Experimentation in Higher Education. With a few exceptions, these associations bring together similar institutions— liberal arts colleges—though the associations themselves may then develop ties with other sorts of institutions, such as the Argonne National Laboratories, the Newberry Library, or universities abroad.

While strengthening these associations, the colleges should, we believe, begin looking to the next step, collaboration with institutions unlike themselves; and public policy should encourage the colleges to carry collaboration into this second stage. Many colleges, for example those that have developed into universities, have already departed from the tradition that a private college should exist as a separate enterprise offering only undergraduate studies for students eighteen to twenty-two years old. The departure we recommend here is of another kind. Some private colleges could well join undergraduate instruction with other enterprises besides traditional graduate work—elementary or secondary school teaching (especially teaching in inner cities or other unusually difficult situations), adult education programs (especially programs, like Goddard's, that depart from the usual night-school pattern), cooperative graduate programs like those now offered by the Connecticut Valley group and the Atlanta University group, postdoctoral programs normally encountered only in universities, and the activities of businesses, industries, and public service organizations that can offer laboratory or field experience for students, a means of support for students, or services essential to the college program itself (e.g., computer services, counseling services). Obviously, a college cannot enter this sort of collaboration casually; but when something in the college's tradition or program or location makes the collaboration natural and when the college as a whole is committed to the idea, it can be a source of energy and economy to the college as well as service to the community.

One kind of collaboration between colleges and other agencies which has proved effective in a number of institutions, though it is not yet widely adopted, may deserve special discussion— work-study programs. In either a concurrent (Berea) or alternating (Antioch) pattern, a work-study program can enhance students' education at minimal cost (by introducing students to laboratories, government offices, social science research groups, businesses and industries of all kinds, social service organizations, and experienced people in every field of work) and can help students pay for an education they could not otherwise afford. Throughout the profile colleges, many students work from ten to forty hours per week while carrying regular or only slightly reduced study loads. Thus the idea of combining work with study is by no means radical or foreign to common practice. Yet typically the colleges have not devoted much organized attention to student work. As a result, students are not as well-paid for their work as they might be in a more deliberately conceived system, and study time is not as well-protected from the competition of excessive work as it might be in a work-study plan supervised by the faculty as an integral part of the educational effort. In most colleges, moreover, there is scarcely any attempt to select jobs, prepare for them, and follow up on them with a view to uncovering their educational value. And that value can go well beyond specific skills and information. Work can help the student develop a realistic grasp of his own capabilities and limitations as a productive person and can give him a chance to exercise his judgment in the use of his time and resources— important aspects of maturity.

Another argument, too, supports work-study programs. A traditional "latent function" of colleges has been to keep young people off the employment market. However, the time is fast approaching when America will have, not a surplus, but a chronic shortage of workers of the caliber of college students. In some fields it will be more costly to put off supplying that labor than to combine the labor with college education. The idea of artificially keeping workers out of employment was never a particularly intelligent one, or one that distinguished our society as particularly acute in its management of human potential and social need. It is high time that colleges played their part as regulators of the labor supply and its allocation in a more socially productive way.

We contend that private and public institutions should compete in trying to render superior or more efficient services of a given kind. And we think some colleges, alone or with other institutions, may well come to perform services that have not ordinarily been in a private college's repertoire. But we would like to insist again that colleges should launch special programs only where they have a clear advantage by virtue of their flexibility, their traditions, their clientele, their location or associations, their faculty or administrative staff. Far Eastern studies and studies of peace and war for Earlham; music and Asian studies for Oberlin; vocational training in library science, medical technology, publishing, etc., for Simmons;

intercultural studies for Morehouse; Appalachian studies for Berea; a general education major for Monteith; a graduate program in theology for Wheaton; a Hawaiian beachhead for Goddard and the other colleges of the Union for Research and Experimentation in Higher Education; programs with the Chicago school system, the Newberry Library, and the Argonne Laboratories for Ripon and the other ACM colleges—all the unusual offerings of the profile colleges, actual or proposed, spring from special strengths or long-standing interests. They could not be invented and then tacked onto any college willing to have them. In each case they had to be discovered and developed from within the college's history and circumstances.

The self-assessment that leads a college to undertake certain programs and not others should be a thorough and candid one. Even the limitations of an institution can sometimes be turned to advantages if weakness can be admitted frankly. For example, a college whose faculty is not suitably trained to offer advanced studies in some of the newer subdisciplines of the social and physical sciences may be in a position to upgrade its faculty for a distinguished venture into the teaching of science to non-science majors. It will never do so as long as it insists on providing its own specialized courses in those newer disciplines. This self-assessment and choice should include, too, a thoroughgoing analysis of the services a college now provides which it could offer at less cost or better quality (or both) by contracting with other institutions or by using some form of network arrangement. Improvement of services and economy of operation are both essential to the staying power of the private colleges on the American scene. This effort will require frank analysis, rigorous application of the findings, and sometimes unconventional partnerships.

Internal obstacles Obstacles of an internal sort may interfere with the colleges' ability to serve society variously and imaginatively. The most critical of these may prove to be the colleges' own preconceptions of what a college ought to be, what liberal education ought to be. Though tradition is important, we are convinced that no dogma or postulate about the meaning of liberal education or the proper business of colleges should make it impossible for the colleges to serve the people who most need or can best benefit from higher education. If adults with only eighth-grade education but with social concerns and questions requiring college-level sophistication come asking instruction, not all colleges may legitimately turn them away because *they have low SAT scores, lack the usual linguistic skills for college, or do not have the prerequisite social studies courses.*

Similarly, traditional ideals about professors' roles, about methods and places of learning, and about the life of students must be reconsidered and altered to provide the many roads to liberal education that are currently called for. This reconsideration may mean campuses in the inner city and abroad, "nonacademic" projects in voluntary national service, and firsthand experience or employment in unfamiliar parts of contemporary society. It may mean the recruitment of some faculty with unorthodox pedigrees of experience and formal education and with a primary commitment to vocations other than teaching. It may mean a mixture of generations of students from teen-agers to grandmothers and from novices in work to managers of major enterprises. Such colleges may have little of the paternal rules and responsibilities of today's American colleges; but they will also be no replicas of the universities of Europe or Latin America. They will be new institutions, new communities—different in tone and climate from any available today within the limited American array, which even so seems confusing in its diversity to visitors from abroad.

A final obstacle springs from the ideals and traditions of governance of colleges. The ideal of academic freedom as practiced today is a mixture of critically important protection for the free competition of ideas, on one hand, and conservative practices of craft protectionism on the other. Under the banner of "faculty responsibility for standards," many a college faculty or department suppresses innovation, refinement of practice, and improvement of instruction.

Christopher Jencks notices the extent to which outside "interference" in the form of government and foundation money has stimulated university research since World War II:

If the conventional wisdom about non-intervention is correct, the American university should have compiled a distinguished record on the teaching side and a rather mediocre record in research. In point of fact, this has not happened. The combination of external financing and individual initiative has encouraged a certain amount of charlatanism and quite a lot of nonsense on the research side, but there has also been an extraordinary amount of brilliant work, a readiness to move into new fields, try new ideas, and respond to real problems. In teaching, on the other hand, collective responsibility and the comparative absence of external financial pressures, far from ensuring a generally high quality of classroom performance, have led to stagnation.*

* The New Republic, Oct. 23, 1965, pp. 17–18.

If Jencks is right, outside support for educational experimentation by inventive individuals, groups, or whole colleges may bring on a flowering of instruction and service comparable to the flowering of research in the last twenty years. We are not content to see this support take the form of waving a checkbook at anyone willing to contrive an "innovation." Charlatanism and nonsense are as easily come by in instruction as in research. But we believe a public policy may be formulated that will discover competence and imagination in individuals and colleges, in both public and private sectors, and nourish them to extraordinary new growth.

Colleges and the superculture   *At this moment in American history, colleges could become the prime agencies of social self-criticism and regeneration. From the eagerness of individuals to get a college education for themselves or their children to the requests of government and industry for the services of intellectuals, institutions of higher education find the demand for their services at a new high. Within higher education, the colleges are probably more open to change than the graduate schools, partly because the strength and prestige of the graduate schools renders them less discontent with themselves and hence more cautious about change. The fact that the graduate schools are specialized also makes them less likely to focus upon the society's needs in the large. Colleges, for their part, have more to gain and less to lose than would the graduate schools by making themselves servants of a larger need.*

A major problem of the next century, according to Kenneth Boulding, will be the preservation of subcultures within the "superculture" of a complex, highly organized world. This technological superculture will standardize goods, ensure efficiency, and spread a certain kind of rationality throughout the world. But it is bound to be incomplete. It cannot fulfill man's need for a full range of thought and feeling. It cannot generate the particularities of language, art, ritual, and social bond that give a culture its emotional drawing power and its aesthetic satisfaction. If people are to be deeply satisfied in a place, a community, or a way of life, it will be because of the union of this efficient superculture with an enhancing subculture. Furthermore, the superculture may well stagnate, become bureaucratic and ponderous, unless new energy and new perspectives are constantly introduced through conflict and hybridization among subcultures.

Up to this point, colleges have largely been servants of the superculture, introducing students to information, techniques, and language that will enable them to move outside their own town or trade or social group. With a solid knowledge of chemistry, a young man can find work almost anywhere in the country, perhaps anywhere in the world. With an easy command of standard English—one of the by-products of higher education—he can talk to the superculture in its own terms. As our earlier discussion makes clear, we do not expect to see colleges desert this role. Indeed, we are arguing that college education should reach far more people than it does now, acquainting them with broadly accepted habits of thought and helping them to intellectual competence that will command respect anywhere in literate society. Colleges, we hope, will continue to take students from the west side of Detroit, from Plainwell, Michigan, or from Anniston, Alabama, and introduce them to the problems that are agitating New York or Peking and to the ideas that informed Byzantium. They will develop skills that can be used, with appropriate variations, in Akron, Bogotá, or Calcutta— and if our prediction about the network is anywhere near accurate, they may well have occasion to try their competence in places as widely separated as these.

But the time is ripe, we hold, for America's colleges consciously to combine this function with another. They must not only free students from the confines of their past but also teach them to relish that past, to respect the local, the particular—this place, this manner of talk, this belief, this odd but traditional way of acting. In short, it is the business of the colleges to preserve and even create subcultures within the superculture. This is a large order. Little is known about the ways in which creative enclaves are born and sustained, and many liberal arts colleges still tend to mistrust their differences. Yet our examination of the profile colleges makes it clear that an institution can generate an identity of its own, a mixture of history and conviction that will help students to define themselves and will provoke the collision of ideas on which society lives. The profiles, as we read them, show that to achieve distinctive character, a college need not pay the price of intellectual isolation, and that extraordinary commitment need not mean neglect of the tasks common to undergraduate education. If public policy is intelligently congenial to the growth of liberal arts colleges and if the colleges themselves can combine imagination, competence, and respect for their differences, the college of the future will not only lead its students into the intricately personal growth we call liberal education but it will also lend color and texture to the fabric of American society.

Three persons were assigned to each profile: the principal author, chiefly responsible for gathering information, arriving at judgments, and writing the profile; an Antioch-based member of the study staff, who was to help gather information and, since he would visit other colleges in the study as well, provide perspective and comparisons; and an "insider" appointed by the college itself to make information available, to assist the visitors in gaining access to students and faculty, and generally to help the outsiders understand what the college is and what it is attempting to become.

The profiles group—principal authors, staff, and insiders—met in September, 1965, in Yellow Springs, Ohio, to discuss the conception of the project, the kinds of profiles and editorial questions they hoped would emerge, and the procedures that would be most likely to yield the desired results. Later in the fall and winter, the teams made two- to four-day visits to their colleges, interviewing students, faculty, administrators, and sometimes alumni or members of the Board of Trustees. Team members had access to documents of all sorts: Presidents' reports, financial statements, registration statistics, minutes of faculty meetings, copies of student newspapers and literary magazines, calendars of campus events, and so forth. In a second meeting at Haverford College, in January, 1966, the group reviewed the first visits, looked over outlines of the profiles, discussed again the aims of the project, and made plans for a second round of visits.

413

Before these second visits, principal authors drafted sections of their profiles tentatively or prepared crucial questions. The second visits occurred during the spring of 1966. Drafts of ten of the profiles were submitted for discussion and criticism at a third meeting of the profiles group at Ball State University in May, 1966. During the summer, principal authors prepared second drafts, with criticism and suggestions from other members of their teams, and Mrs. W. B. Alexander in Yellow Springs gave each profile a first editing. Between January and August, 1967, Conrad Hilberry and Mrs. Alexander did further editing and rewriting, sometimes going to documents the team had collected or to the insiders for additional information.

The evolution of chapters began with working papers prepared during 1965–66 by Morris Keeton and others and distributed fairly widely in mimeographed form. First drafts of five of the chapters were written in September and October, 1966, and criticized at the end of October by a group of educational leaders who had not previously been connected with the study. With the benefit of that criticism, the chapters were almost entirely rewritten during the spring and summer of 1967. Though all are joint endeavors, chapters 1, 2, 5, 6, and 7 were written primarily by Morris Keeton, chapters 3 and 4 primarily by Conrad Hilberry.

Method Though the authors and the teams were at liberty to work in their own ways, the profiles do reflect, we believe, the extensive and repeated discussion among members of the profiles group; the teams employed something like a common method in investigating and reporting. For example:

1. Each team gave considerable attention to the purposes of the institution: what it viewed as its constituency, where it found its students, what it hoped to accomplish with those students or with that constituency, and how it went about accomplishing this. Further, each team began by attempting to see the college from the inside, to understand its mission as the people there understood. This does not mean that the authors withheld judgment or simply adopted the college's conception of education; some of them turned out to be critical of the college's goals or its ways of reaching them. But they attempted, before passing judgment, to understand the college on its own terms.

2. Each of the teams and authors attended to the change occurring within the college—what the college has been in the past, the traditions that directed change, the economic or social facts that set the

limits within which change could occur, the forces working to push the college in one direction or another, and the choices that might be open to it. None of the colleges was viewed as static, cut off from its past or its future.

3. Though each author used his own judgment about the format of his profile, certain questions are answered in virtually every one: Where do the students come from? What are they after in their studies? How do they conduct their extracurricular life? How much has the student revolt or retreat of the mid-sixties reached them? What are the faculty's ambitions, backgrounds, educational ideas? How is the college governed? Who makes decisions on what issues? In what ways is the curriculum distinctive? What parts of the curriculum

PROFILE OF A COLLEGE: ASSESSMENT GRID

Variable	A. Students	B. Faculty	C. Staff and administrators	D. Publics	E. College as interacting group(s)
1 Who? Who are they? What are they like?	A 1	B 1	C 1	D 1	E 1
2 Why? What are their purposes, aspirations, long-range plans, latent needs?	A 2	B 2	C 2	D 2	E 2
3 Where? In what environments? With what resources?	A 3	B 3	C 3	D 3	E 3
4 Interacting how? Among themselves and with other persons of the college? Ways of learning, teaching, administering?	A 4	B 4	C 4	D 4	E 4
5 With what results? What changes occur in them? Impact of interactions on them? How do these effects fit purposes (especially E)?	A 5	B 5	C 5	D 5	E 5

Note: This chart is awkward for representation of the mixes of people, purposes, environments, and modes of interaction, as well as for representing the interactions among these people, environments, and activities. We should therefore keep in mind three questions as we fill in the grid: (1) Show under E anything special about the combinations of A, B, C, and D. (2) Show under E anything unusual about the interactions resulting. (3) Comment on the bearing of these on effectiveness in relation to purposes: consistency of purposes, fitness of environments and resources to aims and of ways of interacting to personnel and aims, etc.

appear to be most successful and what parts least successful? What are the institution's financial resources? How does it balance its budget? In what ways is it affected by its location? Has it developed collaborative arrangements with other institutions? In what sense is there a college "community"? What changes does the college produce in its students and faculty? A grid prepared by the study staff in August, 1965, suggests questions one may ask about each population within a college. Profiles teams used the grid, a copy of which appears here, as a reminder of questions to be looked into, but they did not feel bound to fill in answers item by item.

4. The teams made use of "hard" data of a number of kinds—information already gathered by the colleges in the form of self-studies, financial reports, registration figures, follow-up studies of graduates, College Board aptitude test figures, Graduate Record Examination scores, etc.; information on demographic, economic, and educational trends prepared by Everett K. Wilson for the use of the profiles group; and information collected at ten of the colleges through special administrations of the College Student Questionnaire and the College and University Environment Scales.* But they drew, too, on impres-

* The Educational Testing Service provides these descriptions of CSQ and CUES:

"The College Student Questionnaires have been developed for use by institutional researchers as a means for gathering and processing large amounts of diverse information about college student bodies for a variety of research purposes. This information is for the most part biographical and attitudinal.

"There are two questionnaires—Part 1 and Part 2. CSQ Part 1 is for administration to entering students (freshmen, transfers) prior to the formal beginning of the academic year. Divided into four sections, Part 1 contains questions about (1) educational and vocational plans and expectations, (2) activities, achievements, and perceptions during secondary school, (3) family background, and (4) certain personal attitudes.

"CSQ Part 2 is for administration to any group of undergraduates toward the close of the academic year. It is in three sections, two of which duplicate Sections I and LV from CSQ Part 1. The middle section of Part 2 consists of some 100 questions dealing with what might be called "student functioning," i.e., activities, perceptions, and satisfactions as students at a particular college. The purpose in constructing overlapping instruments is to enable study of student change during the college year. CSQ comparison data is based on the responses of 12,949 entering freshmen at 23 institutions for CSQ–1 and 6,680 undergraduates at 15 colleges for CSQ–2.

"The College and University Environment Scales (CUES) are designed to describe the institutional climate of the campus. CUES consist of 150 statements about college life; features and facilities of the campus, rules and regulations, faculty, curricula, instruction and examinations, student life, extra-curricular organizations, and other aspects of the institutional environment, all of which help to define the intellectual-social-cultural climate of the college as students see it.

sions derived from conversations with people at the college, from firsthand observation of classes, faculty meetings, and student discussions, from student newspapers, bulletin boards, and official publications, and from histories of individual students and of particular campus controversies. Frequently they were able to record in the profile itself the incidents, histories, or bits of conversation or reportage that crystallized their impressions of the college. (For brevity we have omitted much of such material from our final profiles.)

5. Every team except one was assisted by student observers from outside who visited the profile college. A training session for student observers was held at Antioch in March, 1966, the observers trying out their powers of observation on Antioch student life. At the profile colleges the student observers lived in the dormitories or fraternity houses, attended classes, joined in student discussions, became as thoroughly acquainted as possible with the college's student life. Most of the student observers conferred with members of the profile team before and after visiting the college and reported their observations both orally and in writing.

6. The profile teams, and especially the principal authors, undertook not just to report what they saw but also to evaluate the college's mission and its success in carrying out this mission. They attempted to lay out the facts and make clear the reasons for their evaluation so that a reader working from different assumptions might follow the data to another conclusion. Though the insiders and college officials were invited to supply further information when they felt the draft profiles were inaccurate or misleading, they did not censor the final product.

Staff   At the end of each profile appear the names of the principal author, his associate, and the liaison with the institution being studied, as well as the names of the student observers. These names are repeated in alphabetic order on the following page.

"By indicating which statements are generally characteristic of their college, students act as reporters; their aggregate judgment provides an opinion poll which reveals characteristics of the college. Institutions, *not* individual students, are scored. CUES provide a measure of the environment along five dimensions, developed by factor analytic methods, which appear to reflect certain ways in which colleges differ from one another. These dimensions are: practicality, community, awareness, propriety, and scholarship. Normative data are provided from 48 four-year accredited colleges."

Authors, Associates, and College Representatives (Titles at the time of writing, 1965–66, except as noted)

W. Boyd Alexander
Emeritus Vice President and
  Dean of the Faculty
Antioch College

David L. Anderson
Chairman of the Department
  of Physics
Oberlin College

Robert P. Ashley
Dean
Ripon College

George Beecher
Director of Educational
  Experimentation
Goddard College

Edward B. Blackman
Assistant Dean of University
  College
Michigan State University

James R. Bobbitt
Associate Professor of Art
Berea College

Richard W. Burckhardt
Vice President for Instructional
  Affairs and Dean of Faculties
Ball State University

Norman Burns
Executive Secretary of North
  Central Association of
  Colleges and Secondary
  Schools and Professor of
  Education at the University
  of Chicago

William E. Cadbury, Jr.
Then Dean and now Director
  of the Postbaccalaureate
  Fellowship Program
Haverford College

Sherrill Cleland
Then Dean
Kalamazoo College;
Now Visiting Professor
  of Economics
American University
  of Beirut

Paul L. Dressel
Assistant Provost and Director
  of Institutional Research
Michigan State University

Edward J. Drummond, S.J.
Vice President of the Medical
  Center
St. Louis University

Rev. Henri Dulac
Then Chairman of the
  Department of Philosophy
  and now Director of
  Development
College of St. Thomas

Joseph E. Elmore
Vice President for Academic
  Affairs and Dean
Earlham College

Elizabeth Geen
Dean and Vice President
Goucher College

Robert F. Grose
Registrar and Associate
    Professor of Psychology
Amherst College

Conrad Hilberry
Associate Director of the
    Carnegie Study of the Future
    of Liberal Arts Colleges and
    Professor of English
Kalamazoo College

Morris T. Keeton
Director of the Carnegie Study
    of the Future of Liberal Arts
    Colleges and Academic Vice
    President
Antioch College

Melvin D. Kennedy
Professor of History
Morehouse College

Parker E. Lichtenstein
Then Dean of the College
    and now Acting President
Denison University

Hermann R. Muelder
Then Dean and now
    Professor of History
Knox College

J. Garton Needham
Vice President
Simmons College

Carl M. Stevens
Professor of Economics
Reed College

Albert B. Stewart
Professor of Physics
Antioch College

Peter Veltman
Chairman of the Department
    of Education and now Dean
    of the College
Wheaton College

Paule Verdet
Division of Science of Society
Monteith College

Edward K. Williams
Dean
Westminster College

Everett K. Wilson
Then Professor of Sociology at
    Antioch College and now
    Visiting Professor of Sociology
University of North Carolina

Student Observers

Ann Bolt
Antioch College

Richard Bolt
Antioch College

Mike Clark
Berea College

Carol Dressel
Michigan State
    University

Randall Evans
Monteith College

Margaret Hall
William Woods
  College

Melvin Hall
Westminster College

Doug Jessee
Berea College

Ronald Lehmann
Knox College

Elliott Long
Antioch College

Mimi Luebbermann
Goucher College

William May
St. Louis University

Stephen McCarthy
Reed College

Marilyn McNabb
Earlham College

Ruth Mesing
Knox College

Claudene Oliva
Antioch College

James Reed
Ripon College

Barbara Tuttle
Antioch College

Carol Ann Van Zant
Berea College

Nancy Sue Van Zant
Berea College

The persons attending the October, 1966, conference convened to discuss the chapters were as follows:

Laurence Barrett
Professor of English
Kalamazoo College

Mark Benbow
Professor of English
Colby College

W. B. Brentlinger
Dean
Greenville College

Finley Campbell
Assistant Professor of English
Morehouse College

Wayne J. Gerber
Dean
Bethel College

Howard Greenlee
Then Professor of History
  and Dean
Tuskegee Institute;
Now Dean of the Faculty
Antioch College

Sumner Hayward
Then Dean
Macalester College
Now President
Associated Colleges of the
    Midwest

Roy Heath
Dean of Students
Trinity College

Paul Jenson
Academic Vice President
Temple Buell College

William Kolb
Dean
Beloit College

J. Barry McGannon
Dean of the College of
    Liberal Arts
St. Louis University

Leo Nussbaum
Then Dean
Austin College;
Now Dean
Coe College

Richard F. Reath
Professor of Political Science
Occidental College

Byron Youtz
Then Executive Assistant
    to the President
Reed College;
Now Academic Vice President
State University of New
    York at Old Westbury

As noted in the Preface, valuable assistance was rendered by members of the advisory committee, which met several times to discuss the design of the project and the ideas advanced.

Advisory Committee

John Brademas
Member of the House of
    Representatives
Congress of the United States

Victor L. Butterfield
President Emeritus
Wesleyan University

James P. Dixon
President
Antioch College

C. W. Friedman
Executive Secretary
National Catholic Educational
    Association

Algo C. Henderson
Then Director of the Center
    for the Study of Higher
    Education
University of Michigan;
Now Research Professor of
    Higher Education
University of California
    at Berkeley

Steven Muller
Director of the Center for
  International Studies
Cornell University

Theodore M. Newcomb
Chairman of the Doctoral
  Program in Social Psychology
University of Michigan

Willa B. Player
Director of the Division
  of College Support
Bureau of Higher Education
U.S. Office of Education

Lawrence Rogin
Director of the Labor
  Educational Study
American University

James P. Shannon
Bishop of St. Helena's Parish
Minneapolis, Minnesota

Alan Simpson
President
Vassar College

Richard D. Weigle
President
St. John's College

F. L. Wormald
Vice President of the
  Association of American
  Colleges

Theodore O. Yntema
Chairman of Finance Committee
  and Vice President
Ford Motor Company

APPENDIX B

SCIENCE IN THE

LIBERAL ARTS COLLEGE:

A TEST CASE

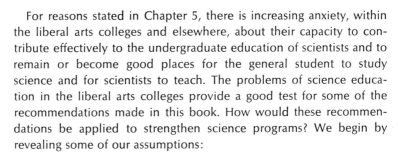

For reasons stated in Chapter 5, there is increasing anxiety, within the liberal arts colleges and elsewhere, about their capacity to contribute effectively to the undergraduate education of scientists and to remain or become good places for the general student to study science and for scientists to teach. The problems of science education in the liberal arts colleges provide a good test for some of the recommendations made in this book. How would these recommendations be applied to strengthen science programs? We begin by revealing some of our assumptions:

1. The world pictures of scientists, technologists, science administrators, and decision makers are important determiners of the shape of the future. Without adequate understanding of the roles of science and technology in the continued adaptation of man to the rapidly changing conditions of his existence, we will get a degradation rather than an enhancement of life.

2. Widespread understanding of the nature of science and technology and of their significance in the modern world is essential to a democratic society. Such understanding must come to include intuitive and affective as well as analytic modes of knowing.

3. To provide a significant liberal education, a college must have effective science teaching. Even much-improved secondary schools will not be able to meet the need for a strengthened science component of liberal education.

4. Support for science education must be based not only on the nation's requirements for scientific manpower but also on the broader needs of society, including the need for greatly increased public understanding of the possibilities and the limitations of science.

Major problems facing colleges trying to become more effective in science education

The problem of engaging students in learning science Only a small minority of college students get far enough into the study of a science to know what it means to be able to use the conceptual and experimental tools of the discipline or to gain an intuitive understanding of the satisfactions of science. Many students who enter college with a central interest in science move into other fields; few students come to take a major interest in science after entering college. The ratio of those moving away from science to those moving toward it in college is estimated at greater than 10 to 1.

The problem of "subcritical mass" In many liberal arts colleges there are inadequate numbers of scientists to provide the cross-fertilization, cooperation, and general excitement to support active and productive scientific work.

The problem of inadequate support for research Appropriate research activity can support the college's teaching of students by (a) leading them to the discovery that it is possible to find things out for themselves, a powerful initiator of interest in science, (b) making clear the character of scientific activity, (c) stimulating the mastery of conceptions, skills, and intellectual tools without losing freshness of conception, independence in thinking, and originality, and (d) indicating the variety of talents and styles of work that lead to scientific productivity.

The problem of working at the frontier of popular research fields Liberal arts colleges find it difficult to bring enough resources to bear on the exploitation of a discovery to compete with larger establishments.

The problem of attracting and keeping science faculty Many of the liberal arts colleges have unfilled openings in their science departments. Even colleges with their budgeted complement of science faculty are unprepared to meet the range of science teaching needs. In the competition for trained people these colleges offer salaries that are too low, facilities (laboratory, library, technical help, secretarial help, computers) that are inadequate, and teaching loads that are too high for sustained professional development. Moreover, a decreasing minority of prospective college teachers have studied in a liberal arts college. As a result, many scientists have no basis for judging the advantages and disadvantages of working in a liberal arts college.

Recommendations for finding solutions Some of these problems may be unsolvable, at least as stated; not all problems have solutions. It seems likely that the frontier in some fields of science is closed to many liberal arts colleges; the scales of activity are too disparate. But liberal arts colleges, with appropriate support, can solve most of these problems. Clearly a federal support program of grants or loans to students that would cover the full educational costs would ameliorate all these difficulties. But it is equally transparent that other forms of support and other sources of strength must be sought.

1. The capital costs in building and equipment are especially great for science instruction. Both public and private capital could fittingly contribute—public capital to increase the nation's resources of educated scientists and other citizens, private capital to put the savings of industry to work developing the talent it needs for survival and growth.

2. Given the present ineffectiveness of science education for the general student, support is required for innovations in science teaching in a variety of undergraduate schools, including those in university contexts. (Harvard is currently seeking some 50 million dollars for science, much of it to be directed to science education of undergraduates.) Studies of the factors that attract students to the sciences as well as those that repel them should be a part of such a program. A national program of summer school scholarships in science for non-science majors and of support for the development of appropriate courses should be initiated as soon as possible.

3. Support is needed for interdisciplinary work in the sciences in liberal arts colleges both to engage students in science study and to contribute to the solution of social problems. For example, making the study of human ecology a major element in the undergraduate curriculum would help develop and extend the practice of thinking about scientific problems in the context of social systems. The integrative possibilities presented by the study of ecology, the need for broader understanding of the interactions among living communities, and the important practical problems posed by finite resources, growing pollution, and expanding human populations all speak for increased research and teaching in human ecology. Other examples can be found in programs to investigate the interrelations between human values and scientific developments in such fields as nuclear physics

and human genetics. Because of their size and tradition of searching for integrating concepts to guide their teaching, liberal arts colleges should play a leading role in these developments.

4. There are a number of forms of association and collaboration that can meet the problems of science education:

a. Support of research institutes on liberal arts campuses by both private and public funds.

b. Joint appointments of faculty to university and liberal arts colleges. Such appointments could provide stimulation in research and in teaching for both the college and the university. If faculty with strong disciplinary interests are to be productive in a liberal arts college, they need to be a part of the scientific establishment, not just in touch with it.

c. An increase in the interaction between the national laboratories and the liberal arts colleges by the expansion of existing programs of cooperation and by the joint appointment of faculty to national laboratories and liberal arts colleges.

d. Specialization of individual liberal arts colleges in areas planned to complement the work in other associated colleges; exchange of students among a group of colleges with designed diversity.

5. Other recommendations:

a. Earmarked research funds for projects that promise well for the undergraduates participating in them. The NSF undergraduate research participation program is one example.

b. Extension of programs for science teaching interns to attract young scientists to the faculties of liberal arts colleges.

c. Increased use by colleges of technicians, secretaries, and other supporting personnel in order to increase the efficiency of utilization of the scarce commodity of science faculty.

The context for distinguished colleges described in this volume is a fitting context for distinguished work in science education.

Albert B. Stewart
Antioch College
January 10, 1968

The Report of the Committee on Physics Faculties in Colleges has
led many of those concerned with the future of the liberal arts colleges to conclude that they are declining as significant sources of
scientists. In an effort to discover how a number of liberal arts colleges were doing as undergraduate sources of doctorates in the
sciences, we have compared the baccalaureate origins of doctorates
in five groups of liberal arts colleges with those in the ten universities
that are the leading sources of undergraduates who come to earn the
Ph.D. The number of graduates earning the Ph.D. in the five years
1961–65 has been compared with the number of graduates earning
the Ph.D. during the period 1950–59. (To make the comparison with
the decade of the fifties, the number earned in the five-year period
of the sixties was multiplied by 2.) All the data were obtained from
the National Academy of Sciences–National Research Council, either
from Publication 1142, *Doctorate Production in United States Universities 1920–1962*, or from tabulations made available by Dr. Lindsey
R. Harmon, director of research.

While the groups of liberal arts colleges show significant differences among themselves, they have all increased their contribution to
science doctorates by a greater percentage than their undergraduate
enrollments. For the ten institutions that are the leading under-

427

TABLE 1

COLLEGES IN THE GREAT LAKES COLLEGES ASSOCIATION

Code Number	Name	Physical Sciences*		Biological Sciences†		Total		Undergraduate Enrollment Fall 1951‡	Undergraduate Enrollment Fall 1958§
		1950–1959	1961–1965 (× 2)	1950–1959	1961–1965 (× 2)	1950–1959	1961–1965 (× 2)		
3402	Albion	8	20	9	18	17	38	1,007	1,384
3102	Antioch	46	70	15	12	61	82	1,017	1,222
3122	Denison	25	22	6	8	31	30	1,124	1,429
3207	DePauw	56	48	41	24	97	72	1,703	2,161
3208	Earlham	8	22	13	32	21	54	648	837
3414	Hope	32	50	15	16	47	66	836	1,156
3415	Kalamazoo	28	42	15	18	43	60	454	637
3131	Kenyon	11	38	8	4	19	42	432	508
3140	Oberlin	131	186	50	84	181	270	1,888	2,109
3144	Ohio Wesleyan	27	44	9	26	36	70	1,988	2,109
3239	Wabash	24	46	18	32	42	78	507	644
3119	Wooster	55	76	9	30	64	106	1,090	1,230
		451	664	208	304	659	968	12,694	15,426
Change from 1950s			+47%		+46%		+47%		
Increase in undergraduate enrollment 1951–1958									+22%

* Chemistry, engineering, physics, mathematics, geological sciences.
† Agricultural, medical (Ph.D.) anatomy, etc., physiology, biochemistry, botany, microbiology, zoology, miscellaneous.
‡ American Universities and Colleges, 6th ed., ACE, Washington, D.C., 1952.
§ American Universities and Colleges, 8th ed., ACE, Washington, D.C., 1960.

TABLE 2

ASSOCIATED COLLEGES OF THE MIDWEST

Code Number	Name	Physical Sciences		Biological Sciences		Total		Undergraduate Enrollment Fall 1951	Undergraduate Enrollment Fall 1958
		1950–1959	1961–1965 (× 2)	1950–1959	1961–1965 (× 2)	1950–1959	1961–1965 (× 2)		
3503	Beloit	23	34	9	20	32	54	932	1,034
4104	Carleton	36	72	14	22	50	94	892	1,054
4205	Coe	13	18	4	6	17	24	610	778
4206	Cornell (Iowa)	19	22	9	16	28	38	654	761
4210	Grinnell	27	48	11	30	38	78	860	944
3347	Knox	18	28	3	14	21	42	781	838
3510	Lawrence	12	24	11	12	23	36	804	889
3360	Monmouth	21	30	5	6	26	36	599	716
3521	Ripon	4	22	4	12	8	34	551	582
4129	Olaf	40	88	11	30	51	118	1,445	1,840
		213	386	81	168	294	554	8,128	9,436
Change from 1950s			+ 81%		+ 107%		+ 88%		
Increase in undergraduate enrollment 1951–1958									+ 16%

TABLE 3

CENTRAL STATES COLLEGE ASSOCIATION

Code Number	Name	Physical Sciences		Biological Sciences		Total		Undergraduate Enrollment Fall 1951	Undergraduate Enrollment Fall 1958
		1950–1959	1961–1965 (× 2)	1950–1959	1961–1965 (× 2)	1950–1959	1961–1965 (× 2)		
3403	Alma	4	4	10	8	14	12	440	677
3307	Augustana	31	44	6	20	37	64	1,191	1,397
3505	Carroll	7	20	2	12	9	32	432	774
4113	Gustavus Adolphus	6	12	13	14	19	26	899	1,120
3343	Illinois Wesleyan	8	4	7	2	15	6	765	1,222
4216	Luther	12	26	7	20	19	46	698	1,210
3355	MacMurray	1	0	1	0	2	0	474	697
3222	Manchester	19	18	6	14	25	32	657	1,015
3345	Millikin	13	24	5	4	18	28	961	1,074
3363	Mundelein	3	2	3	6	6	8	717	1,100
4127	St. John's (Minnesota)	22	24	5	14	27	38	782	1,050
4220	Simpson	3	10	3	6	6	16	440	625
		129	186	68	120	197	308	8,456	11,961

Increase 1950–1959   +44%   +76%   +56%

Increase in undergraduate enrollment 1951–1958   +41%

TABLE 4

THREE REGIONAL GROUPS

Code Number	Name	Physical Sciences		Biological Sciences		Total		Under-graduate Enrollment Fall 1951	Under-graduate Enrollment Fall 1958
		1950–1959	1961–1965 (× 2)	1950–1959	1961–1965 (× 2)	1950–1959	1961–1965 (× 2)		
1402	Amherst	58	104	16	52	74	156	1,051	1,025
1439	Mount Holyoke	13	24	19	20	32	44	1,220	1,350
1451	Smith	9	12	12	22	21	34	2,161	2,256
2305	Bryn Mawr	15	26	9	26	24	52	602	670
2324	Haverford	55	58	9	32	64	90	473	453
2379	Swarthmore	78	144	39	76	117	220	875	918
9341	Pomona	60	102	17	38	77	140	1,041	1,097
9336	Occidental	15	40	5	20	20	60	1,192	1,394
9357	Redlands	15	22	4	10	19	32	1,029	1,211
9363	Whittier	12	8	7	14	19	22	931	1,045
		330	540	137	310	467	850	10,575	11,419
Change from 1950s			+64%		+126%		+82%		+8%

Increase in undergraduate enrollment 1951–1958

TABLE 5

TEN LEADING PRIVATE LIBERAL ARTS SOURCES

Code Number	Name	Physical Sciences		Biological Sciences		Total		Under-graduate Enrollment Fall 1951	Under-graduate Enrollment Fall 1958
		1950–1959	1961–1965 (× 2)	1950–1959	1961–1965 (× 2)	1950–1959	1961–1965 (× 2)		
3140	Oberlin	131	186	50	84	181	270	1,888	2,109
1201	Dartmouth	66	158	30	68	96	226	2,626	2,856
2379	Swarthmore	78	144	39	76	117	220	875	918
1402	Amherst	58	104	16	52	74	156	1,051	1,025
9215	Reed	77	118	21	40	98	158	620	629
3119	Wooster	55	76	9	30	64	106	1,090	1,230
2195	Vassar	15	6	19	16	34	22	1,424	1,383
1460	Wellesley	13	14	15	34	28	48	1,692	1,691
2191	Union	88	114	13	20	101	134	984	1,703
1439	Mount Holyoke	13	24	19	20	32	44	1,220	1,350
		594	944	231	440	825	1,384	13,470	14,894
Change from 1950s			+ 59%		+ 90%		+ 68%		
Increase in undergraduate enrollment 1951–1958									+ 11%

TABLE 6
TEN LEADING SOURCES

Code Number	Name	Physical Sciences		Biological Sciences		Total		Undergraduate Enrollment Fall 1951	Undergraduate Enrollment Fall 1958
		1950–1959	1961–1965 ($\times$ 2)	1950–1959	1961–1965 ($\times$ 2)	1950–1959	1961–1965 ($\times$ 2)		
9356	Univ. of California (Berkeley)	637	888	428	348	1,065	1,236	11,000*	13,633
2188	City College of New York	661	814	201	180	862	994	20,765	24,753
3388	Univ. of Illinois	545	874	298	380	843	1,254	17,857	23,772
3387	Univ. of Chicago	416	340	174	156	590	496	1,100*	2,211
3527	Univ. of Wisconsin	320	498	335	356	655	854	10,139	16,360
1422	Harvard University	440	590	124	170	564	760	4,506	4,538
4133	Univ. of Minnesota	276	418	263	384	539	802	15,598	22,573
3430	Univ. of Michigan	447	684	176	222	623	906	9,805	17,569
2116	Columbia University	298	456	96	120	394	576	4,772	7,501
2120	Cornell University	335	568	310	374	645	942	7,820	8,596
		4,375	6,130	2,405	2,690	6,780	8,820	103,362	141,506
Change from 1950s		+40%		+12%		+30%			+36%

Increase in undergraduate enrollment 1951–1958

* Estimate

TABLE 7

TEN LEADING TECHNICAL SCHOOLS

Code Number	Name	Physical Sciences		Biological Sciences		Total		Undergraduate Enrollment Fall 1951	Undergraduate Enrollment Fall 1958
		1950–1959	1961–1965 (× 2)	1950–1959	1961–1965 (× 2)	1950–1959	1961–1965 (× 2)		
1427	Massachusetts Institute of Technology	687	1,548	48	68	735	1,616	3,154	3,587
9305	California Institute of Technology	343	496	22	38	365	534	611	703
2307	Carnegie Institute of Technology	265	434	5	10	270	444	2,534	4,354
2174	Rensselaer	221	486	12	12	233	498	2,693	3,155
7434	Rice University	114	262	13	36	127	298	1,304	1,616
2332	Lehigh	117	260	13	14	130	274	2,660	2,684
3341	Illinois Institute of Technology	160	262	11	12	171	274	6,013	6,488
2171	Brooklyn Polytechnic Institute	138	298	4	4	142	302	3,616	3,487
5436	Virginia Polytechnic Institute	94	144	59	60	153	204	2,913	4,408
3109	Case Institute	137	330	6	2	143	332	1,287	1,647
		2,276	4,520	193	256	2,469	4,776	26,785	32,129

Change from 1950s   +98%   +33%   +93%

Increase in undergraduate enrollment 1951–1958   +20%

graduate sources of science doctorates, enrollments have risen faster than numbers of undergraduates who go on to get the Ph.D. The ten "technical schools" that lead other such schools as undergraduate sources of science doctorates show increases that are closer to the pattern of the liberal arts colleges than to that of the leading sources (large universities).

The most striking feature of these tables is the large growth in the numbers of undergraduates going on to a doctorate in the *biological* sciences who received their baccalaureate from liberal arts colleges. Here the liberal arts colleges show a much larger increase than the universities and institutes of technology.

Albert B. Stewart
Antioch College
January 23, 1967

TABLE 8

SUMMARY

	Physical Sciences	Biological Sciences	Total	Enrollment
Great Lakes Colleges Association	+ 47%	+ 46%	+ 47%	+ 22%
Associated Colleges of the Midwest	+ 81%	+ 107%	+ 88%	+ 16%
Central States College Association	+ 22%	+ 76%	+ 56%	+ 41%
3 Regional Groups	+ 64%	+ 125%	+ 82%	+ 8%
10 Liberal Arts Sources	+ 59%	+ 90%	+ 68%	+ 11%
10 Leading Sources	+ 40%	+ 12%	+ 30%	+ 36%
10 Technical Schools	+ 98%	+ 33%	+ 93%	+ 20%
35 Ohio Colleges (Non-Ph.D.)	+ 63%	+ 51%	+ 59%	+ 51%
9 Ohio Universities (Ph.D.-granting)	+ 81%	+ 4%	+ 51%	+ 29%

Proposal The new program of federal scholarships, to be included in the Higher Education Act of 1965, should be systematically broadened to include students from higher and higher income brackets. The aim of this expansion should be both to help students who now do not attend college to do so and to help the colleges themselves by enabling them to charge more realistic tuition without excluding students from low- and middle-income families. The federal government should, by 1970, be giving as much financial assistance to individual students as to institutions. A target of 2 billion dollars per year in each category is not unreasonable in the light of prospective costs and numbers. The long-term aim of this program should be to give students from low- and middle-income families the same free choices between attending a commuter college and going away and between the public and private sectors as are now available to students from upper-income families.

Discussion Most advocates of federal undergraduate scholarships rest their case on the importance of ensuring every "able" student a chance to attend college, regardless of his parents' income. Critics reply that able students can already obtain a higher education, even without

* Carnegie Study of the Future of Liberal Arts Colleges Working Paper no. 19.

such a federal scholarship program. If a student has enough confidence in his future earning power to borrow heavily, if he lives within commuting distance of a low-tuition public college, and if he is able to get passing grades while working twenty or more hours per week, he can get a B.A. even if his parents haven't a penny. Such perseverance is not always necessary; there are scholarships.

Today, however, it is apparent that even average students must go to college if they are to be full citizens of the emerging Republic. Those who don't get a degree are condemned to partial or complete exclusion from the affluent sector of society. Since this is so, we can no longer afford to be cavalier about denying or discouraging students of moderate ability from getting higher education. Stupid children from upper-income families have long gone to college; now this "right" must be extended to the rest of the population if they want it. (It is true that many such students, rich and poor, will get very little benefit or pleasure from a conventional academic curriculum. But this is merely an argument for inventing new curriculums leading to the B.A. To make it an argument for excluding such students from college altogether would be justifiable only if it applied to rich and poor alike.)

A student who is neither brilliant nor heroic now has comparatively little chance of getting a college degree unless he comes from an upper-middle-class family. An average student whose family has a below-average income is understandably reluctant to borrow in order to get through college. He usually has little self-confidence and is often uncertain whether he will get a degree. If he doesn't, he knows his chances of getting a lucrative job will be limited, and he doesn't want to be saddled with debts. Even if he does expect to get a degree, he is often uncertain whether he will find his way into a well-paid job. Because college-loan payments cannot be spread over a lifetime the way payments on a house are, the annual cost in the first years out of college looms quite large, particularly for those who anticipate moderate incomes.

Since the cost of higher education is rising faster than middle-class incomes, this problem will grow more serious in the years ahead. (It is already impossible to borrow the full cost of attending most colleges.) For most students this means working either part or full time. Bright students can often manage this without too much academic difficulty; average students, however, cannot give twenty or thirty hours a week to a paying job and still keep up with their academic work. Many get into trouble and withdraw.

Unless these students get some kind of subsidy, they simply will not get a higher education. Studies show that if there is a heavily subsidized public institution within commuting distance, many of these moderate-ability, moderate-income students will attend. Otherwise, very few do so. The result has been a drive to spread public commuter colleges across the nation. This has two difficulties.

First, it would be fabulously expensive. The only state which has moved very far in this direction is California, which has a tuition-free college of some sort within commuting distance of more than nine out of ten families. But California is among the richest states in the nation. Equally important, it is among the most urbanized (or perhaps one should say suburbanized). As a result, a college can be put within commuting distance of almost everyone far more easily than in a poorer or more sparsely settled state. A similar program will not be politically or financially feasible in most states for many years, though many have adopted it in principle.

The second difficulty with the "commuter college" formula is that it leaves most students with only one choice about where to attend college. If a student doesn't like the students or teachers or program at the nearby public institution, his only alternative is to become a dropout. All too often, that is precisely what he does, for most public commuter colleges are discouraging and depressing places to the majority of students. They tend to be big. They tend to be impersonal. They tend to assume that the student is responsible for educating himself, not that they have a responsibility to or for him. Some students, of course, thrive in such a setting. But what of the student who does not? He cannot afford to go away to another public college unless his family has enough money to pay for his room, board, clothes, books, transportation, and "incidental fees." Many parents don't have that kind of money, or at least they won't spend it when it seems to them that there is a perfectly adequate college nearby. A student from a blue- or white-collar family is even less likely to be able to muster the money to attend a private college, which involves not only subsistence but tuition charges. These are climbing considerably faster than blue- and white-collar incomes.

To some, the exclusion of the majority of students from private institutions may seem of little consequence. There is a widespread feeling that private colleges are only for snobs and that their declining role in educating the young (they now enroll only a third of the students, compared with half only a generation ago) is all to the good. It should be remembered, however, that private colleges are many things besides bastions of snobbery. There are many kinds of undergraduate education which are available only in the private sector. (At the graduate level the differences are less important.) One cannot get a religiously oriented education in a public institution. One cannot escape the sometimes unwelcome blessings of coeducation in more than half a dozen public institutions. Except for the military academies, there are no public colleges which draw their undergraduates from all over the country. There are virtually no public colleges small enough to make their students feel they are being treated and valued as individuals. Those that are small are mostly teachers' colleges, where academic inadequacy is only rarely offset by personal concern and responsibility for the students.

The overwhelming majority of students would almost certainly attend private colleges if they cost no more than public ones. Would this be bad? I think not. Students are far better judges of what kind of education they need than are politicians (or educators, for that matter). If students prefer the kinds of education offered in the private sector to the kinds offered in the public sector, they should be encouraged to get the former. If this leads to less rapid growth or even decline of publicly controlled institutions, the moral is that the public does not know how to control colleges and universities as well as private boards do. If that is so (and it is probably only partly so), public control *should* be downgraded. Without doubt, in order to offer students a choice between commuter and residential colleges and between publicly and privately controlled ones, tax subsidies for higher education must be redirected away from institutions and toward individuals.

Obviously, a massive federal program of scholarships for lower-income students would lead to tuition increases in both public and private institutions, for there would no longer be any reason to fear that charging higher tuition would keep anyone out. In a sense, then, scholarships would be providing an indirect subsidy to those colleges which enrolled students from lower-income families. This would enable such colleges to pay higher salaries, offer smaller classes, set up seminar and tutorial programs, provide better libraries and laboratories, and so forth. Furthermore, the colleges would be getting more money not only from their scholarship students but from the affluent as well. The result would be a substantial increase in college revenues (and hence, it is to be hoped, quality) for a comparatively modest federal expenditure.

Such a program would, of course, be expensive. But it would probably be less expensive than subsidizing institutions. By keeping tuition artificially low, especially in public institutions, we are now spending better than a billion dollars in public money each year to subsidize students from families that could afford to pay the full cost of their children's higher education. If the present approach to institutional subsidies is followed in future federal programs, as much as 2 billion dollars a year may be going to these families by 1970. Were everyone else getting what they needed, this would be no cause for alarm. But most students are not. Until we have a system which ensures everyone enough money to get through the college of his choice, such subsidies to the upper middle classes should be kept to a minimum.

As a practical matter, existing state and federal subsidies to publicly controlled institutions could not and should not be cut. It is clear that in the next few years the cost of higher education will climb toward as yet unimagined levels, outstripping both personal incomes and state tax receipts, and that new federal subsidies will be provided. Some of these subsidies will be designed to achieve specific public purposes, like better training for medical technicians, and will necessarily take the form of special-purpose grants to institutions. But there will almost certainly also be subsidies aimed simply at balancing overall college budgets. These should take the form of scholarships to needy students, aimed at facilitating tuition increases, rather than the form of direct grants to institutions. Only in this way could Congress ensure that the subsidies would go to those who most needed them, rather than being spread thin across the whole population. And only in this way can individual students be given real freedom of choice among the many different varieties of higher education which are possible.

Two possible plans for the support of higher education along these lines are outlined below.

Plan I Any student attending an accredited college would be eligible for cost-of-education payments. Payments in the early years of the program would be in "units" of $30, and a student would be eligible to use up to twenty-five units per academic year (i.e., up to $750 per year). Payments would be made directly to the student upon evidence of his enrollment and could be used for tuition, room, board, or other related expenses.

Cost-of-education units would be provided to the student in the form of an ordinary loan at 6 percent interest, with payments deferred, until he reached the age of twenty-one. At that time, the student could choose to convert this loan into a lifetime-repayment plan which would entail a yearly payment to the government of an amount equal to 0.01 percent of his taxable income for each $30 unit received. Thus a student who used the maximum amount of $3,000 over a four-year period would agree to make repayment of 1 percent of his taxable income until reaching age sixty-five. One exception would be permitted: At any time before age sixty-five, the recipient could "buy out of" his repayment contract by paying back in one lump sum an amount equal to his cost-of-education units compounded at 6 percent annually, less his repayments up to that time.

The college graduate today has an average annual income over his lifetime of approximately $10,000. A representative schedule of incomes and tax assessments indicates that a typical person would repay about $3,200 over his lifetime. If about half of the college students availed themselves of this plan (or a larger percentage made less than 100 percent use of the units), the initial outlay would be a little less than $2 billion per year. The annual outlay by the government would rise to over $3 billion after 1975. However, repayments would begin to come in the fifth year of the program and by about 1990 would be greater than the annual outlay. The total amount of loan funds outstanding might rise as high as $35 billion, but would decline after twenty-five years unless the value of the educational units were increased.

Such a program would have a number of advantages. First, if the cost to the government was merely the net interest on the outstanding loan funds, the program would be much less costly than one tax credit proposal which was estimated at $700 million immediate lost revenue, rising to $1.25 billion by 1970. More important, the proposal above would provide immediate funds to help meet college costs two or three times greater than the tax credit proposal. Second, benefits would be available for everyone, regardless of his (or his family's) income. Third, the principle of shifting part of the cost of college forward in time to the direct beneficiary is a sensible development.

Fourth, the participants in the program share the risks of high or low earned incomes later in their lifetimes and also share the risks of death before age sixty-five. The buying-out provision would let persons with high income out without too great a penalty, but the 6 percent cumulative interest would be sufficiently high so that not everyone whose income was above earlier expectations would buy out. And fifth, such a program would permit maximum individual freedom of choice and avoid the criticism of direct federal intervention.

Plan II A federal program of cost-of-education payments to students might be set up with the amount of the payments based on, first, the institution's net annual cost in educating a student, and second, the per capita income of the student's family (family income divided by number of family members).

The net annual cost to an institution would be the total cost less the amount supplied from endowment income or from the state (for a public university). The amount of the net cost that the federal government would assume would vary with the income of the student's family and other claims on that income, as indicated by family income per family member, as follows:

Per capita family-income brackets	Part of net cost covered by federal payment
$0–1,500	All
$1,500–3,000	Half
$3,000–4,500	One-fourth
$4,500 plus	None

The following comments are in order:

1. Endowment income and, for public institutions, state payments are excluded on the theory that their reason for existence is mainly to reduce the cost of education to the student. If this should result in less than justifiable parity between public and private institutions, adjustments could undoubtedly be made.

2. The outer boundaries of the federal payment would be the entire net cost for a family with up to $1,500 family income per family member and nothing for families whose per capita income exceeds $4,500 per annum. The maximum rate of payment would apply to a four-member—or nearly average—family with income of up to $6,000; and the zero rate would apply to a four-member family with more than $18,000 a year.

3. The rate of the federal payment for each family-income bracket was established on a general sense of what people can afford and should pay in achieving the objective of getting into college all the young people who should be there.

4. The program would not be limited to students of superior ability. Every student the college accepts whose family income is as stipulated would be supported.

5. The institution would bill the student only to the extent that the federal payment on his behalf would not cover tuition charges.

This proposal has two major advantages.

First, it offers a new basis and a new rationale for student aid. There is a widespread awareness of, and concern about, the zooming costs of higher education and the pressures which will take them still higher. The proposal offers a way to enable the consumers to afford the product without regulating the price. It maintains the choice— and thus the control—of education in private hands. And it furnishes a defensible justification for helping out the middle-class family with two or more children of college age.

Second, it provides incentives for schools to obtain students from lower-income families and recognizes that access to higher education is a function of family size.

Christopher Jencks
Fellow at the Institute for
    Policy Studies
Washington, D.C.
January 3, 1967